FLAT-RACING SINCE 1900

FLAT-RACING
SINCE 1900

Edited by

Ernest Bland

with a Foreword by

THE EARL OF ROSEBERY, K.T.

LONDON
ANDREW DAKERS LIMITED

First published 1950

Made and Printed in Great Britain
at the BURLEIGH PRESS, *Lewins Mead*, BRISTOL

SO much has happened in the development of Flat
Racing and the Thoroughbred industry in England
during the first half of the twentieth century that it is a
genuine pleasure to contribute a Foreword to a book
which seeks to recapture many of the outstanding events
during that period. I am sure many enthusiasts like
myself whose interest goes back a number of years, and
whose love of the sport and horses is inborn, will welcome
the memories which the various chapters in *Flat Racing
Since* 1900 provide.

Mr. Ernest Bland, who is responsible for editing a
volume of such extreme interest, has exercised a discretion,
born of knowledge, in the selection of his contributors.
The writers on the various subjects are men of acknowledged
authority.

There are references to personalities of the age—
officials, owners, trainers, and jockeys. If some of the
details of a few outstanding characters are not sufficiently
revealing to satisfy those possessed of more intimate
knowledge perhaps that can be attributed jointly to the
wisdom of authors and editor. It will, I am satisfied, be
universally agreed that *Flat Racing Since* 1900 is what it
purports to be—a clear, straightforward and entertaining
record of all that is best in a sport which makes a strong
appeal to all.

We are all entitled to our opinion as to which was the
outstanding colt or filly of the century. Some may, with
justification, claim to be supreme in their judgment.
Others may be influenced by a variety of reasons in their
assessment. Whatever we may think as individuals there
is sufficient material in this book to revive most interesting
discussions and arguments wherever the readers may be
assembled.

Members of the Royal Family have for many years been
staunch supporters of racing and it is encouraging to those
in every walk of life to know that the tradition has been

enthusiastically maintained notwithstanding the upheavals experienced during the twentieth century. The latest members of the Royal Family to own a racehorse are the Queen and Princess Elizabeth, which ensures a depth of public interest comparable only with that which was characteristic of the Turf in the days of the late King Edward VII.

As one who owned his first racehorse in 1905, and went racing long before that, it is interesting to trace the rivalry between our own home-bred stock and horses bred abroad. To those who have not good memories, or who are lucky not to be old enough to remember far back, it might seem that these victories of foreign-bred horses are something quite new to our Turf. On the contrary I should say that by far the best French horse that ever won the Derby was Gladiateur in 1865. He also won the Two Thousand Guineas and the St. Leger. In the 70's French horses were constantly winning all the big long-distance races at Ascot. In 1878 a French horse named Verneuil won the Gold Vase, the Gold Cup, and the Queen Alexandra Stakes in a year when the ground was like iron— a record that I believe no horse has approached. In 1881 Foxhall, a three-year-old, came over from America to win the Cambridgeshire with 9 st., having a fortnight before won the Cesarewitch, and in the summer the Grand Prix de Paris. It is interesting to recall that the papers of that time do not seem to have put forward statements that our horses' merits were declining.

The truth is that, as long as we sell our best or near-best horses and mares abroad, other countries will breed horses as good as ours; but the fact remains that they always have to come back to buy more of our stock to maintain the excellence of theirs, and as we are an export country that is all to the good.

What I have written may be beyond the scope of this book, but you will read in it entertaining stories of those horses and their owners and others who raced in those days when racing was much more of an entertainment and less of a business than it is now.

Rosebery

CONTENTS

The photographs in this book, as indicated by the numbers in parenthesis, are from originals supplied by (1) P.A. Reuter; (2) W. W. Rouch; (3) L.N.A.; (4) Associated Press; (5) Topical Press; (6) *Daily Mail;* (7) Graphic Photo Union; (8) Race-finish Recording Co.; (9) Keystone Press Agency.

ILLUSTRATIONS

ILLUSTRATIONS

x

EDITOR'S INTRODUCTION

FLAT racing during the first half of the twentieth century was fraught with upheavals and vicissitudes such as had never before been experienced in the history of International Sport and, surely, everyone will agree that horse-racing exerts a big influence in the normal lives of sportsmen and sportswomen throughout the world.

Racing during that period has survived two world wars of such magnitude that it might have been excusable and understandable had interest in, and enthusiasm for, the sport been killed. Such, however, was the true appreciation of the Britishers' love for racing that those intimately associated with its control, from his Majesty the King to his humblest subject, were determined that the sport should continue, so long as it did not seriously interfere with, or jeopardize, affairs of far greater international importance.

The accomplishment of such a task reflects the utmost credit upon those members of the Jockey Club who had to exercise wisdom and ingenuity in successfully conducting negotiations of a supremely delicate character to ensure, even in a modified form, the unbroken continuity of racing. Tribute should also be paid to the loyal co-operation of the British public in pursuance of this desirable policy, which the Jockey Club would unhesitatingly acknowledge.

With this brief outline of the situations from which racing had to recover, readers of both the older and younger generations will realize that the task of editing a volume which sought to recapture the spirit of the sport over a period of such extraordinary fluctuations was one of almost frightening enormity. It is doubtful whether any one individual could have done justice to a work of such a comprehensive nature, a work intended to embrace various aspects and developments of a subject with a universal international appeal.

It was, therefore, deemed advisable to engage the assistance of contributors who, by virtue of their experience and knowledge, were qualified to provide authoritative material for the solid foundation upon which a permanent structure could be erected, one calculated to interest and educate racing-folk wherever they might reside.

Rarely, if ever, has such a concise review of racing in America been published as that contributed by Neil Newman, an acknowledged expert on American Turf matters. Racing in France, South Africa, Australia and Eire is also adequately covered to supplement what has happened in the British Isles.

Some contributors have written in reminiscent vein and it is consoling, even to the Editor, to realize that the recollections of such accepted authorities as Cyril Luckman, the distinguished " Scout " of the *Daily Express* ; Major J. Fairfax-Blakeborough, M.C., whose knowledge of personalities associated with racing in the North of England is unsurpassed ; Meyrick Good, doyen of the active members of the English Racing Press and for so long a regular writer in the *Sporting Life*, will stimulate the interest of all followers of the Turf, irrespective of age or nationality.

The influence of Royalty in the maintenance of the Sport of Kings is emphasized by Louis Wulff, M.V.O., whose activities are closely allied with the movements of the Royal Family. Eric Rickman, a former " Robin Goodfellow " of the *Daily Mail*, has probed the history of the Jockey Club, the National Stud and the tests imposed by Classic races.

Other features which, it is hoped, will complete the unique and comprehensive character of the book have been contributed by the Hon. Mrs. George Lambton, Clive Graham, V. R. Orchard (" Rapier "), A. J. Dickinson (" Captain Heath " of the *News-Chronicle*), Frank Harvey, (" Keystone " of the *Sunday Dispatch*), George Bonney, and Raymond Glendenning (B.B.C. commentator).

As to occasional repetitions of facts and names, I confidently rely upon the generous understanding of the reader that these could scarcely have been avoided in all the circumstances.

It is particularly gratifying to me, and all contributors will share in that sense of appreciation, that the Earl of Rosebery, K.T., has graciously written a Foreword to *Flat-Racing Since* 1900. Of him, it can truly be said that few individuals, if any, have a more intimate or expert knowledge of Turf affairs, from all points of view, over the period covered in this volume.

That you derive as much satisfaction and enjoyment from reading the contents, as was experienced by the Editor in their preparation and presentation, is the sincere wish of—

ERNEST BLAND.

CHAPTER I

ROYALTY AND RACING

By Louis Wulff, M.V.O.

FIFTY years may seem a small fraction of the long history of close associations between Royalty and racing, for racing is traditionally the Sport of Kings. To-day, when there are fewer kings in the world, and when the sport is enjoyed to a greater or less degree by everyone who can get to the free side of Ascot Heath or Epsom Downs, or even spare a penny to read the results in the paper, or listen to the bare details announced on the wireless, the tradition still holds good : and, in the past fifty years, our British Royal family have worthily upheld it, not as a matter of duty, but in the true sporting sense, by taking a real and lively interest in the Turf.

In that world of half a century ago, whose gas-lit luxury and easy assurance in the future seem so very remote to us in the uncertain atomic world of to-day, there was no figure more familiar, nor more popular, on a racecourse than that of Albert Edward, Prince of Wales. The sight of his stout, well-dressed frame, his bearded face, a long cigar between his lips, and a twinkle of anticipatory enjoyment in his shrewd eye as he walked slowly round the paddock, appraising the sleek, glossy-coated animals, acknowledging the greetings of friends on all sides, pausing for a few minutes' earnest conversation with his trainer, Richard Marsh, and the Royal jockey of the day, Herbert Jones, or, perhaps, Jack Watts, would draw cheers from the crowds, with cries of " Good old Teddie ! ", a circumstance which, though it may not have pleased the secluded dignity of Queen Victoria, did much to bring monarch and people closer.

That genial Prince, who had such a happy capacity for enjoying life to its utmost, was a true lover of the Turf. In 1899 he was a man of 58, very well versed in all matters connected with racing ; proud of having won the Derby three years before with the famous Persimmon ; eagerly interested in the progress and development of the stud he had established at Sandringham, his country house in Norfolk, and, perhaps, a little more excited than usual over the prospects of the two-year-old Diamond Jubilee, own brother to Persimmon and Florizel II, another big winner for the Royal stable. These three horses represented the height of the Prince's ambitions as an owner and breeder, for they were all of his own breeding and the preliminary reports

1

of Diamond Jubilee gave promise that here was another potential
Derby winner.   That season, the Prince had fifteen horses in
training and it is a striking example of the uncertainties of
breeding that among them was yet another full brother to the
famous " Trinity ", a colt named Sandringham, who in his
subsequent career failed to register a single win.

The colours of King Edward VII were first registered in
1875 and were carried successfully for the first time in a match in
1877.   In that match he ran an Arab which was easily beaten by
an English bred thoroughbred.   His Majesty's first trainer of
any importance was John Porter and in 1886 a filly named
Counterpane, by Hermit-Patchwork and ridden by Fred Archer,
won a small race at Sandown Park.   Counterpane, although well
bred, had a short career, falling down dead during a race at
Stockbridge.   The Sandringham Stud was formed in 1889 under
the management of Lord Marcus Beresford who, in later years,
was instrumental in bringing the American jockey, Tod Sloan,
to this country.   It was in 1893 that the then Prince of Wales
had his horses transferred from Kingsclere to Egerton House,
Newmarket, in the care of Richard Marsh.   In the following
year the first of Perdita II's progeny ran.   This was Florizel II,
and twelve months later this horse won twice at Ascot and
subsequently carried off the Goodwood Cup.   After this came
Florizel II's full-brother Persimmon who first stamped himself
a colt of great distinction by capturing the Coventry Stakes at
Ascot.   As a three-year-old Persimmon excelled himself by
winning what was then described as the " Prince's Derby ",
(1896) and great was the scene on that day at Epsom when a vast
crowd received the Royal success with the greatest enthusiasm
imaginable.   The son of St. Simon also won the St. Leger and
was successful in seven races, including the Eclipse Stakes and the
Gold Cup (both in 1897) the total value in stakes being £34,706.

Perdita II bred another Derby winner in Diamond Jubilee, the
winner of 26 races of the aggregate of £72,912.   When the Prince
came to the throne, he won his third Derby, in 1909, with Minoru.
Although it was only by a short head that Minoru scraped home
from Louviers, that same enthusiastic scene was repeated as
greeted Persimmon's victory.   Persimmon became a great success
when he went to Sandringham as a stallion, siring that illustrious
mare Sceptre, who won the Two Thousand and One Thousand
Guineas, the Oaks and St. Leger, in 1902, and many thought she
was unlucky not to have won the Derby.   Persimmon headed
the list of Winning Stallions in 1906, 1908 and 1912.

But the year 1899 brought disappointment to the Prince and to
his racing-manager, Lord Marcus Beresford, that kindly, patient,
witty man of great charm, who was justly reputed to be one of

the best judges of a horse of the day, for Diamond Jubilee failed dismally at Ascot, finishing fourth in the Coventry Stakes, for which he was favourite at 6 to 5 against. As a two-year-old, he ran six times, and won only once, but Albert Edward and his racing advisers determined to continue, despite the gloomy prophecies of Sir Dighton Probyn, who looked after the Royal accounts.

The following year brought complete justification of their faith for Diamond Jubilee won the Derby convincingly by three-quarters of a length, to a background of cheering and enthusiasm such as Epsom had rarely experienced. It was, perhaps, the supreme moment in the Prince's career as a racing owner. True, he won the Derby again nine years later with Minoru, the first and only time the reigning Sovereign has won the premier race, but Minoru was a leased horse from the Tully Stud of Colonel Hall Walker, afterwards Lord Wavertree, donor of the National Stud, and not a horse of his own breeding.

Nineteen hundred, last full year of the great Victoria era, and his own last year as Prince of Wales, was a magnificent period for the racing Prince. Diamond Jubilee won the Triple Crown —the Two Thousand Guineas, The Derby, and the St. Leger— and the Newmarket Stakes. No owner could ask for more. It was the zenith of the Royal stable, a height of success never reached before nor since. To his justifiable pride in the attainments of his wonder colt, the Prince had the added satisfaction, when the accounts came in for review at the end of the season, of knowing that his horses had won the handsome sum of £29,585, placing him at the head of the list of winning owners for the first year of the new century.

Like a real sportsman, the Prince was generous and open-handed in recognising the services of those who had helped him to win, and after Diamond Jubilee's Derby he sent a gift of £1,000 to his trainer, Richard Marsh, in token of the splendid way he had prepared the horse, and a similar amount to the jockey, Herbert Jones. But with Victorian care for the future, the Prince made the proviso that for some years Jones should only receive the interest on his amount, which was placed in the hands of an official to invest, lest the jockey be tempted to spend the lot foolishly, a charming example of the paternal attitude of wealthy owners of those days towards those who worked for them.

After the great vintage year, luck gradually began to desert the Royal stable, though Diamond Jubilee continued to play a sustaining part in balancing the Royal racing-accounts by his earnings at stud, plus a sum of £30,000 for which he was eventually sold to the Argentine. But there seemed no more Diamonds in the Royal stud. Next year, Queen Victoria died, and King Edward's

horses, according to Royal custom, were run in the Duke of
Devonshire's colours during the long period of mourning.
Whether Diamond Jubilee did not like his new colours so much
as the familiar red blue and gold of the Prince can only be
imagined, but he did not win a single race as a four-year-old,
which naturally was a great disappointment to the King.

One story of Diamond Jubilee, King Edward never tired of
telling. One day, when the horse was a raw youngster, the famous
" Squire ", Mr. Chaplin, went round the Royal stables on a tour of
inspection with the Prince. Richard Marsh, proud of the magnificent animal in his charge, ventured to tell the Squire, who was
reputed one of the best judges of a horse in England, that
Diamond Jubilee was a perfect horse in conformation, without
a single fault. Squire Chaplin refused to believe such an animal
existed, and backed his opinion with a five-pound bet. When the
party came to Diamond's box, Mr. Chaplin remained some time
inspecting the horse with the critical eye of a challenged expert.
When he rejoined the party some distance further on, the Squire
said nothing, but handed Marsh the fiver, to the great delight of
the Prince—and, doubtless, to that of his trainer.

It was not until 1908, after the King had been seven years on
the Throne, that luck began to turn again to the Sandringham
stud, this time in the shape of a filly named Princesse de Galles,
by Gallinule-Ecila. As a two-year-old, she won the Chesterfield,
Boscawn, and Bretby Stakes and aroused hopes of a Royal success
in The Oaks of 1909, but was beaten by Perola (F. Wootton).
She was also second in the One Thousand Guineas. Meanwhile,
among a string leased from the Tully Stud, was a likely-looking
yearling called Minoru. Amid the cares of State and the vastly
increased official calls on his time as King, Albert Edward had
never allowed anything to interrupt his interest in his racing-
stables. Bad years or good, he took them with philosophical
calm, always hoping one day to own another Diamond Jubilee.
Lord Marcus Beresford was charged with the paramount duty of
keeping the King closely and continuously informed of the progress, or otherwise, of affairs at Sandringham and Egerton House,
where the Royal horses were trained. There certainly appeared
to be reasonable prospects of having another candidate worthy
to carry the Royal colours in the finest race in the world. Minoru
made excellent progress in his early preparation and, rather to the
surprise of many people, beat the hot favourite, Bayardo, in the
Two Thousand Guineas. The Royal stable had come back to
form. The delighted King had several conferences with his
trainer and manager about the Derby prospects, and flooded
Egerton House with a series of messages and telegrams. Every
day without fail, a report on the horse was wired to him in

THE KING AND QUEEN DRIVING DOWN THE COURSE
AT ROYAL ASCOT, 1949

THE KING AND QUEEN, PRINCESS ELIZABETH
AND LORD ROSEBERY. Epsom, 1948.

[Facing page 4

KING GEORGE V AND QUEEN MARY. Ascot, 1925

KING EDWARD VII AND QUEEN ALEXANDRA LEAVING ASCOT

London, to be read eagerly and studied closely in between the perusal of documents of State. And no owner could ask for better news.

There was no more popular figure in the carefree England of 1909 than King Edward, and the hint that he had a possible Derby winner was sufficient to set a great flame of enthusiasm alight, a flame which caused Minoru to become favourite at 7 to 2, and which burned brightly among the huge crowds which flocked to Epsom on Derby Day. Lots of people, including the rival owners, were hoping to see the Royal colours defeated, having financial interests in the other runners, but there was something about the prospects of a Royal win that dominated even these considerations.

When Minoru turned Tattenham Corner on the rails, the excitement mounted to new heights. In the Royal box, the King, watching every yard through his glasses, did not try to conceal his delight as his experienced eye showed him his chances improving with every stride. Queen Alexandra at his side, with the Prince and Princess of Wales, watched with almost equal excitement. The nervous tension in the Royal box grew almost unbearable as Minoru passed the post with Louviers, a horse owned by Mr. Walter Raphael, so close that no one could tell with certainty who had won. Then the numbers went up—Minoru had won by a short head.

The King beamed, the crowd redoubled their cheers, and everyone, rival owners, losing punters, and hard-hit bookies forgot everything else in the joy of the King's triumph. The King went down, as he had so often gone before, to lead his horse to the unsaddling enclosure. This time it was a greater occasion than ever, greater even than when he had twice won the same race as Prince of Wales. The King, head of the nation, and living symbol of Britain, had won the nation's greatest race. Someone started to sing " God Save the King ". Thousands took up the anthem as the King proudly escorted Minoru before Herbert Jones dismounted to weigh in with the Prince of Wales (afterwards George V) at his side. It was a scene that is part of English history. Excited orders went from the Royal box to Buckingham Palace for the table to be decorated in the Royal colours for that night's dinner to the Jockey Club, the " stag " party with which King Edward ended every Derby Day. The King, surrounded by friends congratulating him, walked slowly back to his box to watch the rest of the day's racing with a calmer, less-interested eye.

The King, unhappily, lived less than a year after this memorable victory, though no one could have guessed it to look at his genial smiling face and his bubbling good spirits. Of all the happy moments in his life, it is very possible that this was King

B

Edward's happiest, for racing was really an absorbing interest to him.   When he lay on his deathbed at Buckingham Palace 11 months later, on Friday, May 6, his filly Witch of the Air was running at Kempton Park.   The Prince of Wales gave his father news of the Witch's win, and the King's very last words were of delight at the success.   No real racing man, King or commoner, could wish for a better passing.

Among the many other inheritances which came to the new King, George V, were his father's racing-establishments at Sandringham and Newmarket, where Egerton House had, for some time, been constituted as the private Royal training-headquarters. To the great satisfaction of all the racing public, the King soon made known his intention of keeping on the two places as before, with Lord Marcus as his manager and Richard Marsh as his trainer.   The Earl of Derby took over the running of the Royal horses during the period of mourning, as he was to do again twenty-six years later after the death of King George : but little luck came the way of Egerton House.

It was the general view that King George V was nothing like as keen a racing-man as his father, and it is true that the winning and betting side of the sport did not make quite the same appeal to him.   King Edward VII, both as Prince and as King, liked to have a good interest in any of his horses which he fancied, and his betting accounts were in substantial figures.

But King George, even if he did not deal quite so extensively with the layers of odds, took his responsibilities as an owner seriously.   He was reputed to be as good a judge of a horse as his father, if not, indeed, sounder, and his knowledge of thoroughbred breeding was wide and extensive.   Rarely could he be beaten in an argument about breeding or progeny.   King George failed to repeat his father's success in the Derby, though in 1924 there were, at least high hopes at Egerton House, when Knight of the Garter gave promise of being a really " good thing " for Epsom. To the chagrin of the King, his manager and trainer, the horse developed heel bug on the eve of the race and had to be withdrawn.

. In 1911 King George V won six races, one of the first horses to win for him being Dorando, named after the famous Marathon runner of 1908 who collapsed after finishing a great race in the Olympic Games.   Then came Weathervane, who won the Greenham Stakes at Newbury (1922) just as Minoru had done for King Edward a few years previously.   Weathervane won the Royal Hunt Cup in 1923.   His Majesty and Queen Mary were present to see that useful horse, London Cry, win the Goodwood Stakes. Richard Marsh, the King's trainer, was always of the opinion that Friar Marcus was the best horse King George V owned.   This fast horse, like Persimmon, turned out to be a success at the stud at Sandringham. His stock, from 1918 to 1938, won 368 races, valued at £143,672. He became the sire of Friar's Daughter, the dam of the unbeaten Triple Crown hero Bahram. Although King George did not own many top-class horses under Richard Marsh's charge from 1911 to 1924, he won just under 100 races, the best year being in 1923, when he won 19 races ; the next best being in 1933, when he won 10 races of the value of £8,028, and in 1925 he also won 10 races worth £6,134.

On the retirement of Richard Marsh, William Jarvis, a brother to Jack Jarvis, took over the King's horses and trained for him a classic winner in Scuttle and also prepared Limelight, winner of the Prince of Wales Nursery at Doncaster, the Jersey Stakes at Ascot, and as a four-year-old, in 1933 Limelight won the Newbury Spring Cup, the Hardwicke Stakes at Ascot and the Duke of York Stakes at Kempton. In three seasons, Limelight won close on £9,000 in stakes.

Friar Marcus and Scuttle were the two best horses owned by King George. The former, bred at Sandringham, where the King liked to walk round in the evenings feeding carrots to his favourites, won five races as a two-year-old. But he proved a non-stayer in the Two Thousand and was, again to the King's regret, withdrawn from the Derby. Many times King George saw his colours carried to victory in minor races, but it was not until 1928 that he won his first classic, when Scuttle carried off the One Thousand Guineas. But big victories seemed to elude the King. At Sandringham, the King took an eager, expert interest in all breeding-problems, and it probably gave him as much delight that his sire Friar Marcus produced 343 winners in his career at stud as it would have done had all the winners been his own.

What King George V most enjoyed about racing proper was the social side, the friendly atmosphere of Newmarket, where he could stroll with his friends, forgetting the affairs of State for the moment ; the country ease of Goodwood—a meeting he rarely missed—and the more formal elegance of Ascot.

When he went racing, the King liked to leave London behind, making his headquarters in the comfortable Royal suite at the Jockey Club headquarters at Newmarket, or at the Duke of Richmond's home for Goodwood, while for Royal Ascot, of course, he always entertained a large house-party at Windsor Castle. In the Royal Enclosure at Ascot, on the lawns at Newmarket or Epsom, and in the country beauty of Goodwood, he would walk slowly to and fro, greeting his many friends, discussing questions of breeding and other turf-matters with the foremost racing men of the day. He never won vast sums in

prize money, for even Royal owners must have luck on their side
to achieve this. But he always immensely enjoyed a day's racing,
and proved what a good friend he was of the sport when, in the
1914–19 War, he refused to countenance any talk of the suppression of racing—a wise decision and example which his son,
King George VI followed some twenty years later. His two best
years, from a financial point of view, were 1914 and 1928, but
he never achieved the distinction of heading the list of winning
owners of which his father was so proud in 1900.

The Derby, the Oaks, the Two Thousand Guineas, and the
St. Leger all eluded the King's grasp throughout his racing-
career, and, good loser and unshakable sportsman as he was,
King George V was definitely disappointed not, once at any rate,
to have carried off some of the premier awards. He well deserved
better luck, for his interest in breeding was wide and deep, and
he was constantly consulting Lord Marcus, who remained his
manager for many years, and his trainer, about schemes for producing another batch like the famous Trinity. Nearest approach
to a real good'un was the filly Scuttle, who won the One Thousand
(1928), but could only finish second to the late Lord Derby's
Toboggan in the Oaks, beaten by four lengths after starting
favourite at even money. That was one of the greatest disappointments King George suffered on the racecourse, but he allowed
no sign of his regret to be manifest when he offered his congratulations to his friend Lord Derby.

After the unfulfilled promise of Scuttle's year in 1928, the Royal
stable seemed to sink into a trough of bad luck. For the remaining eight years of his life, King George had to be content to see
his carefully bred horses and those he leased from the National
Stud, under the guidance of the foremost racing authorities of
the day, achieving small and occasional successes, while the expenses of the Royal racing establishment were largely covered by
the earnings of his stud horses. The fact that his own colours
were rarely first did not detract from King George's interest in
the sport, and his always immaculately dressed figure, with the
trousers impeccably creased at the side as was his particular
fashion, his bowler or topper placed carefully level on his forehead, his trim beard, was to be seen many times at the big meetings, especially at his favourite Newmarket. Here it was King
George's great pleasure to ride over the Heath in the early morning to watch his own and other owners' strings at exercise whenever he had the chance. That he enjoyed this almost as much as
watching the horses actually racing is added proof of the real
nature of his interest in the sport—a proof that applies equally
in these days, as we shall see presently, to his granddaughter
Princess Elizabeth, whose interest in racing, bloodstock and

breeding is every bit as wide and deep as was that of King George.

King George V took but little interest in steeplechasing, certainly in his later years, and he did not strive to emulate his father's achievement of winning the Grand National. But the Royal interest in " the sticks " was amply maintained in the 1920's and early 1930's by his son, the Prince of Wales (now Duke of Windsor), who, with true sporting instinct, loved nothing better than a fast ride over a difficult point-to-point. He rode with a jockey's seat, perched high up on big-boned, strong-actioned horses, a factor which contributed no little to the several spills he took, as well as to the several cups he carried off. But tumbles or cups, the Prince, though he might come in splashed from head to foot with black mud, enjoyed it all, and spent some of his happiest hours in the racing saddle.

When King George died, the normal procedure was followed with the Royal racing establishment, and the horses were run again in the colours of the Earl of Derby, during the period of Court mourning.

Our present King, like his father, allows his racing activities to take a less important place in his life than did King Edward VII, but it is characteristic of His Majesty to be thorough in everything he undertakes, and the Royal racing establishment is no exception to this rule. It would not be true to describe the King as a real racing enthusiast. He does not, for example, make a point of going to every meeting where he has a runner thought to possess a good chance, as his grandfather was wont to do, but many things have changed since King Edward's day, and, apart altogether from the question of the King's own wishes, the amount of official business and desk-work which the Sovereign, and the Sovereign alone, must do, has increased enormously since those days. But, like any other owner, the King is thrilled when one of his horses wins, particularly if it is one of his own breeding, for in the Royal stables of 1949 were two strings, one consisting of horses bred by the King, the other comprising horses leased by him from the National Stud. It was in the horses bred at Hampton Court, where Captain Charles Moore, the Manager of His Majesty's Thoroughbred Stud, had the mares and foals under his immediate eye—the stallions were kept at Sandringham—that the King's chief racing interest centred.

So far, the most coveted prize of all, the Derby, has not come the King's way, but the Hampton Court stables have produced some good winners for him, and it is not revealing any stable-secret to say that the great ambition of Captain Moore and Captain Boyd-Rochfort, who trains the King's own horses, is to win the Derby for him. Hypericum, who won the One Thousand

Guineas in 1946, Kingstone, Rising Light, Angelola, second in the 1948 Oaks, and Avila, who scored at Ascot in 1949, were some of the successful progeny of the Royal stud, and there were good hopes, at least, of other, and bigger successes to follow.

The King began his stud with about 20 mares, all of which, with the exception of Feola, were disappointing. In 1949 there were a number of promising mares at Hampton Court and the King takes a really close interest in their progress. Of the 12 horses the King has in training to-day, eight are of his own breeding, the other four leased from the National Stud and trained by Noel Murless at Beckhampton.

The National Stud is of considerable importance, of course, in the promotion of the British bloodstock industry, a national asset of whose value the King is well aware, and Royal patronage of the Stud is an incentive to other owners to lease horses. In this connection it may be noted, too, that the King, even if racing does not lie very close to his heart, played no small part in the decision to continue racing throughout the war years. There were strong moves in some quarters to cut the sport out entirely, and it was believed at the time that the King's influence, and the example he set by attending several wartime meetings, including two of the substitute Derbys at Newmarket, did much to counter them. Certainly the King, whose habit is to gauge the public pulse with great accuracy, realised what an important safety-valve racing afforded for the pent-up feelings of those days, as well as the importance of continuity from the bloodstock point of view.

It was a wartime Derby which the King so nearly won with one of the leased horses from the National Stud, the big, well-built Big Game. That was in 1942, the best year the King has had up to date on the Turf. Big Game was a likely-looking yearling, who developed so well as a two-year-old that, at last, it seemed there was a chance of some classic wins for the King, with hopes rising high for the Derby itself. Also in the Royal stable was the National Stud filly Sun Chariot, showing almost equal promise. Big Game won the Two Thousand Guineas in convincing style, starting favourite at 11 to 8 on, and next day, Sun Chariot, also favourite at evens, won the One Thousand Guineas. Everyone, including the King, began to think the elusive Derby was within reach of the Royal stables again, after an interval of 33 years. What added to the confidence was the fact that Big Game had beaten Watling Street, Lord Derby's candidate for the Derby, by four lengths in the Two Thousand Guineas.

With wartime restrictions on travel, it was difficult for the King and Queen to make a special journey to Newmarket to see the race, but the possibility of a Royal Derby victory with the King absent was not to be thought of, so an agricultural tour of Cambridgeshire was planned for the period, which would enable the King and Queen to witness both the Derby and the Oaks. The Newmarket crowd, men and women alike, mostly in khaki or blue, went wild with enthusiasm when the King's colours flashed to victory as Sun Chariot won at 4 to 1 on. No one was more delighted than the King, who went off in high spirits to continue his tour, with the cheers of the crowds ringing in his ears, and in his heart great expectations for the next day. He had won three classics and the fourth seemed very likely to follow. But nothing is certain in racing. Big Game, with the champion jockey, Gordon Richards, on his back, determined to break his own Derby " hoodoo "—for he had never won the Derby either at Epsom or Newmarket—failed dismally, finishing sixth behind Watling Street, whom he had so easily beaten a month before. Groans of the disappointed loyal thousands who had backed the King's horse down to 6 to 4, and thousands of others who wanted the King to win irrespective of monetary considerations, mingled with the cheers for the winner.

It was, perhaps, the King's greatest racing disappointment. Usually, the King shows no signs on his face of his thoughts or feelings in public. But as he stood in his wartime khaki as a Field Marshal in the Royal box at Newmarket on that bright day of June, his expression and a slightly heightened colour showed him high-strung and tense. He watched the horses parade before they wheeled to go down to the post, and from that moment, his race-glasses were not lowered. The Queen at his side, almost equally excited, watched nearly every stride in the race. But Big Game seemed to falter towards the end, as though he could not, after all, stay. Watling Street charged past, and the Royal hopes, so high and eager a few minutes before, faded. It was a bitter blow, one which no man could take with complete equanimity, for victory had seemed so certain; jubilation so near. For a brief moment, the King's face showed something of his inner feelings. Then, as he turned to enter the Royal retiring-room, he smiled a little sadly at the Queen, and said a word of comfort to his bitterly disappointed racing-manager. A few minutes later the King sent for Lady Derby to offer his congratulations, and to ask her to tell her absent husband how sorry the King was he had not been able to see his horse win.

That was a great gesture of Royal sportsmanship which the racing crowds were quick to appreciate. If the King had not been able to win the Derby, as nearly everyone had wanted him to do, he certainly showed he is a good loser. What, later, added a touch of retrospective bitterness to the Derby pill was that Watling Street, already beaten by Big Game in the Guineas, was again trounced in the St. Leger by Sun Chariot, which won by three lengths, so the Royal colours were victorious on two of the three occasions—but not on the most important. Altogether, the King won ten races during that season of 1942, which, if it did not put him at the top of winning owners, brought in £10,535 in prize money, more than the Royal stable had won for several years. It may be remarked, incidentally, that in contrast to the easy-come, easy-go finances of King Edward's day, His Majesty's thorough-bred establishment is run on strict business lines, and is far from being regarded as an easy drain down which good money may disappear.

At the end of the 1949 season, King George VI had won more classic races than his father. His Majesty's best season to date was in 1946, when horses carrying the Royal purple won 16 races of £16,528 following 13 races in 1945, and the same number of events in 1948 to the value of £13,207. One can watch the stud career of the King's Avila with no small interest as the daughter of Hyperion is bred stoutly enough on her dam's side, tracing as she does to the stout-hearted Santoi who won many good handi-caps for the late Mr. George Edwardes.

VALUE OF STAKES WON BY THREE KINGS

PRINCE OF WALES

Year	Races Won	Value £
1899	5	2,189

KING EDWARD VII

Year	Races Won	Value £
1900	9	29,585
1901	nil	nil
1902	2	1,514
1903	3	3,105
1904	5	1,903
1905	2	900
1906	4	2,788
1907	5	2,944
1908	9	5,490
1909	13	20,144
1910	1	216

KING GEORGE V

Year	Races Won	Value £
1911	6	1,649
1912	13	4,008
1913	5	4,480
1914	11	11,744
1915	2	975
1916	3	737
1917	—	—
1918	nil	nil
1919	8	4,171
1920	5	1,837
1921	4	2,146
1922	10	5,289
1923	19	11,369
1924	3	3,095
1925	10	6,134
1926	3	576
1927	8	4,433
1928	6	10,082
1929	7	4,480
1930	2	288
1931	4	2,047
1932	7	3,828
1933	10	8,028
1934	4	729
1935	8	1,597
1936	nil	nil

KING GEORGE VI

Year	Races Won	Value £
1937	3	1,236
1938	2	1,198
1939	5	2,439
1940	1	162
1941	nil	nil
1942	10	10,535
1943	6	2,224
1944	1	262
1945	13	7,736
1946	16	16,528
1947	6	4,300
1948	13	13,207

No account of Royal interest in racing would be complete without mention of Princess Elizabeth, who is the keenest racegoer

of her family. Her first visit to the races was to a wartime
" austerity " Ascot, in 1944, while she was serving in the A.T.S.,
and since then she has taken eager and ever-growing interest in
the sport. The Princess has made a considerable study of racing
records and breeding, and frequently surprises experts by her
detailed knowledge in these directions.

A wedding gift from the Aga Khan, in the shape of a Turkhan
filly, Astrakhan, gave further stimulus to the Princess's racing-
interests, and it was not many months before she decided to race
herself. In August, 1949, she registered her colours of scarlet,
purple-hooped sleeves and black cap, under Jockey Club and
National Hunt Rules. Like many new owners, Princess Elizabeth
began with disappointment. Astrakhan did not seem to stand
up to training and the Aga Khan came forward with another
filly by Stardust out of Bellinzora. But even Royal owners quickly
learn that, in racing, " no one can tell ", for Astrakhan belied
the doubters, trained on, and ran well to finish second in the
Sandwich Stakes at Ascot in October, 1949. A month earlier,
the *Racing Calendar* contained an announcement which gave a
tremendous fillip to jumping enthusiasts. In partnership with
the Queen, the Princess had purchased Monaveen, an eight-year-
old Irish steeplechaser which fell at the nineteenth fence in the
Grand National of 1949.

It was on New Year's Eve, 1949, at Hurst Park, that the young
Royal owner saw her colours carried to victory for the first time.
Monaveen, with " Tony " Grantham up, won by six lengths.

A big crowd gave the Princess a great reception as she went
down to greet the jockey with her trainer, Mr. Peter Cazalet. It
was the Queen Elizabeth 'Chase which Monaveen had won, and
many punters had backed the horse at 10 to 1 in the hope—which
was fulfilled—of an all-Elizabeth day.

Monaveen, which the Princess, with her sister Princess
Margaret, saw finish second in the Grand Sefton at Aintree soon
after she had bought it, was entered for the 1950 Grand National,
and after his series of victories, became a much fancied candidate.
Princess Elizabeth early announced her intention of going to
Aintree to see her horse run—and made no secret to her friends
of her hope that she might follow her great-grandfather's example
by winning.

Before his wedding, the Duke of Edinburgh had not displayed
much interest in racing, but his wife has infected him with something of her keenness, and they have often patronized the week-
end " ordinary " Ascot meetings as well as the " garden-party "
Royal meeting in June, thoroughly enjoying a day at the races
together, so there are certainly no grounds to fear any falling-
off in the Royal support for racing for many years to come.

CHAPTER II

THE JOCKEY CLUB

By Eric Rickman

FIFTY years of Racing is but a span in the long history of this great national diversion. The publication of this book coincides approximately with the second centenary of the sport's ruling authority, the Jockey Club, an event which doubtless will be allowed to pass without particular recognition. There does not seem to exist any precise record of its formation, and even if such information were available, a birthday celebration would be a surprising departure from the club's austere and extremely conservative policy, directed entirely to the control of flat racing and the welfare of the thoroughbred horse.

Its omnipotence has been gradually acquired. Though this supreme authority has been complete throughout the last 50 years, it was not consolidated until 1890, when the over-all powers which the Club had gained, or assumed, during the preceding 140 years were embodied in a completely new set of Rules of Racing. They are substantially those in force to-day, though they have often been revised and amended.

The first reference to the existence of the Jockey Club which has been discovered is in Pond's *Sporting Calendar*, published at the end of 1751 or early in 1752. There, a preliminary announcement of a race to be run at Newmarket on April 1, 1752, reads: "A contribution Plate, by horses the property of the noblemen and gentlemen belonging to the Jockey Club, at the Star and Garter in Pall Mall". The race was eventually postponed until May, 1793, at which meeting this and another Jockey Club Plate, both for horses belonging to members of the Club, were decided. There is other evidence of the activities of the Club at this time.

Newmarket had become the fashionable racing centre at the beginning of the seventeenth century. King James I paid his first visit to this small town on the borders of Cambridgeshire and Suffolk in 1605, though horse racing was not then the sole attraction. There was falconry, cock-fighting and much hunting of the hare. James I built The Palace at Newmarket and, in due course, his son, Charles I, made full use of it and of the facilities the vicinity provided for racing and other sport. During his reign, regular Spring and Autumn meetings were established.

After the Restoration, Charles II and his following of young
" bloods ", passing eagerly from exile and the gloom of the puri-
tanical Commonwealth, hunted, raced, gambled and indulged all
their riotous propensities at Newmarket. The King provided
Nell Gwyn with her own establishment there. The little town
had never seen such times. It has had its ups and downs of fortune since, but owes to the patronage of Charles II its revival and
enduring establishment as the world's chief racing centre. His
nickname was " Old Rowley ", hence the " Rowley Mile ", or,
as it was at first called, " Rowley's Mile ", the course over which
the Two Thousand and One Thousand Guineas are run.

In those days, the racing consisted almost entirely of matches
made by the King and members of his court. They mostly rode
their own horses. Any disputes which arose could be settled
among themselves ; they made all the arrangements necessary for
their sport. There was not any public to be considered ; there
were no bookmakers and very few rules. This was all very well
while the racing at Newmarket was almost exclusively the concern
of the King and his entourage. But King Charles II died in 1685.
His successor James II was passionately fond of hunting and had
ideas about increasing and improving the running of royal horses,
though these were never put into effect. He became increasingly
involved in the disturbed political state of the country and it is
doubtful if he ever visited Newmarket during his short and unfortunate reign. Previously, he was often there. His successor,
William III, maintained the Royal racing and breeding establishments, kept The Palace at Newmarket in good repair and ran his
own horses frequently there and at other places. Queen Anne,
who succeeded him and reigned from 1702 to 1714, was a " good
sport". To her keen support of racing, we owe the start of Royal
Ascot, the first meeting being held by her command on that
Berkshire heath in 1711.

After the death of Charles II, the conduct of racing at Newmarket was maintained, for their own amusement, by great landowners and their aristocratic associates. They bred their own
horses and were steadily improving the breed by the importation
of Arabian, Turkish and Barbary stallions. The early Hanoverian
Kings who followed Anne were of a different type from the
Stuarts and from the sporting English generally. George I certainly paid, at least, one visit to Newmarket, and George II is
known to have kept an Arabian stallion at stud at Hampton
Court. But racing was carried on without any interest of consequence on the part of either of these monarchs. The first
member of this dynasty to become intimately connected with the
sport was the first of the two Dukes of Cumberland, both of
whom made conspicuous contributions to its history. This one

was William, second son of George II, and chiefly famed as the
" Butcher " or hero of Culloden and as the breeder of the two
most predominant progenitors of the present-day thoroughbred,
Eclipse and King Herod.

His nephew, the second Duke, bred and owned many good
horses and had runners regularly for the Derby and Oaks for
several years after the inception of those races, in 1779 and 1780
respectively. But there developed at this time a more notable
Royal association with racing, demonstrated by enthusiasm shown
for it by the young Prince of Wales, afterwards George IV, which
brings us well within the history of the Jockey Club. Indeed,
this Prince of Wales, though a member of the Club, was virtually
warned off Newmarket Heath by the three Jockey Club stewards
in consequence of the inconsistent running of his own horse,
Escape, on consecutive days at Newmarket in October, 1791.
Their spokesman Sir Charles Bunbury (whose name is given to the
" Bunbury Mile " on the existing July course), told the Prince
that as long as he continued to employ the jockey Sam Chifney, Snr.
no gentleman would run against him. The Prince, however, remained loyal to Chifney and withdrew from racing, at least at
Newmarket, for eight or nine years, when the breach was healed.
As George IV, he instituted an annual dinner to the members
of the Jockey Club, continued by William IV and resumed at
Buckingham Palace at intervals since.

It was during the reign of George II that the Jockey Club was
started. The disposition of Englishmen, united by the same
interests, to form a club became a marked social and sporting
development of this period. Most of the Newmarket " set ",
when in London, foregathered at the " Star and Garter " in Pall
Mall, a celebrated and expensive hostelry. Its name is also associated with the history of Cricket. The rules of the game were
revised there by, " a committee of noblemen and gentlemen ",
in 1774.

In those early days, however, the Jockey Club had other
meeting-places. The name adopted for the club was a simple,
straightforward nominative. Several of the founder-members
rode their own horses in races. They were, as their type had been
from the earliest Newmarket meetings, " jockies ", but the term
has since become restricted to professional riders. Use of the
description, " amateur jockey ", frequently encountered at the
present time, is inaccurate. It is a contradiction of terms, inasmuch as according to the Jockey Club's modern Rules of Racing,
a jockey is a person who rides for hire. These rules avoid the
terms, " amateur rider ", and the outmoded, " gentleman rider ",
by merely referring to those who, under certain conditions, are
permitted to ride, " without a jockey's licence ".

It must have been soon after the formation of the Jockey Club that they acquired premises in Newmarket. About 1752 they leased for 50 years a plot of land in the High Street, for the purpose of building a coffee-room, from which has developed on and around the same site the extensive buildings now known as the Jockey Club Rooms.

At this original coffee-room, these aristocratic racing folk and their friends at Newmarket could meet to make their bets, to gamble, dine and wine, together with a degree of privacy and a standard of service unobtainable in other inns and coffee-houses in the town.

These were the days before the start of the Industrial Revolution. The wealth of the country was in the hands of the land-owning patricians and the upper squirearchy. They were the governing class, exercising an almost unchallenged feudal power and taking all its privileges as a matter of course. A large proportion of those who belonged to the Jockey Club fulfilled, according to their lights, dispositions and talents, public and patrimonial duties and responsibilities. Some were men of outstanding ability and attainments, but the pursuit of gaiety and diversion tended on the part of many to be intense, lusty and unbridled. Heavy gambling was the fashion, and betting, one with the other, on the relative merit of their horses was the preoccupation of most of those who raced.

As far back as can be traced, membership of the Jockey Club has been obtained by ballot, each candidate being proposed and seconded by members. Notwithstanding the enormous development of horse racing since the Club was formed, the gradual extension of its authority from its own Newmarket meetings to practically every detail in the conduct of flat racing throughout the United Kingdom, and the sweeping advance of democratic thought, the Jockey Club remains no less exclusive than when it began. From that day, its members have jealously assured that their successors shall be of their own social pattern, most discriminately selected from owners and breeders of thoroughbreds and the sons or relatives of past members.

Except for a few years in the reign of Queen Victoria, at least one member of the Royal family has been an elected member of the Jockey Club, including George VI and his three immediate predecessors on the throne. Apart from honorary members, the list for 1949 contains less than 60 names. In 1900, there were about 70. One hundred years ago the number was 74. When Newmarket races, lacking the interest of George I and George II, ceased to be run as a Court diversion, the responsibility for their conduct fell to those chiefly interested in the continuance of the meetings. And according to the social set-up of the time, the racing aristocrats and others who were included in their most exclusive set, not only constituted the only available authority at Newmarket but assumed it in the manner born.

Some disputes arising from racing at Newmarket during the reign of Charles II had been referred to, and settled by, the merry Monarch himself. The need of an authority to deal with such objections as are inevitable in any competitive sport is as obvious as is a set of rules. Doubtless, certain individuals of prestige and experience undertook a measure of control at Newmarket, before the Jockey Club was constituted, as others did in the form of a race-committee or panel of stewards at meetings elsewhere. There were very few generally accepted rules, but custom or precedent was gradually shaping the conduct of the sport in a primitive way.

Considering all the known circumstances of the time, however, I am inclined to accept the view that the leading lights among the frequenters of Newmarket did not form the Jockey Club under pressure of any actual need for a prescribed, constituted authority to govern the racing there, but to ensure an exclusive meeting-place for themselves and those socially acceptable to them. That they also intended, collectively, to keep the racing at Newmarket in their own hands, chiefly if not entirely for their own pleasure, also seems consistent with the known facts.

About 1770 the Jockey Club decided that three of their members should be elected to act as Stewards. Certain powers and duties were delegated to them, and one of the chief, if not the most important, of their responsibilities was to adjudicate on disputes arising from the racing at Newmarket. One Steward had to retire each year, nominating his successor, with the main weight of responsibility passing annually to the third-year man—the senior Steward. That arrangement has been maintained ever since, though occasionally some particularly dominant man has held office for longer than three years, notably Admiral Rous, paramount dictator and famous turf-reformer during the third quarter of the last century.

As the reputation of the Newmarket Stewards, as an authority became more widely recognised throughout the country, the Stewards, or Promoters, of other race-meetings began to seek and obtain their ruling on knotty problems. There were few written rules or orders of the Jockey Club and such as existed in its early days were concerned chiefly with betting and the offence of watching the trials of racehorses. The conduct of each of the scores of meetings held away from Newmarket was very much a law unto itself. When matters arising from these meetings were referred for settlement to the Stewards of the Jockey Club, there must have been created the desire on their part, at least, for a greater degree of uniformity of rules and the application beyond Newmarket of a procedure of which they approved and could uphold.

The most important early step the Jockey Club took to extend its authority beyond racing at Newmarket occurred in 1816, when the Stewards published the conditions to which the disputants must agree before submitting matters arising at other meetings for decision. The parties had to sign an agreement to abide by the ruling of the Jockey Club Stewards, and the dispute could only be submitted through, or with the sanction of, the Stewards of the races where the matter arose. Sixteen years later Jockey Club authority was immensely strengthened by the publication of a notice pointing out that though the rules and orders of the Club applied only to Newmarket races, they recommended, " for the sake of greater uniformity and certainty ", that the same rules should be adopted by the Stewards of other meetings. The notice concluded with the statement : " the Stewards of the Jockey Club will not receive any reference of disputes from any places except those at which the Rules and Regulations of New-market shall have been declared to be in force in the printed articles of those races." This policy was further tightened in 1870, when the Jockey Club ruled that neither the programme nor the result of any flat-race meeting in Great Britain would be published in the official *Racing Calendar* unless the meeting was advertised to be subject to the Club's own established Rules of Racing.

But while the Jockey Club was steadily gaining, in this way, a closer control over racing away from Newmarket, they had taken effective action which, though primarily of a domestic nature, was to prove a most important contribution to their complete author-ity. From the beginning of the nineteenth century, the Club began to acquire at Newmarket, either by lease or purchase, first the land over which the horses raced and, later, large areas around the town used chiefly for training purposes, so that it is now the owner of about 3,500 acres, including two racecourses, the train-ing grounds, and two farms. The Club's legal right to " warn off " their property at Newmarket an offending person was estab-lished in the High Court in 1862.

New rules of 1877 gave more specific and extensive effect to the control which, by this time, the Jockey Club had obtained over racing in general. They gathered up a number of loose ends in their administration. The " recognised " meetings became those the programmes of which were accepted by the Jockey Club for publication in the *Racing Calendar* and which conformed to their regulations. Any horse which ran at an unrecognised meet-ing was disqualified from racing under their rules. Defaulters and persons found guilty of corrupt practices were barred **from**

THE DERBY FIELD AT THE MILE POST, 1948

THE START OF THE 1924 DERBY, SHOWING THE EARLY TYPE OF GATE

THE START OF THE GREAT METROPOLITAN AT EPSOM, 1939, SHOWING
THE MODERN TYPE OF GATE

making entries at any " recognised " meeting and from having any horse under their care, training or superintendence. In 1879 all jockeys were required for the first time to obtain from the Jockey Club a licence to ride, which could be withdrawn at the discretion of the stewards. All race-meetings became subject to the licence of the club, for the grant of which the fulfillment of certain conditions, including minimum prize money, was required.

With the re-casting of the rules in 1890 the Jockey Club had achieved complete control of the sport, and a new period, the present period of racing, may be said to have begun. There was, in all truth, great scope for improvement and reform. The number of runners had substantially decreased during the previous 20 years. The funds of the Jockey Club were so low that when in 1890 a second July meeting was introduced at Newmarket, nine of the 26 events were selling-races or those in which horses could be entered to be sold, all calculated to produce a surplus for the Club on the sale of the winner. It accepted in that year the offer of £3,000 from a non-member, to be used as prize money for three races during the season for the encouragement of stayers. One of these was included in the mean programme of that July meeting.

Writers of the period make frequent and pointed references to " in and out " running and unscrupulously prepared " coups " ; there are details of a number of scandals and many suggestions of the existence of others. It is not surprising that large and influential sections of the public were strongly opposed to racing, believing, in their limited knowledge of it, that the thoroughbred horse was maintained solely as an instrument of gambling. Starting by flag, often wearisome and unsatisfactory, made lotteries of short races and placed a premium on ill-discipline among jockeys when under the starter's orders. Jockeys, too, were betting quite openly until the practice was forbidden in 1900.

As is natural, the administrative energy and enterprise of successive Stewards of the Jockey Club and their ability, not only to perceive the need for action or reform, but to secure the adoption of their ideas, have varied greatly. One of the most active and boldest Turf rulers and legislators of the last 50 years was the Third Earl of Durham (born 1855 ; died 1928). He was senior Steward in 1899, when he and his two colleagues, including Lord Crewe (later Ambassador in France), ordered the newly invented starting-gate to be tried at the Epsom Summer meeting. It was adopted for all courses the next season—1900—though horses above the age of three were not subject to the change until the following year.

Another feature of 1900 was the sensational termination, by the Stewards, of the riding career of the brilliant and successful

C

American jockey Tod Sloan, who had revolutionised the style of
race-riding in this country by his crouching seat, short leathers,
and pace-forcing tactics. He had offended against the new rule
which prohibited betting by jockeys. His general behaviour, too,
had incurred official disapprobation and he was told that he need
not apply again for a licence. Lord Durham was re-appointed
senior Steward in 1902 and, in that year, the conduct of jockeys
occasioned further action. One leading rider was " warned off ",
another had his licence withdrawn, and others were severely
cautioned for associating with persons of bad character.

The Stewards also tackled the practice of doping, which up to
that time had never been forbidden. From the earliest days, such
stimulants as whiskey and port had been administered to faint-
hearted horses, just before a race, but the invasion of American
trainers with their horses and company of gamblers in the last
quarter of the nineteenth century was responsible for the extensive
use of drugs for the same purpose. On the recommendation of
the Stewards in 1903, the Jockey Club approved an addition to
the rules, which prohibited the practice and decreed that any
offender would be " warned off " Newmarket Heath, " and all
other places where these rules are in force."

After Lord Durham's campaign against some opprobrious features of racing at the beginning of this century, the policy of the
Jockey Club up to the outbreak of the First World War, in 1914,
was not particularly eventful or progressive in a popular sense,
though men of great talents and distinction in public life continued
to take a conspicuous part in its deliberations. Its standing had
achieved world-wide recognition and, during this period, many
racing authorities overseas applied for, and were accorded, reci-
procal agreements with the Jockey Club. These agreements
included the mutual exclusion from any participation in racing,
under the rule of the bodies concerned, of " disqualified persons ",
leaving little scope anywhere in the world for the activities of
anyone " warned off " Newmarket Heath. In purely domestic
matters, at this time, the Jockey Club were on occasions positively
reactionary. Races of 4 furlongs, previously discontinued as un-
desirable, were revived in 1905, though restricted to two-year-
olds up to the Epsom Summer meeting. These " scurries ",
however, were stopped again in 1913. By a small majority, the
Jockey Club first agreed to forbid the use of an assumed name
by owners, for racing purposes—which was a common practice—
but the proposal was defeated when submitted for confirmation.
This desirable reform was not adopted until 1919.

Up to 1913 a considerable number of horses had run unnamed,
being distinguished only by the name of their dam, such as the
Golden Knot filly, or the Wheelabout colt. Any reason which

could be advanced as an excuse for the tardiness of owners in this matter was greatly outweighed by the claims for the abolition of the practice, urged persistently for at least 50 years. The Jockey Club ruled, in 1913, that no horse, *three-years-old or upwards* was to run unnamed, and it was not until 1946 that they went the whole hog by ordering that *no* horse would be allowed to run until he had received a name.

When the war started in 1914, the Stewards—Captain J. H. Greer, Lord Wolverton, and Lord Villiers (soon to become Lord Jersey), called a special meeting of the Jockey Club to ascertain the views of members about the continuance of racing. The meeting decided unanimously that the season's fixtures at Newmarket and elsewhere should be carried out " where the local conditions permitted, and the feeling of the locality was not adverse to the meeting being held ". In May 1915, at the request of the Government, all remaining fixtures for the year were cancelled except those for Newmarket, " the peculiar circumstances and industries of which combined ", the Government admitted, " to make this exception expedient ". The reason given for the ban was the necessity for keeping the railway-system free for the rapid and unimpeded transit of troops and munitions. Extra meetings were arranged for Newmarket, the added prize money for which was guaranteed by the proprietors of other race-meetings. No call was made on them, though the Jockey Club did accept gifts to a total amount of £6,000 towards the £28,000 distributed in " added money " at the extra 1915 Newmarket meetings. Early in 1916 Captain Greer (who had continued in office) and the other Stewards, by the unanimous wish of the members of the Jockey Club, applied to the Government for additional racing facilities. The President of the Board of Trade, " saw no objection ", to a limited number of meetings at Gatwick, Lingfield, Newbury and Windsor, which were duly arranged in addition to the ordinary, and three extra, fixtures at Newmarket.

There was persistent and clamorous opposition in Parliament and the Press to the continuance of racing, and it was fortunate for the future of bloodstock-breeding that among the members of the Jockey Club at that time were men of great wisdom, tact, repute and influence. Lord Jersey became senior Steward in 1916 and assumed that responsibility again in 1918. He was exceptionally able and, as his views were wider and more progressive than had previously characterised the general policy of the Jockey Club, racing suffered a great loss when in 1924 Lord Jersey died in middle age. Other wartime Stewards who most capably sustained the heavy burdens of office at that time were Captain Greer and Sir John Thursby. Invaluable support and assistance to the Stewards was rendered during these years of trial by men of such character and political experience as the late Lord Derby (Secretary for War in Lloyd George's Cabinet), the late Lord Rosebery (a former Prime Minister), Lord Crewe, and Lord Durham.

Most of these men were members of the deputation to the Prime Minister (Mr. Lloyd George) when he was persuaded on July 4, 1917, to remove the ban which had been imposed on all racing by the War Cabinet from April 5 of that year.   Hurried preparations were made to resume the Newmarket meetings, including the New Derby and New Oaks, and authority was granted for some fixtures at Manchester, Stockton, Windsor, and Brighton.   Steps were taken by the Jockey Club to implement the request of the Government that the number of horses in training should be reduced to 1,200.   (At the start of the war the number in England and Scotland had been over 4,000.)

Two points expressly acknowledged by the Government during that war have an important place in the history of the Jockey Club. They were : (*a*) That the Jockey Club was the supreme racing authority, and (*b*) the full recognition, by the Government, of " the national importance of horse-breeding ", to maintain which, the War Cabinet admitted, somewhat tardily perhaps, " a limited amount of racing is essential " (President of the Board of Trade to Lord Jersey, May 22, 1918).

The sweeping German push in the Spring of 1918 was, while it lasted, an intense crisis for the Allies, and a revision of the racing fixtures arranged for that season was imperative.   Some meetings were being held away from Newmarket, but none of these was permitted after the Manchester Whit-week fixture.   For the rest of the year, racing was again limited to Newmarket, where the season ended on November 1, ten days before the Armistice.

Racing was resumed with a full fixture list and with enormously increased attendances in 1919.   Conditions and arrangements on many race-courses were severely strained, by the large crowds. The activities of thieves and gangsters became a scandal. Members of the Jockey Club, naturally, saw little of what was going on and were slow to believe what they heard about it.   In 1920, as the result of proceedings instituted by the Jockey Club, several persons were " warned off " for fraudulently substituting three-year-olds for two-year-olds in races for two-year-olds, and other offences.

Sir Samuel Scott became senior Steward in 1922 and, before he retired at the end of his year of office, the Jockey Club had decided to appoint their own officials to supervise and tighten arrangements made by race-course managements for the protection of the public.   Sir Samuel was succeeded as senior Steward by Lord Jersey, who also pressed this reform, and the Jockey Club and National Hunt Racecourse Personnel, as this new organisation was called, has functioned most effectively ever since. In 1923 the Jockey Club instituted an insurance scheme for the benefit of jockeys and apprentices killed or injured in the course of their profession.

During the 1914–18 War, a number of owners and trainers combined to request the Jockey Club to consider the introduction of the Totalisator, an innovation which had for some years been widely recommended. The petition was not unfavourably received, but it was pointed out that before this form of betting could be introduced, legislation would be required and that the middle of a world-war was not the time to press for it. However, when in 1927 the Government imposed for a short time a tax on betting and racecourse attendances were greatly reduced in consequence, the Jockey Club set up a committee, with Lord Hamilton of Dalzell as chairman and including representatives of the National Hunt Committee and the National Coursing Club, to enquire " how betting might best be made to contribute to the maintenance of sport ".

As a result of the recommendation of this committee, the Racecourse Betting Act of 1928 was prepared and passed by Parliament, legalising Totalisator operations on British racecourses and providing for a special charge on race-course bookmakers. The Totalisator, conducted by the Racecourse Betting Control Board (which is responsible to Parliament) was first operated on July 2, 1929, at Newmarket and Carlisle. This momentous innovation, which has proved of inestimable benefit to racing, is attributable largely to the zeal and influence of Lord Hamilton of Dalzell. He was one of several effective and liberal-minded administrators who made the period 1921–31 one of exceptional progress in the history of English racing. The reported proceedings of the Jockey Club at that time reveal, as never before, a refreshing and repeated concern for the interests of the general racing public.

It has always been the policy of the Jockey Club to control and administer the sport, to maintain its good name, to protect and advance the welfare of the English thoroughbred horse. So long, however, as race-course proprietors have complied with the Jockey Club's rules and regulations, the comfort and convenience of the race-going public have been regarded as a domestic matter, dependent on the degree of enterprise actuating individual executives. In due course, the Totalisator began to provide, from its profits, grants for the general benefit of racing or particular improvements on race-courses, which were also reaping substantial revenue from the levy on bookmakers. As we shall see, the Jockey Club has controlled the expenditure of these funds, devoting them either to purposes of general advantage or ensuring that they are used to good purpose.

Other notable changes of a technical nature were made in the 1920's. Always, entries and nominations for races had been rendered void by the death of the person in whose name they stood, a rule which, in some cases, deprived horses of exceptional merit of fulfilling their classic engagements and adversely affected the interests of a deceased estate. In 1929 Mr. James de Rothschild earned the thanks of his fellow-members of the Jockey Club for his successful efforts to alter this condition. As the result of a friendly law case in which the late Edgar Wallace, author, playwright and race-horse owner, was concerned with the Stewards of the Jockey Club, it was established that all rights, privileges and liabilities attached to entries standing in the name of an owner passed on his or her death to his or her personal representative. An early consequence of this change was that Cameronian, who had been nominated for the Derby by Lord Dewar (died 1930), was able to run for, and win, that and other important races in 1931 for his nephew and heir, Mr. J. A. Dewar.

Among the ancient practices abolished at this time were the " running off " of dead-heats, and the provision that when an owner ran two horses in a race, he could declare to win with one and have his other runner pulled if such was necessary to allow the " declared " horse to win. In the case of dead-heats, the stakes must now be divided, while it is laid down that every horse must run on his merits, however many an owner may start in a race. The present type of unbreakable starting-gate replaced in 1929 the " tapes " through which impetuous jockeys could burst with impunity, a great improvement effected during the late Lord Ellesmere's term as senior Steward.

The huge sweepstakes newly organised in Ireland on English races received the official notice of the Jockey Club in 1930. The prizes had included a substantial sum to everyone who drew a runner. In consequence, some entries were started only because the owner had received an inducement to that effect from the person who had drawn his horse in the sweepstakes. Some enormous fields were the result until the promoters gave effect to the expressed desire of the Jockey Club that they would " co-operate to safeguard the interests of racing by not discriminating, in the amount of prize money offered, between entries and runners, other than placed horses ".

At the 1930 Kempton Park August meeting, the horse Don Pat was examined by order of the local Stewards after he had won a race. As there was evidence of the administration of a stimulant, he was disqualified and his trainer subsequently had his licence withdrawn by the Stewards of the Jockey Club. The trainer brought an action against the Stewards of the Jockey Club which he lost on appeal.

From the earliest days of organised racing, every race-meeting has been controlled by a panel of local Stewards, usually three in number. At first, they were big-wigs of the neighbourhood and as sportsmen and owners of horses closely interested in the meeting. As racing became more popular, more highly organised, and the governing rules of the Jockey Club more exacting and circumspect, the responsibilities of local Stewards increased. Some race-course managements were more successful than others in securing Stewards of personal repute with an adequate degree of racing experience, and zeal. Many local Stewards, lacking practice as race-readers, or disinclined to make a burden of their honorary duties, failed to notice incidents in the running which, to more experienced observers, seemed to call for official enquiry. Some of the criticism to which this method of supervision was continually subjected for longer than many can remember was doubtless ill-informed and not always disinterested, but generally the shortcomings of the system were obvious to all.

The call for Stipendary Stewards was insistent and, in 1931, the present Lord Rosebery, initiated a discussion at a meeting of the Jockey Club on the matter. His suggestion was not the replacement of local Stewards by Stipendiaries but the provision of paid secretaries to assist and advise the local Stewards. Three years later the Jockey Club decided to proceed on these lines if the necessary finance could be provided from the grants forthcoming from the operation of the Totalisator. The scheme was passed before the commencement of the 1936 season. On the whole, it has produced a great improvement in the supervision of the actual racing. It was in 1936, too, that the appointment of all officials, except that of the Clerk of the Course, was taken out of the hands of race-course managements and undertaken by the Jockey Club.

Throughout the period between 1921 and the outbreak of the second World War there was on the part of successive Stewards of the Jockey Club a notable concern for the interests of the ordinary race-goer. Though progress in that wide field was slow, it was a new and welcome feature of Jockey Club policy. Directly the war started, most race-course buildings were requisitioned by Government departments chiefly for the occupation of troops. The Rowley Course at Newmarket was taken over by the R.A.F. and all racing there during the war was run over the July course.

As soon as war was declared, on September 3, 1939, sports gatherings were prohibited and racing was not resumed until October 18, at Newmarket. For the rest of the season, there were also fixtures at Newbury, Thirsk, Stockton, and Manchester. Several courses were used for racing in 1940 until, on June 19, the Jockey Club announced that, after consultation with the Government, all racing was suspended until further notice. A list of fixtures was resumed on September 14th. Meanwhile, a great reduction in the number of horses in training and at stud was being effected.

A limited amount of racing was maintained for the remainder of the war period, though in 1942 the number of courses available was greatly reduced and a regional system introduced, whereby racing at Newmarket, with the exception of the substitute classic races and a few other important events, was confined to horses trained there. The Salisbury and Windsor meetings were for horses trained south of the Trent (Newmarket excluded), and Pontefract and Stockton provided for those trained in the North.

No decision taken by the Jockey Club in the last 50 years has revealed a higher degree of administerial foresight and reforming zeal than that, proposed in 1941 by Lord Ilchester and seconded by the late Lord Derby, to appoint a small committee " to consider the whole future of racing in general and in particular with reference to the encouragement of owners and the greater comfort and convenience of the public ". It was called the Racing Reorganisation Committee. Lord Ilchester was appointed chairman and the other members were the Duke of Norfolk, Lord Zetland, the late Lord Harewood, the late Lord Portal, and Sir Humphrey de Trafford. They received evidence from representatives of many organisations and a large number of individuals interested in the future of racing in its various aspects. Suggestions were invited from the public and received in great abundance and variety.

The Committee submitted their report to the Stewards of the Jockey Club in 1943, prefacing it with the observation that it was clear that a strong demand prevailed for change in many directions. " The attractiveness of racing in England ", the Committee stated, " has fallen far behind that in the countries in which it is of more recent origin, from the point of view of the general public as distinct from the regular race-goer."

These members of the Jockey Club who formed the Committee burst with surprising frankness into a sweeping indictment of many features of the sport they had assisted to regulate and govern. They confirmed what had been obvious for at least 100 years, that " race-course executives, with few exceptions, have shown little disposition to cater for the individual man or woman outside the fringe of those directly concerned with the business of racing ". The Committee added that, from the occasional race-goer must be drawn those increased attendances from which the new money required for improvements would be forthcoming.

The recommendations made by the Committee concerned the breeder, the owner, the public, race-course executives, and finance. On the whole, their report was remarkably comprehensive and detailed and most progressive in its outlook. It was fully discussed at a meeting of the Jockey Club in 1943 but, of course, nothing could be done about it as long as the war lasted. The following year, Lord Rosebery moved and the Duke of Norfolk seconded, that a committee should be set up to consider the question of photographing finishes of races, a matter which had not been dealt with by the Reorganisation Committee. This was done, with the result that the first camera was installed and operated at the first Newmarket July meeting of 1947, and its use has been gradually extended until all courses will be equipped with it, for the assistance of the judge, and the satisfaction of the public, when the finish of a race is close.

After further consideration of the Reorganisation Committee's report, the Stewards issued, soon after the conclusion of the war, a declaration of policy which they stated would be concentrated on the provision of cheaper and better accommodation for the public and increased prize money and a reduction of expenses to owners. They appointed an experienced journalist, Mr. J. H. Freeman, as Public Relations Officer, who acts in the same capacity for the National Hunt Committee and the Racecourse Betting Control Board.

As the Stewards predicted, restrictions on the supply of building materials, labour and the maintenance of an entertainment tax of nearly 50 per cent. on admission prices at race-meetings, greatly restricted the fulfilment of their post-war policy, but much that could be done in the way of minor improvements has been carried out on race-courses by the more enterprising executives. The supervision by the Jockey Club of race-course managements and their policy has been intensified, and the grants from the profits of the Totalisator applied in accordance with the Club's declared concern for race-horse owners and the race-going public.

The Reorganisation Committee expressed the opinion that, whilst the responsibility and authority of the Jockey Club should remain " undiluted and unimpaired ", closer contact was desirable between the Stewards and race-horse owners. The Committee suggested that, to facilitate discussion between the parties, the Stewards should invite all owners to meet them in London once a year. That has not been done. In recent years, an organisation called the Racehorse Owners' Association has gained in strength and accomplished much useful work. One would have thought that its executive committee was a suitable body with which this proposed contact could be made with excellent effect. So far, the attitude of the Jockey Club towards the Association has been slow to reveal that degree of cordial co-operation and encouragement which would appear to many to be desirable.

It would be interesting to have some authoritative amplification of that word, " undiluted ", in connection with the Jockey Club. No one interested in racing would wish their authority to be weakened.   There is among racing-people an unequivocal, universal loyalty to its rule, inspired by an innate respect for the manifest and incalculable benefits the sport has derived from it, the remarkable orderliness of its present administration and a deep faith in the Club's undeviating fairness and predominant concern for the virility and reputation of the sport and the welfare of the thoroughbred horse.

The Jockey Club has been, and continues to be, a generally acceptable autocracy.   Whatever its shortcomings, there is not the slightest suggestion on the part of anyone who submits in any way to its omnipotence that its authority should be " diluted " in the sense that it should be watered down and weakened.   The greater part of the life of the Jockey Club has coincided with the growth of democratic government and social conditions in this country.   Its completely despotic rule of a great national sport with an integral industry of considerable magnitude, by this self-elected, class-restricted body, has been gradually established and exercised almost unaffected by the popular trend.   Whether its membership can be maintained as an aristocratic preserve, strongly hereditary in character, in face of changing social and economic conditions and whether men of ripe racing experience and credit should, with advantage, be co-opted from a wider social field are questions which may, in time, become pressing.

In the second half of the nineteenth century the number of people who were attracted to racing as owners and breeders began to increase.   To a large extent, they were men whose wealth was more or less self-made in commerce.   Many of this class raced in the best style and achieved conspicuous success as thoroughbred breeders, but rarely was one of them acceptable as a fellow-member by the titled folk and squires of the Jockey Club and then only when the candidate had outlived his generation and had one foot in the grave.   To-day, few apart from those whose money has been derived from commerce can afford to race in a big way.

The extreme conservatism of the Jockey Club, though doubtless the mainstay of the successful fulfilment of their responsibilities, is at times open to particular complaint.   What they do is far less subject to criticism than the time they take to do it.   It has been said with an element of truth that 50 years has been the average interval between the first public advocacy of a desirable innovation, and its adoption by the Jockey Club.

Behind the Stewards of the Jockey Club, and always at their elbow, is the famous family firm of Weatherby and Sons, fulfilling in some respects functions broadly comparable with those which the senior permanent officials of a Government department render to transient ministerial chiefs. But there is much more than that in the relationship between the Jockey Club and Weatherby's and in the family's connection with racing.

In 1773, James Weatherby published his first *Racing Calendar* in succession to similar racing records compiled by others. In it, he describes himself as " Keeper of the Match-book at Newmarket ", a Jockey Club appointment which still exists, combined with that of Secretary. Whether or not this James Weatherby was also Secretary in 1773 is not clear, but in all probability he assumed the dual capacity. In any case, a Weatherby has filled the two appointments ever since.

The private firm of Weatherby not only provides a secretary and administrative organisation for the Jockey Club. On their own account, they act as general stakeholders, collecting and distributing among race-course executives and owners, prize money, entry fees and forfeits, a centralised procedure which gradually replaced the custom by which race-horse owners and the stakeholders of individual race-meetings themselves collected direct the sums due to them. Weatherby's also debit to the account of owners, every jockey's riding fee and similar disbursements, acting much in the way of bankers, with, of course, a charge for keeping the account. They have their own printing-plant and are owners and editors of the *General Stud Book*, begun with a supplement by James Weatherby in 1791, and followed by Volume I in 1808, " to correct the increasing evil of false and inaccurate pedigrees ". A new, up-to-date volume is published every four years, containing a record of the pedigree and the thoroughbred produce during that period of every mare eligible for entry. The price of Volume 19, published in 1901, was 25s. Recently, Volume 31 was produced, the cost being £8 8s. The Jockey Club has no official connection with, or direct authority over, the *General Stud Book*, though the Editors have occasionally asked its advice when a particularly important development has called for the consideration of some variation in the rule of admission to this exclusive record of pure blood.

In 1902, however, the Jockey Club became the owners, by purchase from Messrs. Weatherby, of the *Racing Calendar*, which includes the annual calf-bound volume, *Races Past* (in much the same form as James Weatherby's 1773 edition, but of greatly increased bulk), *Races to Come*, and the weekly *Sheet Calendar*, which, as the official organ of the Jockey Club, has proved to be an instrument of great effect in the extension and consolidation of their authority.

No account of the development of the power of the Jockey Club would be complete without reference to an existing scheme, which, if ever carried out, will be the consummation of the policy pursued from the time the Club first concerned itself with the affairs of race-meetings other than those at Newmarket.

As the result of a recommendation of the Reorganisation Committee, a company, called the Jockey Club Racecourses Ltd., was registered with the object of acquiring, by negotiation, the share-capital of existing race-courses. So far, the Treasury has been unable to grant permission for the scheme to be implemented, as the Jockey Club has announced it can be as soon as the control of capital-issues is relaxed. Fixed-interest bonds would be issued in place of the dividend-yielding share-capital of the race-course companies acquired, an arrangement which would usually provide a larger proportion of the profits to be devoted to the benefit of the sport generally. The ultimate aim of the scheme is to bring all proprietary, dividend-paying race-courses into the management of this Jockey-Club-controlled Trust of beneficent purpose.

CHAPTER III

THE NATIONAL STUD

By Eric Rickman

AS soon as I found, as a schoolboy, that the racing news interested me I became a devoted partisan. The first Derby to raise my enthusiasm was that won by Diamond Jubilee for the Prince of Wales, shortly to become King Edward VII. A romantic attachment to the fortunes of the Royal stable followed. I had another favourite owner, Colonel Hall Walker, doubtless because he was winning many races at the time and was very much " in the news " in consequence.

Colonel Hall Walker was born December 25, 1851. As a young man, he bred, raced and rode ponies, known as Galloways, the racing of which had considerable popularity and support, particularly in country districts. He also won many point-to-points and steeplechases on his own horses, but it was not until 1895 that he registered his colours, blue-and-white check, with the Jockey Club, adding a cerise cap the following year.

In 1902, Colonel Hall Walker established the Tully Stud bordering on The Curragh, Co. Kildare, and immediately produced the succession of high-class winners which were to fire my boyish interest.

The first of importance was Cherry Lass, by Isinglass out of Black Cherry, by Bendigo. Having won three of her five races as a two-year-old in 1904, she was the best of her sex the following year, winning six races of a total value of £13,319. Such triumphs at the present time would have netted at least double that sum, as they included the One Thousand Guineas, the Oaks and the St. James's Palace Stakes. During that season, her two-year-old half-brother, Black Arrow, won three races, including the Coventry Stakes, failing on other occasions through being fractious at the start. He was a 100 to 7 *on* chance when, in a field of three for the Lavant Stakes at Goodwood, he was left at the post.

The rapid success of the Tully Stud may be judged from the Ascot results of 1905. Colonel Hall Walker had five winners at the meeting, all of his own breeding. Three of them were two-year-olds and another of that age was second, beaten a neck. One of the winners, the filly Colonia (New Stakes) was successful in five consecutive races that year, including the Gimcrack Stakes.

The stud's next classic winner was the filly Witch Elm (Orme-Cannie Lassie) ; she took the One Thousand Guineas of 1907. By this time the racing fortune of King Edward VII and his Sandringham Stud had sadly declined.   There was an impression that the King was losing interest in racing and breeding and it was known that the yearlings he sent into training in 1907 gave no promise of a change of luck.   Colonel Hall Walker showed a generous appreciation of the position by offering to lease his yearling colts to the King and the proposal was accepted.   These colts included Minoru (Cyllene-Mother Siegel), destined to win in 1909 for King Edward his third Derby, following a Two Thousand Guineas victory in the Royal colours.

Prince Palatine (Persimmon-Lady Lightfoot), bred at Tully, won the St. Leger of 1911 for Mr. T. Pilkington and, later, two Ascot Gold Cups.   Night Hawk (Gallinule-Jean's Folly) was successful in the St. Leger of 1913 for Colonel Hall Walker himself.

Other notable winners bred at this stud up to the outbreak of war in 1914 were : Charles O'Malley (Ascot Vase), White Eagle, William Penn, Challenger, Carrickfergus, Let Fly, Ulster King, Polar Star, and Lily Rose.   Colonel Hall Walker headed the list of winning owners in 1905 and 1907 and was third in 1906.   The produce of the Tully Stud kept him among the five most successful breeders in every season, except one, from 1905 to 1914.

There is in this record clear evidence of a studious, resolute, and well-founded breeding policy.   Apart from this, Colonel Hall Walker, being deeply interested in astrology, applied the medium of horoscopes to his racing and breeding ventures.   He acted only if the portent of the horoscope were favourable.

Whatever influence astrology may have had on the unquestionable genius of Colonel Hall Walker (created Lord Wavertree in 1919) as a breeder of bloodstock, there are attributable to him two developments of great consequence to racing and the English thoroughbred.

The late Sidney Galtrey ("Hotspur" of the *Daily Telegraph*) quotes, in his delightful book, *Memoirs of a Racing Journalist*, a letter he received from the Aga Khan in which the latter declared that it was due to Lord Wavertree and to his personal friendship that he started to race on the English Turf.   " I would probably never have been known ", writes the Aga Khan, " as an owner west of Suez had he not, during and after my visit to Tully in 1904, urged me to take up racing in England.   He undoubtedly gave me much good advice, and up to the last I never took an important decision without asking his opinion."

The Aga Khan mentions in the same letter, that Lord Wavertree's successes were the outcome of comparatively little expenditure, adding : " He always told me that had the money

I invested in horses been spent according to his views there would have been no limit to the successes I would have had. Looking back, I see . . . it would have been true in practice, year by year."

This is a remarkable tribute to the judgment of the founder of the Tully Stud; it is almost incredible that the Aga Khan could have been more successful than he has been on the English Turf during the last 30 years.

Lord Wavertree was not elected a member of the Jockey Club until 1919 (when he was 68) and he died in February, 1932. His outspoken opinions on breeding were dogmatic; there was no mistaking his pride in his own achievements. I never knew him personally (I began racing regularly in 1920) but can well understand that, whilst he was evidently pleased by favourable publicity, his demeanour was too oracular to make him generally popular among racing people.

Yet this is the man who spontaneously surrendered a future Derby victory to the pleasure of his King, fathered the Aga Khan's stupendous influence, as a breeder, on the modern thoroughbred and, finally, in 1915 gave to the nation the Tully Stud, at the height of its strength and fame, together with his racing establishment at Russley Park, Wiltshire.

The terms of this munificent and far-sighted gift were, briefly that all Colonel Hall Walker's stallions, brood-mares, female yearlings, the foals, cart-horses, half-bred horses, their provender and tackle, 600 head of cattle, and the Tully residence (including the furniture and valuable pictures) should be handed over to the Government to be run as a National Stud.

All that the Government were asked to pay for was the land, which they were to have at their own valuation. Following two months of indecision and after Colonel Hall Walker, becoming impatient or despairing of the Government's wavering, had sent most of his splendid mares to England with the intention of selling them by public auction, the offer was accepted in December, just in time to avert dispersal, and the mares were returned to Ireland.

The Government paid £47,625 for Tully and £18,000 for Russley Park, for which figures and much other information I am indebted to the Ministry of Agriculture and Fisheries. At Tully, there were nearly 1,000 acres, divided into about 100 paddocks.

In the early summer of 1915, the Jockey Club, at the request of the Government, abandoned all remaining racing fixtures for the season, except those at Newmarket. One of the considerations prompting Colonel Hall Walker's offer was his desire to stiffen the Government's interest in light-horse breeding and, consequently, in the maintenance of as much racing, during the war, as the conditions allowed.

As to Russley Park, his idea was that the establishment should be devoted to light-horse breeding, chiefly for military purposes. He envisaged it as a depot for a number of thoroughbred stallions, for whose services only a nominal fee should be levied. His vision could not have comprehended the fast developing mechanisation of warfare. The almost ageless era of armed horsemen had already closed ; my own regiment had landed that year on the beaches of Gallipoli in breeches and spurs, but with infantry equipment. They were never to see their horses again. The few subsequent achievements of cavalry, as such, were merely the afterglow of their departed glory.

Colonel Hall Walker thought that the income from the National Stud at Tully could be used to maintain Russley in accordance with his views. He hoped that some of the horses included in his gift would form the nucleus of a group of stallions there and that others would be purchased. Russley Park was in fact used, but not in this way, by the War Office for military purposes throughout the war. In October, 1924, the Ministry of Agriculture, to whom responsibility for the National Stud was delegated, handed over Russley Park finally to the War Office, when the administration of the Light-Horse Breeding Scheme was transferred to that department.

The stallions taken over at Tully were : White Eagle (fully booked at 60 gns.), Royal Realm (60 gns.),Great Sport (48 gns.), and Night Hawk (25 gns.). Count Schomberg, of whom Colonel Hall Walker had made extensive and successful use, had died in 1914. Minoru had been sold to Russia in 1913 after only two years at stud, first at Tully and finally at Newmarket.

Forty-three brood mares were included in the gift, an almost priceless collection. So great has been the subsequent influence of many of them that no record of the achievements of the National Stud would be adequate without the full list, which is :

> Bella Roba, by Count Schomberg out of Black Cherry
> Belle Royal, by Royal Realm out of Belle Vale
> Belle Vale, by Isinglass out of Meddlesome
> Black Cherry, by Bendigo out of Black Duchess
> Blanche, by White Eagle out of Black Cherry
> Burnt Almond, by Gallinule out of Jean's Folly
> Canidia, by Count Schomberg out of Cannie Lass
> Colonia, by Persimmon out of Sandblast
> Countess Zia, by Gallinule out of Order of Merit
> Crucible, by Count Schomberg out of Sandblast
> Dolabella, by White Eagle out of Gondolette
> Dorothy Court, by Robert le Diable out of Cherry Lass
> Dutch Lady, by Count Schomberg out of Elm Twig
> Elm Twig, by Orme out of Lucky Hit

LORD WAVERTREE

MR. PETER BURRELL, WITH SUN CHARIOT

[*Facing page* 36

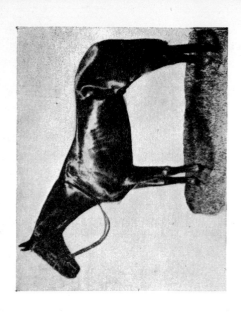

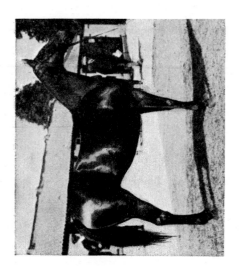

Left
SCEPTRE
Persimmon-Ornament

Right
BARHAM
Blandford-Friar's Daughter

Left
GAINSBOROUGH
Bayardo-Rosedrop

Right
BLANDFORD
Swynford-Blanche

Empyrean, by White Eagle out of Imperatrix
Fine Art, by Songcraft out of Belle Vale
Flaming Vixen, by Flying Fox out of Amphora
Flash of Steel, by Royal Realm out of Flaming Vixen
Honey Sweet, by Laveno out of Honeydew
Imperatrix, by Ladas out of V.R.
Jean's Folly, by Ayrshire out of Black Cherry
Lady Lightfoot, by Isinglass out of Glare
Lily Rose, by Wildflower out of Rose Ronald
Meinhart, by County Schomberg out of Tully Lass
Merry Gal, by Galopin out of Mary Seaton
Mindful, by Minoru out of Noble Martha
Mine Own, by Minoru out of Meinhart
Miss Cue, by Orme out of Lucky Hit
Mountain Eagle, by White Eagle out of Black Cherry
Mountain Pine, by White Eagle out of Witch Elm
Northumbria, by St. Aidan out of Honeysweet
Order of Merit, by Collar out of Lady Rayleigh
Osca Marah, by Songcraft out of Colonia
Petroline, by St. Aidan out of Lady Lightfoot
Purple and Gold, by Royal Realm out of Dorothy Court
Queen Mother, by Diamond Jubilee out of Barbara
Sea Eagle, by White Eagle out of Mother Siegel
Sweet Waters, by Count Schomberg out of Benedictine
Tillywhim, by Minoru out of Lily Rose
Tully Lass, by Isinglass out of Tullia
Weldam, by Count Schomberg out of Miss Gunning II
White Lie, by White Eagle out of Jean's Folly
Witch Elm, by Orme out of Cannie Lassie.

Sir Henry Greer was appointed Director of the National Stud and continued in that capacity until December 31, 1933, when he was succeeded by Mr. Noble B. Johnson. Mr. Peter Burrell was appointed Assistant Director a few weeks later and became Director on the death of Mr. Noble Johnson on March 4, 1937.

At one time, Sir Henry Greer also managed the Aga Khan's Irish stud close to Tully. Much credit for the great and consistent success of the National Stud, from its inception, is due to Sir Henry's skilful and careful management.

The policy from the first was strictly commercial, though, following criticism of the sale by the National Stud of Blue Train in 1947, some important changes emerged from representations made to the Minister of Agriculture (Mr. Tom Williams) by The Thoroughbred Breeders' Association, to which development I will refer in due course.

From the time Tully was taken over by the Government, most of the young stock bred there were sold regularly, as yearlings, at auction. To replace old or drafted brood mares selected fillies

D

bred at the stud have been retained. The policy has been to lease them for their racing careers either to the late Lord Lonsdale (up to 1939) or, subsequently, to King George VI. In 1927 four yearling colts, including Lyme Regis, winner of the Prince of Wales's Stakes at Ascot, were leased to King George V, and, throughout the existence of the National Stud, some colts of particular promise have not been offered for sale as yearlings, but leased for racing to Lord Lonsdale or to King George VI. The terms of lease were, up to 1939, that the Stud should be credited with 33 per cent. of the stakes won. In that year it was changed to a fifty-fifty basis. In 1943, the allocation of winnings reverted to 33 per cent. for the Stud.

The first substantial fruits of this leasing policy came with the 1922 St. Leger victory of Royal Lancer (Spearmint-Royal Favour) in the colours of Lord Lonsdale, to whom, at the same time, Diligence had been leased. A. Sadler, jun. trained Royal Lancer. Diligence was with Fred Darling at Beckhampton, to which stable all the horses leased by the National Stud for racing have since been sent, with the exception of the four colts trained by the late W. R. Jarvis for King George V.

Diligence, having dead-heated for the Kempton Park Jubilee (1923) and won the Newbury Summer Cup, besides other races, returned to Tully as a stallion, in which capacity he gained distinction as sire of Clarence, dam of Sun Chariot. He was eventually sold to Russia, but died there soon afterwards.

Warden of the Marches, won many races, including the City and Suburban, Chesterfield Cup and Champion Stakes of 1926, while leased to Lord Lonsdale and was then sold by the National Stud to Lord Dunraven for £20,000.

In 1930, the National Stud mare, Dolabella, by White Eagle out of famous Gondolette, produced a grey filly to Tetratema. Named Myrobella, this youngster seemed to Sir Henry Greer of great potential value to the Stud, and so was leased to Lord Lonsdale and sent to Beckhampton. After being narrowly defeated, through inexperience, by a much inferior rival, in her first race as a two-year-old, she was not beaten again that season, her victories including the National Breeders' Produce Stakes at Sandown and Doncaster's Champagne Stakes. She was rated the best of her age, topping the Free Handicap at 9 st. 7 lbs.—3 lbs. above her closest rival. The next year, she finished third to Brown Betty (Friar Marcus-Garpal) in the One Thousand Guineas, having led to the Dip. She never raced afterwards over a longer course than 6 furlongs, winning among other events the Fern Hill Stakes at Ascot and the July Cup. She had two races in the first half of 1934, one of which she won, and then returned to Tully, to become the dam of a succession of winners, including

Snowberry (dam of St. Leger winner Chamossaire) and Big Game, both retained by the National Stud.

Big Game was foaled January 24, 1939, as the result of Myrobella's mating to unbeaten Bahram. By the time he was a yearling, the war had started and bloodstock values touched bottom. Big Game, the filly Sun Chariot, and others were leased to King George V and sent to Beckhampton. Big Game's conformation was superb and he soon displayed exceptional promise. But for a long time as a two-year-old Sun Chariot failed to show any ability. Fred Darling, who has never tolerated mediocrity at Beckhampton, was at first so disappointed with this filly that he was on the point of sending her back to Tully when, one morning, he noticed a distinct improvement in her action. With each gallop, progress was revealed and, when she made her first appearance in public, at Newbury on June 6, 1941, she started second favourite at 11 to 4 for the Acorn Plate and won by two lengths. She also won her other three races as a two-year-old, including the substitute Queen Mary Stakes and the Middle Park Stakes. She was placed top of the Free Handicap, 1 lb. above Big Game.

Her three-year-old career began with a reverse, the only one she suffered. Started for a 6-furlong race at Salisbury in April, in the course of her preparation for the One Thousand, she was unable to go the pace in this sprint, won by Ujiji (Umidwar-Teresina), and dead-heated for third place. This exceptionally good, though at times alarmingly wilful, filly proceeded to win the One Thousand, Oaks, and St. Leger at Newmarket. Gordon Richards, her partner in these triumphs, has said that she is the best he has ever ridden.

On her return to the National Stud, she produced in 1944 her first foal, Blue Train (by Blue Peter). He was unbeaten, winner of three races, but after his Newmarket Stakes victory he could not be trained satisfactorily for the Derby and never ran again, being eventually sold privately as a stallion to the Kildangan Stud, Co. Kildare, for £25,000.

Big Game, having won all his five races as a two-year-old, began the next season by beating six others for the Salisbury Stakes (7 furlongs) and then won the New Two Thousand Guineas by four lengths, from Watling Street (Fairway-Ranai). He started a 6 to 4 *on* favourite for the New Derby, but ran much too freely to stay the distance successfully. Weakening in the last quarter of a mile, he finished sixth, Watling Street winning by a neck from Hyperides (Hyperion-Priscilla). That was Big Game's only defeat. He won the Champion Stakes (1¼ miles) easily and began his stud career as a four-year-old.

Obviously, he was a stallion of high repute and promise. His

superb breeding, glorious conformation and his brilliant race-
course performances combined to create a demand for nominations greatly exceeding the customary maximum of 40 mares per
season. This was something new for the National Stud. Of the
stallions taken over from Colonel Hall Walker, Royal Realm was
destroyed and Great Sport sold for 420 gns. in 1922. Silvern
was bought for £16,000 from Sir Edward Hulton to join White
Eagle and Diligence at Tully in 1924, but these were never top-
class sires ; Silvern, in fact, was completely disappointing. White
Eagle, many of whose daughters did well as brood-mares, was
destroyed in 1928 and Silvern died of a ruptured artery in 1931,
from which time up to Big Game's return to the stud, a thoroughbred stallion had not been kept there.

Big Game being the property of the nation, there was clear
need for the available nominations to him to be allotted according
to a specific plan, as fair as possible to all applicants for his services and in the best interests of the breed generally. The
Ministry of Agriculture invited the Council of Thoroughbred
Breeders' Association to nominate two members to act with Mr.
Burrell, the Director of the National Stud, in carrying out a plan
of procedure, and Captain J. Farr and Captain A. E. Brice were
chosen. Big Game's fee was fixed at 250 sovs. and 1 gn. for the
groom. The scheme adopted by the Ministry was published on
November 7, 1944. Limiting nominations to 40 mares for 1946,
it divided these into three categories. Twenty were reserved for
mares the property of the National Stud and of those owners to
whom the National Stud " is under an obligation ".

Five nominations were to be allotted to approved mares which,
in the opinion of the Director, were of a higher class than the
average and which it was not desired to miss by the lottery of a ballot.

The remaining 15 nominations were to be distributed by ballot
among approved mares, the two representatives of the Thoroughbred Breeders' Association acting with the Director in approving
mares eligible for the ballot. The Ministry's conditions provided
that the result of the ballot would be made known on July 14,
and a waiting-list of six additional mares announced. Nominations were made strictly non-transferable.

Big Game's first produce ran in 1946. Nine of them won 13
races of a total value of £7,686 between them, the most notable
being Combat, son of the Oaks winner, Commotion (Mieuxce-
Riot). The next year he had 14 winners of 27 races (£19,413),
unbeaten Combat being again the most successful. Big Game
was eleventh in the list of winning sires.

In 1948, he leapt to the top. Twenty-five of his offspring won
42 races worth £40,690. They included Queenpot (One
Thousand), his first classic winner.

The glorious achievements of Big Game and Sun Chariot afford a striking epitome of the history of the National Stud. They reflect the consistent success with which it has been developed from the foundations so masterfully laid by Lord Wavertree.

One of the first " outside " mares purchased by the National Stud was Ecurie, bought in 1918 from Lord Woolavington for 1,900 gns. She had been covered that year by Hurry On, and duly produced Diligence, to become the sire of Clarence, dam of Sun Chariot. But Sun Chariot goes right back through the tail female line to Blanche (by White Eagle) and her dam Black Cherry, both of whom were among the mares presented by Lord Wavertree.

What the National Stud has accomplished in Big Game from its original stock can best be presented by his pedigree, which is :

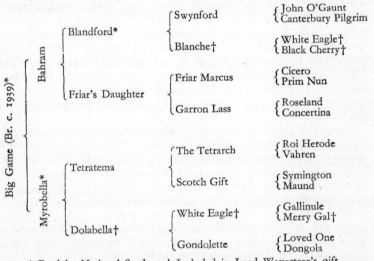

Big Game (Br. c. 1939)*			
Bahram	Blandford*	Swynford	John O'Gaunt / Canterbury Pilgrim
		Blanche†	White Eagle† / Black Cherry†
	Friar's Daughter	Friar Marcus	Cicero / Prim Nun
		Garron Lass	Roseland / Concertina
Myrobella*	Tetratema	The Tetrarch	Roi Herode / Vahren
		Scotch Gift	Symington / Maund
	Dolabella†	White Eagle†	Gallinule / Merry Gal†
		Gondolette	Loved One / Dongola

* Bred by National Stud.   † Included in Lord Wavertree's gift.

Blandford, sire of four Derby winners, Bahram (1935), Windsor Lad (1934), Blenheim (1930) and Trigo (1929), was bred by the National Stud, and was among the yearlings sent up for sale in 1920. He was bought by Mr. S. C. Dawson and his trainer-brother, R. C. (Dick) Dawson for 730 gns. Being difficult to train, he only ran four times, twice as a two-year-old. He won three races, and his career ended with his success in the Princess of Wales Stakes (1½ miles), which showed him to be one of the best of his age. He headed the list of winning stallions in 1934, 1935, and 1938.

For the greater part of its existence, the National Stud has relied on the sale of young stock for its revenue. The practice has been to send drafts annually to the yearling sales, but in 1926 the Director effected a notable deal with the Aga Khan. The latter bought two yearlings privately from the National Stud for £20,000, one of them Feridoon, by Hurry On out of Ecurie (and so, brother to Diligence), being valued, for the purpose of this transaction, at £17,000, the highest price ever given, up to that time, for a yearling. Feridoon was a complete failure as a race-horse and was eventually sold in France for about £13. From the proceeds of this transaction with the Aga Khan, Sir Henry Greer bought a few mares, including Sister Stella and Simon's Shoes.

Some notable winners bred by The National Stud and sold as yearlings have been mentioned. They are too numerous to list entirely, but they also include The Panther (Two Thousand Guineas), Poisoned Arrow, Seminole (Cesarewitch), Orleans (Irish 2,000 Guineas), Anetta (Irish One Thousand), Ankaret (Coronation Stakes), and Sword Play's brilliant two-year-old colts, Challenger and Poise. Challenger was rated third best of his year (1929), 2 lbs. below the top (Diolite), but four National Stud products have headed the Free Handicap for two-year-olds: The Panther, Myrobella, Poise, and Sun Chariot. Stardust, among the two-year-olds of 1939, was assessed only 1 lb. inferior to the champion Tant Mieux, who had beaten him a length for the Gimcrack.

The National Stud has been conducted with considerable satis-faction to the taxpayer. From 1916 to the end of 1948, the accum-ulated *net* profit was £250,000. In each of 21 years, there has been a net profit, varying from £251 in 1939 to £50,589 in 1947. Losses were sustained in 10 years, but have been heavy only in 1931 (£21,634), 1932 (£15,269), and 1933 (£9,944), a period of general and world-wide economic depression.

In 1922, the Irish Provisional Government claimed ownership of Tully Stud, both land and stock. It was eventually agreed that the British Government would retain the stock and pay a net sum of £21,300 in lieu of rent, as user of the property between 1922 and 1943, when the stud was transferred to Gillingham, Dorset.

The first property bought at Gillingham was the Sandley Estate (157 acres), to which were added, by purchase, Begley, Lower Bugley, and New Barn, together with six individual fields, bring-ing the total area to over 400 acres. Much of this property had been used by the late Lord Furness as a stud, but much old stabling was generally in a poor condition. Great improvements were begun in 1948, particularly in the replacement of the old, dilapidated wooden structures by lofty, convenient and well-ventilated brick boxes for the mares and foals. There are over

40 paddocks, none of which is used, as a rule, for more than three months at a time.

Paddocks which are being rested from bloodstock are grazed by bullocks. In more than one instance during those few bad years at Tully, the bullocks were more profitable than the blood-stock!

The private sale in 1947 of Blue Train and Howdah out of the country was widely criticised, the opinion of many English breeders being that the horses should either have been re-tained as stallions by the National Stud or that English stud-masters should have had an opportunity to bid for them at public auction. At the annual meeting of the Thoroughbred Breeders' Association, the Duke of Norfolk said that he believed most of them thought that colts retained by the National Stud and leased for racing, should, if good enough, be placed eventually by the Government at stud at reasonable fees throughout the country. As a result of this discussion, the Thoroughbred Breeders' Association requested the Minister of Agriculture to consult with their representatives " as to the policy of the National Stud ".

Mr. Tom Williams readily acceded to this request. He in-formed the representatives of the Thoroughbred Breeders' Associ-ation that the general rule would be to sell the Stud's surplus stock by auction. Blue Train, being unsound when withdrawn from racing, had not been regarded as suitable for sale in that manner, and the disposal of Howdah provided the revenue with much needed dollars.

The deputation suggested that selected colts not necessarily of classic-race quality should be kept by the National Stud to stand at reasonable fees for the benefit of the " small " breeder and that suitable horses might be purchased for this purpose. They ex-pressed the view that such stallions should not necessarily stand at Gillingham.

The Minister's reply was : " There would be no hesitation in keeping suitable colts, bred at the National Stud, as stallions. Nor would there be any objection, in principle, to purchasing stallions, or prospective stallions, by the National Stud. Where such stallions should stand would be in accordance with the position ruling at the time."

The policy expressed in this announcement was considerably wider in its scope and closer to what Lord Wavertree himself had envisaged than it had been at any time since his gift was accepted. When the deputation emphasised that the primary purpose of the National Stud should be to enhance the standard of the thorough-bred horse by assisting breeders to the utmost, the Minister did in fact declare that it was the policy of the Government to fulfil Lord Wavertree's wishes.

Up to now, there have been two important steps by the Ministry of Agriculture to explicate Mr. Williams' assurances. Arrangements were made in 1948 with Signor F. Tesio, owner of Tenerani, for that fine Italian horse to join the National Stud in 1951, on a three-year lease with an option to purchase.

Tenerani, after winning the Italian Derby and other top-class races in his own country, came to England as a four-year-old in 1948, to win the Queen Elizabeth Stakes ($1\frac{1}{2}$ miles) at Ascot and the Goodwood Cup (2 miles 3 furlongs). In the latter race, he beat Arbar, the year's Ascot Gold Cup winner and champion of France. Tenerani is by Bellini (son of exported English mare Bella Minna) out of Tofanella, by Apelle out of Try Try Again (winner of the Goodwood Stakes, 1927, and Newbury Autumn Cup, 1926).

The intention to keep more than one stallion created the need for additional accommodation. At Gillingham, there is room only for the visiting mares to Big Game, possibly Tenerani, besides the existing bloodstock owned by the National Stud. In 1949, therefore, the Ministry of Agriculture arranged to lease for 99 years another establishment at West Grinstead Park, Sussex, where the late Mr. J. P. Hornung bred many good winners and kept the 1923 Derby winner Papyrus (Tracery-Miss Matty) at stud. It is here that two or three stallions, other than Big Game and Tenerani, will stand at comparatively small fees.

In 1944 the filly Pukwana, by Papyrus out of Concorda, was acquired for the National Stud for 4,000 gns. and the next year 5,600 gns. was given for Fair Profit, by Fair Trial out of Molly Bawn. Latest addition to the young mares at Gillingham is Mombasa, by Taj Ud out of Nairobi. Mombasa was probably the best three-year-old filly of 1947, though she was not engaged in the Classic races. Mr. Peter Burrell bought her privately for the National Stud at the end of 1948.

CHAPTER IV

FAMOUS THOROUGHBRED SIRES

By Clive Graham

EVEN though this may only be regarded as a cursory, and not an exhaustive, treatment of the breeding of race-horses during the first 50 years of the twentieth century, there will be found much of absorbing interest. It would be wrong to enter into any such discursion, however, without examination of the various trends which have contributed to the present qualities, good and bad, which distinguish the British-bred thoroughbred.

The most important point to bear in mind is that for fully 100 years the goal of every owner and breeder has been to rear and/or own a horse capable of winning the Epsom Derby, run at the end of May or in early June, over 1½ miles. The stoutness which stamped the winners of 4-mile heats was considered to be a less desirable characteristic than speed over the Epsom gradients and around the twisting, horseshoe-shaped course, as this race (founded in 1780) gathered ever-growing fame.

In the years preceding the dawn of the twentieth century, the great names of St. Simon, Ormonde, Hampton, Galopin, and Balcaldine were dominating the Turf statistics. One only has to trace pedigrees of any modern Derby winners back a few generations, to discover these five stallions represented—in some cases several times over. A different generation, however, has come into being since the era of their immediate dominance. The institution of valuable two-year-old races created a demand for speed coupled with precocity.

The high-class horses of the 1890's, thanks largely to the stoutness and toughness of their near ancestors, were able to go on running and winning from two years to four, and longer. Fred Archer died in 1886, but his classical style of race-riding still prevailed. An examination of times for the Derby suggests that My Love (2 mins. 40 secs.), the 1948 winner, would have beaten Ormonde (1886) ridden by Fred Archer (2 mins. 45¾ secs.) by 100 yards.

It is not my intention to pose as one who believes that there have been no real generals since Julius Cæsar or poets since Shakespeare. But: *was* Pearl Diver better than Flying Fox (1899, 2 mins. 42⅘ secs.) or Mid-day Sun superior to Islinglass (1893 : 2 mins. 43 secs.)? Pearl Diver (2 mins. 38⅖ secs.) and Mid-day Sun (2 mins. 37⅘ secs.) ran the Derby in faster time than the two great horses named, primarily because the riding-fashions had changed in the years between.

A famous trainer, now dead, expressed the opinion that Bend Or, the 1880 Derby winner (2 mins. 46 secs.), could only stay a mile. He was able to win a Derby, for the sound reason that the race in those days developed into a sprint from Tattenham Corner to the winning-post. Start-to-finish racing was not encouraged. The changes that took place, gradually, during the formative years of the early 1900's are easily perceptible now. A plough-man as he glances back at a completed furrow can see flaws which could not be noticed at the moment of commission. The accent, one must remember, in those years was on speed. Man was just awaking to the discovery that the horse, after all, was not the swiftest means of transport, and the horse's pre-eminence was being superseded gradually, and for ever. The "American invasion" helped to reinforce this feeling. The Americans intro-duced the idea of doping horses in order to make them run full-tilt from the fall of the flag. Sloan popularised the crouch-seat, which lessened wind-resistance and also placed the rider's weight more exactly over the centre of gravity. The innovation of the starting-gate and the draw for places lent added importance to the craze for speed.

This trend, fostered by £5,000 races for two-year-olds, by in-creased taxation which made attractive the prospect of getting quick and lucrative returns from horses bought as yearlings, and by close inbreeding to the St. Simon strain, undoubtedly produced the type of horse most in demand by race-horse owners. Speed became a dominating factor, and the effect on our bloodstock was emphasised when Anglo-French racing rivalry was resumed in 1946 after a break of seven years. The French horses won three successive Gold Cups, two Derbys and innumerable other good-class races for stayers.

In the light of this basis for argument, let us proceed to examine the five decades from 1900 to 1950.

1900–10 : The Golden Years

The twentieth century was heralded on the Turf by Diamond Jubilee, owned by King Edward VII, winning the Triple Crown. The Royal colt was a son of St. Simon, whose progeny succeeded in winning 17 Classic races. The career of the Duke of Portland's brown horse, which he acquired for 1,600 gns. on the death of his previous owner (Prince Battyany), in 1883, is familiar to those who will be interested in this treatise.

St. Simon was unbeaten on the Turf, winning 12 races.

Contemporary critics were uncertain whether he was a stayer of the first order, but there could be no doubting his brilliant speed. He stood at stud for 22 seasons, until his death at the age of 27 in 1908. During his stud-career, St. Simon got 554 foals from 775 mares, and in 1896 achieved the remarkable fertility percentage of 40 foals from 46 mares. His success at the stud was regarded at the time as phenomenal, and he earned for his owner nearly £250,000 in stud-fees in the course of his reign over the paddocks at Welbeck.

The brilliance of St. Simon, however, has been fated during the major part of the whole period under review to be transmitted mainly through the female side of his progeny. Persimmon, St. Frusquin, Chaucer, Desmond, and other of his sons were all unable to propagate a strong consecutive male line. Twelve out of 17 Classic victories won by produce of the Duke of Portland's great horse went to fillies, and it is through his fillies that he became established in modern blood-line charts.

Persimmon, most-famous son of St. Simon, is remembered in this country, not for Zinfandel, Prince Palatine, or Royal Realm, but for the peerless Sceptre. St. Simon's son Desmond sired Charles O'Malley, whose name endures through his daughter Malva, dam of Blenheim. Bromus, mother of Phalaris, was a grand-daughter of St. Simon; Popinjay, one of the foundation mares of Lord Astor's stud, granddaughter of St. Simon; Rosedrop, dam of Gainsborough, granddaughter of St. Simon; Prim Nun, another granddaughter, produced Friar Marcus, famous, in his turn, for the progeny of Friar's Daughter. And one need hardly mention the Derby taproots, Scapa Flow, Canyon, and Selene.

We are in the position of owing gratitude to the French for maintaining the St. Simon sire-line. France has also provided a recuperative influence, not only on the St. Simon inheritance but also on the semi-defunct Herod and Ormonde heirs-apparent. The sire line Chaucer-Prince Chiney and their male descendants—such as Prince Rose, Prince Chevalier, Vatout, Vatellor, My Love, and Bois Roussel—have kept the flag somewhere above half-mast.

It was in 1900 that the Duke of Westminster's horses were put up for sale, and the whole story of British bloodstock might have been different if M. Edmond Blanc had not bought Flying Fox for 37,500 gns. Flying Fox sired Ajax, who, in turn, produced Teddy. Teddy's son Sir Gallahad, exported to the United States, has had an incalculable effect on race-horse breeding in that country.

Flying Fox was a son of Orme, whose blood-line was kept alive in England through the agency of Orby (owned by Mr. "Boss"

Croker), winner of the 1907 Derby. We had the worst of the bargain, for Orby was a glorified sprinter and, although he got a Derby winner in Grand Parade (1919), his progeny were notable for speed rather than stamina, and so contrived further to weaken our staying-strains.

The first 10 years of the twentieth century were made notable by the doings of two wonderful fillies, Sceptre and Pretty Polly. Sceptre was one of the lots in the Duke of Westminster's sale, and the late Mr. Bob Sievier created a sensation by giving 10,000 gns. for this yearling filly by Persimmon out of a sister to Ormonde. If he had not insisted on training her himself, it is possible that Sceptre would never have known defeat. She won four Classics—her only failure being the Derby won by Ard Patrick—but had to be sold after failing to win the Lincolnshire Handicap as a four-year-old (as she had done the previous year), and became the property of Sir William Bass.

When the time came for her to go to the stud, she had won 13 races worth £38,200. Her stud-career did not seem successful at the time. She produced eight foals, not one of whom *nearly* approached her ability on the racecourse. Maid of the Mist, by Cyllene, her first foal, was the one destined to perpetuate Sceptre's name. She won three races worth £1,850 and became the dam of Hamoaze (who bred Buchan, for long a leading sire of brood-mares ; St. Germans, a successful sire in the U.S.A., and Saltash, who went to Australia), Sunny Jane (winner of the Oaks), and Craig an Eran, sire of the Derby winner April the Fifth and of Admiral Drake, winner of the French Grand Prix. April the Fifth has so far not been a conspicuous success, but Sceptre's star still shines through the descendants of Admiral Drake.

Sceptre's career was still at high peak when Pretty Polly—two years younger—also began to dazzle the watchers on the race-course with a sequence of brilliant victories. The breeding of Major Eustace Loder's filly gave little hopes of the fame that was to be her destiny. Two years before this exceptional filly was foaled in 1901, Gaze, her granddam, was sold at public auction for 7 gns. The buyer, incidentally, subsequently regretted his purchase and resold her as a hack for 15 gns. Major Loder bought Gaze's daughter as a yearling for 510 gns. in 1892, and named her Admiration. She could not win in England, but eventually succeeded in two insignificant Irish races to offset a dozen failures.

Imagine, therefore, your reactions if you had had to make an offer for a big, common-looking filly by Gallinule (an unsound horse) out of Admiration, by Saraband out of Gaze (ran once, nearly last in a selling race at Warwick), by the handicapper Thuringian Prince out of Eyepleaser (never raced), by Brown

Bread out of Wallflower (winner of selling-plates at the now-defunct meetings of Odiham and West Drayton).

Admiration, however, was to prove herself a remarkable brood-mare, for in 13 years at stud, she produced 13 foals, and her name still survives, not only through Pretty Polly but also through other daughters—notably Miranda, great-granddam of Tehran. P. P. Gilpin had no great opinion of the filly until, in her first race at Sandown, she astounded the crowd by winning by 100 yards from John O'Gaunt. Fourteen consecutive victories followed, and they included the One Thousand Guineas, Oaks, and St. Leger (1904). In the last Classic, she easily defeated the Two Thousand Guineas and Derby winner St. Amant. Two failures only chequered the 24-race record of this amazing filly. One was in Paris, after a bad journey, the other as a five-year-old in the Ascot Gold Cup.

Was it the effect of this long succession of training and racing which caused her to be barren for her first two seasons at stud? In her third season, she slipped twins and Major Loder was seriously minded to return her to his racing-stable. However, he persevered and from 1911 to 1924 Pretty Polly produced 10 foals. The six colts were of no lasting account, but four fillies—Molly Desmond, Dutch Mary, Polly Flinders and Baby Polly—although not outstanding race-mares, have kept evergreen the name of their famous dam. Colonel Giles Loder's stud is still strong in Pretty Polly blood-lines, while other of her descendants are now scattered all over the world.

Although they could produce no mare to equal the race-course feats of Pretty Polly and Sceptre, it was in these years that the studs of Lord Derby, Lord Rosebery, and Lord Astor became firmly founded. Lord Derby's key mares Canterbury Pilgrim (1893), Glasalt (1898), Santa Brigida (1898), and Anchora (1905), have since mothered and grandmothered horses who have become famous, not only in this country but also in America and in France.

Lord Astor had the first of many successes in the fillies' Classics when Winkipop, a hardy daughter of a mare called Conjure, which he had bought while an undergraduate, won the One Thousand Guineas in 1910. Lord Rosebery had already won two Derbys in the '90's, but Cicero (1905) was an undoubtedly good horse, who still appears in many Classic pedigrees through the agency of his son Friar Marcus. The champion colt of the decade, however, now appears to have been Bayardo. A tail-male descendant of Newminster, he retired in 1910 winner of 22 of the 25 races he contested. An untimely death from thrombosis restricted his stud-life to seven seasons, but before he died he had sired, not only Gay Crusader but also Gainsborough.

1910–1920 : WORLD WAR I ; THE TETRARCH ; PHALARIS ;
THE JERSEY ACT

An era ended when King Edward VII died on May 6, 1910,
not long after his filly Witch of the Air had carried his colours
to victory at Kempton that afternoon. The 10 years which followed were doomed to be distinguished by one of the most bitter
wars in history, which was to have far-reaching effects on Britain's
economy. Repercussions on the narrower world of the race-
course were inevitable.

In 1915, the German Kaiser achieved something of which not
even Napoleon could have boasted. For the first time since its
inception 135 years previously, the Epsom Derby was abandoned
and a substitute race run at Newmarket. Important as was its
impact and its consequences, the war was not the only factor
which shaped the destinies of the British Turf during this
troubled and tragic decade.

The passing of an administrative measure in 1913, and the foaling of two thoroughbred colts, one in 1911, the other in 1914,
formed a combination of circumstances which exerted an incalculable influence on the future of the British race-horse. In
1908, legislation restricting betting on horse-racing was enacted
in the U.S.A. Owners and trainers in that country directed their
horses to England, and so did several breeders. More than 100
American mares and yearlings were submitted for sale at Newmarket, in that year, and the population of American-bred stock
in England, already considerable, increased sharply.

Many of these horses were produce of parents exported in the
first place, but others had been crossed with indigenous strains.
As early as 1901, the subject was vexing the compilers of the
General Stud Book, and the following notice appears in Vol. XIX :

" The increased importation of horses and mares bred in
U.S.A. and Australia, which . . . though accepted in the
Stud Books of their own country, cannot be traced back in
all cases to the Thoroughbred stock exported from England,
from which, more or less, they all claim to be descended,
induced the publishers to refer the question of admission of
such animals into the Stud Book to the Stewards of the
Jockey Club, as the highest authority on all matters connected with the Turf.

" The Stewards, after finally consulting most of the principal breeders, came to the conclusion that any animal
claiming admission should be able to prove satisfactorily some
eight or nine crosses of pure blood, to trace back for at least a
century, and to show performances of the immediate family on
the Turf as to warrant the belief in the purity of its blood..."

When Volume XX was published in 1909, it was discovered that there were 180 American-bred mares included, not all of whom could fulfil the clauses of the 1901 preface. Another Commission was appointed, under Lord Villiers (afterwards Lord Jersey), and in May, 1913, the sentence which was to cause such an outcry 30 years later, was conceived. " No horse or mare ", it ran, " can be considered eligible after this date unless it can be traced without flaw on both sire's and dam's side of its pedigree to horses and mares themselves already accepted in the earlier volumes of the Book." Messrs. Weatherby, editors and publishers, reserved to themselves the right to exclude or to admit.

And so the Jersey Act came into being, primarily to preserve the purity and the essential qualities of the British thoroughbred, which had taken so many years of scrupulous care and selection to evolve. At that time, the measure was regarded in Great Britain as, not only necessary but also eminently fair, there was a feeling of righteous self-satisfaction that the British thoroughbred, then in its heyday, could no longer be " contaminated " by association with the cross-bred stock of foreign countries.

By one of the amiable quirks of Fate, these sentiments received their first shock in the following year, when the French " half-bred ", Durbar II, won the Derby. Much was made at the time of the opinion that this winner lacked quality and that he owed his triumph to the unusually moderate character of that particular season's three-year-old generation. Durbar II was by Rabelais out of Armenia, by Meddler out of Urania, by Hanover out of the unauthenticated American mare Wanda. No one could have foretold that Durbar II was to sire Durban, who, mated with Ksar, produced the potent Tourbillon, sire, in turn, of Djebel and progenitor of the great Boussac line.

At this period before the First World War, the strongest tail-male ancestry was that which sprang from the Darley Arabian, especially through the Birdcatcher and Voltigeur branches. The Godolphin Arabian line, due soon for a remarkable resurgence, still had a few descendants flourishing at stud : among them being Chaleureux, sire of Signorinetta, winner of the 1908 Derby and Oaks. The third great House of racing-stock, the House of Herod and the Byerly Turk, had not had a notable horse since Flying Dutchman (foaled in 1846) and Thormanby, winner of the 1860 Derby. This line was virtually dead in England, but through the two Buzzard stallions, Dollar and Atlantic, it was still strongly established in France.

With the object of reviving the Herod descent, Mr. E. Kennedy, of the Straffan Stud in Kildare, imported the grey French horse Roi Herode, foaled in 1904 by La Samaritain, by Le Sancy, a son of Atlantic. In his first year at stud, Roi Herode was mated with

the Bona Vista mare Vahren, the produce being the famous
" Spotted Wonder," The Tetrarch.   Mr. H. S. Persse, on behalf
of Major D. McCalmont, gave 1,300 gns. for this colt at the Doncaster Yearling Sales.   The Tetrarch, tried amazingly speedy, won
all his seven races as a two-year-old in 1913, but could not
be trained the following season and was promptly retired.   At
stud, his progeny included three St. Leger winners—Caligula
(1920), Polemarch (1921), and Salmon Trout (1924)—but his
stamina-index figure was less than a mile and he is remembered
mainly for transmitting his brilliance to his son Tetratema (won
Two Thousand Guineas in 1920) and to his daughter Mumtaz
Mahal (second to Plack in One Thousand Guineas in 1924).

Two-year-old racing was, as I have remarked earlier, becoming
increasingly popular with owners : there were nine races at Ascot
and ten at Goodwood open to horses of this age in 1914.   So the
patronage due to The Tetrarch was assured, despite wartime
conditions.   Racing had to suffer during the four succeeding
years, and by 1916 there were only 2,363 horses in training, compared with the 4,100 three years previously.   The scene of the
Classic races moved to Newmarket, where Pommern, Gay
Crusader, and Gainsborough were each Triple Crown
laureates.

One searches those wartime records in vain to find the name
of Phalaris inscribed among the list of horses placed first, second
or third in the Classic races.   Lord Derby's son of Polymelus-
Bromus ran only in one Classic race, the Two Thousand Guineas
of 1916.   Starting among the " 20–1 others ", he finished eighth
in a field of 17, behind Clarissimus, Kwang Su, and Nassovian.
His racing career was thenceforth shaped on sprinting lines,
although he contrived to win one modest race against two runners
at 1¼ miles.   He was unbeaten over short distances as a four-year-
old in 1917 until an impost of 9 st., and the 9 furlongs of the
Cambridgeshire, confirmed his stamina limitations.

The late Hon. George Lambton never considered Phalaris as a
stayer, and Mr. Persse has always entertained similar doubts about
The Tetrarch.   These two horses, therefore, exerted a powerful
predisposition towards speed among their descendants.   The
Tetrarch's male line was only of brief flowering : Tetratema, The
Satrap, and Salmon Trout were the best of his sons.   At the end
of the half-century, there were only Auralia, Alisha, the elderly
Mr. Jinks, and Jamaica Inn to represent at stud the sensation of
the 1913 racing season.

The Phalaris line, however, has bloomed prolifically.   There
are more than 50 grandsons and great-grandsons, in the immediate
line, represented by winners in the 1948 and 1949 seasons, in
England and Ireland.   Many more are to be found in France and

Left
BLUE PETER
Fairway-Fancy Free

Right
HYPERION
Gainsborough-Selene

Left
NEARCO
Pharos-Nogara

Right
BIG GAME
Bahram-Myrobella

CAMERONIAN (Pharos-Una Cameron)
J. CHILDS UP

FELSTEAD (Spion Kop-Felkington)
H. WRAGG UP

BLENHEIM (Blandford-Malva)
M. BEARY UP

in America. The process of the years and careful crossing with staying strains has eliminated the tendency towards mere speed in excess of stamina.

Felicitation, Ocean Swell, Sayajirao, Scottish Union, and Fairford are examples of the success enjoyed by breeders in this direction. Brief reference has already been made to Orby, who, like Phalaris, was in the direct line of descent from Bend Or. It is true that he was a Derby winner (1907), but speed has characterised all his posterity. One has only to glance at some of the stallions which have taken their turn at stud : Orpheus, Vencedor, Flying Orb, The Boss, Gold Bridge, Denturius, Sir Cosmo, Bellacose, and Panorama. All these were sprinters and sires of sprinters. Whiteway, out of a Gold Bridge mare, was the only horse connected with this branch, to develop into a stayer of class. The outlook would have seemed bleak if two horses of the Hampton family and one descendant of Sterling and of West Australian had not made their appearance in these years.

Opinion would be divided as to which of these four horses —Gainsborough, Son-in-Law, Swynford, and Hurry On—would have prevailed in a weight-for-age race at 2 miles. Swynford, a product of Lord Derby's famous stud, was foaled in 1907, by John O'Gaunt out of the Oaks winner (1896) Canterbury Pilgrim. He was half-brother to the St. Simon horse Chaucer, whose success as a sire of brood-mares was phenomenal and who headed the list of winning stallions for seven consecutive years, from 1927 to 1933. He broke his fetlock-joint in 1911 and was only saved for the stud by great veterinary skill.

Son-in-Law (1911) was bred by the South African millionaire, Sir Abe Bailey, by Dark Ronald out of a mare by the Galopin horse, Matchmaker. He could not win as a two-year-old, but his ability and stamina found scope in the next season, when his triumphs included the Goodwood Cup. He set up a new time-record (3 mins. 47 secs.) for the Cesarewitch (1915) as a four-year-old, and also won the Jockey Club Cup. In normal times, his career as a stayer would have attracted much greater attention.

Hurry On (1913) was probably the most brilliant stayer to race during the war-years. He was a big, overgrown two-year-old, and did not race until he was three. He was then unbeaten, winning six races, including the substitute St. Leger. Lord Woolavington, his owner, did not breed him, but bought the Marcovil-Tout Suite colt as a yearling for only 500 gns. As The Tetrarch revived the semi-defunct Herod line, so Hurry On performed the same services for Matchem. At the time of Hurry On's birth, the succession of the male descent from the Darley Arabian hung by a mere thread. Kilwarlin had won the 1887 St. Leger, and the filly Signorinetta, at the time of her Derby

E

victory, gave hopes that Chaleureux might also have a son to perpetuate the line.

Lord Rosebery's Sir Visto, winner of the 1895 Derby and St. Leger, and a half-brother to Bona Vista, had seemed another hopeful prospect, but after seven years at stud his fees were reduced to £49, and he produced no winners of any account. The ancestry of Hurry On offered no great encouragement that he might achieve distinction where Sir Visto had failed. Marcovil had won the Cambridgeshire (1908) as a five-year-old with a weight of 7 st. 11 lbs., which was fair comment on his racing-status. Marco, his sire, had also won the same race, when three years old with 7st. 9 lbs., and one has to go back another three generations before finding in West Australian, Triple Crown winner of 1853, a horse of superlative merit.

The stud career of Gainsborough, who won all three of the colts' Classic races in 1918, was not besmirched by similar doubts. Lady James Douglas's beautifully modelled colt was a son of Bayardo (Hampton), the outstanding horse of the twentieth century's first decade : out of Rosedrop, by St. Frusquin, out of a mare by the Musket horse Trenton. He was beaten in his last race, but each of his three Classic victories had been gained in impeccable fashion.

That was the general scene as the war-clouds rolled away : a depleted mare-population, a choice of stallions whose racing-worth had been difficult to gauge owing to restricted racing during the war-years, taxation which made desirable the prospects of quick returns from the buyers at the yearling sales, and a change in the wealth of the community which attracted a new class of owners to the fascination of racing and breeding.

1920 TO 1930 : THE GROWING ASCENDANCY OF LORD DERBY'S STUD ; THE DAZZLING SONS AND DAUGHTERS OF HURRY ON ; THE RISE TO FAME OF BLANDFORD ; THE ARRIVAL OF A NEW AND SPECTACULAR BUYER, OWNER, AND BREEDER IN H.H. THE AGA KHAN

In the years leading up to 1920, the black-and-white colours of the Derby family had once more been establishing themselves among the most notable on the Turf. Family association with racing had for some 30 years been disrupted, but in 1893, both the sixteenth Earl, and his son Lord Stanley, who succeeded him, decided simultaneously to renew them.

Reference has been made to Canterbury Pilgrim, winner of the Oaks in 1896. She was one of the foundation mares of the Derby stud. Five more Classic successes were recorded : Keystone II (Oaks 1906), Swynford (St. Leger, 1910), Canyon (Two Thousand

Guineas, 1916), Ferry (One Thousand Guineas, 1918), and Keysoe (St. Leger, 1919). The four last, carried the colours of the seventeenth Earl, whose successes were destined to continue on an upward trend for the remainder of the period under review.

In 1924, Sansovino carried the colours to victory in the Epsom Derby, which had been founded by the twelfth Earl, but only once previously, in 1787, had it been won by a holder of the title. The 1920's saw the fruition of the plans, initiated by John Griffiths, Walter Alston, and the Hon. George Lambton. Scapa Flow (1914), destined to produce eight winners of £86,000 in stakes, threw Pharos in 1920 and his full-brother Fairway five years later.

In 1925, Glacier (dam of seven winners of nearly £42,000) foaled Toboggan, who later won the Oaks in 1928 and, eventually, became ancestress of the American champion Citation. Glacier's half-sister Canyon (whose seven winners gained £51,000) foaled Colorado, her most famous son, winner of the 1926 Two Thousand Guineas and the instrument of Coronach's downfall in the first of that season's Classics. Coronach, however, had his revenge in the Derby when Colorado was third.

Selene (1911) got 10 winners. Among her early ones were Sickle and Pharamond, exported to the U.S.A., where they ranked for many years among the leading stallions. Hunter's Moon achieved fame in the Argentine, and in 1930 Selene foaled to Gainsborough the little chestnut colt Hyperion.

It has been argued that one of the bases for the success of Lord Derby's stud was inbreeding to St. Simon. The passing of the years, however, has brought about the necessity for finding a new formula, perhaps with Hyperion as its focal point.

The '20's also witnessed the sudden upsurge of West Australian blood, through the agency of Hurry On. The Classic successes of Captain Cuttle (1922), Plack (1924), Coronach (1926), Call Boy and Cresta Run (1927), Scuttle and Toboggan (1928), and Penny-comequick (1929) seemed to vouchsafe that the Hurry On line was here to stay. The wheel turned with equal abruptness, and revival in 1949 depended on the stud career of Precipitation, Chamossaire, and the Italian-bred Niccola dell'Arco.

By no stretch of the imagination could Blandford be listed among the outstanding horses to race during this decade, for although he won the Princess of Wales's Stakes at Newmarket in 1922, he only ran a few times and was then taken out of training. And yet, 1929 brought him his first Derby winner in Trigo, and linked his name as a sire with that race and other Classics for the next ten years. Blandford, great-grandson of Isinglass, through John O'Gaunt and Swynford, was owned and trained by R. C. Dawson. It was a fortunate coincidence for H.H. the Aga Khan, who transferred his racing and breeding interests from India to England soon after the conclusion of the 1914–18 War. He chose George Lambton to buy his yearlings and mares, and " Dick " Dawson to train his race-horses.

The latter was always, rightly, an enthusiastic champion of Blandford, who sired two of His Highness's Derby winners : Blenheim, bought at auction, and the unbeaten Bahram, which he bred at his own stud. Blenheim, in turn, sired Mahmoud in this country, and Whirlaway when he was exported to America, where both Mahmoud and Bahram later joined him. Blandford's influence continues strong in Europe, however, for Bahram left behind Big Game and Persian Gulf, while Blenheim's son Donatello II is sire of Lord Derby's Gold Cup winner, Alycidon.

The rise of H.H. the Aga Khan's stud was one of the salient features of this period. Success came early, for by the end of 1924, his horses had already won two Classic races and had been placed in three others, while his fillies, bought in the open market regardless of expense, included Cos, Mumtaz Mahal, and Teresina. Many reductions were made during the 1939–45 War, but the shrewd purchase of a half-share in My Love (1948 Derby winner), and the victories attending the crop of 1949 two-year-olds suggests that the foundations laid in the 1920's were on a firm basis.

The theories of Colonel Vuillier, a French student of breeding-lines and trends, appealed to the imagination of the Eastern owner-breeder. These theories, which propound an admixture of the blood-lines of many famous stallions in certain percentages, have prompted the reason for many of the matings of the Aga Khan's mares. The theories can only be proved over a long period of years, and must be allied with the other prerequisites for success in stud-management. His Highness, in his business affairs, has always shown himself to be a brilliant picker of men to work for, and with him. Perhaps that is half the secret of the reputation won by his priceless collection of horses at stud and in training.

1930 TO 1940

Durbar II had won our 1914 Derby, Massine and Filibert de Savoie had outdistanced all comers for the 1924 Ascot Gold Cup, in which year Sir Gallahad III triumphed in the Lincolnshire Handicap. Tapin also won " the Lincoln " in 1925 for France, and in the same year, the French-bred Masked Marvel and Forseti landed the Autumn Double of the Cesarewitch and Cambridge-shire handicaps.

Insight II, Palais Royal, and Asterus added more big-handicap wins, and in the four years between 1929 and 1933, the French annexed the Oaks (Brulette, 1931), the Two Thousand Guineas

(Rodosto, 1933), and the One Thousand Guineas twice (Taj Mah, 1929 and Kandy, 1932). The process might have continued in the 1934 Classics had not Easton met a brilliant miler in Colombo for the Guineas, and Windsor Lad, probably Blandford's best racing-son, in the Derby.

Mesa's win in the 1935 One Thousand Guineas was unlucky not to be capped by the Oaks won by Squashed. Le Ksar came over to beat French-bred Goya II for the 1937 Two Thousand Guineas, and next year, Bois Roussell, who had been in England only a few weeks, recorded a hollow victory in the Derby.

Galatea II won both Classic races confined to fillies in 1939, when the French also scored a notable series of Ascot wins. Two champions were stabled on either side of the Channel in 1939 : Blue Peter, winner of the Guineas, Derby and Eclipse Stakes, and Pharis II, whose worth had been proved in the Prix du Jockey Club at Chantilly and in the Longchamp Grand Prix. Their encounter in the St. Leger had to be cancelled owing to the outbreak of war. Djebel came over to win the Middle Park Stakes and returned next Spring, the last challenger for six years, to win, the 1940 Two Thousand Guineas.

This brief summary, which excludes details of many other important races won by the French in this period, nevertheless emphasises the remarkable advance of the French-breds. In 1919, 1920, and 1921, and again in 1925, the Grand Prix had been won by an English horse. We have not prevailed in that race since. Indeed, the pendulum had swung so far the other way by the end of the '30's, that the 1936 and 1938 winners, as well as the 1937 runner-up, were purchased as stallions for English studs.

All three have proved their worth. Mieuxce has been a consistent sire of winners. Nearco, of Anglo-Franco-American strains, has been, not only a sire of winners, but a sire of sires, while Donatello II has finally made his name through the medium of Alycidon. One of the few important events which evaded the French through the 1930's was the Ascot Gold Cup. This race, in 1934, proved the downfall of Hyperion, but this failure, after his brilliant three-year-old career, was soon overlooked in the light of his immediate and unmistakable propensity at stud.

His first year was in 1935, so the outbreak of another world-conflict in 1939 could scarcely have appeared more unpropitiously. He topped the list as sire of winners in 1940, 1941, and 1942, and again in 1945–46. One could be pardoned for fancying a slight similarity to St. Simon, for Hyperion, on balance, is already more famous for his fillies than for his colts.

There are strong hopes of the Owen Tudor-Tudor Minstrel, and the His Highness-Beau Sabreur branches. Nor should sight be lost of Alibhai, Ponder, and Heliopolis in the U.S.A., or of

the lightly-rated Helios who has proved the old adage, " blood
will tell ", so amply in Australia.

1940 TO 1950

The 1939–45 War affected racing and breeding even more
adversely than its predecessor. Racing was severely restricted
and organised on a regional basis. Events for two-year-olds
dominated all the programmes, and stayers' races were few and
scattered. Many paddocks were ploughed up on the orders of
the Ministry of Agriculture, and the reduction in the area for use
by mares and foals greatly increased the risk of infestation by red-
worm. Breeders, who would normally have bought busily in the
foreign market in an endeavour to stem, by outcrossing, the tide
of French successes, were thrown back on the stock already
available.

Descendants of Hampton (12) and Bend Or (eight) won 20
out of the 24 Classic races in the war-period. There were, however, some stout horses raised, notably Ocean Swell, Borealis, and
Tehran, while Sun Chariot (who beat Watling Street, the Derby
winner by three lengths for the 1942 St. Leger) would have been
an exceptional filly in any year. Dante was another brilliant race-
horse of the war-years, and Nasrullah, also by Nearco, would
probably have proved his worth if he had not been forced to race
only at Newmarket.

In the first war-free year, the French challenge was renewed
and we were speedily convinced that the French breed had been
improving, not deteriorating, during the isolation period. The
Boussac stayers, Caracalla II and Marsyas, took all the worthwhile
long-distance stakes, while Monsieur l'Amiral and Sayani
triumphed in the Autumn double. Sayani's victory was a blow,
for he had carried a record weight and had shown that lack of
stamina was not the only defect of our horses.

There was one consolation : Sayani's pedigree, except for one
generation, might have been that of an all-Knowsley product.
Souverain's defeat of Airborne was the prelude to another Ascot
Gold Cup. Worse still, two successive Derbys, an Oaks, and a
One Thousand Guineas also went across the Channel. Not all
these good horses were excluded from the stud-book, but the
bar was up against the Djebels and the Tourbillons. Breeders,
however, began to question the sense in labelling such horses as
Arbar and Caracalla II " half-bred ".

Black Tarquin's St. Leger win in 1948 lent added point to the
debate, and in that year, Messrs. Weatherby again invited a committee to discuss the possibility of altering the terms of admission
to the *General Stud Book*, not by restriction but by extension. The

committee decided that some alteration was advisable, and suggested that the terms of Vol. XIX (quoted previously) should be reintroduced.

Race-course executives were also taking a hand in shaping the future stamp of our horses. Special allowances were given in valuable Autumn races to two-year-olds which had not raced in the first half of the season. Clauses barring the progeny of sprinting sires were also applied in several races, both for two-year-olds and three-year-olds. By 1949, it was already becoming preferable to own a staying rather than a sprinting horse. Sprint prizes had been reduced, and opportunities limited.

Many French mares, and French and Italian stallions were imported, with the object of outcrossing, although most of them traced back, after two or three generations, to purely British stock. The economic situation, however, prevented breeders from tapping the American market. In the next 50 years, the clash between American and European strains promises to be one of absorbing interest. In this time, the New World may have to be called upon to redress the balance of the Old.

CHAPTER V

THE BLOODSTOCK INDUSTRY

By V. R. ORCHARD

ON February 15, 1900, General Roberts sent home the long-awaited news that the siege of Kimberley had been raised ; a fortnight later, dusty columns of British cavalry rode into Ladysmith. The tide of reverses in the Boer War was beginning to turn in our favour.

The country, in spite of jingoist symptoms, and of the inability of the masses to realise the importance of a war so distant, concentrated on what at the time was considered to be a national effort. Its immense riches were being poured out for the equipment of the Army. Business was good.

Money was being made in the industrial areas, when manufacturers and contractors added to their fortunes in an unexpected and unprecedented fashion. North and Midlands combined in the production of war munitions. The Remounts Department combed the four kingdoms for horses ; agents in the Americas created a boom in the export trade in mules.

What better augury could there have been for the start of the racing season ? There were plenty of race-horses, plenty of money, and no lack of people willing to spend it. The war, after all, was the concern of the professional soldiers—and South Africa was a long way away. It may further be reflected that racing, as a form of amusement was as popular as drinking. It had no serious rivals, although professional football was beginning to attract the crowds. But, at least, there was no greyhound-racing, nor were there any cinemas.

It was in such an atmosphere that the 1900 flat-racing season got under way. Its start at Lincoln—apart from the institution of a revolutionary contraption known as the starting-gate—followed the traditional pattern. Ambush II scored a thrilling and popular success in the Grand National in the colours of the Prince of Wales. Continental bookmakers were circulating their lists of prices on the Derby. Income-tax was 1s. in the £1.

" Teddy," as the Heir Apparent was known to the populace to the end of his life, had a great racing year. Not only did Ambush II win for him the Blue Riband of steeplechasing, but Diamond Jubilee won the Triple Crown, taking the Eclipse Stakes *en route*.

Otherwise, the first year of the new century produced few good horses. Merman, who won the Ascot Gold Cup for the lovely

Lily Langtry, might have been an exception ; but the greater ones were still in their infancy : Sceptre was as yet a yearling ; Chaucer and Rock Sand were still foals.

Bloodstock values were not seriously affected by the war. The 37,500 guineas which Monsieur Edmond Blanc paid for the Duke of Westminster's Flying Fox (then at the end of his racing career) certainly created a sensation. *Per contra*, Lord Rosebery, whose racing stable was out of luck, sold his yearlings and most of his horses in training ; the prices realised were reasonable, including the 1,050 guineas for the embryo Eclipse Stakes winner, Epsom Lad.

The war, by 1901, had entered upon its long guerilla stage, and it was not until the Spring of the following year that the Peace Treaty was signed at Vereeniging. Racing, however, blossomed into a new heydey. Edward VII was King of the Realm ; Horatio Bottomley and Robert Sievier were Princes of the Turf.

Bob Sievier walked into the Rutland Arms Hotel at New-market on the evening preceding the opening of the July Yearling Sales and asked for Mr. Somerville Tattersall. " I am going to buy the Persimmon filly out of Ornament," he told him. " As I have no account with you, I thought you might like a deposit." With that, he thrust £20,000 in Bank of England notes into " Sommy's " reluctant hands. " It is far too much," said the auctioneer, " and I don't know what to do with so much money at this time of the night." Eventually, the notes were secreted at the top of a bedroom wardrobe, but they were taken across the road to the bank next morning as soon as the door was opened.

The sale became a sensational duel between Sievier and the young Duke of Westminster's agent. Sievier's first bid was 5,000 guineas ; his last was £10,000. " Bob " walked away, delighted with his bargain. The bargain was Sceptre.

The Edwardian era, which ended in 1909, may be regarded as a brilliant period in Turf history, inasmuch as it produced many great horses and a company of great racing men. The King spent more money on the Turf than any of his royal predecessors and certainly enjoyed a success unequalled, before or since, by any British reigning Monarch. Money in bulk, however, flowed into the sport in ever increasing quantities, as a result of its popularity among the great industrial barons. Commoners, and even Americans and foreigners, it is true, occasionally won the Derby ; but what did it matter if a few thousand pounds went out of the country. It would all come back.

A high proportion of the prize money won was provided by owners and breeders themselves. Stake money exceeded £500,000 per annum during the period and was divided between approximately 4,000 horses. The proportion between prize money and horses, as will presently be seen, was very low compared with present-day figures, but the £ sterling in the 1900's was, at least, worth 20s. It was prized and sought for all over the world, like the British thoroughbred himself.

PRIZE MONEY (GT. BRITAIN AND IRELAND) 1900 TO 1948

Year.	No. of Horses.	No. of Races.	Value of Stakes £
1900	3,921	1,924	526,492
1910	3,877	1,964	518,459
* 1915	3,169	1,011	243,080
1920	4,095	2,095	708,010
1930	4,792	2,302	823,771
* 1940	3,357	958	184,787
* 1945	3,242	1,120	363,916
1948	5,748	2,684	1,306,211

* War years.

It might be possible to attempt to relate prize money in any given group of years or periods, to bloodstock values. I prefer, however, to set out a table of sales prices and averages—made possible by the industry of former Editors of the *Bloodstock Breeders' Review*.

It is, perhaps, necessary at this point to explain that the only practical method of recording price-tendencies is that of taking the *yearling* as the standard, or measuring-stick. Annual sales turnovers, which include sales of stallions, brood-mares, fillies, foals, and horses in training can easily be misinterpreted. A brood-mare and her foal, for example, might be sold for £500 in December of one year—only to realise possibly five, or even ten times as much a year later. Many brood-mares may be sold many times over : yearlings, only once.

Sales of bloodstock, in general—that is to say, with the exception of yearlings—may be described, roughly, as a process whereby capital-assets are realised and redistributed. Sales of yearlings, on the other hand, represent dividends on breeders' capital ; or, regarded in a more practical fashion, they stand for the sale of a commodity, or a crop ; as such, they realise and represent current market values.

Thus, a few averages and aggregates may be examined :

	DONCASTER YEARLING SALES.			DECEMBER SALES.		
Year.	Lots Sold.	Aggregate (guineas).	Average (guineas).	Lots Sold.	Aggregate (guineas).	Average (guineas).
1910	272	93,325	344½			
1911	298	113,583	381			
1912	304	150,070	493½			
1913	321	221,456	690	713	308,658	432
1914	220	54,860	249	359	68,795	191
*1915	260	51,178	196	497	84,208	169
*1916	280	88,074	314½	523	90,529	173
*1917	269	105,751	393	651	112,224	172
*1918	287	149,830	522	551	217,259	394
1919	230	223,425	971	645	344,882	534½
1920	271	274,595	1,013	711	370,262	520½
1921	265	172,090	649	632	255,907	404½
1922	299	195,505	653½	649	236,089	363½
1923	321	199,775	622	661	354,036	535½
1924	329	327,353	994½	857	380,319	443½
1925	326	320,460	983	761	353,287	464
1926	325	344,990	1,061½	811	433,776	547
1927	325	323,810	996	768	389,206	506½
1928	344	398,130	1,157	838	478,427	570½
1929	313	288,705	922	802	319,220	398
1930	294	183,065	622½	777	233,254	300
1931	302	143,778	476	848	163,528	193
1932	295	155,595	527½	655	142,793	218
1933	325	188,738	580½	754	164,329	218
1934	343	298,280	869½	669	196,543	293½
1935	364	273,620	751½	714	207,276	290
1936	362	258,755	714½	795	239,964	301½
1937	366	226,745	619	781	218,369	279½
1938	357	232,495	651	843	242,279	287
*†1939	114	13,350	117	645	111,599	173
*†1940	131	6,786	52	346	74,008	217
*†1941	103	42,203	410	404	74,865	185
*1942	137	55,006	401½	417	162,613	390
*1943	193	140,300	727	597	259,585	434½
*1944	305	344,920	1,131	679	517,722	762½
*1945	321	539,280	1,680	745	580,887	793
*1946	273	536,270	1,964	788	882,173	1,119
1947	327	597,725	1,827	877½	748,673	853
1948	345	524,670	1,520	831	678,522	816
1949	334	542,189	1,623	808	614,609	760

* Held at Newmarket.　　† Sold in October.

It would be interesting to analyse the figures more deeply. Other matters affecting breeding, however, remain to be discussed. Readers are, therefore, invited to study the tables and to consider, if they will, to what extent the rises and falls in prices were influenced by political or economic conditions.

Low prices in the two war-periods are easily understood. It is less easy to account for the absolute regularity with which each boom-period has been followed by a decline. The 1929–31 slump may be attributed to the Wall Street crisis and to our own domestic difficulties ; it should be remembered that, during the Ramsay MacDonald administration of that period, there were in the country 3,000,000 of unemployed persons. To explain the rise in prices in 1943 and 1944, when the World War was raging, is not so easy. On the other hand, all commodity-prices were steadily rising from that date. The 5,000-gn. yearling of yesterday became the 10,000-gn. yearling of the morrow—which, perhaps, is the natural and most simple explanation of the matter.

It was true, until the war, that British bloodstock was exported to nearly every country in the world. In the year 1938, for example, thoroughbreds were sent to the following countries :

Argentina.	Egypt.	Norway.
Australia.	France.	Panama.
Belgium.	Germany.	Poland.
Brazil.	Gibraltar.	Roumania.
British Guiana.	Holland.	S. Africa.
B. West Indies.	Hungary.	S. Rhodesia.
Burma.	India.	Sweden.
Canada.	Italy.	Switzerland.
Ceylon.	Japan.	Thailand.
Chile.	Kenya.	Turkey.
Columbia.	Malay States.	U.S.A.
Czechoslovakia.	Malta.	Venezuela.
Denmark.	Mauritius.	Yugo-Slavia.
Dutch E. Indies.	New Zealand.	

India took 115 ; South Africa absorbed 63. Australia was, as ever, another good customer. The majority of the horses shipped were moderate animals, but, as I think I was the first writer to point out some years ago, they made good friends for us, as well as showing a profit to our breeders, our steamship and insurance companies, and to the exporting agencies.

In addition to what might be termed the bread-and-butter business, there has always been a small, but regular, flow of horses —notably stallions or embryo stallions—of the highest class, especially to the Americas. Some have been sold privately, others by agents. It is not necessary to single out any particular horses for attention ; it is a commonplace that nearly every big country

in the world—Russia, latterly, excepted—has in its stud-books
the names of thoroughbreds exported from this country. In many
instances, they have headed the lists of leading sires in the countries of their adoption.

One series of exports must be referred to in some detail, inasmuch as it represents an achievement of historic interest. The
story begins in 1936, when the Aga Khan decided to sell his 1930
Derby winner, Blenheim (Blandford-Malva) to an American
syndicate. The price was agreed at £45,000 and the horse was
duly despatched.

The sale of a Derby winner for export to the United States was,
of course, no novelty. Diomed, the winner of the first Derby
(1780), was exported to America in 1798 and his blood made a
lasting impression on American stock. Twelve more Derby
winners, including the mighty Ormonde, followed him at intervals
between the years.

Blenheim, however, was the first of the series under notice. In
1940, negotiations were begun for the sale of Bahram (Blandford-
Friar's Daughter) and the 1935 Derby winner was safely shipped
and escorted across the Atlantic in the month of July. He
realised £40,000, which was a very high price indeed considering
that horses at home were selling, as it were, two for a penny.

Scarcely had Bahram arrived in America, when a new transaction took place. This time, it was Mahmoud (Blenheim-Mah
Mahal), again a Derby winner and again the property of the Aga
Khan. Mahmoud's price was only £20,000, but American breeders may agree that he was a better bargain than Bahram and, in
fact, dirt cheap at the price.

The three sales were all effected by the British Bloodstock
Agency Ltd.—a notable achievement on their part. But they
themselves were surprised when it fell to their lot in the following year—1941—to dispose of Mr. John Dewar's 1931 Derby
winner, Cameronian (Pharos—Una Cameron). The buyer on
this occasion was the French breeder Mr. Simon Guthmann, whose
Normandy stud was seized by the Germans and who wanted
Cameronian for the new stud he was establishing in Argentina.

Thus, with half the enemy's undersea fleet on the look-out for
fresh kills, the British Mercantile Marine and the proud ships of
the Royal Navy took their precious cargoes, without hurt, and
delivered them safely and on time—a new record to be added to
their long and faithful list of achievements.

Cameronian was shipped in dramatic conditions, due to changes
of shipping- dates and times necessitated by the submarine war.
Short notice of the sailing-time meant that the groom who had
brought him to Liverpool had to run with him through the

crowded dockside for the best part of a mile to the quay at which the ship, steam up, was waiting.

The war—reference, of course, is to the Great War—was responsible for many changes in stud management. Breeders were urged, at an early stage of the conflict, to reduce their establishments, owing to the need for converting their pasture into arable land and because of the shortage of oats.

Negotiations between influential members of the Jockey Club and Government departments concerned were conducted with the greatest tact and consideration on both sides and what amounted to a gentlemen's agreement was effected. Breeders reduced their studs to a minimum ; the Government arranged a system of rationing—admittedly inadequate, but the best that could be devised. Scales of rationing were laid down for all types (e.g., brood-mares, foals, stallions), of stock at various periods of their stud life. Horses in training were similarly rationed, the management and organisation of the system being virtually controlled through Messrs. Weatherby's offices.

The Duke of Norfolk, at that time Joint Parliamentary Secretary with Mr. Tom Williams (who became Minister of Agriculture under the Socialist administration), Mr. Williams himself and the Minister, Mr. Robert Hudson, co-operated to good purposes with Lord Rosebery, acting in an unofficial capacity, an invaluable adviser and ally.

The reduction process was effected largely by eliminating the older and unprofitable mares. As broad policy, this was undoubtedly a sensible makeshift, although who can tell that one of the " eliminated " mares might not have produced a Sceptre or a Pretty Polly had she stayed in the paddocks !

As a result of the reducing policy, the whole of the thoroughbred population temporarily diminished, as the following table shows :

Foaling Season.	Mares indexed in the General Stud Book.	Foals Reared.
1939	8,210	3,675
1940	7,904	3,224
1941	7,547	2,691
1942	6,666	2,282
1943	6,073	2,450
1944	6,113	2,573
1945	6,896	3,248
1946	7,523	3,506
1947	8,062	3,553
1948	8,475	3,945

The figures, seen in retrospect, are remarkable. It will be observed that, by 1942, the foal-population—which is to say, the birthrate—had fallen to 2,282, an alarming decline from that of 1939, when 3,675 foals were born.

Had the rate of decline continued, the thoroughbred population would have been in danger of extinction. Fortunately, the effect of the culling began to show itself. By breeding from the better, and younger mares, although their number had fallen, in 1943, to its lowest for 18 years—namely, 6,073—more foals were born and reared—a complete justification of the policy pursued.

High prices obtained for yearlings in 1944 and 1945 tempted many of the amateur breeders—mostly farmers—who had bought mares at this time to send them to cheap stallions. Thus, fortuitously, the foaling returns went up, as the table shows. What the table does not show, is that a lot of rubbishy stock was bred—so defeating the objects of the scheme—and found its way to the yearling markets. It was from that date, approximately 1944–5, that scores of yearlings worthless for racing-purposes were sold for what they would fetch as meat.

Meanwhile, there had begun what amounted to a revolution in farming on practically every stud-farm in the country. Breeders, even the smallest among them, were compelled by their local War Agricultural Committees to plough up a proportion of their grasslands, so reducing the acreage necessary for maintaining their stock to a minimum. In the early stages of the war, many injustices occurred, due to the inability of the Committee executives to understand the needs of breeders. In more than one district, owners of stallions were told that they only needed pasture for their stallions—or stallion—regardless of the fact that, in the covering season, each breeder had to provide accommodation for 40 mares and their foals !

Matters, however, were gradually smoothed out and breeders made the best of what many of them regarded as being a bad job. Some of them, impressed by the teaching of Sir George Stapledon, began " to take the plough round the farm ". The process entailed, not only the growing of arable crops, but the re-seeding of old, ploughed-up, pasture.

Whether this was advantageous in every instance is doubtful. In many stud-farms, however, old and unprofitable permanent pasture was opened up to the sun and air for the first time and, in due course, re-seeded with pedigree mixtures on the advice of agricultural specialists.

The growing of grass as a crop is now a recognised practice. The most progressive of our breeders are experimenting on a large scale with the comparatively new form of husbandry and

are working in the closest touch with the experts at the agricultural colleges and research stations which are concentrating on
grass production.   One breeder, at least, is establishing a grass-
drying plant, with the object of cutting and preserving young
grass in the leaf for Winter consumption.

The formation of the Veterinary Educational Trust (now called
the Animal Health Trust) in 1942 has widened considerably the
outlook on thoroughbred-breeding.   It is too early to appraise
the value of this great institution, as it is as yet in its infancy, but
much progress has been made.

Its functions, in relation to thoroughbred-breeding, may
roughly be summed up as follows : (1) The establishment of a
corps of specialists in veterinary medicine and research ; this is
being accomplished by the granting of scholarships and fellow-
ships at the appropriate institutions ; (2) Research in all matters
affecting the race-horse, notably infertility, the control of parasitical
infestation and diseases in foals ; (3) Instruction.   This important
function is in its infancy, but courses which have been arranged
for stud-men have been amazingly successful ; the training of the
younger men in the elements of stud-management will, it is hoped,
raise the standard of stud practice to an entirely new level.

Infertility in brood-mares has long been a cause of anxiety and
loss among breeders.   During the war-period, it was undoubtedly
due in a considerable measure to lack of trained stallion grooms.
It is, however, realised to-day that it is a subject which must be
much more scientifically tackled than has been the case in the past.

For many years breeders have accepted with apparent compla-
cency the fact that the average brood-mare produces or rears only
two foals in every three years.   When it is realised that breeders
pay up to 400 guineas and more per mare for services from the
stallion, it is clear that the financial loss involved is considerable.

A well-known writer recently established the fact that the
fertility rate among brood-mares in the years 1945–48 was approximately less than 54 per cent.—an appalling state of affairs.   The
all-over figures, however, did not give credit to the better-class
breeders, whose well-bred and well-managed mares produced
considerably better results.

The economics of stud-management are hardly a subject for
this article.   There has developed a system since the war which
has affected the account-books of nearly every important breeder.
This is the system of syndication as applied to stallions.

It may briefly be explained that syndication, as generally practised, grew out of the high rate of taxation to which the country
has been subjected in recent years.   In the ordinary way, an owner

P. P. GILPIN

A. TAYLOR

F. HARTIGAN

S. DARLING

[Facing page 68

F. DARLING   R. MARSH

J. JARVIS   F. BUTTERS

who wishes to maintain a stallion is able to stand him at his stud at a fee varying from £48 or even less, per mare, to 400 or, in exceptional cases, 500 gns. Thus, the annual receipts from stud-fees from 40 mares visiting a £200 stallion amount to £8,000, less expenses and overheads.

The £8,000-per-annum income is, of course, a thing of the past, and owners paying sur-tax have been obliged to make complicated arrangements with the Inland Revenue authorities in order to obtain for themselves any semblance of a reasonable return for their outlays.

Syndicating stallions thus became a common practice. The method employed was to capitalise a stallion at a certain sum, possibly up to or beyond £100,000, and to form him into a syndicate or company. Shares were issued in denominations of £2,500, or less, members of the syndicate having the right to nominate one mare per share per annum for the services of the stallion.

In the case of successful and long-lived sires the shareholder need have no regrets. The curse of this system, however, is that the breeder, wishing to use the best stallions available, finds himself obliged to take shares in anything up to a dozen syndicates, so locking up capital on what, after all, is as likely to prove a gamble as an investment.

The small breeder, unable to find capital even for one syndicate, is thus—in theory, at any rate—debarred from sending his best mare or mares to the stallion he would like to have. The only person, in fact, who really benefits from the system is the original owner of the stallion. If he can syndicate him for a considerable sum, he receives that sum in cash. What he is able to do with such cash—a capital, and, therefore, untaxable asset—is another matter.

Here are some of the facts established to show the progress made in the world of thoroughbred-breeding since 1900 :

1. Racing, despite two wars, has maintained its popularity.
2. Prize money has increased from £526,492 in 1900 to £1,306,211 in 1948.
3. The foal-population, now standing at approximately 4,000, ensures, as far as can be seen, an adequate supply of racehorses for the future.
4. Prices of bloodstock have appreciated, on the whole, steadily. (Compare the average price of 344½ gns. for yearlings in 1910 with the figures, all well above 1,500 gns. in the post-war period.)
5. Stud-farm management has been improved and the education of studsmen has been undertaken on a comprehensive scale.
6. Research into infertility and diseases of the thoroughbred is being developed on an ambitious scale.

F

CHAPTER VI

PERSONALITIES OF THE NORTH COUNTRY

By Major J. Fairfax-Blakeborough, M.C.

QUITE recently, a few North Country sportsmen, who have been prominently associated with the Turf in various capacities for over half a century, discussed (as the older hands are given to do), the changes in connection with racing of which they are living witnesses. I was one of the company, and, if my memory does not go back quite 50 years, it does, alas, cover by far the greater part of that period, for very shortly after the dawn of this century I went to the historic Hambleton training-quarters, there to learn some of the mysteries of the science of riding race-horses and of preparing them for their engagements.

Those of my contemporaries who remain as active participants in the great game, have seen more dynamic changes in the whole system, conduct, and economy of racing than can ever occur in another single generation.

We have watched it emerge, as it were, from the chrysalis-stage through the evolutionary flight of gate-money meetings, to become a mighty industry rather than a leisurely sort of open-air club, more or less patrician, at many places. Moreover, we have seen the end of the heavy plunging, " break-the-ring " era, and the exodus of all the best horses from northern to southern training-quarters. Happily, in recent years, there has been a partial revolution in this connection. There came a time very early in this century, when outstanding owners—even those living in the North Country—deserted Malton, Middleham, Richmond, Hambleton, and other training-quarters in their homeland, and sent their horses with Classic pretensions to Newmarket. This was not because they thought there was any more skill at " Headquarters " (as Newmarket is termed), or that the gallops there were any better than those in the North : but rather that they wished to have their horses nearer London, so that, during the season, they would be able to see them at work and to witness trials.

That is the explanation of the paucity of northern-trained Derby, Oaks, Guineas, and St. Leger winners during the twentieth century. Prior to that time, John Scott turned out from Whitewall, Malton, a very long succession of winners of all the great races mentioned. The I'Ansons contributed, so did Middleham, Richmond, and Hambleton. Despite the North being robbed of this distinction through the exodus mentioned, my old friend the late Wm. I'Anson, jun., trained, at Malton, more winners on the flat than any man living or dead.

Amongst other changes which strike those of us of the older generation, none are more impressive than those borne upon us in the weighing-room, say at York, Doncaster, Newcastle, and Hamilton Park. We could almost count on our fingers those whose business brought them there in our salad days, and who are still at grips with racing. We have seen several generations of jockeys come and go. We have seen a whole generation of trainers pass on; and it is the same with owners and officials. The remarkable fact is that in all these various sections of Turf *personnel*, as one has dropped out, two or three others have immediately taken his place. Hence the strength of the army responsible for what may be termed " the behind-the-scenes " of racing, has year by year gone on increasing in numbers.

I have referred to the days of our youth on the Turf as " spacious and leisurely ", and to the open-air social and sporting-club atmosphere associated with them. In this respect, too, we find marked changes, many of them, it must be admitted, for the better. Nevertheless, there is a great spirit of commercialism pervading the sport, more discussion of form, chances and odds, than of the make and shape and breeding of the horses walking round in the paddock. There is greater precision as to time, a closer observance of the Rules of Racing, and, withal, more clash, hustle and rush than there used to be.

This had begun prior to the introduction of the Totalisator, but " The Tote " undoubtedly did much to accelerate it. The demands of the Racecourse Betting Control Board for the working of " The Tote " seemed largely to change the character of the weighing-room—that holy of holies, which is the nerve-centre, lever, and focal point of every race-meeting. It is, now, more so than ever it was, a place of intense activity, often at top speed, in which the clerk of the scales, jockeys, clerk of course, starter, Stewards' secretary, declarations official, stakeholder, jockeys' valets, number-board telephonists, Tote liaison officer, and others, often work at high pressure when fields are big. They carry out their various duties amid a clamour of voices and continuous tumult of hither-and-thither dashings. It was otherwise in the first decade of this century, when there were fewer runners, fewer officials, less hectic haste, and, incidentally, when the overhead charges in connection with running a race-meeting were negligible.

For the purpose of this review, let us, in backward flight, re-people a Yorkshire weighing-room—say, that at Thirsk—as I remember the *personnel* found there and on other northern courses, meeting by meeting, in the early years of this century. First arrival would be dear, gentle, Miles I'Anson, clerk of the course, and owner of the Blink Bonny Stud at Malton, with his two lieutenants—Jack Atkinson (his nephew), and liverish Michael Pigg, his managing-clerk, who had previously been with Craggs, clerk of Stockton and one or two other race-courses. Miles I'Anson's father (of Blink Bonny and Blair Athol fame), had been dead nearly a decade (January 10, 1881, to be exact), but brother William had a big string of horses at Malton and was always ready to enter a few to fill up blanks in races which threatened not to fill.

Miles I'Anson and his two assistants had begun their duties at the Fleece Hotel before coming to the course. For an hour, they had sat available to anyone who would consult them, the majority of their clients being those (many of them "dead-heads"), who pleaded all manner of reasons why their names should be put down on the list for free admission to the paddock. To these, Mr. I'Anson usually listened with so sympathetic an ear that he was much imposed upon. Kindliness, and fear of giving offence, were among his outstanding characteristics, and the culminating point was reached when, at a York meeting, the new manager (the late Colonel Eason Wilkinson), took I'Anson's free-list from the man at the owners' trainers' and jockeys' gate, and tore it up. So hurt was I'Anson that he told me that afternoon, with tears in his eyes, that he was going to resign.

He was the fourth son of the famous trainer, William I'Anson, and was born at Spring Cottage, Malton, in 1850, so was but seven years old when his father's immortal mare Blink Bonny, won the Derby and Oaks. He inherited the Blink Bonny Stud and continued to run it until 1907, when he leased it to Sir John Thursby. Among the sires Miles I'Anson had at his stud during his time were: Beauclerc, Bread Knife, Selby, Waterford, Bosphorous, and Petros, and to his credit as a breeder, he had Roysterer, Coromandel II, Chitabob, Selby, Incendiary, Lady Muncaster, Jim Selby, Cardrona, Bonny Doon, Monte Cristo, Highfield, Belle Mahone, and others of more or less note as winners. He was the embodiment, and controller, of northern racing to a greater extent than it had ever been before, or ever will be again, in the hands of one man.

Brig.-Gen. Sir Loftus Bates, a little later in the century, and until quite recent times, had the management of a considerable number of courses, from Pontefract to Perth, but even he did not so completely rule the destinies of what is known as " The Northern Circuit ", as did Miles I'Anson. Almost every meeting between, and including, Doncaster, York, and Scotland was under his control as clerk of the course until 1911, when, owing to Bright's disease, from which he had long been a sufferer, he resigned several of these appointments. The following year he died, leaving £38,262. He began his career in connection with Turf administration as assistant to his brother-in-law, T. S. Dawson, an ex-trainer, and son of Thomas, who at Tupgill, Middleham, trained the 1869 Derby winner, Pretender, after which there was no Epsom honour for Yorkshire until Matt Peacock's success in the Derby with Dante.

Eventually, Miles succeeded "The Young Pretender" (as T. S. Dawson was often called), as clerk of the course at Doncaster, York, Malton, Pontefract, Beverley, Ripon, Redcar, Thirsk, Catterick, Newcastle, Edinburgh, and a number of others, some of which have dropped out of the list. He lived to see far-reaching changes in the conduct of race-meetings, but not those of recent times which have saddled executives with heavier burdens in the shape of overhead charges resulting from compulsorily increased stake money, additional fees for officials, and new officials created by the Jockey Club. When Miles I'Anson began to function at his many meetings, the cost of policing them was negligible, owners paid for their own stabling and their lads' lodgings, at not many places were owners and trainers entertained to free luncheons and teas, and stake money was everywhere comparatively small.

We are, in imagination, at Thirsk's two-day Autumn meeting in 1900. The stake money offered there was £1,072 on the first day and £635 on the second, the two "big" races being the North Yorkshire Foal Plate of £300, and the Thirsk Autumn Handicap of £200. The total number of runners was 147, so that the executive received in entry-fees and forfeits practically half the money they put up for competition. I do not recall that, at that period, there was any great outcry among owners about, "running for their own money", or much demand for increased stakes. Somehow, owners were more content with the honour and sweets of victory, and with small prizes.

To-day, Thirsk, in the Spring, gives £1,000 for a Classic Trial Stakes and, at their Autumn fixture in 1949, on the opening day there was a £600 race, three worth £400 each, two of £300. On the second day, there were three £500 races, the other three being worth £300 each. This would have been thought unnecessary and heading for bankruptcy in the days of Miles I'Anson. When he died, his nephew, Jack Atkinson, got only Beverley of the many meetings at which he had assisted his uncle, but to the time of his death at the age of 70, in 1936, he continued to act as clerk of the scales at a number of meetings in the North. Very efficient, he was, too, his returns always being a model of neatness and accuracy. An outstanding memory of my old friend was his unfailing kindness and patience with nervous little apprentices who came to the scale, and to whom he gave confidence. He and I, together, were responsible for getting a number of clerks of courses in the North to put apprentice races first on the card, instead of last, thus saving a lot of young lads several hours of mental anxiety waiting for the race in which they were to take part.

William I'Anson—big, burly, cigar-smoking Bill—ought to have been a very wealthy man, but he had an expensive family, was fond of the good things of life, and was a heavy and courageous wagerer. When he began life on the Turf, his father's counsel to him was : " My advice to you is, don't bet. . . . But if you *do* bet, then *BET !* "—and William certainly carried out the latter part of the suggestion. He tried Newmarket for a time but didn't like it. He trained at Hambleton, and eventually settled down at Highfield, Malton, a big and expensive place to keep up, and now occupied by Captain Charles Elsey.

At the outset of his career, William had Mr. (later, Viscount) Henry Chaplin as his main patron, but that was before the commencement of this century, so does not come within the scope of this chapter. He was undoubtedly a clever trainer, although (like Tom Coulthwaite) he was no horseman himself. William, however, regularly rode a hack with his string, and even occasionally put in an appearance with the Middleton Hounds, whereas Tom Coulthwaite of Hednesford (trainer of Grand National and many big jumping winners) never got on to a horse. At Highfield, Malton, William I'Anson had had three Northumbrian patrons who were partners—a confederacy who raced as " Mr. Northern ". The trio consisted of : (1) Mr. Charles Perkins (the guiding and leading spirit), who lived near Morpeth, and was responsible, in 1881, for moving Newcastle Races from the old Town Moor to the present excellent Gosforth Park track. (2) Mr. John Blencowe Cookson, of Meldon Park, Morpeth, who, in 1875, had succeeded his father as Master of the Morpeth Hounds. Mr. Cookson's mother was a daughter of Sir Matthew White-Ridley of hunting-fame, and he himself married a Fenwick of Bywell, one of a family prominent as bloodstock breeders in early days and, later, in the hunting-field. (3) Mr. Bullman, a sleeping-partner, who was connected with banking on Tyneside, and did not continue to have any share in race-horses when the confederacy was dissolved.

Mr. Perkins was really responsible for Malton Races coming to an end, for some reason, taking exception to the course at Highfield where his horses were trained. He was a great horse-lover and disliked motors intensely. Strangely enough, the first time he was induced to travel in one was when he wanted to catch a train at Belsay and, on that isolated occasion, he met with an accident which proved fatal, in the August of 1905. The Perkins Memorial Plate at Newcastle perpetuates his name, although few now going racing remember him. His best horse was Chitabob, which William I'Anson trained for him, as he did Jenny Howlet, the 1880 Oaks winner.

Eventually, Mr. Perkins spent a lot of money in laying down a training-ground at his own place, Gallowhill, Morpeth, and appointed Tom Connor (who afterwards trained at Middleham) his private trainer. The real reason for leaving I'Anson was that he objected to Peter Buchannan having horses in the same stable as himself, and, as I'Anson would not get rid of Buchannan, Mr. Perkins' horses left Malton for the Northumbrian gallops, which soon proved useless for training-purposes. Mr. Perkins then sent his horses back to Highfield for a couple of years, at the end of which time Captain Percy Bewicke, one of an ancient North-umbrian family, started to train in his home county, and Mr. Perkins' horses went to him.

Captain Bewicke later went to Newmarket, and has never set foot on a race-course since he gave up training in 1927. He was a first-rate amateur rider in his day, and when he turned trainer, brought off a number of coups for a stable which gambled to some purpose. His nephew, Major Calverley Bewicke, is now training at Close House, Wylam, near Newcastle-on-Tyne. William I'Anson was a clever trainer, although not all the horses under his charge could stand his severe preparation. Just after the dawn of this century, he got a new patron in the person of Mr. John Hill, who lived at Saltburn, was a Middlesbrough iron-master, and was quite blind.

I have known two or three others in the North who continued to go racing after they had lost their sight. Lance Barker (who was a good amateur rider in the second decade of this century, and whose brother Horace, now trains at Redcar), is one. Another is Fred Holland, whose father, after being in racing-stables, went into Hunt service and for long hunted the Bedale. The former (" Young Fred ") now lives at Masham, and was blinded through colliding with the branch of a tree when jumping a fence in the Old Berks country, where he made such a name for himself as a brilliant huntsman. John Hill, with the exception of Mr. Mandaras, was the only blind owner of race-horses I ever knew. For 500 gns., William I'Anson bought him Mintagon (by Martagon, out of the One Thousand and Oaks winner, Mimi), which won him the 1906 Cesarewitch. It is on record that there was once a blind jockey named M'Gilvray in Scotland, who rode for the grandfather of the Malton trainer W. A. Binnie. A story is told, too, that when Godding trained for the short-tempered Lord Glasgow, he had a blind patron, a joke regarding whom so irritated the Earl (much given to changing his trainers) that he took his horses away from Godding. That trainer remarked to Lord Glasgow as they were walking round the boxes, " That's old Volunteer. He's won 17 races, and his owner has never seen him." On the Earl expressing surprise at such apparent lack of interest, Godding remarked, " You see, the owner is blind."

Mr. Hill's Mintagon was bought cheaply because two southern trainers had decided that he would never stand a preparation, and I remember I'Anson remarking to me, apropos this : " I've heard it said I break horses down, but all my best winners have been unsound animals, and Mintagon was one of these. He never really trotted soundly, and yet it took two horses to lead him in his work." Mr. Hill was very anxious to win the 1906 Ebor at York, but was beaten a head by Danny Maher on Golden Measure. Hill seemed to have an added sense, for after the race (which I'Anson " read " to him on the stand), Mintagon's owner said : " Most people seem to think the winner didn't get up, but I could see that he just ' pipped ' my horse."

Like so many others connected with the Cleveland iron trade, Hill fell on hard times. He died at Kingston in 1921 at the age of 71. Another of his horses was Mondamin, much fancied for the 1908 Cesarewitch. I'Anson had bought him at the December Sales, despite being told that he was such a bad-legged horse that he would not stand a canter. He ran twice only in 1907, and then Hill sold him to H. F. Clayton, another of I'Anson's patrons, for whom he afterwards won the 1908 Derby Gold Cup. I'Anson often told me he was sure that Mondamin would have won that year's Cesarewitch had he not bolted when at exercise on the morning of the race, and galloped the length of the course, and then down the hard road into Newmarket High Street.

Mr. Clayton had to wait until 1931 before he won a big race, and in that year, again, he had hard luck in the Cesarewitch. His horses were still at Highfield, but then, of course, with Captain Elsey. Disarmament secured him the Cambridgeshire in 1931, but his Cesarewitch runner, Six Wheeler, was second to Noble Star. Had Six Wheeler been successful, his owner would have brought off a £100,000-to-£100 double. Born in 1856, Mr. Clayton won his first race at the defunct Scarborough meeting in 1890. He never lodged an objection during his long innings on the Turf, loved others to back his horses when he fancied them, and continued at his Leyland Motor Co. at Huddersfield, and as an owner of race-horses, until his death in 1935. His Six Wheeler (named after a type of motor-vehicle his firm manufactured) went to Colonel B. C. Fairfax's Blink Bonny Stud (adjoining Highfield) at the end of his racing-career. The Colonel, by the way, died in January 1950—a great loss to the northern turf.

Reverting to William I'Anson's day at Highfield, the last important winner he trained was Rathlea, and his final patron was the late Sir John Robinson, who founded the famous Worksop

Manor Stud in 1890. The very last of I'Anson's winners was Dormant, owned by Sir John. William was then living at Wold Cottage, having leased Highfield to Sir John Thursby when he rented the Blink Bonny Stud. Fred Archer (a nephew of the immortal Fred, and very like him), came, a very young man, as private trainer to Sir John, and later became a public trainer at Danby House, Malton, but in 1924 returned to Ellesmere House, Newmarket, following the death of his father. In 1926, he took charge of Lord Glanely's horses at The Grange. He met a tragic end, his car crashing into a 'bus at Woodford, Essex, causing instantaneous death.

In 1912 William I'Anson retired from training but continued to live at Wold House until a few years before his death, when he moved to Scarborough. There, he died suddenly after returning from church on April 31, 1934. He had reached his eighty-seventh year, and, some 10 years previously, I had written the story of his life. He always used to say that the greatest jockey he ever saw ride (drunk or sober) was Jim Snowden, who died at Bentley, near Doncaster, in 1889. Jim Fagan, he also spoke very highly of. Mr. Perkins secured him for I'Anson's stable in 1877, and among many disappointments he had in his life was when Chitabob failed to withstand his preparation for the 1889 Derby. Jim had set his mind on winning the race with the son of Robert the Devil, out of Jenny Howlet, for Mr. Perkins and I'Anson. He would, in any case, have been taking on something to beat the Duke of Portland's Donovan, a colt only once defeated that year, when, by a head, Enthusiast beat him for the Two Thousand Guineas.

Jim Fagan gave up riding in 1903, and began to train at Grove House, Malton, spending a lot of money on the place. He was unfortunate in some of his patrons, who failed to pay their accounts and put him into Queer Street. Born at Knutsford in 1855, he died at Malton in 1932, rarely coming racing in his later years, as he was in receipt of the Bentinck Memorial Fund allowance and felt it was not " quite the thing " to be seen on a racecourse. I believe the very last meeting he ever attended was Thirsk, on Friday, October 31, 1930, and I find recorded in my diary :

"Jack Atkinson brought Jim Fagan racing to-day. He really came to have a chat with Dobson Peacock, who unfortunately was not at the meeting. Fagan came and had a chat with me in the weighing-room and told me that, with the exception of George Manser, old George Taylor, Sir Loftus Bates, Bob Armstrong, and one or two more, there was no one in the paddock whom he knew. He was very interested in the automatic scale, and as he went out I watched him walk across the paddock, and thought he seemed as sprightly and active as ever."

We had laughed over the incident at York, when, after wasting hard to ride 7 st. 11 lbs., he undid it all by eating a small pear in the paddock to quench his thirst. He had already got Mr. Manning to try him, but when he went to pass the scale, he was over a pound heavier than when he " tried ". There are other instances of jockeys putting on weight after severe wasting, out of all proportion to what they have eaten or drunk. For instance, the very year Fagan died, I was officiating in the weighing-room at Hamilton Park when Joe Marshall (who had won the 1929 Derby on Trigo) passed the scale at 8 st. 2 lbs. to ride Caress in a selling plate. He had been wasting hard to do the weight, and, feeling faint, had half a bottle of " fizz " brought into the weighing-room, in a tea-pot, by one of the valets. He was beaten a neck in a desperate finish, and when he came to scale to weigh-in as rider of the second, he was about 3 lbs. overweight. Caress was in consequence disqualified. Jim Fagan, by the way, like Tom Bruckshaw and George McCall, did not believe in physic or Turkish baths, they put on sweaters and walked for miles to get off every possible ounce.

Tom Bruckshaw was training at Whitehall, Malton, in the early years of this century, and, peculiarly enough, Thirsk was the last meeting he attended. Born 1853, he was apprenticed to John Fobert, who trained Van Tromp and the Flying Dutchman at Middleham. He rode his first winner at Lanark in 1870, and it was in Scotland he read his own obituary after being taken to hospital following an accident on Musselburgh race-course. He rode the 1873 Cesarewitch winner (Lord Lonsdale's King Lud), for which he received a present of £100, then considered a hand-some gift to a jockey. When he gave up riding, he bought the once-famous Whitewall training-quarters at Malton (now occu-pied by W. Bellerby), from which John Scott had sent out so many Classic winners, most of them ridden by his brother William, who, after a lean time, was heard to say in his evening prayers, " Thank God, You've sent us a —— smasher at last ".

There had not been a race-horse in the Whitewall boxes since John Scott's death 20 years before, his widow refusing to sell or let. Bruckshaw had not much luck as a trainer, and latterly managed Lord Durham's bloodstock until he retired to Scar-borough in 1928. I occasionally met him there and had many interesting chats. He died in November, 1943, having celebrated his ninetieth birthday the previous August. He once told me he hoped, when his time came, he would pass out in his sleep—and his wish was gratified.

We are still, in fancy, re-peopling the weighing-room at Thirsk in 1900, and at that fixture George McCall and his brother John both rode winners. George then had the world at his feet. He

was just 20, and to the end was a lad's weight with a man's head
and strength, but he had a better-balanced head for race-riding
than for keeping the fees he earned in his profession. A really
good horseman on any sort of horse, particularly sympathetic
with two-year-olds, and able to get the last ounce out of a lazy,
sluggish horse, or " a thief ", he came much into the limelight
in 1901, and for some seasons afterwards was much in demand
although he once told me when I apologised for giving him only
" a pony " (£25) for riding a winner in which I had an
interest :
" I very often don't get even ' Thank you ' for riding winners."

In 1901 he rode four winners and a dead-heat at Beverley one
afternoon when there were five races only on the card, and that
year he finished third to Otto Madden and Danny Maher in the
Winning Jockeys' list. Among George's winners were : Cumberland Plate, 1901 (Old China) ; Lincolnshire Handicap, 1902
(St. Maclou), in which race he beat Sceptre ; One Thousand
Guineas, 1905 (Col. W. Hall-Walker's Cherry Lass), and Northumberland Plate, 1908 (Old China). He was second to Ard
Patrick on Rising Glass in the 1902 Derby, but was never on the
winner of the Epsom Classic. George and John M'Call were both
apprenticed to their father John M'Call, who trained at Dunbar,
and had been an athlete in his younger days, winning the Powder-
Hall Foot Handicap in 1879. A neat, smart, modest little man
was John, who trained White Bud on the sands at Dunbar to win
the 1923 Lincolnshire Handicap, and in 1904 had G. Tod's
Powder Puff, which twice won the Cumberland Plate.

Like John McGuigan (the Ayr veteran), Jim Russell (who
trained at Mablethorpe), and Burns of Ayr (whose son and grandson have done well as jockeys in Ireland), John smiled indulgently
at those who asked if training on sea-sands did not make horses
slow. Old John M'Call once replied to such a query in my
presence : " The trouble with nearly all the horses I have ever
had to train was that they were not speedy enough when they
came to me. They certainly never got any slower because I
galloped them on the sea-shore—rather the contrary." John
Osborne once tried this out with certified surveyors to measure
horses' strides, both on the moor at Middleham, and then the
same horses on the sands at Redcar, and found there was very
little in it.

John M'Call, sen., was born at Kelso and died, in 1931, at
Dunbar. George died there in 1948, almost a forgotten personality. One rarely saw him racing for the last 25 years of his life,
and one of the rare occasions on which he put in an appearance
was in 1931 at Hamilton Park. I got him to sit in the scale, and
we found he was 7 st. 11 lbs.—exactly the same weight as when

he gave up riding. He belonged to an age when jockeys quickly spent the fees and presents they received, and were left with little or nothing when it was assumed—sometimes inaccurately—that they had lost their nerve and dash, and so got fewer and fewer mounts. Always rather a heart-break thing to those who are made to feel they are " has-beens ". With nearly all his generation of jockeys, it was a case of " a short life and a merry one " : for I do not think, in view of privation, the uncertainty of continued popularity, and the disappointments associated with the pro-fession, that it is correct to apply to them the hackneyed slogan, " Easy come, easy go ".

Looking through the list of those who ran horses at that 1900 Thirsk meeting and flitted in and out of the weighing-room, one feels rather like a museum-piece—one of the " last of the Mohicans ! " Tommy Weldon, who later trained at Beverley, then bought Tupgill (which he sold cheaply to the veteran Bob Armstrong), was riding. He never really recovered from an accident in the 1901 Oaks, when his mount Arta, and also March-cress (ridden by K. Cannon), fell. Tommy died in his chair at Beverley in 1905, at the age of 45. George Sanderson, who rode four winners at the Thirsk meeting, was the son of William Sanderson, then training at Malton, whither he had gone in 1886 after being for several years at Hambleton. Originally, he was stud-groom to Major Stapylton at Myton-on-Swale, and went to Hambleton about 1866 with some horses owned by the major. Sanderson retired in 1909, and died at Malton at the age of 80, in 1920. His son Walter, trained for a time for Mr. Lanarch.

Among other good jockeys Sanderson turned-out, were Jim Griffiths, the Woodburn brothers, and Fred Finlay. The last-named rode a lot of winners in his day, and died at Malton in 1909. In 1893 he was on four successive winners at York, and that season he finished fifth in the Jockeys' List with exactly 100 winners to his credit. Another of the real " old school " riding in 1900 was Seth Chandley, then over 40. He went on riding for four years afterwards, and Dobson Peacock of Middleham was very good to him latterly. In the end, Seth went as " boots " to a Stockport hotel. He was born at New Mills, Derbyshire, and died at the age of 63 in an institution. Such was the end of a good jockey who rode three successive winners of the Cumberland Plate, and won the 1888 Lincolnshire Handicap, Ascot Stakes, and Cambridgeshire.

The " bottle " was also responsible for Tiny Heppell's down-fall. He was apprenticed to Dobson Peacock, and spoiled a brilliant career by lack of restraint. As Peacock more than once said to me : " They can't stand corn ! If you bring field-daisies

in to hot-houses, they only grow into bigger field-daisies."
Heppell was a Durham lad and died at Dawdon in his home
county, in 1937, at the age of 60.   Latterly, he was employed as
a checkweighman at a colliery, and almost to the end, he used to
put in an appearance in the paddock at Gosforth Park to see the
Northumberland Plate, the winner of which (Palmy Days) he had
ridden, together with other successes at the same meeting, in
1904.   The last time I saw Tiny was at Gosforth on Plate-day.
He was smoking a big cigar, wearing a brilliant waistcoat, as perky
as a banty-cock, and living in the past.   Unlike C. Foy, and some
other fallen stars from the jockey firmament, Tiny Heppell never
lost his self-respect, and never asked for, nor accepted, charity
from those whom he had known in the days when he had money
to burn—and burnt it !

Still taking the Thirsk 1900 meeting as the text upon which I
am hanging these notes reviewing the past half-century, the
youngest jockey riding at the Yorkshire meeting was Melton
Vasey, who is still hale and hearty, and training at Doncaster,
whilst his brother Percy trains at Wetherby.   As a matter of fact,
although only 15 years old when he rode at Thirsk, Melton had
had his first ride in public five years earlier when he rode Mrs.
Knight filly at Thirsk.   Indeed, he had ridden winners : the first
being at Redcar in 1897, in honour of which the folk on Hambleton
presented him with a gold watch, which he carries to this day.
No one looking at Melton now, would imagine that he was ever
able to go to scale at under 6 st., but so it was.   His father, the
late Joe Vasey, trained at Hambleton for some years before going
to Doncaster, where he died in 1905, through blood-poisoning
contracted from the colour in some socks he wore.

Melton was born in 1885, the night before Melton (that year's
Derby winner) won the St. Leger.   He rode under National Hunt
Rules after becoming too heavy for the flat, and then had some
interesting experience as a trainer in Brazil before returning to
Doncaster, where he has trained ever since, apart from the inter-
ruptions of two wars.   His brother Percy, was training in Malaya
until 1936, when he returned to this country, and took out a
licence to train in this country.   Melton's early start as a jockey
is unusual but by no means exceptional, for Syd Menzies, who
now lives at Sedgefield, commenced to ride over hurdles when
he was 12.   At that time, his uncle George was training at Coxhoe,
quite near Shincliffe race-course, on which there has been no
racing since the First World War.

Horses trained by the late George Menzies (according to the
late Jimmy Deans, a " vet " very prominent on the northern
Turf), were the first to be " doped " in this country.   Before
" doping " was illegal, Deans regularly made up what he called

" speedy balls ", first for Menzies, and then for other northern trainers, who found that they put " pep " into horses which were not inclined to " put it all in ".   George Menzies' Durham stable was most successful in the days when he had Rising Falcon and Weather Eye, and when quaint, old East-Riding Bob Harper (who used to ride as " Mr.", and was, later, many years henchman for George Gunter, when he sent out a lot of winners from Wetherby, and was leading amateur rider), was his head man. Syd Menzies was for a long time a successful steeplechase jockey in the North, then he trained a few jumpers, farmed at Stokesley, and later acted as starter at Sedgefield, Wetherby, and Hexham.

Percy Woodland rode in his first 'chase when he was only 12, and his brother William had a mount in the Grand National when 13, Fred Archer lending him his boots and breeches. Herbert Woodland, another brother, who later trained in France, rode a winner on the flat when he was nine years old. The prize " baby " jockey story (which one always revives when the subject of juven- ile prodigies is under discussion), concerns my old friend Mr. George Stafford Thompson. His father (who had the Rawcliffe Stud at York), made a match at York, and was under the im- pression that it was to be " owners-up ". He discovered, how- ever, that his opponent had engaged a featherweight from Scott's stable at Malton to ride for him. Mr. Thompson walked over to the carriage in which his wife sat with her little son, then about eight years old, and said, " Hand me out George ". His bodily weight was then about 2 st. 13 lbs., and his riding orders were : " Hold your reins tight, and as soon as they say ' Go ', come home as fast as you can." He won his first race by several lengths, and became one of our best amateurs on the flat.

On Lord Zetland's Hardrada, he once beat Fred Archer (on Oxlip) in a great finish at Stockton, but said : " I can hardly crow over Archer, for I had three close finishes with Johnny Osborne, and he beat me a head in each of them. I spoke to his mother, a dear old soul, of his heartless conduct to me, and begged she would give him a good talking to." Mr. Thompson declined several offers to ride in the Derby, but did ride once in the St. Leger. That was as long ago as 1860, and I think I am correct in saying that he is the only amateur rider to have competed in the Yorkshire Classic, although one or two amateurs have ridden in the Derby. He had given up race-riding before the dawn of this century, but I often saw him out hunting on a small blood- 'un, and once or twice stayed with him at Newbuilding, under the Hambletons, near Thirsk, to hunt on the hills with the Bils- dale. To the end, he always put in an appearance at Thirsk and York Races. He was born in 1832, for some years had the

Moorlands Stud at York, and it was a great joy and education to sit and listen to him talking of days, and people, of the past. He died November, 1916.

The reference in the foregoing to Johnny Osborne, reminds me that his son Fred was riding at the 1900 Thirsk meeting. Fred never approached his father in jockeyship, and never rode in a Classic. He lacked, too, his father's personality—for old John had *that*, in addition to his great skill and knowledge. John was one of the most modest and retiring of men—so different to some jockeys of to-day when they have ridden a few winners! Although known in his younger days as, " The Pusher ", that was the last thing he was out of the saddle. He never spoke unless spoken to, he never advanced an opinion unless asked, he never criticised jockeys who rode for him, and I never heard him say an unkind word about anyone. All this was intensified in Fred. A true story gives one an index into his temperament and lack of self-reliance and initiative. Once, after Newcastle Races, old John and he were leaving the course when John found he had left his coat in the weighing-room. He told Fred to sit down until he returned. In the weighing-room, John was asked by someone to look at a horse at the course stables, and did so, forgetting all about Fred, who did not put in an appearance at dinner, and was still missing when the meal was over. Eventually, John and Dobson Peacock, who were staying at the same hotel, walked back together to the race-course, and found the obedient Fred still sitting, patiently awaiting his father's return.

Fred, by the way, died at Richmond in 1944, at the age of 72, at once-famous Belleisle, from whence the Watsons' turned out so many winners in the merry past. Fred's final winner was on Tarboy at Catterick in 1906. After his father's death at the age of 89, in 1922, Fred trained at Middleham, but never had more than a few horses, and nothing outstanding. I had a few words with his father at York two or three days before his death, and marked him the runners on his card, as his eyesight was failing. He was one of my earliest turf mentors, and with him I went to the first race-meeting at which it was necessary to stay away all night. This was the opening of the new course at Carlisle, when the races were moved from The Swifts to Blackwell in 1904. John took me to a little temperance-hotel near the station, and when I suggested that we went to a music-hall in the evening, he replied that he always went to bed at nine o'clock, and that he was going to be up and on the race-course as soon as it was light.

John was not a spender, was almost a teetotaller, a non-smoker, never swore, and was one of the most honourable and purest-minded men it has ever been my good fortune to meet. He was not a great conversationalist, and was not easy to draw, unless someone made an erroneous statement on some historical Turf event, and John was appealed to as referee. His memory for facts and details then astounded one. He had ridden in 38 consecutive Derbys ; won the 1869 Derby and Two Thousand Guineas on Pretender (and five other Two Thousands) ; had ridden two winners of the One Thousand ; the 1874 Oaks and St. Leger, on Apology ; an earlier St. Leger on Lord Clifden, and was a jockey from 1846 to 1892, so that he had had a wealth of experience.

In the many talks I had with him, both at his home at Middleham and travelling to and from race-meetings, I gained the impression that highest in regard amongst the Osborne's owners was the Rev. J. W. King, B.D., vicar of Ashby-de-la-Launde, in Lincolnshire, who raced under the name of " Mr. Launde ". It was for him that Johnny rode Apology to victory in the 1874 Oaks and St. Leger, and it was the winning of these two important events which made " Mr. Launde's " Bishop sit up and take notice. The Bishop of Lincoln wrote a letter of remonstrance, with the result that the bloodstock-loving parson sent in a very dignified resignation of his benefice. After saying, " It is true that for more than 50 years I have bred and sometimes had in training horses of a breed highly prized, which I inherited with my estate, and which breed has been in my family for generations ", he went on : " I resign the living I hold in your lordship's diocese, not from any consciousness of wrong, or from fear of any consequences which might ensue in the ecclesiastical courts, but simply because I desire to live the remainder of my life in peace and charity with all men." He died very soon afterwards (May, 1875), so that his Holy Friar, much fancied for that year's Derby, could not run. There were quite a number of clergymen owning race-horses about this time and a little later. William I'Anson, for instance, trained for the Rev. H. Ramsden, who had a living near Peterborough, bought Fred Archer's house at Newmarket, and came to be known as " The Bishop of Newmarket ".

Then, of course, there was Parson Parkes, who left the Church and turned trainer, and was often seen on The Northern Circuit. He died from pneumonia in 1920. Jim Adams, the oldest living ex-trainer, at one time trained for a parson, although I don't think the horses ran in the cleric's name. One could go on extending the list, but I will mention just one more—the Rev. Sir John Barker Mill, of Mottisfont Abbey. He owned part of Stockbridge Race-course, had horses in training, and in 1837 founded and hunted a pack of hounds in the Hursley country. One who knew him well, thus described him in *Baily* in 1874 :

R. C. DAWSON   W. EARL

S. WOOTTON   V. SMYTH

[*Facing page* 84

C. BOYD ROCHFORT   LORD ROSEBERY

MR. and MRS. M. MARSH. SIR HUMPHREY AND MISS C. DE TRAFFORD

He soon dropped the outward and visible signs of being a clergyman when he bought the Sandbeck hounds, which had hunted the North Notts country. He only continued as M.F.H. three years, for the Revd. Sir John (who wore the loudest plaid trousers and cherry-coloured ties), had his heart more in the racing snaffle than the scarlet, and up to the time of his death delighted to drive over to Danebury to see Day's horses at work. He was owner of Cymbra, which won the Oaks in 1848, entered in Hill's name, and in later years had Flying Englishman and a few other fair horses. A very bumptious squire-parson told him he had had a well-known trainer and his brother to dinner, and had given them champagne as a treat. " They have drunk more champagne out of tumblers than you have ever seen ", replied Sir John.

William Day, in his *Reminiscences*, tells us that the sporting parson-baronet suffered much from gout, and adds :

When he came to the races or to Danebury to see his horses, he came in a carriage with four horses, two postilions and two outriders, all dressed in blue livery with red cuffs and collars, and although he could scarcely step out of his carriage, he would set gout at defiance and have some champagne, if nothing else. He had running, about this time and later, Cerva, Bar One, Cymbra (which he bought from Harry Hill after the Oaks), Volunteer, Giantess, Miss Elis, Pugilist, Margaret of Anjou, Red Doe, Deer Stalker, Black Doe, Pet of the Herd, and Remus. I have always heard he was very fond of cocking, and many mains were fought at the two inns on his property.

John Osborne was a great churchman, and for years acted as churchwarden or sidesman at the little church at Coverham, near his Middleham home. I once remarked to him, when riding out with him on Middleham Moor, " You have never adopted the American monkey-crouch, short-leathers, Mr. Osborne ", to which he replied, " It's as much as I can do to ride in the old English style, although I always rode much shorter than Archer, Fordham, and other jockeys of my time ; but then I had shorter legs, apart from believing in the forward seat, though not to the extreme it has now got." When well over eighty, his family insisted upon him riding a pony rather than a blood-'un on the moor, to superintend the work of the few horses he had under his charge. He was most indignant at this, but gave way. So late as 1913, however, he rode The Guller the full length of the Chester Cup course the day before he won it, and also gave Mynora her final pipe-opener before she won the 1912 Northumberland Plate, which, strangely enough, was the only race the

G

mare won out of a dozen attempts that season. Like The Guller, she was ridden by James Ledson, who was apprenticed to Hugh Powney, successor to Godfrey Miller at Hambleton. Ledson met his death riding a motor-cycle on the Darlington-Richmond road in 1924.

It was John Osborne who gave the late Mathew Dobson Peacock his winning ride as an amateur. This was at Catterick in 1877, a meeting at which Osborne told me he remembered jockeys having to dress in a tent. Peacock had "ridden out" a lot for Harry Hall, then training at Spigot Lodge, and Osborne had seen him on Middleham Moor, and also going well across country with the Bedale Hounds, with which they both hunted. To the end, there was a close friendship between the old Middleham ex-jockey trainer and Dobson Peacock, and when the former died and the family sold their Middleham property, Harry Peacock, who had bought Belleisle at Richmond, let it to Fred, Phil, and their sisters.

Dobson Peacock started to train in the early '80's, but went on riding in public as an amateur until 1895, his last mount being Mr. Chatterton's Grasp, on which he won the Club Plate at Manchester. Mr. Peacock was born at Harmby, near Leyburn, in 1856, and died Sept. 13, 1935. Although continuing to take an interest in his string and going up to the moor in his car to the end, his son, Mr. Mathew J. Peacock, for a couple of years prior to 1935, was virtually trainer. After the First World War there was, year by year, an increasing number of horses in the Manor House stables at Middleham, and during the last 10 years of his life, the following was the Peacock record on the flat:

			Horses.	Races.	Value. £
1926 ..	..	..	27	47	11,445
1927 ..	..	..	34	54	17,543
1928 ..	..	..	36	48	11,708
1929 ..	..	..	33	46	12,661
1930 ..	..	..	35	69	18,882
1931 ..	..	..	51	98	22,803
1932 ..	..	..	52	100	30,742
1933 ..	..	..	35	78	16,937
1934 ..	..	..	54	89	22,624
1935 (to Sept. 15)	..		32	48	11,366

The best of his earliest horses was Golden Drop, and possibly the outstanding horse he trained was Denbigh. Naturally, it was Mr. Peacock's great ambition to train a Derby and St. Leger winner, but the Classics eluded him, something always happening to the one or two animals he thought had rather more than an outsider's chance at Epsom. Almost at the same time as he started to train, Mr. Peacock founded the Manor House Stud, and, born of agricultural stock, he farmed all his life, latterly having about 600 acres in his hands. Indeed, often when one saw him in deep conversation in the paddock at race-meetings, and " information-hunters " wished they knew what secrets the Middleham trainer was imparting, it was about sheep, bullocks, or crops he was talking. He was a great-hearted, kindly man—in his young days, a very handsome one—and in his latter years, when he tired of standing about at race-meetings, he came into the weighing-room and had long chats with me.

Several times I suggested he should write his " Life ", but he never did, which is to be regretted, for, like John Osborne, he was a link between the past—which some call " the good ", and some " the bad ", old days—and the present. Dobson Peacock always said they were very pleasant, full of fun and of sport for sport's sake. It is often said that jockeys find the Turf much more profitable than trainers, who have months of anxiety and work " readying " horses for jockeys, who are on their backs only a few minutes, but trainers get neither the same reward or kudos when they win. Not many trainers have died well off, and for that matter, not many jockeys of the early part of this century left behind them much of the money which came their way. Dobson Peacock's will was proved at £60,364, the goodwill of the training-establishment being left to his elder son Mathew, to whom he gave the option (which he took) of purchasing the Manor House property.

" Matt " Peacock, as he is known to all and sundry, continues the high tradition of the Manor House stable, accepting (as his father did), new patrons with care and discrimination. Blunt, brusque, and a call-a-spade-a-spade Yorkshireman, Matt Peacock hates veneer ; he is forthright, and has no damned nonsense about him. Also, he is a very shrewd judge of character, and dislikes nonsense in others. He has succeeded in doing what his father, with all his skill and all his years at the game, failed to accomplish : send out a Derby winner from Middleham. This was Sir Eric Ohlson's Dante, who won at Newmarket in 1945. Dante was the first Classic winner by the unbeaten Italian-bred Nearco, and out of Rosy Legend. He was bred by his owner at his Friars Ings Stud, adjoining Peacock's training-stables. It was one more instance of beginner's luck, for Sir E. Ohlson, who gave 3,500 gns. for Rosy Legend in foal to Nearco, was a newcomer to the Turf.

William Nevett, who rode Dante, was successful in three of the wartime Derbys : Owen Tudor (1941), Ocean Swell (1944). and Dante (1945). Prior to the St. Leger, it was said that Mr, Martin Benson offered £125,000 for Dante. The colt, however,

did not run in the Yorkshire Classic owing to his preparation
being interfered with.   There was a sort of day-to-day bulletin :
that there was nothing wrong with him, that he would run, that
he wouldn't run, and so on.   He went to Mr. A. McIntyre's
Theakston Hall Stud, near Bedale, at a fee of 400 gns.   Nevett,
the Manor House jockey, and many years champion jockey of
the North, was apprenticed to the late Dobson Peacock, but is
not, as is often stated, a Yorkshireman.   He was born near Manchester in 1906, his father having been one of Peacock's earliest
employees.   Nevett's apprenticeship ended in 1930, and he then
(and since) had tempting offers to go south, but remained loyal
to the Middleham stable.

    In 1931 he rode 91 winners, and had the best average among
jockeys.   Next season, he was third in the Jockeys' List with 97
wins and 59 seconds.   In 1934 his total was 109 winners, and
in 1936, one less.   Several times he has been runner-up to Gordon
Richards.   Now he is an estate-owner, having in 1948 bought
Patrick Brompton Hall and estate from Mr. Robert Dand, a
quondam amateur rider, afterwards breeder of bloodstock, and,
incidentally, a kinsman of Mr. Adam Scott, who trained such a
lot of winners in Northumberland, and rode them himself.   Adam,
who met his death riding in a 'chase at Kelso, had the great
moment of his Turf career when he saw his home-trained Jazz
Band win the Northumberland Plate, counted a Classic by those
in the far North.   Fond of shooting, and at one time keen on
football, it is interesting to recall that it was the still-living Jim
Adams who gave Nevett his first winning mount.   This was
Stockwood, at Carlisle in 1924.   Adams was one of four brothers, all fine horsemen, particularly over country.   Born in 1863,
Jim was the son of a race-horse owner and horse-dealer, who
lived until he was over 90.   Dobson Peacock thought most highly
of Nevett, which reminds me that he missed by a hair's-breadth
having the services of Steve Donoghue.   Steve went to the Manor
House, but being under a wrong impression that the police were
making enquiries about him running away from home, the great
jockey-to-be departed from Middleham at dead of night.   Not
having given him his indentures, Peacock did not bother further
about the unknown star.

    There is now a third generation of the Peacock family coming
along to continue the Manor House tradition, for Matt's only son,
Richard (who served with the Scots Greys during the Second
World War), has been assisting his father for a year or two, and
is already well-known and much liked in racing-circles.   His uncle
Harry—Mr. Henry Dobson Peacock—has been training at Hurgill Lodge, Richmond, since he left Spigot Lodge, Middleham,
in January, 1937.   For some years Harry had run Spigot Lodge

as a stud-farm, but in 1931 took out a licence as a trainer at the persuasion of the veteran Scottish owner, Mr. Alex McKinlay, and his Turf partner Mr. Tom Stevenson. The following year, Harry won them the Lincolnshire Handicap with Jerome Fandor (40 to 1) and again in 1937 with Marmaduke Jinks (33 to 1). It was the Marquess of Zetland who influenced H. Peacock to go to the new Hurgill training-establishment his lordship had built so that his horses might return to Richmond to be trained as soon as his brother, Lord George Dundas, gave up training at Newmarket.

Alex McKinlay, of Glasgow, is another link with the distant past, for well over half a century ago his Fair Ellen II ran second in the Grand National. He is the third generation to have a big horse-dealing business in Glasgow, and at one time never had less than 1,000 horses in his stables there, and sold, on an average, 300 a week. Alex was born in 1868, is a bachelor, often went to France to buy bloodstock, but now that his legs are not as trustworthy as they once were, he confines his racing and journeys to the Scottish circuit. His racing-partner, Mr. Tom Stevenson —one of the wittiest, cheeriest, and most delightful companions— is a Glasgow stockbroker, whose father had horses both with the Osborne's and the I'Ansons, and acted as steward at a number of Scottish meetings. Incidentally, it is often said that the I'Ansons were Scotsmen. As a matter of fact, they are an old North-Yorkshire family, long-seated in Richmondshire and Wensleydale. Certainly, the elder William was one of the trainers who migrated from over the Border—the Dawsons, I'Ansons, Binnies, and Ryans from Gullane to Yorkshire, the Waughs to the South.

W. Binnie, who trains at Malton, is the third or fourth generation of the family to follow each other in the profession. The astute William, who was born 1863, and died March, 1937, was for some time secretary to the famous Mat Dawson. When Binnie set up as a trainer, it was at Middleham, but he soon left there for Malton, and one of the most remarkable horses he had was Wrinkles, which won 14 races in one season. It was not a record, for The Bard was never beaten as a two-year-old in 1885, winning 16 races, whilst in 1925 Lord Londesborough's Dudley won 17 races. I remember the days when the late William Binnie spent a great deal of his time painting—Napoleon on a white horse was his favourite subject—and when, in the winter, he hunted a pack of harriers, to which his then-tiny apprentice, Charlie Ringstead, whipped-in.

Charlie was much in demand in his apprentice days, and rode some good winners later. He lost a lot of money in a bloodstock concern in Ireland, which afterwards became very prosperous. Contemporary with Charlie in his apprentice days was Elijah

Wheatley, who, in 1905, when still an apprentice, was top of the Winning Jockeys' List with 124 winners. Known as " Whip" (or " Whippet "), he was born at Ilkeston in Derbyshire, and served his time with the late William Elsey at Baumber in Lincolnshire. He married a daughter of Marie Lloyd, and has been training in Egypt for the last 20-odd years.

In his day, at Baumber, the late W. E. Elsey had one of the biggest strings in the North, and did not keep horses to look at. Indeed, so frequently did some of them run, that it used to be said he trained them on the railway lines. He was a tower of strength to The Northern Circuit, always ready to supply a few entries for any race that did not fill. He bred bloodstock before he began to train in 1893, being persuaded so to do by Taylor Sharpe, who bred Galopin, the 1875 Derby winner. Sharpe for many years had a large stud at Baumber, but latterly lived at Newmarket, where he died in 1911. In 1904, 1905, and 1906, the late W. Elsey turned out more winners on the flat than any other trainer, but was never fortunate enough to have a real smasher. He gave up training in 1911, and died at Baumber in 1922, at the age of 67.

His son, Captain F. Elsey, now training with such success at Highfield, Malton, followed in his footsteps but did not remain at Baumber, trying both Middleham and Ayr before settling down at Highfield. Another brother is the Rt. Rev. Bishop Elsey. The Captain was born in 1881, and in recent years has had Royal patronage, in addition to that of three dukes and the late Lords Harewood and Derby. He has his own private training-ground and never goes on to historic Langton Wold at Malton. During the last two or three years success has followed success in big races, Musidora winning him his first two Classics when capturing the 1949 One Thousand Guineas and Oaks. It does not seem, however, that the long family connection with the Turf is to be continued, for Captain Elsey's son takes little interest in horses or racing, so that continuity seems certain to be broken.

It is remarkable how in some families the mantle of the father has fallen on the son from generation to generation. For instance, the Taylors (who were originally Yorkshire), the Rickabys (also hailing from the same county), the Waughs (who were Scots), Sadlers, Jarvises, Collings (also Yorkshire), Armstrongs, Dawsons (Scots), Peacocks, and others one could mention. Possessing a charming manner, Captain Elsey has had a long innings, and is one of those trainers against whom one has never heard a breath of scandal. He trained some of the late Lord Harewood's horses, as already stated. His lordship, who died in 1947, acted as steward at a number of Northern meetings, but never *appeared* to be enjoying racing. I once heard the late Lord Lonsdale say to him in a stewards'-room, " Lascelles, don't look so miserable. One might think you'd been welshed, or had your pocket picked of your last fiver."

Lord Lonsdale, who passed on in 1944, was always bubbling-over with good-nature, and seemed to enjoy every minute of life. R. W. (" Bob ") Armstrong trained for him for over 40 years, and they never had a wrong word. Bob is still fit and well at Tupgill, Middleham, and still holds a licence as a trainer as he has done since it became necessary for trainers to hold such authority, which was as recently as 1905. I believe he was the last to hold both a licence to ride and train under Jockey Club Rules. I cannot recall a time when I did not know Bob Armstrong, or on occasion when we met and he had not a good story to tell. As a matter of fact, he was riding as a jockey before I was born, for his natal year was 1863, and he commenced to ride and train when he was very young. The secret of Lord Lonsdale's popularity was that he was just as genial and friendly to the man at the gate at a race-meeting as he was to Royalty. Yet, although he was all things to all men, no one ever thought of presuming on his generous nature, or of taking a liberty.

Armstrong twice won for his Lordship the Cumberland Plate —with Melayr (1910), and Ornamentation (1926)—and I know that these successes (on his own heath, so to speak), gave the Earl as much pleasure as when he won the St. Leger with Royal Lancer in 1922. The last-named was trained by A. Sadler, jun. Lord Lonsdale loved to see his horses at work when Armstrong trained near Penrith, and quite near Lowther Castle. He prepared Dan Dancer on these Cumbrian gallops to win the 1888 Ascot Stakes, he rode at the long-defunct Penrith Races, as he did those at Durham and Richmond (also no more), on the Swifts at Carlisle, and other places which sound almost prehistoric to modern ears.

In 1923, he left Cumberland for Tupgill, Middleham, which he had bought years before from Tommy Weldon. Captain Nat Scott, who died that year, had had a lease of the old training-quarters, his best horse being Bibiani. Armstrong's sons, Gerald and Fred (the latter always known as Sam), had left Rossall School, and were anxious to embark on a Turf career, so that Middleham offered more scope. Gerald, after serving with cavalry in the First World War, came home to assist his father, then followed the late Joe Cannon as assistant to the Hon. George Lambton at Newmarket for a time, before settling down as a Middleham trainer. He saddled his first winner when Blue Stem won at Carlisle in 1923, and was one of the leading amateur riders on the flat until he had a bad accident in 1937 when riding Fad at Lewes. He did not ride again in public until 1947, when he won a race at Hamilton Park on his wife's Thyme.

Fred Armstrong trained in Ireland for a while, but in 1924 had a string at Ashgill, which erstwhile home of the Osbornes his father had bought. Fred rode a bit under National Hunt Rules, but did not continue long, and soon began to turn out his share of winners. Then came the Gaekwar of Baroda as a patron in 1946. The Maharajah was anxious to have his horses more access-ible, so installed his young trainer (he was born in 1904), at Warren Place, Newmarket, from whence he has turned out a lot of winners, until the sudden decision of the Gaekwar to change trainers in 1949.

It was to Bob Armstrong that Harry Carr, now the King's jockey, was apprenticed. Incidentally, Harry's father ("Bobby" Carr), was also apprenticed to the same veteran trainer, and still remains with the family, breaking-in yearlings and supervising generally. Harry was born at Eamont Bridge, near Penrith, and had his first " ride ", at Redcar, when only 13, and still at school. He rode his first winner at Ayr, in July, 1931, on Knight's Folly, and for some years after he had finished his apprenticeship, went each winter to India, where he was one of the leading jockeys.

It was to R. W. Armstrong, too, that Robert Weston Colling was sent when his family found that nothing would deter him from becoming a jockey. The Collings had long been landowners and prominent hunting-men in Yorkshire and Durham, and known as outstanding horsemen. The veteran Newmarket trainer was born at Marske-by-the-Sea, a mile or two from Redcar Race-course, in 1872, and rode his first winner at Newcastle in 1889, on Mortaigne, which later turned out to be D'Orsay, the two having been confused as yearlings. Both won races before the late Mr. F. Harrison—who bred them, and had the Aislabie Stud, near Ripon, and transferred it to Stetchworth—spotted the error. The facts were laid before the Jockey Club by Captain Machell, and neither of the horses was disqualified for the races they had won in each other's names.

From Armstrong, Colling went to William I'Anson at Malton, and rode a lot of winners for him before increasing weight com-pelled him to relinquish his licence. He then started farming at Habton, near Malton (Walter Easterby's brother is now on the farm), and got together a little pack of hounds. Not many flat-race jockeys have gone really well across country to hounds, but Bob Colling was one of the exceptions. He was one of a number of Yorkshire sportsmen who at that time were bad to catch, be the country or pace what they may. R. I. Robson (who trained near Knaresborough), Jack Hett (who had a few horses near Piecebridge), Leetham Whitwell (who trained a few jumpers at Croft), " Gab " Leatham, T. S. Petch (still officiating as race-auctioneer, founder of the Northern Bloodstock Sales at Stockton, and father of Major Leslie Petch, Jockey Club judge and M.F.H.), were all members of the select band of " first-flight " men.

Messrs. J. R. and George Colling, Newmarket trainers, were born at Habton, which their father left in 1899 to return to the Turf as a trainer. He took historic Spigot Lodge at Middleham, his first patron being Mr. Viginti Thompson (not to be confused with Vincent T. of Newcastle-on-Tyne), who later moved from the North to Hampshire, and died in 1946. He married a sister of Mr. Hubert Allison, the Jockey Club Starter. It was mainly due to Mr. Thompson that Bob Colling left Middleham for Newmarket in 1917. His heart has always been in the North, but now only a handful of his friends are alive and he rarely visits his old haunts. A couple of years ago, however, he stayed with his old patron, Major L. B. Holliday, Master of the York and Ainsty (North), and went as straight as ever to hounds. By a perfectly friendly arrangement, Major Holliday's horses, in 1948, went to R. Warden, at Newmarket, to be trained. In 1949, Geoffrey Brooke was appointed his new trainer. The Major has for some years now ranked as one of our leading bloodstock-breeders. He has the Cleaboy Stud (named after a favourite old point-to-point horse of his) at Kilpatrick, Mullingar, and divides his time between his chemical works in Yorkshire, his thorough-bred-breeding and racing concerns, and the hunting-field. He has been M.F.H. since 1922, when he took the Derwent country, later Mastering the Badsworth and Grove before taking the York and Ainsty (North).

Mr. Colling married a daughter of Robert I'Anson, a brilliant steeplechase jockey, and afterwards Starter. Colling's sons were both jockeys prior to setting up as trainers at Newmarket. The elder son, Jack, loves to come back to Yorkshire in the hunting-season and to make raids on the northern racing-circuit in the summer, with conscientious " Sheff " Davey (originally appren-ticed to his father) as travelling head-lad. George Colling, in 1949, trained his first Classic winner when Nimbus won the Two Thousand Guineas and then followed this by winning the Derby with the same horse.

They never forget that they are Yorkshiremen : as, by the way, are T. Weston and the Wragg brothers. There was a time when there were three of the latter jockey-brothers holding licences together, and, at the same period, three Yorkshire brothers Taylor riding. This, of course, pales before the Doyles, one of whom is now training at Wetherby. There were five brothers Doyle all simultaneously holding jockey's licences, and, at least once, they all rode in one race in Ireland. Weston commenced his career at Middleham, with George Drake, a Leeds bookmaker, who, be-fore assumed names were barred, raced as G. W. Smith. He built the Warwick House training establishment at Middleham, and must have spent a lot on his racing exploits. Eddie de Mestre had his first training appointment with him on coming to this country, Weston then being an apprentice in the stable, which Ned McCormick had been supervising. Weston won the Derby in 1924 on Sansovino, and on Hyperion in 1933 ; the St. Leger on Tranquil (1923), Fairway (1928), and Hyperion (1933).

At the same time as Weston was at George Drake's place at Middleham, George Formby went as apprentice, but having failed to make his mark as a jockey, he succeeded in doing so on the music-halls, following his father, who was a popular comedian. Nowadays, Captain Neville Crump has Warwick House, and from there sent out Sheila's Cottage to win the 1948 Grand National—the first National winner trained at Middleham. The Captain commenced to train at Upavon in 1937, but the war resulted in his stable being broken-up whilst he was on active service. He was educated at Marlborough and Oxford, and his father was Master of the South Oxfordshire Hounds from 1932 to 1935. At the end of the war, Captain Crump was stationed in Yorkshire, liked Middleham, sold his place at Upavon to W. Payne, bought Warwick House for £6,000, and soon had a string of horses on Middleham Moor.

It was on this moor that a race-meeting was held in very early times, largely sponsored by the ancient Scrope family, whose descendants are to-day prominently associated with both blood-stock- breeding and racing, and hunting, as the Scropes always have been. Mr. Adrian Scrope married a sister of Sir Richard Sykes, who continues the famous Sledmere Stud, which is as successful as ever it was. He has a few useful horses in training and has been M.F.H., so maintains the long-standing Sledmere tradition. Although crippled by the taxation, and by death duties, which together are slowly but surely annihilating the old land-owning classes, one finds sons following in the Turf footsteps of their fathers (if on a much less ambitious scale) throughout the North.

The Earl of Feversham has revived the Duncombe interest. Lord Irwin (joint-Master with his father, Lord Halifax, of the Middleton Hunt), has a few horses in training and acts as Steward at a number of northern meetings. Sir Thomas Dugdale, M.P., of Crathorne Hall (whose father's Picton was so unlucky to meet a horse like Spearmint, who beat him in the 1906 Derby), is also very keen, a patron of Matt Peacock's, and Steward at several meetings. The Marquis of Zetland carries on the Aske tradition of over a century, breeds bloodstock at his stud near Richmond, has his horses trained at home by Harry Peacock, and, as his forbears did, hears the crowd cheer when the historic "Aske spots" carried by Voltigeur, flash past the post at Redcar, Stockton, Catterick, Thirsk, and York.

In the closing years of his life, the late Lord Londonderry had but a few horses in training. Little, however, was seen of them, or their owner, in the North. Many will remember the procession of carriages containing distinguished guests from Wynyard Park, a few miles away. There were liveried outriders, all the panoply of State, and all the house-party wearing buttonholes made up into the Vane-Tempest colours—the lilac-and-yellow registered by Hambletonian's owner in 1798. This procession was one of the sights of Stockton Races, and, bringing together some of the prominent owners of the Turf, resulted in their running horses at the meeting. It was the same well into this century at Redcar, when the Rt. Hon. James Lowther, the Marquess of Zetland, and Lord Durham, all entertained on a big scale for the local meetings, as did Mr. R. C. Vyner (of Minting fame) at Newby for each Ripon fixture, and the Fitzwilliams for Doncaster.

Private luncheon-rooms, or tents in the paddock, flowed with champagne, and all manner of good things, to which hunting-men and racing-men were invited, both gentle and simple, if they were known to be sportsmen. Those were days which, with their atmosphere, may never return—days when motors had not ousted horses, and when those who *were* somebody travelled *as* somebody, and spent their money on their estates, and in giving pleasure to others. Surely, those who lived in those times, and treasure still their memory, saw the happiest days of racing, notwithstanding all the admitted improvements which have taken place.

The memories of few go as far back as those of Brig.-General Sir Loftus Bates, D.S.O., of the Spital, Hexham, who has, perhaps, done more for northern racing than any other man, and who is still Managing Director of Thirsk, Catterick, Carlisle, and Hamilton Park Race Co's. He was one of the most efficient Clerks of the Course ever, notwithstanding the fact that when he had passed his eightieth year, and was (and is) still as much at grips with racing as anyone, and as full of activity in mind and body as most, the Jockey Club, in 1946, thought he ought to give place to younger men. Born in 1863, Sir Loftus is one of the Bates family who, together with the Collings, made the Shorthorn breed of cattle. For over 50 years, he has been officially connected with race-courses, but his reminiscences go back still further, for he can recall the Northumberland Plate won by Lily Agnes in 1874. After Eton, he joined the Dragoon Guards, and on leaving the service in 1896, he trained a few horses in Cumberland, and, when offered the Clerkship of the Course at Hamilton Park, he began a long career of race-course management which later

included Thirsk, Catterick, Pontefract, Perth, Hexham, Carlisle,
Kelso, Lanark, Dunbar, Shincliffe, Rothbury, and other meetings.
It is interesting to quote what he has often told me of Turf
officialdom at the commencement of this century. Here are his
own words :

" When I took over Hamilton Park I found the Company
in very low financial position, although the Directors certainly did their best to economise : for Hugh Patrickson,
my predecessor, acted as clerk of the course, clerk of scales,
handicapper, judge, stakeholder, and secretary. No doubt
he would have acted as Starter, too, had the starting-points
been nearer. The Starter received £2 2s. for each meeting.
Hamilton Park was started in 1888, and was one of the first
meetings to provide free-stabling."

Even this inducement did not produce increased fields, a
paucity of runners having always rather marred Scottish racing,
although the travelling-allowance given in recent years by the
Race-course Betting Control Board has done something to improve this. Scotland has ever had to rely upon the Yorkshire
stables, even when there were a lot of horses in training at Ayr :
when the Burns's, Wyllies, Steel, Ruby Thomson, and John
M'Guigan all had their stables full, and John M'Call had a fair
string at Dunbar. Now Andrew Keddie (who began his career
with Ruby Thomson), is the only trainer at Ayr. George Boyd
has the M'Call's old place at Dunbar.

No official living has seen so many changes in the conduct of
racing as Sir Loftus Bates. I have been associated with his meetings for many years in various capacities, including that of judge,
and was always astonished with his self-composure, and how he
kept his head under all emergencies, when all around him were
losing theirs. Another characteristic has always been his loyalty
to his staff, albeit their loyalty to, and affection for, him. Unlike
some Clerks of the Course, he has ever been most kindly disposed
to old-timers, particularly those who have not made a success of
their time on the Turf. None of these was ever refused free-
admission to his meetings so long as interest in the sport, rather
than " tapping " those they had known in better days, was their
object.

For some years, Sir Loftus had the assistance of his son Captain
E. Giles Bates, M.C., who eventually took over the National
Hunt meetings, and who was one of the most efficient Clerks of
Scales and officials generally with whom I have had the pleasure
to work. He retired from racing, however, when he inherited
the Langley Castle estate in Northumberland. In 1947 the whole
racing-community combined in presenting Sir Loftus with a

handsome testimonial. Apart from maintaining his active connection with race-course management, he has a few horses in training, under both rules.

Another family long connected with Turf officialdom in the North is the House of Ford. The first of them was William (born Lincoln, 1808), who became Clerk of the Course at Lincoln, and founded the Lincolnshire Handicap over a century ago. He died at Nottingham in 1891 and was succeeded at Lincoln by his son, Mr. W. J. Ford (born Derby, 1842 ; died Nottingham, 1912), who controlled Derby, Nottingham, and other meetings, was judge and handicapper and held other offices. Before he gave up handicapping, he had made 21 consecutive " Lincolnshires ". Many of us recall him as " the man in the box ", in frock coat and silk hat. He had three sons who all became Turf officials.

William followed his father as judge and continued until his death in 1912, when Mr. Stanley B. Ford took his place, his first appointment on the flat being at Ayr at the final meeting on the old course. He gave up judging a few years ago, but continues as Clerk of the Course at a number of Midland meetings. His son Francis acts as Clerk of the Course at Pontefract, and as Clerk of Scales at many meetings, also judging under National Hunt Rules. Mr. John Ford (who married a daughter of the well-known owner and commission-agent, Charlie Hibbert), died in 1944. He was a race-course auctioneer, a keen hunting-man, and for some time secretary of the South Notts, and Earl of Harrington's Hunts. Charlie Hibbert, by the way, left £103,498 when he died in 1915. He won the Lincolnshire Handicap with Mercutio in 1911. Five years after his death Joe Pickersgill, the big Leeds bookmaker, passed on. He had a few horses in training at one time at Richmond, but soon gave up owning, and when he died his will was proved at £746,459.

Major Leslie Petch, M.F.H. (born at Liverton, North Yorks, 1900), became judge under Jockey Club Rules in 1933. A bold horseman, though a welter-weight, winner of point-to-points, Master of the Cleveland Hounds, he comes of a family long prominent as hunting-men, hunter judges, and hunter breeders. He is also Managing Director and Clerk of the Course at Redcar, and at Catterick. Since 1944 Mr. L. L. Firth has been Clerk of the Course at York's important meeting, in succession to Mr. Fred Wilmot, who had held the position from 1912. Mr. Firth was at one time an amateur rider, and succeeded the late Captain E. Willoughby (afterwards Lord Middleton), as starter after the 1914 war. He has bred a few bloodstock, and sold Nitsichin, the 1932 Cesarewitch winner, as a yearling at Doncaster.

The Tophams, who still control Aintree, were originally a

Yorkshire family, being landowners near Middleham and prominent there in the world of sport. Prior to 1848, the first Topham to become a Turf official was manager of Chester Race-course, and, in the year mentioned became lessee of Aintree, where he founded the Grand National. He was well-known as a handicapper, and died in 1873, being succeeded by his son Joseph, who, in turn gave place to Mr. E. A. C. Topham, of our own generation. He died in 1932. Now, " Topham's Ltd. " consists of Messrs. A. R. and M. D. Topham, who are jointly managers and secretaries of the Liverpool course with which the family has so long been identified.

CHAPTER VII

MEN, WOMEN, JOCKEYS, AND HORSES

By CYRIL LUCKMAN

FIFTY years of following practically every sport—what a gorgeous cavalcade of memories!

Racing has been the dominant factor in most of them, but there were those grand days when, as an old Rugby footballer I went round with Dave Gallaher and the first epoch-making "All Blacks" team in 1905—as I did also the South African " Springboks "—with grim Paul Roos as Captain—the following winter. Likewise, when the Australian " Wallabies " came over to remind us then that more came from " down-under " than cricketers and horses like mighty Carbine—" five furlongs to five miles " : distance didn't trouble him, and he could win twice in the same afternoon!

And I saw the cricket Tests, including some of the only triangular series ever likely to be staged. It had always been an ambition with Sir Abe Bailey to get Australia and South Africa over here at the same time and the noted South African sportsman achieved it in 1911.

Most readers of this volume will, however, associate "Abie" more with Son-in-Law and his many Turf successes in two lands. His horses were so invincible at one time in South Africa that he had to " buy money " whenever allowed to bet on them. Though Reggie Day was his chief trainer over here at Newmarket, Sir Abe believed in spreading his favours. Harry Cottrill produced many good winners for a patron who liked to bet. They included the 1936 Oaks' heroine, Lovely Rosa (33 to 1), with Weston in the saddle, and Tommy was also on Dan Bulger (7 to 1) the same year, when Cottrill provided the Cambridgeshire winner in the famed black-and-gold colours.

Joe Lawson had won the 1933 Cambridgeshire for Sir Abe with 33–1 chance Raymond, and the ill-fated South African jockey, " Ticky " Nicol seemed made then. But, poor chap, he never seemed to recover his position after one race he rode for Templeman at Doncaster : didn't look after himself well and committed suicide.

Over many years, the Turf has had its tragedies as well as its glamour and high spots. Apprentices ride a few winners and seemed booked eventually to bid for honours achieved by men like Steve Donoghue and, now, Gordon Richards : but there are hundreds of such lads I've seen drop out and become forgotten. Some went back to the stable yard, others just became members of that great, ever-increasing crowd of " might-have-beens " and found " spivving " an easier outlet.

Mention of South Africans, perhaps Strydom would have gone on showing his worth, but he was killed in a road smash on his way back from riding a big Ascot winner.   And so was trainer Fred Leader when returning on the first day by car to Newmarket after winning the Gold Vase (1933) with Gainslaw for my friend Mr. H. L. Simms.   Royal jockey Crouch flew his own plane and fatally crashed.   Speed is a mania with many lads, and I suppose race-riding teaches them to take a risk.   Charlie Smirke no longer drives himself, but they still speak of " Smirke's Corner " on the road between Royston and Newmarket !

So now back for a spell to 50 years ago—and 1900 was made more than memorable by the varied triumphs of the Prince of Wales—afterwards King Edward VII.   Late-Victorian crowds and, of course, crowds during the Edwardian period later, idolised him.   He was so definitely the *grand seigneur*, who could be starchy if he thought etiquette was being overlooked, but he could also be " Teddy ", and he never forgot a face.

Perhaps there were more stories—only a small percentage true—told about him than about any other reigning monarch since Charles II.   He loved racing and tried, perhaps vainly, to make Queen Victoria realise what a lot its patronage meant in linking the Throne to a national sport.   Persimmon had already won the Derby—flooring the 13 to 8 laid on Mr. Leopold de Rothschild's St. Frusquin in that neck affair of 1896—and St. Leger, when starting 11 to 2 on : Jack Watts had been the jockey each time.

I did not see Persimmon ; by general consent, he will be voted the pick of the three Royal Derby winners for King Edward, but Diamond Jubilee was the Triple Crown winner of 1900 and associated with many dramatic elements.   And there was a specially satisfactory side to the Two Thousand Guineas and Derby successes of Minoru in 1909, for this colt—leased from Colonel Hall Walker (afterwards Lord Wavertree and the donor of the National Stud)—was the confident tip for both races in the daily paper with whose editorial staff I have had the pleasure of being closely allied for nearly half a century.

The flat-racing season of 1900 was indeed memorable.   It began as right royally as it went along.   There were many who came away from Lincoln, after Morny Cannon had won the big Carholme handicap easily on Charlie Archer's 100-to-12 chance Sir Geoffrey, with " live " vouchers with the Prince of Wales's Ambush II for the National.

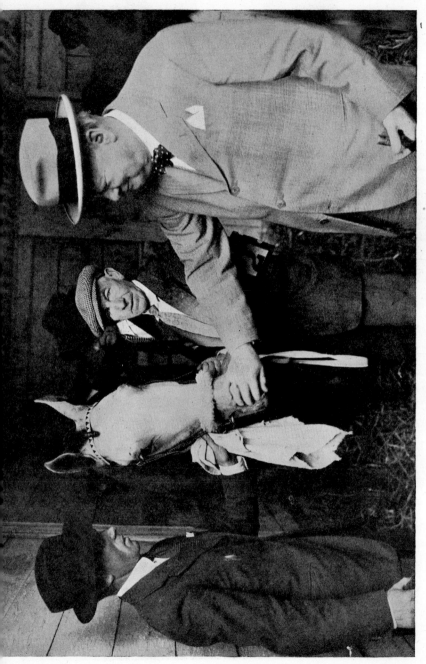

MR. WINSTON CHURCHILL WITH COLONIST II

MR. JAMES DE ROTHSCHILD, 1921   THE HON. DOROTHY PAGET, 193?

MR. R. ("BOSS") CROKER LEADING IN ORBY, J. REIFF UP. Derby, 1907

Incidentally, you *dared* not then (as a small punter) bet " cash " in England, and such firms as Topping and Spindler—did Hardaway and Topping come first ?—and Robert Masters, Crook & Co. catered for the ready-money in Holland. First at Flushing, then at Rotterdam and, still migrating (when the law ordained), to Switzerland and the smaller independent State of Luxemburg.

But the days of overseas' betting (except for commissions in South Africa) are over : we used to be mulcted with a reduction of 2½ per cent. on all winnings, which were, of course, only at multiplied odds at the time of booking and, naturally, " all-in-run-or-not ". One of those firms in Holland was started on the " never-pay " basis, but was so profitable from the outset that " Honesty became easily the best policy ".

A flashback to rubicund, well-bellied " Bob " Topping walking disconsolately, but still belligerent, off the course at Lincoln with his open waistcoat exposed to Carholme winds, a loose, heavy gold chain flapping, and his doubly-heavy gold watch missing. " They can't do this to me ", he kept ejaculating. But, " boys " had been no respecter of persons. Happy ending: Bob paid the intermediary a price and got back his " two-ton ticker ". Even if you should in these immaculate days lose your binoculars —no youngster seems to wear other than the wrist-watch—don't shout " blue murder ", but " have a chat "!

In my amateur theatrical days—and "rails"-bookmaker Lord " Tommy " Graves and Frank Hartigan's pal Harvey Solomon (so closely associated with Mr. Jim Joel's horses) will recall them—a " short " play by a noted playwright like Pinero, Henry Arthur Jones or any other " comedy " writer, was prefaced by a " curtain-raiser ". It lasted about half an hour. This preamble to Ambush II won't last nearly so long, but it will have a good curtain. So back to our " mutton " and the Aintree scene of 1900, where the Topham family (who celebrated their centenary in 1948) ruled the roost. The Prince of Wales had bought Ambush II in Ireland and, with " Algy " Anthony in the saddle, he beat " Bill " Halsey on Barsac, by four lengths. Greatest " National " performer of all time was Manifesto—winner in 1897 and 1899—and third, again, in 1902. When he won in 1899 he was ridden by George Williamson, one of the best-turned-out of men, whom I liked to meet in the Midlands many years later.

I have seen scenes which were " terrific " in the expression of the modern reporters, for there was a greater sense of proportion 50 years ago—at least, an old-time journalist cares to think so. But it was certainly a " bubbly ", and not merely a Barsac, celebration that afternoon, and the Royal party could not find " ambush " from the most enthusiastic crowd ever at Aintree. They were on a 4-to-1 winner in the *right* colours.

How many riders of National winners have found that the "limelight" was not the road to riches. "Algy" Anthony certainly did not die in luxury, nor did Arthur Nightingall—the most successful "daddy" of them all. And "Sunloch" Smith, after his all-the-way 1914 win, could not wear it well. Then there were the ill-fated men who "rode to death": like George Parfrement (Lutteur III, 1909), Captain "Tubby" Bennet (Sergeant Murphy, 1923), and W. Watkinson (Jack Horner, 1926). The last war claimed "Sailor" Bob Everett (Gregalach, 1929), and Frank Furlong (Reynoldstown, first time, 1935). Poor Tommy Cullinan (Shaun Goilin, 1930), committed suicide on his gun-site in an A.A. station.

So now for Diamond Jubilee: so aptly named when the "little" Queen celebrated her Diamond Jubilee in 1897. And a colt, with such a distinct will also of his own, was destined to cause almost as much sensation. Jack Watts had been in the saddle when Tod Sloan, on Democrat, beat Diamond Jubilee in both the Middle Park and Dewhurst Stakes and Mornington Cannon was third each time on Goblet. Richard Marsh's charge started, however, at good odds each time and was expected to come into his own as a three-year-old.

"Morny" had been on the Duke of Westminster's great Triple Crown winner Flying Fox in 1899: and just a reminder that, on the death of the famed racing Duke, M. Edmond Blanc (top-notch owner-breeder in France) bought Flying Fox for his Jardy stud, but offered John Porter the opportunity to train the champion for the 1900 cup races. The master of Kingsclere would not accept the responsibility. "Morny" would have been associated with Diamond Jubilee in the Classics, but realised that the "colt with a kink" did not exactly take to the handling of a very great horseman and one of the very best jockeys of all time.

History repeated itself, in a sense, 40 years later in the case of a filly, Godiva, in the stable of another Royal trainer, the late William R. Jarvis, whose son Ryan is carrying on the tradition at Newmarket. Godiva, however, was a wayward miss and owned by the present Lord Rothermere. The only lad she really got on with was Douglas Marks, who also "did" her. So he got the chance of winning the One Thousand and Oaks. Poor Douglas has had many bad smashes—it seemed impossible, once, that he would ever come back to the saddle—but was still riding winners over jumps in 1948–49.

In Dick Marsh's Egerton House stable at Newmarket was a promising lad named Herbert Jones, but they called him Bert. His job was to "do" Diamond Jubilee and ride him out. He was about the only one who could really get on with the colt. There seemed an "affinity" between them. So the venture was considered and Bert Jones got his chance of Classic fame. He gripped it like the good rider he was. Four lengths to spare over Lester Reiff's mount Bonarosa in the " Two Thousand ", and three-quarters of a length at Epsom, when " Morny " Cannon's Simondale was second and Tod Sloan a moderate third on Disguise II. Then the St. Leger, as a 7-to-2-on chance, and again Cannon was runner-up, beaten a length on Elopement, with Tod third again, on Courlan. Herbert Jones remained the Royal jockey for many years. I have rather lost touch with him in retirement. Like Percy Woodland, who became the Starter at Plumpton and Fontwell jumping, Bert had rather hankered after a job as an official. Always the same " honest-to-goodness " chap, he was one of the finest examples of " boy makes good " I could quote. Sam Darling—who was with his prospective brother-in-law Dick Marsh at the time—told me, when I was writing this, that he had a photo of Diamond Jubilee about to leave the paddock at Doncaster. " He had reared up and was practically perpendicular, but Bert stuck it stoically and won." When sold to the Argentine as a sire, I believe he gave no trouble there.

As Classic interest is paramount, I will stick to it for the time being. It is impossible, of course, to discuss all the winners over 50 years. But many colts and fillies have come into the " outstanding " category. I once asked that particularly good Jockey Club handicapper Mr. T. F. Dawkins, how he would like to frame a handicap embracing all the Classic winners he had seen. He shivered at the thought and said, " It could only be a personal opinion : to disagree is the spice of racing. And just imagine the wrath of the owner who considered his Derby winner the best ever, if I put the colt a stone below Flying Fox and a few others! " So I suppose some corns will have to be trodden on when a personal view is expressed about some of the top-notchers I have seen. All in good time.

It was strange that, in the year following Diamond Jubilee, there should be another " peculiar cuss " in Volodyovski—which the bookmakers translated into " Rum, Gin and Whiskey ". Rhyming slang was far more popular in those days, but has ever been inseparable from a race-course. The " boys " simply wouldn't call the paddock anything but " Finnon Haddock ", and one of them told me once how many abortive meetings had been held without finding a satisfactory rhyming slang for *sugar !* Anyway, though English bred, Volodyovski was all-American otherwise—owned by Mr. W. C. Whitney, trained by Huggins and ridden by Lester Reiff—the only noted jockey I can recall who never had his licence restored by our Jockey Club. He was Johnny Reiff's elder brother.

Doricles beat odds-on chance " Voddy " by a neck in the St. Leger and Kempton Cannon, so long Mr. Leo de Rothschild's jockey, rode a 40-to-1 winner. It had, however, been an American- owned and ridden double at Epsom, for Mr. Foxhall Keene's good filly, Cap and Bells II, piloted by Milton Henry, was a very easy successful Oaks favourite. She was trained by Sam Darling—father of Sam, Fred, and Dick Marsh's widow— at Beckhampton. Sam Darling—who always reminded me of " Mr. Punch "—soon cropped up again in that very distinctive 1902 season. He had won the 1897 Triple Crown for the rather strange owner John Gubbins with Galtee More—ridden by Charlie Wood—and now the little American " Skeets " Martin was the successful Derby pilot on Ard Patrick. Sceptre, not even placed at Epsom, had trounced Ard Patrick in the first Classic and she also won the One Thousand, Oaks, and St. Leger that year.

Former amateur Bert Randall had won the Guineas' double on Sceptre and rode her in the Derby. Owner-trainer " Bob " Sievier—a heavy gambler when he ran into funds—was a man of his own opinions and they could be truculent too often. He always admitted that Sceptre was the gross type who needed a race whatever work she had at home—incidentally, I knew Mr. Sievier for well over 50 years and he trained at my cousin's (Miss Mills) former " Manor " at Shrewton. So I'm not going to revive Epsom " inquests ". Randall lost race-course interest and pre-ferred golf when he retired. So did " Morny " Cannon when his brother, " young Tom ", retired and there was no longer a family reunion on the race-course when Tom had a fancied one.

When Ard Patrick—now ridden by Manton jockey Otto Madden—and Sceptre (Hardy) renewed rivalry as four-year-olds (1903) in one of the best races I have seen for Sandown's Eclipse Stakes, the colt again won—only by a neck. Sceptre was sold to race later in Sir William Bass' colours, and I recall how Bob, with his feather-weight Happy Slave, had run his pet filly—then with Alec Taylor at Manton—to a head in Kempton's Duke of York Stakes in 1903.

This Sceptre story automatically brings me to the best filly I've ever watched " go by ". I did not see La Fleche, the winner of the One Thousand, Oaks, and St. Leger for Baron Hirsch in 1892, but I did see Sceptre, Pretty Polly and, in the last war, Sun Chariot. And I also watched, in my spell in Paris, a grand grey filly named Semendria win the 1900 French Oaks and Grand Prix for the late Baron de Schiekler. I mention her again in connec-tion with Sloan and Codoman, but am sure Willie Pratt—still as dapper (as I write) as when he was No. 1 and countering, with George Stern, the American invasion—will endorse my high opinion of that grand-looking filly.

Comparisons only bring a ton of bricks. It will continue to be said and written that, in the hands of a professional trainer, Sceptre might never have been beaten. It is so easy to make such an assertion. Sievier may have been an amateur in the training sense—but he *did* know his idol. Obviously, she would not, in other ownership, have made a big-money bid for the Lincoln Handicap *as a three-year-old* (1902) with a brilliant and Classic career ahead. It was almost unthinkable that George McCall's mount St. Maclou (who won the Manchester November Handicap that year with 9 st. 4 lbs.) carried 7 st. 12 lbs. to her 6 st. 7 lbs. and just beat her by a head. St. Maclou was 100 to 8 and Sceptre a 11-to-4 favourite. The third, Over Norton, won the Lincoln the following year with his same weight, 7 st. 6 lbs. That was the poundage Otto Madden could ride in those days.

I am still working up to the best Derby winner so many old-timers have seen. If I also added the St. Leger, apart of course, from those who won both—it would become far more intriguing. Old Sam Darling, at the time he handed over the reins to Fred—who had been earlier making his name in Germany—was inclined, when we discussed it informally with his sons, to rate his big, late-maturing last-Classic winner Hurry On in the Newmarket substitute of 1916, at least the equal of the John Gubbins' cracks, Galtee More and Ard Patrick, but the old adage of " latest is best ", does apply to many stables. Incidentally, Galtee More went to Russia and Ard Patrick to Germany—Mr. Gubbins always preferred to cash in.

Visions still remain of Leopold de Rothschild going out into the violent Epsom thunderstorm of 1904 to lead in St. Amant. The colt may have been a bit more fortunate than John O'Gaunt, ridden by Mr. George Thursby for his brother Sir John. George was also runner-up on Picton to Spearmint in the Derby of 1906 —the last association of an amateur rider with the Derby. Fred Rees was a " daddy " occasionally on the flat as a young amateur and I should have liked to see John Hislop try his hand. But 9 st. wants doing.

Though St. Amant won the Two Thousand and Derby with lengths to spare, that was definitely a filly's year when Pretty Polly won the three other Classics. And that brings Sceptre and Sun Chariot into the perspective again. All at their very best, shall I say a personal leaning is towards Pretty Polly as "peerless"?

And now I'm going to be prepared for a heap of disagreement over Spearmint—another from old Peter Purcell Gilpin's famed Clarehaven establishment, which turned out champions at all distances. His various jockeys, over all the years, would probably vote the tall and essentially starchy " P.P. " a martinet. Yes, he did put some riders into the place they thought they had discarded when chewing straw and shovelling had given way to Turkish baths, silk shirts, and being accepted as an intimate of a patron and his family—like Danny Maher on the old Rosebery yacht.

Nobody could, I'm afraid—not even dear Marie Lloyd—be sufficiently a " martinet " with Bernard Dillon. From rough clothes and boots, this devout Irish Catholic—unused to the " harpies " who will ever be eager to take a likely jockey " round west "—simply found the " glamour " too much. It ended a tight regime enforced by association with Mr. " Nut " Purejoy and the famed Druid's Lodge stable, for which Bernard Dillon had made good in big-handicap coups. A chequered career has long finished, but there must still be a good word from me for " Berny " Dillon. R.I.P.

Spearmint's year is an old story in the Luckman household. It is in all the intimate chronicles of 1906—and ever since—that the Clarehaven representative for the Derby would be Sir Dan Cooper's fine One Thousand winner Flair. She went wrong and a resident Newmarket correspondent "Archie " Falcon—he wrote in the name of " Franklin " then—found out the full strength of the gallop he had seen with Pretty Polly and other inmates of the stable. " Here is the Derby winner ", he told my father " Dick ", who was well in advance of publicity values in national dailies. So Spearmint was plugged day in and day out until he beat Picton and the less-certain Kingsclere colt Troutbeck (" Skeets " Martin).

Troutbeck (G. Stern) won the St. Leger for the old Duke of Westminster, but there was no surviving Spearmint then. Dillon had gone to Paris to supplement Classic gains in the Grand Prix. I shall never forget the race he rode on the gallant son of Carbine and Maid of the Mint at Longchamp. He had to win about ten races in one, finally taking on Mr. W. K. Vanderbilt's good French-Derby winner Maintenon, and licking him, in probably, the greatest " catch-as-catch-can " race I've ever seen. That was however, the last of Spearmint, but he links as much in my memory (as an Australian-born) as did his mighty sire. Oh! to find another Spearmint in the Derby of any year. Mr. Vanderbilt won several French Classics, but you never hear now of a horse-racing Vanderbilt. Famous colours fade out, though tall, former-Guardsman Colonel Giles Loder (who won a Derby with Spion Kop in 1920) races in those of his uncle, Major Eustace (Pretty Polly and Spearmint) Loder. The present Duke rarely sports the Westminster livery. Kingsclere glories, when the colours of Westminster, Portland, and the " magpie jacket " of Lord Falmouth were so dominant, are but memories.

Incidentally, " Morny " Cannon promised to leave me the true story of the " poisoned " Orme—" never to be published until after my death "—who could not emulate the Triple-Crowner, Ormonde. " Ormonde was the greatest of them all ", the oracles would say. Then they would work round to St. Simon !

The first wartime produced vintage years, and it is remarkable that there should have been three colts all capable of winning the Triple Crown in Newmarket substitutes and that the Hulton filly Fifinella should take the 1916 Derby. I would not put Mr. Sol Joel's Pommern (1915) on the same mark as the Manton pair, Gay Crusader (1917)—for whom the late Mr. Jack Joel vainly offered £100,000 for his stud—and Gainsborough (1918). Dear old Gainsborough : he lived to emulate another old pal in Sir Abe Bailey's Gold Cup and Cesarewitch winner Son-in-Law and be an amazing sire, both for success and longevity, at the stud. Could there be better examples of " old sires never die, they simply fade away ". Another wartime feat of Alec Taylor's was to supply the second (Blink) to Gainsborough in the Derby, and second (My Dear) and third (Prince Chimay) in the Leger.

So the glorious Classic years rolled on. There were, of course, the Beckhampton winners for Fred Darling to come between world wars—and his own more modest colt Pont L'Eveque, in 1940 at Headquarters, where that tantalising and erratic Derby and Gold Cup winner, Owen Tudor, also scored in 1941 substitute Classic. I doubt if Pont L'Eveque would have beaten M. Boussac's Djebel if he could have crossed from France again, to supplement " Two-Thousand " spoils. But Gordon Richards had chosen the wrong Beckhampton representative, though he still claims he would have stuck to Owen Tudor (25 to 1 in " Squire " Nevett's hands) if he had not been mending a broken leg. I shall always regard Beckhampton's Coronach, on his Derby and Leger days (1926), as a greater Beckhampton colt than Captain Cuttle (1922) and little Manna (1935), but Joe Childs would agree that Coronach had a temperament.

Lord Astor has always been fated to be as unlucky as Gordon in the Derby at Epsom. St. Germans failed to plough through the mud like Sansovino (who changed Lord Derby's luck in 1924). That was the year of Salmon Trout's St. Leger : and will the true story of Carslake's belated win on the Aga Khan's colt ever be told. Trainer " Dick " Dawson was not wise to it.

Harking back to 1913, the Epsom scene was certainly lurid when the Stewards—lodging their own " objection "—disqualified the public favourite Craganour and gave the spoils to Mr. Cunliffe's 100-to-1 chance Aboyeur from the Druid's Lodge stable. That was the year when the suffragette threw herself in front of the King's Anmer, and there were many other unlucky Derby colts, including Louvois, Shogun, and another Nimbus.

Though Reiff did some "roughing" most of the way on Craganour—Billy Saxby had been sacked after losing the Two Thousand by a head to Louvois—it always struck me as a harsh decision. Mr. Bower Ismay soon sold Craganour to the Argentine, and fiery trainer "Jack" Robinson was unapproachable for weeks.

There was the general feeling that Rae Johnstone got into so much trouble on the Two Thousand winner, Colombo, that the Derby favourite (11 to 8) was unlucky to be only third in 1934 to Windsor Lad : but a considered opinion is, that Windsor Lad (subsequently an easy winner of the last Classic) would always have outlasted Lord Glanely's colt. "The Lad" *was* a good 'un.

Even trainers do not always divulge their innermost thoughts. Listen-in to Frank Butters, years after Fairway had funked and misbehaved himself at Epsom (1928) : " He was the best horse I trained and ever hope to train ". But there was the compromise answer, when I tackled him again, far more recently : " apart, of course, from the Aga Khan's Bahram ". Well, we all know this representative of an existing patron remained unbeaten, but he never met Frank, one older than himself, and I would earmark my special pets Spearmint, Fairway, and Blue Peter as greater Classic colts. What would have been a real Classic climax had to be scrapped when war came in 1939, for unbeaten Boussac challenger Pharis was to take on Triple Crown aspirant Blue Peter. I'm not sure that Caracalla II (Grand Prix and Gold Cup winner) was better than Pharis. I would have remained loyal to Lord Rosebery's Blue Peter on firm ground and he remains not very far behind the best in my long time. Fortunately, I have not to embrace Persimmon and Flying Fox in a 50 years' retrospect. A big pointer to Ard Patrick and Sceptre is that the younger Triple Crown winner, Rock Sand, was well beaten by them in the Eclipse Stakes (1903).

You can, more or less, confine the Classics, but it is like getting out to the wide-open spaces when endeavouring to recall other great popular horses : sprinters, milers, middle-distance, and stayers. That also brings in noted handicappers of their day, though, in my earlier race-going, there used to be more of a gulf between the Classic winner and the mere handicapper. That has long been bridged now, and I can only wish that a few of the so-termed handicappers had been available for the Classics. Take Polymelus and Irish Elegance, and Frenchmen Epinard and Sayani—to name only four at random—on their day of days.

Which was the best youngster who never was able to supplement two-year-old achievements with three-year-old fame? I've told you about Pretty Polly—who made a most sensational juvenile debut—but I think The Tetrarch (famed "Spotted

Wonder ") will remain my idol, and, of course, Dermot McCalmont colours were also carried by Tetratema. The Tetrarch had to miss that 6-furlong race at Kempton for the Imperial Produce Stakes : it was in the Imperial, that the Aga Khan's grand filly Mumtaz Mahal (9 to 2 on) failed, in the mud, to give Arcade 7 lbs. in 1923. Persse intended to train The Tetrarch for the first Classic, but, shortly before, realised the risk might be dangerous and the grey retired in all his unbeaten glory.

Though the modern purchaser is so eager to secure the likely sprinter or the middle-distance performer—and you can hardly blame the breeder-for-sale if he sees a quicker way to £ s. d.—I think that it is in the heart of every Britisher or Irishman, and certainly Frenchmen, to feel most sympathetic towards stamina.

So let's have a dive into the Ascot Gold Cup. You know how, in the years following the last war, French owners got us on the raw and produced Caracalla II and Souverain—both Grand Prix winners the previous season—and Arbar (now at an American stud) before young Lord Derby put England on the map once more with a true and good stayer, Alycidon in June 1949. I know his sire Donatello II is one of the famous Tesio-breeding, in Italy, but the blood is all English.

One day, perhaps, the strange, Hollywood-like story of Souverain ownership will be told : the other two carried the Boussac colours and I would give the palm to Caracalla II. He can probably be included among the giants, though his way was not hard on the Royal Heath. I know Souverain—reputed a bad traveller—beat another compatriot in Chanteur II more easily the following June, but Chanteur II (now at an English stud) did not look an odds-on favourite in his second venture. Just one of many time-honoured Gold Cup upsets. Great mares like Sceptre (only third to Throwaway in 1904) and Pretty Polly (11 to 4 on when licked by Bachelor's Button two years later) were not so happy as another of the sex in the late Lord Stanley's Quashed, a filly only officially ranked, then, as half-bred, who short-headed Mr. Woodward's American-bred Omaha in their great 1936 duel. You'll continue to hear arguments that Omaha did not seem to have been beaten. Like Verdict, Quashed traced back to the winner of an Ascot selling-plate—yes, there was one in the dim and shadowy past, at the Royal meeting—who had been bought by the Lord Coventry of the time.

Mr. James de Rothschild always loved a likely outsider, and what a sensation when Freddy Fox (destined to be killed in a wartime car-smash) rolled up in the Ascot Gold Cup (1909) at 25 to 1 against, to beat Leo de Rothschild's favourite Santa Strato. And Goodwood's stands nearly collapsed in 1910 when Billy Rickaby's father, Fred (a first-war victim), on Magic, floored by a neck 20 to 1 laid on the mighty Bayardo with Danny Maher in the saddle—Bayardo (a St. Leger winner) had beaten Gaelic-invader Sea Sick II easily in the Gold Cup and did look a "sitter".

Fifty years ago, men in chimney-pot toppers and women in long, flowing skirts and conservatory hats, were still discussing whether there would be another Persimmon (who had licked grand handicapper, Winkfield's Pride), successful French invader Elf II, or a Cyllene, always reckoned by old Bill Jarvis (father of Basil and Jack) the greatest colt to have missed Classic fame because he became ineligible, in a modest outsiders' year, owing to the old "nomination-void" rule.

One of the most discussed women, on and off a racecourse, actress Lily Langtry (we called her the "Jersey Lily") won the Ascot Gold Cup in 1900 with old Merman, the great Australian stayer which had won the Goodwood Stakes in 1899. She used a *nom-de-course* (which was common then), and Jack (W. T.) Robinson's eight-year-old was handled by Tod Sloan, to lick the brothers Cannon. The third horse, The Grafter, had been the means of a big City and Suburban coup which had put meteoric Bob Sievier into the big money and enabled him to spend so lavishly later at the Westminster sale. He went through life making and losing fortunes.

"Gaiety" George Edwardes (The Guv'nor) scored in 1901 with another true stayer in Santoi, at 11 to 10, and "grand-father" Fred Rickaby rode. Santoi became the sire of stayers, which reminds me of a true story. George Edwardes had seen, later, what he considered an unlucky "Park" defeat of Santoi by Epsom Lad, and challenged Mr. "Jimmy" Buchanan —afterwards, Lord Woolavington, and then racing as "Mr. Kincaid"—to a match. A canny Scot, however, countered an Irishman by saying, "Certainly—provided the winning owner takes *both* horses". Nothin' doin'—Epson Lad was a gelding!

And just another little digressive anecdote. It occurred after the present Lord Brassey (then Sir Leonard) had, with Catmint, beaten Aleppo a neck in the Goodwood Cup of 1913—the year in which Jack Joel's overnight purchase, Prince Palatine, had signally failed to live up to his proved form as a fine St. Leger and dual Gold Cup winner. Would-be purchasers (or their touts) pestered Mr. "Fairie" to put a price on Aleppo for export as a sire. The owner was not feeling particularly good that after-noon—which was not altogether unusual—and struck me as looking like a "dream walking". Brushing aside one very im-portunate individual, he expleted: "I've not made up my mind yet to sell him or (pause) have him gelded".

That must surely take me back to a stayer who was one of the stoutest and best in my time—The White Knight. He figured in that sensational Gold Cup disqualification of 1907, when French challenger Eider—first past the post—lost the spoils to Bill Halsey's mount. Halsey always claimed that his knee was " locked " so he could not get ahead and would produce a photo to substantiate it. Without doubt, justice was done, though it rankled with Frenchmen for years.

Another Gold Cup disqualification (in 1920) was just as tantalising—that of the automatic odds-on chance, Buchan, in the Astor colours. Australian Frank Bullock seemed to be winning comfortably when he had a look round. He lost, momentarily, control and the little colt darted sideways and interfered with George Hulme's mount Tangiers. Would there be an objection? Shipping- and meat- magnate Sir William Nelson had no use for the " not-done-at-Ascot-old-chap " stuff and he got the spoils. I shall never forget an excited Lady Astor darting as near as possible into the weighing-room—" no-woman's land "—while the Stewards were holding their enquiry.

The White Knight landed 7 to 4 laid on in the Ascot Gold Cup of 1908 without untoward incident. Without doubt, he was the greatest horse to run in, but not win, a Cesarewitch. Just take that 1907 bid with 9 st. 12 lbs. Australian trainer Brewer had a " rod in pickle " in another four-year-old named Demure. And that good boy Frank Wootton had only 6 st. 9 lbs. to carry. The coup came off by three quarters of a length for inseparable owners, Messrs. Clark and Robinson, but all the honours undoubtedly went to the " Knight "—a 100-to-8 chance.

Winning weight-carrying record in the Cesarewitch, over the proper course, was that of Willonyx with 9 st. 5 lbs. in 1911, when he came out well over 2 st. in front of his nearest rivals. What a proud day that was at Newmarket for Mr. C. E. Howard (whose firm designed and built the stands at Goodwood and elsewhere), old Sam Darling, and jockey " Billy " Higgs (who was on top at that time). It only rounded off a great Willonyx year. His four-year-old career was that of continued progress. Leading-off with only 8 st. 2 lbs. in the Chester Cup, he justified 5 to 4 favouritism in the Ascot Gold Cup, but only beat Donoghue on Charles O'Malley by a neck.

It may be thought that I hark back to the earlier years. There has been no intentional overlooking of the broad spaces between the two world wars, but I feel that memories since can be easily captured by the younger generation. So what father, or even grandfather, told me is something that can be reconstructed when the younger reader visualises his pre-natal generation. Anyway, here's a special word for 1931 and 1932 Gold Cup winner Trimdon, who was a maiden four-year-old when he first won for Manton the Gold Vase. His owner, Brig.-General Charles

Lambton, survived all the famous Lambton brotherhood and is Turf's G.O.M. as I write. (He has since died.—Editor.)

What a stable was Druids Lodge! Look at the Cambridgeshire record alone. Jack Fallon's charge Hackler's Pride, twice (1903, when Jack Jarvis did 6 st. 10 lbs., and 1904, with Dillon, carrying 2 st. more), and again with Christmas Daisy (1909 and 1910), when improvident Jack Fallon had been succeeded by E. Lewis as trainer.

Mention of lightly-weighted " certs " recalls Velocity, who had only 6 st. 5 lbs. when winning the Cambridgeshire in 1905, and he became a great Irish horse. Dumbarton Castle (7 st. 4 lbs.) was a terrific gamble, down to 4 to 1, when John Powney's three-year-old won the Stewards Cup of 1903. Incidentally, Royal Flush—slammed by Eager in the famous Hurst Park match—was a seven-year-old when the American combination of Wishard and Johnny Reiff landed the Hunt Cup and " Stewards " in 1900.

National Spirit has proved himself worthy to join Count Schomberg and Roughside (both Chester Cup winners), Trespasser, Wrack (who became a leading sire in America), Brown Jack, and 'chasing Balscadden among those in my time who could mix jumping and the flat so effectively. I leave the fond memory of Brown Jack to you: he gave up hurdling after a Champion Hurdle win, and that plaque at Royal Ascot extols his six successive wins in the Queen Alexandra Stakes (1929–34); he never lost one. And Donoghue rode him every time.

Brown Jack, Victor Wild, Dean Swift—only three among the many "handicappers" who were idolised. And what a cheer Irish Elegance got when, with 9 st. 11 lbs., including a 10 lbs. penalty, he won the Hunt Cup in 1919. And I think he should have defied 10 st. 2 lbs. and given elder King Sol 44 lbs. in the subsequent Stewards' Cup. He was only beaten three quarters of a length.

There have been hundreds of contemplated great coups, but how many have come off? Tod Sloan, and all concerned with French three-year-old Codoman in the 1900 Cambridgeshire had gone for a coup which would have made Tod laugh at officialdom and a licence! He was pretty thorough in his " approach " to some of the other interested riders. Connections of the Irish four-year-old decided, almost at the eleventh-hour, to put J. Thompson on Berrill, who beat Codoman by three lengths.

Other noted handicappers, no doubt, enter into the great perspective—but equally so do my friends and great companions. It is always easier to name than eliminate. Once again, fill in your own blanks and ejaculate : " Fancy Cyril Luckman forgetting one of the greatest winners, or men, of all time ". So I shall remain rebuked—but plead that the task was too much in an " article " so personal.

So much for great, or popular horses. The human element always appealed to me, and I think also of some of the wonderful men who have been associated with our favourites. Inevitably, over a period of 50 years, I cannot treat the subject on a " Who's-Who " basis, but just catch up with a few old pals—gradually getting less—and the men there has been so much good reason to admire.

Royalty first. King " Teddy " was, as I have written, a personality distinctly his own and of his time. It was the day of the spectacular, lavish entertaining, big house-parties at Goodwood and elsewhere—and toppers were still sported at Goodwood and for Sandown's Eclipse Stakes function—and that versatile old sportsman Lord Lonsdale—the " yellow Earl " in his yellow phaeton—was never one to let the team down !

Both King George V and the present Monarch—and, of course, their respective Queens—have always kept up the tradition of setting an example in their ownership and enthusiasm, but they never sought the glamour of Victoria's son.

Racing had already changed since the famed autocracy of Admiral Rous—in more recent years there has ceased to be a " no-man's-land " between Stewards of the Jockey Club and the rank and file of a race-course. It has, naturally, been all for the betterment of the Turf. Two of the greatest legislators of my time have been noted : Lord Durham—the maker of a most sensational Gimcrack speech which involved more than one of our leading owners—and Lord Hamilton of Dalzell. I once had the pleasure of being with Lord Hamilton on the P. & O. liner *Strathmore* on a cruise to the West Indies and, on arrival at Kingston, we knew King George was dead. In all our many conversations, Lord Hamilton showed a kindly tolerance as well as shrewdness, and he was such an excellent controller of Royal Ascot before he handed over to much-younger and very keen Duke of Norfolk.

That cruise also recalls to me other shipmates : Lord Glanely (plain " Bill " Tatem) and his inseparable Sir " Troops " Carter, who held sway so long as Ascot's Clerk of the Course. Major Crocker Bulteel is keeping up the tradition there now. So very different in type and one of the best " clerks " I ever want to meet. But once you got under Sir Gordon's old-soldier's skin you found a very lovable man. At least, I did.

Two very great owner-breeders I would class as distinctly kind of nature, were Mr. Leopold de Rothschild—whose generosity spread even to every London 'busman with a gift of game—and the late Lord Derby. He was still Lord Stanley when his father

won the Oaks with Keystone II in 1906, but for the greater part
of the next 40 years, he made himself surely the most successful
and lavish owner-breeder of all time. Just recall a Swynford and
a Phalaris, a Fairway, or a Hyperion—and then some. I shall
never forget, soon after the late Colledge Leader had taken over
the stable from George Lambton, how Lord Derby explained to
me that every new trainer must take time to understand the
breeding. " George will always stand alone in that respect ", he
emphasised.

There has been more contacting of the present Lord Rosebery
—since his hard-hitting Oval days as Lord Dalmeny when skip-
pering Surrey at cricket—than his political father, who had such
a grand Derby record. The Earl of to-day is a real hard worker
and takes his racing very seriously. Never oppose his views
unless you know you have the stronger cards to play.

Naturally, I would meet occasionally the Kingsclere pillars,
like the old Duke of Westminster, the Duke of Portland, and
Lord Falmouth. It is not so easy, in these restricted times, to run
stables like Kingsclere and Manton on the old lines, though
Beckhampton has retained its position all the time. John Porter,
of Kingsclere, will always rank with the Taylors of Manton.
" Young " Alec Taylor—he was still so-called as an old man—
had a delightful manner and betted only in trifles, but he died a
very rich man. I have referred to a patron like eccentric Mr.
" Fairie " Cox. Then came Lord Astor and so many who knew
the Taylor tradition, which was certainly sustained by the former
head-man, Joe Lawson.

I did not know Sir James Blundell Maple or Baron Hirsch so
well as I did the brothers Joel, Sol and Jack—now succeeded in
ownership by their respective sons Stanhope and Jim. Jack Joel's
trainer, Charlie Morton, was not only the superman at his job,
but one of the greatest little gamblers there have been in that
capacity. But it all went in his old age.

The whisky magnates " Tommy " Dewar and " Jimmy "
Buchanan—first and only Lord Woolavington—were not a bit
alike. Lord Dewar was the wittiest after-dinner speaker I knew :
he stored up a stock of epigrams. The term " wisecrack " had
not yet come from America. As you know, he was succeeded
by his nephew, and the Woolavington Stud and stable-interests
are carried on by his daughter and her husband—one of his two
adopted sons.

There is nothing much fresh to say about the Aga Khan.
George Lambton put him on the way to become one of the most
successful owners and breeders after the First World War. He
can rightly be termed an expert. You might think some of the
present leaders are not being given enough space, but let time

mellow the associations of the Gaekwar of Baroda and others
with our racing : and old American Turf-pillar Mr. William
Woodward had not been in England for many years.

My earlier recollections in France were of Edmond Blanc, and
also brother Camille, and of George Stern as a " real tough
guy " when riding against the invading Americans. And we
always called immaculate Willie Pratt the " ' Morny ' Cannon
of France ".

M. Marcel Boussac—a bit " dressy "—has, however, proved
perhaps the most amazing of French owner-breeders. A big
industrialist, he is the hardest worker in any country and
thorough in his successful schemes to produce the greatest of
thoroughbreds.

It is as well always to play for safety and avoid discussion as
to who was the greatest trainer and rider of all time. Reference
has been made liberally to some of the trainers who will always
be quoted. I have not attempted to " place the first three ", and
I must add men I know pretty well, in Frank Butters—a " No.
1 " season in and out—so worthily upholding, with Cecil Boyd-
Rochfort, what a fashionable trainer should look like !

The Jarvis and Leader families I have always counted as friends
—unnecessary to add as shining lights in their calling. Jack
Jarvis has had a fairly long innings : it was still, however, the
younger brother of Basil—plus " Young William "—in those
Newmarket days of 1910, when my father had fostered a Counties'
Club venture there. The time was not ripe, socially, to mix up
the " snobbery " of Turf H.Q. " Shall we invite the jockeys to
join ? " : how often I heard that put forward. How we could do
now with a place at Newmarket, which is surely the worst-catered-
for in entertaining race-week and other " working " visitors.
I've never been to Saratoga or Miami—but !

Thank goodness, when writing of the jockeys, I've not to compare Fred Archer with George Fordham, for there are quite
enough men who must be given at least a brief mention in such
an extended review. " Morny " Cannon retired later than I
thought he had done, but this grand horseman and jockey will
always link me with the American and Tod Sloan period. Tod
was just one of those " seven wonders of the world ". There
will never be another Sloan. Don't try to tell me it would be so
very different in 1950—what he attempted came off. A lad without any balance, inconsequential and hard to get down to brass-
tacks, he was, but never so black as many tried to paint him.
Tod's worst enemy was Tod himself.

Going backwards once more, one recalls Charlie Hibbert's
jockey, Charlie Trigg's win at Lincoln on Mercutio : Otto Madden
trying always to find " change for a fiver " at a railway-station

bar, Pretty Polly's ill-fated rider W. Lane, and those who have already had a passing thought and praise in the earlier years. Danny Maher was the consummate artist and—" always the gentleman ". He was, in the general sense, the leading product America sent us after the days of Sloan and the Reiffs. There were also Frank O'Neill, Milton Henry, Lucien Lyne, and a crop of invaders both over here and in France.

Nowadays, it is all Australia. Like Maher, Frank Bullock and " Brownie " Carslake were the perfect riders of a finish and such stylists, though Frank had learned his jockeyship—with his hur-culean old " Pop "—in the rough " down under ". So the talk of Australia gets us from a Carslake and a Bullock to successful Edgar Britt—a topnotcher on a free-running horse—" Last Race " Cook and moody Rae Johnstone, who refuses to forget his Colombo days in England, but is an outstanding rider, nevertheless.

Freddy Fox, Tommy Weston, " Squire " Billy Nevett (not only in the north), the brothers Eph and Doug Smith—known them since their horse-show days at Reading—you can throw-off successful riders easily. I thought that Rickaby, the father of " Billy ", had a great future before him, and the smooth races which Dick Perryman rode—modelled on Steve Donoghue—come back to me. So do many others I can't include.

Even then, I nearly omitted to mention Frank Wootton, the most wonderful young apprentice—and also rider under both codes later. Brother Stanley (now a " big noise " in his way and Kempton director) will agree that Frank was the " best horse " in old Dick Wootton's Epsom stable. He had the brains for race-riding and the knowledge of what had happened to others. Like Sloan, he was never so good at " managing " himself : but how few of the successful, in any walk of life, can claim they can do that.

I'm still dodging the Gordon Richards v. Donoghue issue——and we're forgetting Archer and Fordham and those who flourished when so many present old 'uns were not foaled—but must emphasise my special belief in long-standing Charlie Elliott—he beats so many of them as " best-timer "—and another Charlie, in the mercurial and terrifically pugnacious Smirke. Watch both when the money is down and you can polish binocu-lars and know it is probably the best bet of the day. And Irish-man Michael Beary—horse and hunting are in his blood—is perhaps the grandest horseman of the lot and keeps up his form in the saddle—and the inevitable charm and handshake out of it.

Harry Wragg must have a special paragraph to himself. Harry had always been the " problem child " in the saddle, though you'd never accuse " Brains " (as other Wragg brothers call him) of

LORD LONSDALE, 1931   LORD MARCUS BERESFORD, 1921

[*Facing page* 116

LORD ROSEBERY LEADING IN BLUE PETER, E. SMITH UP.   Derby, 1939

H.H. THE AGA KHAN LEADING IN MAHMOUD, C. SMIRKE UP.   Derby, 1936

being childish. Only time I've ever seen the "Head Waiter" really relax was on the lawn-tennis courts at Madeira. It was said of him by a disgruntled tout at Newmarket—where there had not been a liaison with his "unreported" horses—that it was rumoured locally he would wake up sometimes and "tell himself his probable plans". Charming Madge Wragg—whose sister married "Chubb" Leach—thought that becoming a trainer would lessen the strain. But has it? There may not be enough Ovaltine in any tin to allay that "nightly" combination with peaceful sleep.

So it comes about that I have left Donoghue and the reigning champion to the last. And if you expect me to say "my few bob would always be on Steve against Gordon", or vice versa, you need not go on reading this "happy haphazard". One great asset they had in common—their very infectiousness inspired the horse below. Donoghue found the combining forces of experienced restraint (when necessary), essential pushfulness, and daring strengthened his natural genius. Socially, he was a delightful little man, and in any business affair, he was best cut out. Steve always possessed, nevertheless, the gift of making friends and keeping them—despite financial disruptions.

Nothing of that about Gordon Richards. I don't profess to have seen any man's investments or bank-credits, but it would be a surprise of my long experience, to find the reigning champion other than a "Hollywood star" in modern money-gathering. Yes! I know Mr. Income Tax, thank you! Steve liked a bet, or somebody to make it for him : what a scream to know that officially "jockeys must not bet". It doesn't interest our Gordon and he has known, and seen, more "pigeons" disappear than even did his own birds which he races from his Marlborough home.

Let us try to take Gordon Richards on balancing results over umpteen years. You might hear, "He's losing his dash. . . . This is no longer his course" : but watch the racing and say now't until you ejaculate, "Nobody but Gordon could have got that one home", and draw your money, and you'll agree with Cyril Luckman. Once he gets a horse in front, he has that compelling "fluence" which makes the mount say to himself, "No supper to-night, unless this 'little stiff' rides me into the winner's unsaddling enclosure". This may seem light-hearted and unreasoning, but just as it was Tod Sloan, it is now Gordon. Academically, I might punctuate his perfect balance—that does mean a lot—but put most of it down to flair, and you won't be wide of the mark.

It is a long cry back, Gordon, since you came from Oakengates and we first called you "Moppy" and my good friends Pat and

I

Martin (your master) Hartigan—George still remains one—were alive. But may we still continue to tread the old turf which " gets " all of us. Anyway, nobody will ever beat your continuing champion " records ".

So we pass on to the women and men, trainers and jockeys, owners, horses, who will (I hope) find a place in the reminiscences of someone writing in A.D. 2000.

CHAPTER VIII

TESTS IMPOSED BY CLASSIC RACES

By Eric Rickman

DIAMOND Jubilee's triple triumph in 1900, when he won the Two Thousand Guineas, the Derby, and the St. Leger for the Prince of Wales (later King Edward VII), is as good a mark as any from which to review those Classic races which, coming more or less within memory, may be regarded as modern. But, having selected that starting-point, one soon realises that any satisfactory history of twentieth-century racing in England cannot be arbitrarily circumscribed. What is happening on the race-course to-day is the outcome of evolution, in some respects, almost limitless. What has been achieved in the Classic races of the last 50 years is rooted in the preceding centuries. It cannot be appreciated fully without reference to, and comparison with, what went before.

Before starting this chapter, I made a comprehensive study of the simple details of all five Classic races from their inception, the numbers of entries made for each, the number of starters and the recorded time taken by the winners to cover the course. Vividly, and in striking relief, those facts present the outline of racing-history for the last century and a-half. They provide indisputable evidence of the steady improvement, despite occasional setbacks, made during that period by British breeders in the general racing-merit of the thoroughbred horse. No other feature of our system of racing has contributed as much to that improvement as the progressive tests provided by the five Classic races for the best three-year-olds of each season.

The St. Leger, for three-year-old colts and fillies, was first run in 1776, though not until two years later was it given the name as a compliment to Lieut.-General Anthony St. Leger, of Park Hill, near Doncaster. There were six subscribers of 25 gns. each and five starters, the winner apparently taking the £131 5s. subscribed by the others. The distance was 2 miles, and so it remained until 1813, when it was reduced to 1 mile 6 furlongs 193 yards, henceforth to be described as the St. Leger course.

The St. Leger idea probably inspired the twelfth Earl of Derby to organise a sweepstakes for three-year-old fillies only, run at Epsom on May 14, 1779, and which he named after his local residence, " The Oaks ". The distance was about 1½ miles, there were 17 subscribers of 50 gns. each, and 12 starters. The young Earl won it himself with Bridget.

The next year, 1780, Lord Derby and his racing friends origi-
nated The Derby Stakes, for three-year-old colts and fillies, run
on May 4 over 1 mile (the distance was extended to 1½ miles in
1784). Colts carried 8 st., fillies 7 st. 11 lbs. There were 36
subscribers of 50 gns. each, and nine starters. The race, seemingly, was worth £1,837 10s. to Sir C. Bunbury, who won it
with Diomed.

These three races, the St. Leger, the Oaks, and the Derby did
not, of course, achieve great fame or importance immediately, but
their success gave impetus and permanence to a comparatively
new development in horse-racing. From the earliest recorded
meetings in this country up to the latter part of the eighteenth-
century race-programmes consisted chiefly, if not entirely, of
matches between two horses, or sweepstakes which, having more
than two entries, were run in heats. Except for any animal withdrawn after any heat, the same horses ran against each other
in successive heats until one had twice finished first. He or she
was the winner.

As the most usual distance of these heats was 4 miles, the
runners had, in one afternoon, to race that distance at least twice,
at half-hourly intervals, and sometimes three or four times before
a decision was achieved. Whatever other reason there may have
been for this custom, heats served to spin out an afternoon's sport
where few runners were available. Four or five starters for a
small sweepstake, or prize subscribed by local people, might have
to run the course several times for a decision, and, in many cases,
one or two sweepstakes or plates, decided in this manner constituted the whole programme.

When the St. Leger, Oaks, and Derby were inaugurated, the
method of heats prevailed at all meetings. They were rare only
at Newmarket, where most of the contests were matches, or
sweepstakes decided by a single contest. Prizes were still being
decided by heats at some of the smaller country meetings less
than 100 years ago, and it was not until the Rules of Racing were
completely revised by the Jockey Club in 1877 that they ceased
to state conditions governing the running of heats.

On the day that the first Oaks was decided, the only other event
on the Epsom programme was the Ladies Plate of £50, run in
heats of 2 miles. As Leapfrog, winner of the first heat, finished
first again in the second, that settled it, and the crowd saw only
three races altogether. None could have realised, however, the
extent to which history was made that day by one of those events.

Shorter races, too, even when settled by heats, were increasing
and gradually displacing the 4-mile tests. The originators of the
St. Leger, Oaks, and Derby followed the marked tendency of the
time, not only by settling the issue by a single contest but by

deciding it over a distance which was reasonably within the compass of a three-year-old and demanded a combination of speed and stamina in the winner.

A thoroughbred is not thoroughly mature at three years of age, though, of course, his physical development normally advances steadily throughout the season. Whilst Lord Rockingham who was chiefly responsible for founding the St. Leger, considered that by the last week in September, a 2-mile course was a fair test for a three-year-old, the twelfth Earl of Derby and his friends chose shorter distances for their new Epsom races in May, when the powers of a colt or filly are less developed than later in the season.

It was not, however, until more than 20 years later that two other races were introduced to be run over a straight 1-mile course at Newmarket in the Spring to establish the set-up of the five "Classics", which, ever since, have tested the best three-year-olds progressively from 1 mile to $1\frac{3}{4}$ miles over courses of different conformation.

The Two Thousand Guineas, a sweepstakes of 100 gns. each (half forfeit) for three-year-old colts and fillies, was first added by the Jockey Club to their First Spring Meeting in 1809 and run, as it still is, over the Rowley Mile. There were 23 subscribers and eight starters.

The One Thousand Guineas is the youngest of the Classic races. This event was first run in 1814, five years after the initial Two Thousand Guineas. The purpose of the new race was to give the fillies a mile test to themselves, and in its earliest years it was run over the Ditch Mile. This course being practically level, is regarded as less exacting than the Rowley Mile with its up-hill finish. There were 10 subscribers and only five starters for the first One Thousand Guineas. The race was not transferred to the Rowley Mile until the early '70's.

The national popularity—and world-wide fame—of the Derby developed steadily. It flourished more rapidly from the start than any other of the four races which were to become its complement. I hope Yorkshiremen will not feel that this comparison is any slight on the St. Leger, the oldest of them all. Only twice (1785 and 1786) did the number of subscribers to the Derby at Epsom drop below 30. There were 29 in those two years. Not until the first decade of the nineteenth century did the number of entries for the Doncaster race exceed 30. Only once in its first 27 years did the St. Leger entries rise above 20.

Each of the five Classic races has had its ups and downs according to the influence of national or international affairs, such as wars and periods of economic stringency at the time the entries closed. The reputation of the sport and the public interest in it has fluctuated, too, in the last 150 years, but, notwithstanding occasional setbacks, the popularity of racing has tended during that period to increase, and the number of thoroughbreds providing the sport has advanced enormously. Some idea of these trends, particularly in the last 50 years, may be gained from the following details of the number of subscribers and runners for the Classic races :

Year	" 2,000 " Subs.	R'ners.	" 1,000 " Subs.	R'ners.	Derby. Subs.	R'ners.	Oaks. Subs.	R'ners.	St. Leger. Subs.	R'ners.
1800	—	—	—	—	33	13	24	8	17	10
1825	10	6	8	walk-over	58	18	50	10	88	30
1900	94	10	81	10	301	14	233	14	222	11
1925	213	13	179	11	324	27	232	12	286	15
1938	247	18	269	20	294	22	289	14	294	9
1949	377	13	400	18	417	32	386	17	445	16

The year 1938 has been included, being the last normal season between the two world wars, a period of great general extension of almost every phase of racing.

A hundred years ago, the Epsom executive did not add a single penny to the owner's sweepstakes for the Derby. The conditions of the race stipulated that the owner of the winner *paid* " 100 sovs. towards the police and regulations of the course and 50 sovs to the judge ". The subscription then was still 50 sovs. each (half forfeit) and the second received £100. With the number of subscribers topping the 200 mark for the first time at this period, the stakes for the winner began to exceed £5,000. But for long afterwards, the value of the race varied, according to the number of entries and runners between £4,000 and £7,000.

In 1890, the executive guaranteed £5,000 for the owner, and £500 for the nominator of the Derby winner, with £300 for the second and £200 for the third, but, even so, the race cost them nothing. The entry fees yielded a surplus of £430, which went to the owner of the winner. There were similar conditions that year for the Oaks (£4,000 for the winner) and the Epsom Grand Stand Association had in this case to find £320 to make up the prize money, which must have been a great disappointment to them !

The first time any promoting executive offered any sum to be added to the sweepstakes for any Classic race was in 1892 when £1,000 was added to the Derby Stakes (making £6,960 for the winner) and £500 to the Oaks (£5,270). But there was nothing forthcoming from that source the following year.

At this time a far-reaching change was developing in racing. New courses, like Sandown, Kempton, and Hurst Park, and several elsewhere, completely enclosed and able to levy gate-money on everyone, were presenting races of unprecedented value by adding substantial sums to owners' stakes. On "open" courses, including Epsom and Doncaster, only those people who used the enclosures and stands could be charged, and for a while the Classic races were of less value than some of the new prizes, like Sandown Park's Eclipse Stakes. In 1895, Epsom were forced to do something to keep the Derby in step with this development, but they did not give much away. They raised the guaranteed total value of the race to £6,000, adding whatever was required on top of the owners' sweepstakes to make up this sum.

Fifty years ago, those conditions still prevailed for Diamond Jubilee's Derby, and if the winning owner was also eligible for the nominator's £500, he received £5,450. The Guineas were still devoid of added money, owners racing for their own money (100 sovs. each, half forfeit), in each event. In 1890, the Two Thousand, won by Diamond Jubilee (St. Simon-Perdita II) was worth £4,700 to the winner and the One Thousand (Winifreda) £4,150. The St. Leger, in which Diamond Jubilee completed his Triple Crown, was still a sweepstakes of £25 each with nothing added. The first prize was £5,125.

In 1903, the total value of the Derby was increased, £6,500 (net £6,450) being guaranteed to the winner. This cost the executive £1,570. Gross value to the winner of the Oaks—Pretty Polly (Gallinule-Admiration)—in 1904 went up to £5,000. Her St. Leger was worth to her owner, Major Eustace Loder, £4,625. There was no change in the conditions of the Classic races until 1908, when those for the St. Leger were altered to conform to those of the Derby, the cost to run being raised to 50 sovs. each and the winner taking £6,500, less his £50 stake.

To the twelfth Earl of Derby, we owe the most famous race in the history of the Turf. His even more distinguished descendant, the seventeenth of his line, who died in 1947, was largely responsible for the introduction of the modern practice of adding a specific sum to the entry-fees and forfeits of owners subscribing to the Classic races.

On May 20, 1915, owing to the circumstances of the war, the Jockey Club, complying with a request from the Government, cancelled all race-fixtures forthwith—other than Newmarket— and proceeded to arrange extra meetings both for the Summer and Rowley Mile courses. As the Epsom Derby, Oaks and the St. Leger were abandoned, substitute races were arranged with fresh entries, to be run at Newmarket. The Derby was re-opened as " The New Derby Stakes " of £100 each with £1,000 added (given by Lord Derby), for entire colts and fillies which were entered in the Epsom Derby, 1915. There were 18 entries, and the late Mr. S. B. Joel took a prize of £2,400 with Pommern (Polymelus-Merry Agnes). To the New Oaks Stakes of £50 each,

the Jockey Club added £1,000, and a similar sum was added to
the September Stakes of £50 each, run over the last 1¾ miles of
the Cesarewitch course as a substitute St. Leger, to give Pommern,
who had won a normal Two Thousand Guineas, his Triple
Crown : a comparatively austere adornment in this case.

This improvised pattern of the Classic races was adhered to
throughout that war, the Two Thousand and One Thousand
Guineas being run each year, with the original entries, and over
the Rowley Mile. The New Derby, New Oaks, and September
Stakes, with fresh entries, replaced the Epsom and Doncaster
Classics. Throughout the war, entries were made at the customary
time for the original Derby, Oaks, and St. Leger, though, as long
as hostilities lasted, they were eventually abandoned. When peace
came and more-or-less normal fixtures were resumed in 1919, the
five Classics were ready for revival, under the old conditions,
with the original entries made for them as a matter of course in
1917. There was no mention of added money, the guaranteed
value of the Derby, Oaks, and St. Leger being the same as in
1914.

This eventually produced an unusual contrast in values, the
Two Thousand Guineas of 1921, entries for which closed in the
first year of peace, yielded the record sum for a Classic race of
£8,300 to Lord Astor, owner of the winner, Craig an Eran
(Sunstar-Maid of the Mist). The Derby—Humorist (Polymelus-
Jest)—and the St. Leger—Polemarch (The Tetrarch-Pomace)—
of that season were worth the usual £6,450.

Racing was booming. There were, for one or two seasons
after the war, record crowds everywhere. A welter of war-made
wealth flowed into racing, but the value of money had greatly
depreciated compared with 1914. Up to the war, most owners
thought that 50s. per week was enough to pay for the keep and
training of each horse. By the time the war was over, trainers
found that they needed 4 to 5 gns. a week to meet their increased
overheads and to maintain the standards of their establishments.

Owners felt, too, that they should have a larger share of the
swollen race-course receipts, in the form of richer prizes. The
time had long passed when they were content to run only for the
money they themselves subscribed. Executives, they maintained,
should contribute more. The Stewards of the Jockey Club shared
this view. When they advertised, in 1920, the conditions of the
1922 Two Thousand Guineas and One Thousand, they added
2,000 gns. and 1,000 gns. respectively to the sweepstakes, whilst
their authoritative views were reflected by a complete change in
the conditions of The Derby, Oaks, and St. Leger for the same
year. The Epsom Grand Stand Association added £3,000 to the
Derby stakes of £50 each, and £2,000 to the Oaks, while the

Doncaster Corporation fell into line with a contribution of £4,000 to the St. Leger Stakes, and for the first time in their long history, the Two Thousand, the Derby, and St. Leger of 1922 were all worth over £10,000 to the winner.

For the Derby, Oaks, and St. Leger of 1926, the full contribution from the owner of each runner was raised from £50 to £100, and at that figure it has remained ever since. This did not immediately produce new records in prize money, but the following year (1927) Mr. Frank Curzon, the owner of Call Boy (Hurry On-Comedienne) took the unprecedented sum of £12,615 for his Derby. That was surpassed when, a few months later, the St. Leger victory of Lord Astor's Booklaw (Buchan-Popingoal) netted £13,280. From that point, the economic depression, which touched bottom in 1930, had its effect on the number of entries for the Classic races, and up to the outbreak of the Second World War, in 1939, the average value of the Two Thousand Guineas, the Derby and the St. Leger was roughly £10,000, with the One Thousand and Oaks usually producing for the winner about £8,000.

For the Derby of 1939, won by Lord Rosebery's Blue Peter (Fairway-Fancy Free), the Epsom Grand Stand Association introduced a trophy valued £200 for the owner of the winner, a cup valued £50 for the trainer (Jack Jarvis), and a cup valued £25 for the jockey (E. Smith).

Blue Peter proceeded to win the Eclipse Stakes, and exceptional interest developed in the prospective St. Leger rivalry of this clear-cut English champion with M. Boussac's Pharis, outstandingly the best three-year-old in France. War was declared on September 3, all racing was stopped, and was not resumed until a Newmarket meeting was started on October 18. The Doncaster meeting, with its Yearling Sales, was abandoned, a substitute race for the St. Leger was not arranged and Blue Peter retired to the stud.

During the war, the Classic races were substitute events similar to those improvised while the First World War was in progress, except that, as the Rowley Mile course was requisitioned—this time by the R.A.F.—the Guineas were run over the Bunbury Mile on the July course, entries being made afresh.

While the New Derby and Oaks were decided for five years over the Suffolk Stakes course (1½ miles) "behind the Ditch", a substitute for the St. Leger was found in 1940 in the Yorkshire St. Leger Stakes of 1 mile 7 furlongs at Thirsk. In 1941, a New St. Leger Stakes of 1¾ miles was run at Manchester, and from 1942-44, a similar race with the same name was held in September of each year at Newmarket, the distance being 1 mile 6 furlongs 150 yards of the Summer course. On some of these occasions, especially for the 1945 Derby, won by Dante (Nearco-Rosy Legend), the crowd severely overstrained the accommodation available and the arrangements made for dealing with extraordinary conditions on the Newmarket July course. The stands and enclosures were planned for quiet meetings in July and not for great popular attractions.

The war in Europe was officially terminated on May 8, 1945, the day Sun Stream (Hyperion-Drift) won the One Thousand Guineas for Lord Derby. Earlier that year, the Stewards of the Jockey Club had given notice to exercise their power to order any race, for which entries had closed, to be run on any course selected by them. Most race-courses had been requisitioned by the Government for war purposes and could not be vacated, in a large number of cases, in time to permit meetings during the remainder of the season. This authority was invoked by the Stewards to transfer the St. Leger, with its original entries, from Doncaster, which had not become available, to York, where it was run on September 5 and won by Squadron-Leader Stanhope Joel's Chamossaire (Precipitation-Snowberry).

In 1946 all five Classic races returned " home " to be run over their customary courses, with more or less the same conditions as to entry, forfeits and stakes as before the war ; though, at the request of the Government, both the Derby and St. Leger took place on a Saturday, that being made the final day of the meeting in each case. The purpose was to avoid attracting large crowds from work and over-burdening public transport in midweek. This arrangement is continued from 1947-50.

The Classic races run in 1948, entries for which closed in 1946, sharply revealed a boom similar to that which blazed in 1919. With 357 entries, the 1948 Two Thousand Guineas, won by My Babu (Djebel-Perfume), was worth £14,099 15s. to the winner, while the One Thousand brought £12,433 10s. to Sir Percy Loraine, owner of Queenpot (Big Game-Poker Chip).

My Love's Derby (Vatellor-For My Love) had a first prize of £13,059 5s., and Masaka's Oaks (Nearco-Majidal) £10,679 15s. But again the St. Leger provided a new record. There were 438 entries, and the Doncaster Corporation added the unprecedented sum of £5,000 to the stakes. The result was that Mr. William Woodward, Chairman of the New York Jockey Club, was credited with £15,268 by the victory of Black Tarquin (Rhodes Scholar-Vagrancy). And for the first St. Leger, be it remembered, there were six entries : the winner took £131 5s. !

Nimbus (Nearco-Kong), 1949 Derby winner, after a thrilling finish with the French colt Amour Drake (Admiral Drake-Vers l'Aurore) which will be discussed for years to come, earned the distinction of crediting his owner, Mrs. M. Glenister, with the richest stake ever won in the history of that race up to date. Only two women have won the great race at Epsom, the other being Mrs. G. H. Miller who, in partnership with her mother, Mrs. Talbot, owned Mid-day Sun (Solario-Bridge of Allan), 1937. Gainsborough (Bayardo-Rosedrop), winner of a wartime Triple Crown at Newmarket, was bred and owned by Lady James Douglas.

The Classic races, almost from the beginning, have been the pre-eminent and most coveted prizes of the British Turf, in the whole structure of which the Derby became the keystone. The winner of that race is usually accepted as the champion three-year-old and, unless his subsequent performances are very dis-creditable, he is assured of the best possible opportunities as a stallion to propagate his superior qualities conjointly with some of the best mares. The Classics, and particularly the Derby, provide the supreme annual test of the prevailing trends and achievements in bloodstock-breeding, exposing mistakes and weaknesses and emphasising what is best and most worthwhile in the ceaseless efforts, studiously and selectively to improve the racing attributes of the British thoroughbred.

What then has been effected and demonstrated in this respect by the Classic races of the last 50 years? I have shown that the number of entries has increased tremendously and with fair con-sistency through their long existence and that, except for a lengthy period in the middle of the nineteenth century, the average number of runners has been larger in recent years than ever before. This tendency suggests increased competition, but is not proof-positive of improved general quality. There does exist, how-ever, strong evidence that, on the whole, the Classic races have become more exacting tests in the course of time, revealing a higher degree of racing-merit in many modern winners than was demanded of their successful predecessors.

Until a reliable device is installed on English race-courses for recording the time taken by the winner to cover the course, the supply of this interesting information is dependent on the manipu-lation of a stopwatch by a regular racing-reporter on the Press stand. From this position, the finish is viewed at an angle, often acute, and the quickness and concentration necessary to strike the watch simultaneously with the rise of the starting-gate also creates the possibility of inaccuracy. On the whole, however, the work has, in my experience, always been done at the principal meetings conscientiously by a practised hand. A mistake of a fraction of a second is always possible, but the times returned for Classic winners of the last 100 years have improved progressively to such a marked extent that the general trend can be accepted un-questionably.

In 1849, the Flying Dutchman's time for the Derby course was 3 mins. dead, and subsequently two winners of the race took longer, according to the existing records. There is no need, for the purpose of this review, to consider the state of the going from year to year, though it may reasonably be claimed that improved care of the turf and minor alterations to the rails of a race-course may have been partly responsible for faster times. It was not until Blair Athol beat 29 others (1864) in 2 mins. 43 secs. that the watch-holders of those days (when races were started with a flag) recorded less than 2¾ mins. for the Derby. That stood as best for 32 years, though it was equalled on a few occasions meanwhile.

In 1896 Persimmon (St. Simon-Perdita II) covered the Derby course in 2 mins. 42 secs., which brings us to the last 50 years, his brother Diamond Jubilee taking exactly the same time in 1900.

That record was beaten the next year by Volodyovski (Florizel II-La Reine) with 2 mins. 40⅘ secs., since when there has been an improvement of 7 secs. at Epsom, as revealed by the following table :

Year.	Winner.				Mins.	Secs.
1905	Cicero	..	..	..	2	39-3/5
1906	Spearmint	..	..	..	2	36-4/5
1910	Lemberg	..	..	..	2	35-1/5
1920	Spion Kop	..	..	..	2	34-4/5
1922	Captain Cuttle	..	..	..	2	34-3/5
1927	Call Boy	..	..	..	2	34-2/5
1933	Hyperion	}	..	..	2	34
1934	Windsor Lad					
1936	Mahmoud	..	..	..	2	33-4/5

The pace at which Classic races have been run since 1900 seems to be the most telling point which can be made in any attempt to compare the modern race-horse with his ancestors. As I see it, there is definite proof that the qualities demanded by our system of racing were steadily improved up to 1939. Reference may be permitted to the temporary decline in the stamina derived from the fashionable strains developed exclusively in England and Ireland. My own view is that this was brought about chiefly by the delay on the part of most breeders in seeking stout out-crosses for the exceptionally successful Phalaris blood, and other speedy strains which, between the two wars, produced brilliant two-year-olds which were generally deficient in staying-power.

The red light flashed for the first time when Mr. P. Beatty and the Aly Khan bought and imported Bois Roussel (Vatout-Plucky Liege) from France to win the Derby of 1938. The champions of both countries in 1939, Blue Peter and Pharis, were grandsons of Phalaris, but the following year Djebel (Tourbillon-Loika) came from France to win the 2,000 gns. just before the great

German advance closed the Channel ports. Even so, the New Derby winner of that year, Pont L'Eveque, had come from France *in utero*, his dam (Ponteba) being imported in foal to Barneveldt. Ponteba was daughter of the French-Derby winner Belfonds, but Barneveldt, Grand Prix winner, was of entirely English pedigree though bred in France.

War-conditions excluded any further runners from France for our Classics and other principal races until 1946, when they were soon to reveal the sorry extent to which wartime restrictions had accentuated the deterioration, in stamina and general merit, of the English thoroughbred.

The pre-war importation of Mieuxce, Nearco, and Donatello II, stallions of brilliantly stout racing performances on the Continent, produced Classic winners here during the war, notably Dante (by Nearco), winner of the 1945 Derby. Bois Roussel having gone to the stud in this country, sired in his first crop a New St. Leger winner (1944) in Tehran, but this new blood was not sufficiently widely established, effectively to resist at once the most powerful and successful French attack on our Classics and other high-class races since the days of Gladiateur, Fille de L'Air, and other famous winners of the Count Legrange-Tom Jennings era.

There was not any French opposition when Airborne (Precipitation-Bouquet) won the Derby of 1946 and only the non-staying Nirgal was sent from France to run against him in the St. Leger. Airborne was decisively beaten soon afterwards by the Grand Prix winner, Souverain, for the newly-created King George VI Stakes over 2 miles at Ascot.

French colts, Pearl Diver (Vatellor-Pearl Cap) and My Love, won the Derby in 1947 and 1948 respectively. Another, Amour Drake was beaten a head by Nimbus (by Nearco) at Epsom in 1949, by which time there was already considerable grounds for the belief that English breeders were overcoming the consequences of pre-war trends and wartime conditions. The patriation of stout strains which had thrived on the Continent, but languished in England seems to be rapidly restoring the English thoroughbred to his customary pre-eminence. Meanwhile, the French also won the One Thousand and Oaks of 1947 with Imprudence (Canot-Indiscretion). My Babu, winner of the 1948 Two Thousand Guineas, was bred in France and the St. Leger winner of that year (Black Tarquin) in the United States, though his sire Rhodes Scholar was an English horse.

But back for a moment to 1900. All five Classic races of that season were won by the progeny of St. Simon. They were: Diamond Jubilee (Two Thousand, Derby, St. Leger), Winifreda (One Thousand), and La Roche (Oaks). St. Simon, a mighty, unbeaten race-horse, was at stud from 1896 to 1907 ; he headed the list of winning stallions on three occasions, was second twice, and third three times.   He has been by far the most dominant factor in the breeding of the thoroughbred horse since Eclipse (1764–89).   In all, he sired 17 Classic winners and, though the last were those of 1900, his subsequent influence may be judged from the fact that it would be difficult to find to-day a thorough-bred which does not trace back to him through at least one line. Most of the Classic and other important winners of the last 30 years have had from two to five strains of St. Simon.

In the last half-century, only four colts have won the Triple Crown (Two Thousand Guineas, Derby, and St. Leger).   They were : Diamond Jubilee (1900), Rock Sand (Sainfoin-Roquebrune 1903), Gainsborough (1918, at Newmarket), and Bahram (1935), the last-named having an unbeaten career.   Of the famous fillies of the period Sceptre (Persimmon-Ornament), in 1902, won all the Classic races except the Derby (in which she was unplaced).   Pretty Polly took the One Thousand Guineas, Oaks, and St. Leger of 1904. Sun Chariot (Hyperion-Clarence), leased from the National Stud to King George VI for her racing career, won in 1942 the New One Thousand, Oaks, and St. Leger, while Big Game (Bahram-Myrobella), another National Stud product running in the Royal colours, was succeessful in the Two Thousand of that season.

Other Classic winners of the last 50 years who may reasonably be accepted as being above the average merit of this exalted class, are : Spearmint (Carbine-Maid of the Mint), Derby and Grand Prix, 1906 ; Bayardo (Bay Ronald-Galicia), St. Leger, 1909 ; Swynford (John o' Gaunt-Canterbury Pilgrim), St. Leger, 1910 ; Sunstar (Sundridge-Doris), Two Thousand and Derby, 1911 ; Hurry On (Marconi-Tout Suite), Substitute St. Leger, 1916 ; Solario (Gainsborough-Sun Worship), St. Leger, 1925 ; Coronach (Hurry On-Wet Kiss), Derby and St. Leger, 1926 ;   Fairway (Phalaris-Scapa Flow), St. Leger, 1928 ; Toboggan (Hurry On-Glacier), Oaks, 1928 ; Hyperion (Gainsborough-Selene), Derby and St. Leger, 1933 ; Windsor Lad (Blandford-Resplendent), Derby and St. Leger, 1934 ; Rockfel (Felstead-Rockliffe),One Thousand and Oaks, 1938, and Blue Peter (Fairway-Fancy Free), Two Thousand and Derby, 1939.

The Aga Khan, having bought from M. Leon Volterra a half-share in My Love shortly before his 1948 Epsom triumph, is credited with four Derby victories, his other winners being Blenheim, Bahram, and Mahmoud, each of whom was sold to the United States when the Second World War started.   Between 1782 and 1836, Lord Egremont won the Derby five times.   The Aga Khan had four runners for the St. Leger of 1932 ; they finished : first (Firdaussi : Pharos-Brownhylda), second (Dastur:

Solario-Friar's Daughter), fourth (Udaipur : Blandford-Uganda), and fifth (Taj Kasra) in a field of 19. They were all trained by Frank Butters.

In the last half-century, Lord Astor has had five Oaks winners: Sunny Jane (Sunstar-Maid of the Mist), 1917 ; Pogrom (Lemberg-Popingoal), 1922 ; Saucy Sue (Swynford-Good and Gay), 1925 ; Short Story (Buchan-Long Suit), 1926, and Penny-comequick (Hurry On-Plymstock), 1929. But a Derby triumph has been just beyond the reach of this otherwise most successful breeder : he was five times second between 1918 and 1924. It is the only Classic race he has not won.

The supreme influence on the evolution of the thoroughbred horse in modern times by the stud of the late Lord Derby is reflected by the following personal records of success in the Classic races of the last 50 years, begun, in a few instances, prior to 1900 :

OWNERS.

	"2,000."	"1,000."	Derby.	Oaks.	St. Leger.	Total.
Late Lord Derby	2	7	3	4	6	22
The Aga Khan	2	—	4	2	5	13
Lord Astor	3	2	—	5	1	11
Late Duke of Portland ..	1	2	2	4	2	11
Late Lord Rosebery ..	3	3	3	1	1	11
Late Mr. J. B. Joel ..	1	2	2	4	2	11
King Edward VII	2	1	3	—	2	8
Mr. "Fairie" (A. W. Cox)	1	1	2	1	2	7
Late Lord Glanely ..	1	1	1	1	2	6
King George VI	1	2	—	1	1	5

TRAINERS.

	"2,000."	"1,000."	Derby.	Oaks.	St. Leger.	Total.
Alec Taylor	3	1	3	8	5	20
Fred Darling	5	2	7	2	3	19
Frank Butters	1	1	2	6	5	15
George Lambton	1	4	2	2	3	12
C. Morton	1	2	2	4	3*	12
R. Marsh	3	1	4	—	2	10
J. Lawson	4	3	—	3	—	10
P. P. Gilpin ..	1	4	2	1	1	9
J. Jarvis	3	2	2	—	1	8
R. C. Dawson	1	—	3	2	2	8

* C. Morton is credited with Tranquil (St. Leger).

JOCKEYS.

	"2,000."	"1,000."	Derby.	Oaks.	St. Leger.	Total.
J. Childs	2	2	3	4	4	15
S. Donoghue	3	1	6	2	2	14
E. C. Elliott	5	4	3	2	—	14
G. Richards	3	2	—	2	5	12
H. Wragg	1	2	3	4	2	12
T. Weston	2	1	2	3	3	11
D. Maher	2	1	3	1	2	9
H. Jones	4	—	2	1	1	8
B. Carslake	1	2	—	1	3	7
M. Cannon	1	—	1	2	2	6
F. Fox	2	1	2	—	1	6

CHAPTER IX

THE EPSOM DERBY

INFLUENCE OF THE DORLING-LANGLANDS COMBINATION IN THE
SUCCESSFUL DEVELOPMENT OF THE EPSOM MEETINGS

By GEORGE BONNEY

EPSOM roared into the twentieth century under the guidance of Henry Mayson Dorling. Number five in the line of Dorlings who ruled the fortunes of the famous race-course for 121 years, Henry Mayson was a lion of a man. He reckoned to count his true friends on the fingers of one hand.

In the season of 1900, he had occupied the position of Managing Director to the Epsom Grand Stand Association for four years and that of Clerk of the Course for some 20-odd years. That such a man, brusque to the point of rudeness, could successfully handle negotiations with the racing hierarchy, the professionals of the industry, and the non-racing public is somewhat paradoxical. The plain truth is that Henry Mayson Dorling's opinions were right for the general betterment of the sport and for Epsom in particular.

History has labelled him reactionary, but without his dogged enthusiasm and insight for business, the world's greatest race-course might to-day have been a very different proposition. A few years prior to the turn of the century, he and Edward Jonathan Dorling jointly purchased Walton Manor, part of which covered a stretch of the race-course near Tattenham Corner. Together, they also obtained a 29-year lease of Epsom Downs, thus gaining control of exercise-grounds, gallops and all private stands to augment the wealth of the Grand Stand Association.

On his own initiative, Henry Mayson Dorling increased still further the Association's property by buying the Warren Estate for £9,000. Then, in 1903, he surrendered the existing lease, paid a premium of £25,000 to the Lord of the Manor of Epsom and agreed to a yearly rental of £3,354 for a new lease covering a term of 106 years.

The terms authorised the Association to conduct two race-meetings a year, namely the Spring Meeting of two days and the four-day Summer Meeting. Up to this time, the Lord of the Manor had enjoyed the sole right of income from the parking of vehicles, but a clause in the new lease empowered the Grand Stand Authority to make charges in those enclosures which

BOIS ROUSSEL EASILY WINS THE 1938 DERBY; SECOND, SCOTTISH UNION; THIRD, PASCH

SANSOVINO WINS THE 1924 DERBY; SECOND, ST. GERMANS; THIRD, HURSTWOOD

THE FIRST PHOTO FINISH OF THE DERBY (1949): FIRST, NIMBUS (13); SECOND, AMOUR DRAKE; THIRD, SWALLOW TAIL (9).
The Recorded time between First and Third is 1/20 sec.

stretch east of the stands to Tattenham Corner, and on part of
the Hill.   There cannot be any doubt that this enterprise set the
foundation for what has been the most progressive 50 years in
the history of Epsom Race-course.   It is appropriate to recall the
overwhelming enthusiasm with which the vast crowds welcomed
the success of Diamond Jubilee in the Derby in 1900.   The colt,
which started favourite at 6 to 4, carried the Royal colours.   It
was the second Derby victory for the then Prince of Wales before
he became King Edward VII.

In those days, going to Epsom was something of an adventure.
A contemporary writer described the scene on the roads as, "Very
patrician and very plebeian," and 50 years later there cannot be
any arguments with that, for the duke and the dustman still
journey to the Downs.

The manner in which they make the trip has to-day, for all
its speed and clean comfort, robbed the cameraman of a worthwhile break in picture-stories.   That is, of course, provided he
could have taken his shots through the pall of swirling dust.

The roads then were packed with horse-drawn vehicles, and
a thirsty ride it was for those in open carriages.   There was variety
in makes and shapes that has no parallel in the modern car.   They
ranged from the lumbering horse-omnibus, to the four-in-hand,
the phaeton, the tandem ; perhaps the solitary driver in a sulky,
and certainly the coster in his donkey-cart.

In the early morning before people in the quiet suburban
houses were about, the barrow boys of the period trundled their
loads of nuts and oranges ; flashily decorated carts known as
ginger-beer engines, and waggons laden with lemonade, started
the stream to Epsom.   Later in the day it was an occasion, not
only for those going to the races, but a roadside spectacle for
people living on the route.

Then, as now, the railway catered for great numbers of the
crowd.   According to the class by which they travelled, Epsom
was reached in an hour for a few shillings.   From the station, a
ride in a hansom cab would relieve the uphill trek to the Downs.

Whichever way the race-goer journeyed, it was a carnival.
Certainly it was noisy and sometimes rowdy, but twentieth-
century progress changed all that.   Modern cars and electric
trains allow no time for boisterous trippers.   Nevertheless, the
atmosphere of the Downs has not dimmed to such a degree.
The refreshments and the side-shows are there, but their proprietors smartly whisked them out in spacious motor vehicles.

In 1900, the Derby offered a straight prize of £6,000 and the
actual cost to the executive in added money amounted to £635.
It was the practice of the Grand Stand Association to offer a
guaranteed figure and, after receiving entrance fees and forfeits,

K

to add the sum necessary to achieve the total. The guarantee was raised to £6,500 in 1903 and thereafter until 1922 the system persisted with the prize varying according to the number of entries. For instance, an example taken at random shows that in 1913 the sum was £7,100. The figure was made up in this way. Of the original 325 entries for the race, 108 declared forfeit for £5. At the second acceptance, 202 withdrew for £25, and the owners of the 15 runners each paid £50. Simple arithmetic proves that the executive added only £760 to the stakes.

The cost to run a horse in the Derby remained at £50 until, in 1922, the Grand Stand Association doubled the entry fee and offered £3,000 in added money. With the stakes also making-up the prize, the value rocketed and, gradually, the executive increased their commitment. Last year (1949), with £4,250 added, Mrs. M. Glenister, the owner of Nimbus, received the record prize of £11,565 and a gold cup worth £250. Total value of the race, £14,845, was a record in prize money. Of this sum, the late M. Volterra received £1,620 for Amour Drake's head defeat into second place, while Swallow Tail, also a head away third, claimed £810 for Lord Derby. The breeders of the three horses received £850 between them. It was, perhaps, the most spectacular Derby finish in the history of the race and for the first time the photo-recording camera was used to determine all three placings.

Before leaving the subject of figures, one or two other comparisons in a gap of 50 years can serve to tell of progress and the high cost of racing to-day. In 1900, the Epsom executive's responsibility for rent, taxes, and insurance demanded £4,569. Of this, they paid £252 in income-tax at 8d. in the £, and entertainment-tax was not in existence. In 1948, the amount necessary to cover these commitments was almost precisely £80,000 more than in 1900.

The tax-demands were less than a third of the entire cost of operating the race-course and, to inspect one other increased item, the expense of employing policemen to maintain law and order on the Downs is interesting. The gap in their case has widened from £1,268 to a figure that, nowadays, is always in the region of £6,500.

One distinctive happening of historical interest to the Turf took place at Epsom in the opening year of the century. The starting-gate was introduced and its trial quickly influenced its adoption on other race-courses throughout the country.

Events in the next several years were marked by occurrences that affected the Royal household. There was the occasion, in 1909, when the Derby success of Minoru gave King Edward VII his third triumph in the great race. It was a day when people in the stands and on the open Downs let their excitement run riot, for he was the only reigning Sovereign to carry off the coveted prize.

The following year the famous Downs had lost their sparkle, the crowds were thin and Lemberg, the Derby winner, was led into the unsaddling enclosure through a silent gathering of those racing-folk whose duty alone had brought about their presence. The genial, friendly King Edward had died three weeks before the major Classic event was due to be run.

In 1913, history records a tragedy of a different kind. A woman named Emily Wilding Davison deliberately chose to risk her life under the pounding feet of King George V's horse, Anmer. She did it in the cause of woman's suffrage and, of course, she died. The story is an old one now, but it is linked with another extraordinary happening on that Derby Day nearly 40 years ago and the bare facts will stand re-telling.

For the only time in the history of the Derby Stakes, an objection was raised against the winner. Craganour, who had passed the post barely a head in front of Aboyeur, was declared by the judge to be the winner. So intense was the excitement of the spectators in the stands watching the final bitter struggle between these two horses that the tragedy down the course was missed by many.

Herbert Jones, the King's jockey, who rode Anmer, was carried through the unsaddling enclosure on a stretcher as the " Objection " flag was hoisted on the number-board, but, apart from the jostling throng in the immediate vicinity of Miss Davison's still form, interest centred on the outcome of the Stewards' enquiry.

Oddly enough, the Stewards had themselves made the objection on the ground that Craganour had jostled the second horse. The owner and trainer of Aboyeur had made no move to disagree with the judge's verdict ; nevertheless, they were awarded the race. The Stewards ruled that Craganour, besides interfering with others in the field, had " bumped and bored the second horse ".

While all this was going on, Herbert Jones was receiving medical treatment in the ambulance-room and Miss Davison was on her way to Epsom Cottage Hospital, where later she succumbed to her terrible injuries without regaining consciousness. The incident had taken place in the straight, just round the bend from Tattenham Corner. The King's horse who was not a fancied runner, was well behind the leaders and turned the Corner behind Agadir. Walter Earl, Agadir's rider, saw a woman rush on to the course and, with great skill, avoided running her down by a matter of inches. Jones, on Anmer, who was lying close up to Earl's mount, had no chance of escape. He ran full-tilt into Miss Davison, the horse stumbled and he fell off. He suffered temporary concussion and, except for a nasty gash on his cheek, he recovered in 24 hours.

Interest in Emily Davison's unfortunate end was more than equalled by the heated discussion over the Craganour verdict. In fact, three days later an appeal against the disqualification was lodged with Henry Mayson Dorling, but the Clerk of the Course received it after the time prescribed by the Rules of Racing.

The decision of the Stewards was upheld and Dorling hardly could have been blamed for that, although his career frequently was subject to unfair accusations. On more than one occasion, he was fined by the Jockey Club because the state of the course was considered unfit for racing. The faults were brought about due to the thoughtlessness of hack-riders who cut up the turf. Dorling remedied the matter by placing " dolls " and bushes about the Downs, but, at once, he was attacked by the local authority. He had, they said, interfered with public rights and upset the recreation of equestrians. Eventually, by detailing the damage done to the course, he won his point.

Perhaps the unkindest remarks suffered by this fiery man were those levelled at him soon after the start of the First World War. Like everybody else in those days, he could not have foreseen that the struggle would last four years. So, in the true spirit of patriotism, he induced the Association to convert part of the Grand Stand into a military hospital for a period of six months. The time-limit was unfortunate and Dorling was publicly lampooned as being without a care for his fellow countrymen. Strictly, of course, criticism was directed at the Association, but it was the man who felt the barbs.

While letters appeared in *The Times* and the question of the selfish consideration for race-goers was being aired, Dorling was, in fact, negotiating a new arrangement at the War Office. Even before the detail was finally settled between the hospital authorities and Whitehall, the merciless campaign upset his usually hard indifference. For perhaps the only time in his professional career, he went on the defensive and wrote a letter to *The Times*. Through this medium, he told his critics of an impending meeting to arrange new details for a prolonged occupation of the building. He told them, also, that the Association had freely given up the building, together with the use of beds and furniture. Not unnaturally, he failed to commit to writing that a great deal of the cost of installation was contributed out of his own pocket.

Editorial comment in *The Sportsman*, taking up the case, pointed out that, " it was indeed an utter impossibility for any

Dorling to act in the manner suggested ". As for the accusers, they had only to carry out the penned advice of the Clerk of the Course, " to wait and see what happens, instead of condemning us unheard," for very soon the Grand Stand hospital was fully operative.

When the Derby meeting of 1915 took place soldiers who were able to get about had the run of the Grand Stand. However, it was the last fixture on Epsom Downs until the Spring of 1919. All meetings except those held at Newmarket were abandoned and Epsom was requisitioned by the military authorities.

The resumption of racing in 1919 proved to be the beginning of Epsom's brightest period, although many changes foretold the story of present-day admission charges. Income-tax had jumped to £7,589 and entertainment-tax was introduced for the first time. It demanded payment of £7,320 in that first season and, to quote the most up-to-date figure available, in 1948 the Chancellor's Budget was enriched by £68,546 from the pockets of Epsom race-goers.

All the gaiety returned to the Downs in the year following the Armistice (1919) and, up to that time, the greatest crowd ever known turned up to see Grand Parade win the Derby for Lord Glanely. The success of the meeting hinged directly on the tireless activity of Henry Mayson Dorling. It delighted him to know that once more Epsom was a going concern, but he was 84 years of age and the effort must have proved too much for him. At any rate, this martinet-of-a-man died five months later.

His passing did not end the Dorling régime. Two other members of the family, who had worked unobtrusively on the Committee of the Grand Stand Association quickly found prominence. One, a half-brother to Henry Mayson, was Walter Dorling. He, together with his nephew, Edward Earle Dorling, was appointed joint General Manager. Walter, whose temperament was directly opposite to that of his predecessor, filled another dual position. He was made joint Clerk of the Course with Walter Gerald Langlands. The latter's family association with Epsom Race-course started in the early years of the nineteenth century when his grandfather rented part of the Downs from the Lord of the Manor.

The Langlands family operated a private stand, first paying ground-rent to the Lord of the Manor and then to the Grand Stand Association. So, in the course of more than a century of close-working agreement, it was not surprising that a Langlands should take his place in the administration of the racing.

That the selection of a Dorling to fill a managerial rôle caused no little astonishment might have been difficult to understand, except that Edward Earle was in Holy orders. The Rev. E. E.

Dorling, M.A., F.S.A., enjoyed the newspaper headlines and, as it happened, the " Novel Job for a Clergyman " came at a time when he could justifiably accept the appointment. He was a demobbed chaplain-to-the-Forces and had not then settled down to a civilian living. Furthermore, he had succeeded to certain shares in the Grand Stand Association and, incidentally, to the printing business set up in Epsom by William Dorling 100 years earlier. Anyway, whatever it was that prompted him to leave his ministerial duties and engage actively in race-course management, he was a man of remarkable achievement. After taking his degree at Clare College, Cambridge, the Rev. Dorling became a master at Derby School. Before service in the Army, he had been Headmaster to the Cathedral School, Salisbury, and was appointed a minor canon in the Cathedral.

Even his work for the Grand Stand Association failed to disturb his energy in other directions. Earle Dorling took an active interest in heraldry and archæology and in 1928 he was appointed a Member of the Royal Commission on Historical Monuments. He designed the coat of arms for the Borough of Epsom and in 1937 became the town's third substitute Charter Mayor. However, it is certain that Epsom Race-course did not suffer by these varied interests. Indeed, the Dorling-Langlands trio quickly proved themselves expert in the technicalities of racing. In their first year, the somewhat abrupt turn at Tattenham Corner was remade and, laid out in the perfect segment of a circle, has remained a gentle curve into the straight.

Another of their early reforms was the introduction of a temporary line of running-rails at the Summer Meeting. From Tattenham Corner to the winning-post, they are set out 20 feet from the permanent rails. The Derby, The Oaks and, of course, all other events at that meeting are run for the last half-mile on turf on which no horse sets foot for 12 months. The trio were, perhaps, the more determined to improve general conditions because of their predecessor's poor relationship with the Jockey Club. If they wanted any urging, the Summer Meeting of 1924 provided the necessary momentum. It was the year in which Sansovino streaked through the mud to win in a canter by six lengths from St. Germans, who passed the post only a neck in front of Hurstwood. The race was run in a torrential downpour.

Rain had been falling all day and the course was very soft, but by the following day it was almost impossible to race. Several events had to be abandoned because heavy Derby-Day traffic, ploughing across the course at Tattenham Corner, had churned up a quagmire. The Jockey Club and the Police demanded certain alterations. These embodied alterations to the enclosures to allow additional free-way for the public and, among other things, requests for more adequate accommodation. Plans were made to carry out rebuilding, but they were not approved and it was decided to knock down the existing building and erect a new stand. It was not practical to do this on land of which the Association were only lessees. They decided to buy the freehold of Epsom Downs and all the Lord of the Manor's rights attached to it, and this they did in 1925 for £57,000. To help meet the cost, they sold the greater part of Walton Downs, excluding that part of the Derby Course in the Manor of Walton, to Stanley Wootton for £35,000.

The balance of £22,000 which the Association provided to meet the land-purchase was only a fraction of their requirements. The contract to build the new stand on the plans approved by the Jockey Club and their architect, was estimated at about £119,000. To cope with this, the directors of Epsom Grand Stand Association were authorised to issue £100,000 new capital, of which £64,000 was subscribed. Unfortunately, Walter Gerald Langlands was only on the fringe of this new era of Epsom progress when he died in August, 1924, and, in 1925, before the final detail was completed, Walter Dorling also passed away. The clergyman was left as sole General Manager, but his task was made the easier by the able assistance of Charles John Laurance Langlands. Charles, an experienced surveyor, was the son of Walter, and, over the years, he had acquired a practical knowledge of his father's duties. Clearly, he was the man to fill the position of Clerk of the Course, and he took up the appointment in January, 1926. He was also made a director of Epsom Grand Stand Association, and within two years was elected chairman.

Meanwhile, his inaugural year proved to be an exceedingly tough proposition. The old stand was demolished and the new stand started, but scarcely before the work was under way, the Coal Strike had become the General Strike. Essential material was held up, thousands of tons of steel girders were frozen in transit, and, of course, the building operatives downed tools. The new Grand Stand was scheduled for completion in time for the Summer Meeting of 1927, but with only a few days to go, the chance of success appeared to be slender. The prospect affected the workmen, and their industry flagged until Lord Lonsdale took a hand.

One of the greatest figures on the Turf since the time of Lord George Bentinck a century before, Lord Lonsdale arranged a dinner for all the workmen. He gave it in the almost finished building, and, what with the quips of his Lordship and the general feeling of good-fellowship, the carpenters, the plasterers, and the painters decided to speed-up their efforts. They were still at work on the eve of the Derby and their activity lasted far into the night, but on the morning of June 1, 1927, the present Epsom Grand Stand was ready. The task had employed 500 men working day and night. They put in over 1,000,000 rivets and used 2,700 tons of steel. The whole structure, measuring 700 feet in length, comprised three sections. The first is the Club Stand, which houses Their Majesties' Suite. Next is the Grand Stand, rising 70 feet in height, and adjoining is the East Grand Stand.

The new buildings, without fanciful decorations, were designed on good clean lines, but, largely due to the General Strike, the original estimate was exceeded and the final cost amounted to £250,000. To meet the expense, the Association had to raise their capital, and a further £28,000 was subscribed, bringing the capital to £245,713. In addition, they had to borrow £180,000 from the Bank to make up the balance of the cost of the new stand. In 1928, owing to the new stand being twice the length of the old one, it was found necessary to build a larger number-frame on the Hill so that it could be seen from all parts. Before work on this could be started, a public enquiry was held at Epsom, and, with the assurance that the natural scenic beauty of the Downs would not be impaired, the Ministry of Agriculture and Fisheries authorised the construction of the frame. It is the largest number-frame in the country and operates on the telescopic principle, the supporting columns being wound down so that they disappear into the ground when racing is finished.

At this time, the Association's foresight in acquiring the freehold of the Downs enabled them to carry out a drastic reform in car-parking arrangements. Except for specific enclosures, motorists had enjoyed the privilege of parking free of charge, wherever they chose to leave their cars. They might be doing it to this day, but for the fact that they complained to the police. From a few isolated grumblings over several years, annoyance had become almost a public outcry by 1928. People were being fleeced by gipsies and the variety of unscrupulous characters who frequented race-meetings. Up on the Downs, early in the morning, groups of these vagrants selected areas and enclosed them with the aid of ropes and stakes. Motorists, obliged to use the roped-off areas on crowded race-days, were charged excessive prices to leave their cars. The rogues charged whatever they thought a person could pay; a nondescript driver in a shabby car would fare better than the obviously-wealthy in a sleek limousine. Similarly, if business was brisk, up went their prices all round, or of it was slack, they reduced their charges.

Once again Lord Lonsdale gave the Association the benefit of his influence in matters affecting racing. He convened a conference in his Town house. Among those present were the late Lord

Byng (then Commissioner of the Metropolitan Police), the late Admiral Royds (his Assistant Commissioner), Sir Percy Laurie (who was Deputy - Assistant Commissioner), with Charles Langlands and others representing the Grand Stand Association. It was decided that the Association should control the whole of the Downs for parking purposes and that prices should be agreed between them and their tenants prior to each meeting. The conference covered, also, the system of traffic control to and from the Downs. The problem of keeping vehicles moving had always been difficult to solve, particularly on Derby Day. There was an occasion when an airship patrolled the sky over the arterial roads leading to Epsom. That was in 1921, a year in which another coal strike forced the railways to close down. In consequence, the roads were jammed and the ill-fated R 33 wirelessed details of congested areas to police-control from her floating observation-points.

The system devised in Lord Lonsdale's house was dependent on the co-operation of the police, the Grand Stand Association, and the public. It was decided that the Association should pre-pare a plan showing the position, names, and prices of every car-park on the Downs and that this should be made available to the public. The object was to give motorists an opportunity of deciding before they left home exactly in which park they pro-posed to leave their cars. The plan was developed until a system of colour-routing ensured a constant flow of speedily moving traffic. The aeroplane that took over duty from the R 33 was no longer necessary. Race-goers consulted the annual brochure produced by the Epsom Grand Stand Association, applied to National Car Parks for the appropriately coloured windscreen-label and the drive to the course was simplified. The Automobile Association sign-posted the routes, the police directed the various colours from control-points and, without delay, the driver found himself in the parking-spot of his choice.

It works well enough now, but, when the Association first tried to operate the scheme, they were faced with the task of keeping gipsies and other casual race-track followers off the Downs. The job was doubly difficult because the Law of Property Act, passed in 1925, gave the public right-of-access over any part of the Downs. They could, if they were fortunate enough to avoid the fate of Emily Davison, walk out on to the track during the running of a race. Between races, it was com-mon practice for thousands of people to crowd on to the track.

Seriously disturbed by the amount of damage to the turf, the Stewards issued a notice requesting people going from the stands to the paddock, to use a special footway at the back of the stands. Decent folk obeyed, but the usual cranks, insisting on their rights, ignored appeals by the police. No action could be taken against them. In 1928, anxious to define public rights, the local Council petitioned the Minister of Agriculture for a Conservancy Scheme. In the interests of their own protection, the Epsom Grand Stand Association at once followed suit, and it was eight years before negotiations were settled between these two bodies. The Epsom and Walton Downs Regulation Act was approved and passed in 1936.

This Act of Parliament is administered by a Board of Conservators made up of Epsom councillors, members of the Grand Stand Association, and Mr. Stanley Wootton, who owns a portion of Walton Downs. They issued a set of bye-laws, and any infringement was, on summary conviction, punishable in a magistrate's court. While the Act preserved the " natural state of beauty " on the Downs, the public still have access for " air and exercise " at suitable times. The terms allow the Association to conduct their business on their own land, unhampered by dolts and vagabonds.

It was the start of a new era in Epsom history. Rogue-gipsies, described for so many years as the colour-feature of the scene, were forbidden to encamp on the Downs. To-day, a few of them still make the journey for the Derby meeting, but they sneak their caravans into the hedgerows several miles from the course. The public suffer the begging only of those few who complete the journey on foot, and the Association's property, in the shape of wooden fences and posts, no longer kindle gipsy campfires. Legally, the course and the training gallops are protected from the thoughtless as well as the unscrupulous. A man can freely ride a horse as long as he steers clear of these places. As for the honest trader, whether palmist or beer-salesman, he or she need only first obtain a licence from the Association to erect a tent at a race-meeting.

There was another alteration in 1936 which, although of minor significance, compared with the Conservancy Act, improved amenities for those race-goers who enjoy their sport from the paddock. The oddly shaped parade-ring was abolished and an extra-large symmetrical ring was made on level ground. The stabling was doubled and a second " walking " ring for horses installed near the boxes. And, more important from the public point of view, a large " tote " was erected and a miniature grand stand built. From the stand, people can see a good deal of the course over the fence. A record of all happenings is made by loud-speaker, and they can, between events, enjoy the colour of flower-beds and the restful green of the turf. Such a setting would not, perhaps, appeal to the inveterate race-goer, but, for these people, there is not the jostling bustle of the betting-rings. It is the distinctive quality of Epsom that it is designed to please all comers.

Spacious as are Epsom enclosures, they cannot begin to swallow the hundreds of thousands who make their way to the races. The overflow spreads out on the Downs. These are the people who get their racing free of charge, although, for the most part, they see little of the horses. For them, it is a carefree occasion with the sport thrown in, and it is they who create the story-book colour of Epsom. There are others, of course, who arrive in 'buses and motor-coaches to picnic beside the rails and take their racing seriously.

Some idea of their numbers may be estimated by the sale of race-cards. Only a percentage buy them, and often family groups are contented with one card. On Derby Day, 1948, 138,386 race-cards were sold.

It is on the Hill, in the centre of the course that the jellied-eel merchants, the icecream-men, the drink-salesmen, and the preachers of the gospel vie with the bookmakers and tipsters to make themselves heard. There also are the roundabouts and swings and the tents of the palmists. Nothing of this, really, has altered throughout the years, unless it is up-to-date equipment and the changing style of dress.

At the start of World War II, Epsom was once again taken over by the military authorities. Bombs damaged the Grand Stand during the war, and many great holes were torn in the enclosures. For the safety of the public, licences were granted to carry out repairs. It is well that the work renewed the strength of these fine stands, for post-war crowds at all meetings have so far proved greater than at any time in the history of the course.

Edward Earle Dorling, the last of his line in race-course management, died in 1943. His name is commemorated by a race called the Earle Dorling Memorial Stakes, to be run annually over one and a quarter miles. This event was inaugurated in 1947 when a third meeting was granted to the Grand Stand Association.

Mr. Charles Langlands who, in addition to his duties as Clerk of the Course, was appointed Chairman and Managing Director of the Association, framed two additional races for this meeting, thereby further commemorating the tradition of racing on the Downs. They are : the Diomed Stakes, named after the winner of the first Derby, and The Nell Gwyn Stakes, so called because of the orange-girl's association with Epsom during the reign of Charles II.

While Charles Langlands has a mind for the history of Epsom, he has also an interest in the future. After the war, he was the first Clerk of the Course to install that most recent piece of race-course equipment, the photo-finish camera. There is little doubt that, when circumstances permit, he will follow with character-istic enthusiasm the progressive lead of his predecessors.

CHAPTER X

OWNERS AND TRAINERS

By Meyrick Good

IT is a profound truth that flat racing has made more pro-
nounced progress during the last 50 years than in the
preceding half-century. Furthermore, the improvement of
the British thoroughbred, taken collectively, has also been outstanding. The times taken by Derby winners since 1900 endorse
that view. That great horse of the early days of the sport, Eclipse,
left his indelible mark on the best of present-day race-strains.
His race-track deeds prompted the saying in those days of,
" Eclipse first and the rest nowhere ", just as the horse of the
century, Ormonde, was repeatedly referred to as the " Ormonde
of the age ". Mention of the late Duke of Westminster's famous
horse reminds one of the fact that Flying Fox, the best Derby
winner of my time, was a grandson of the " Eaton Hero ".
Flying Fox, after being purchased by Edmond Blanc for 35,700
gns.—a record price for a horse at that time—became the sire
of Ajax, who bred Teddy, the progenitor of Asterus, who got
many of the good horses with which M. Marcel Boussac, in
recent years, invaded this country and carried off stakes to the
value of over £30,000. The Ascot Gold Cup winners, Arbar
(1948) and Caracalla II (1946), and Goyescas, Corrida, Marsyas II,
Goyama, and Nirgal all have strains of English thoroughbred
blood coursing through their veins. The late Duke of Westminster named his son Bend Or after the son of Ormonde. Flying
Fox was of the Doncaster and Bend Or branch of the Whalebone
family, while St. Frusquin and Persimmon came of the Whisker
branch of the Galopin and St. Simon families.

The racing-world generally, and the writer in particular, lost
a very great friend by the death of Lord Derby in 1948. There
has never been a greater personality in England or France or anyone more universally loved than his Lordship. He was a great
friend to me, and many an interesting letter on racing-matters
have I received from him. Lord Derby's influence on the breeding of the English thoroughbred has reached to the far ends of
the world, especially in America where the greatest horse that
has raced there for the last ten or a dozen years, Citation, is a
grandson, on his maternal side, to Hyperion.

It was in 1896 that Canterbury Pilgrim won The Oaks and
became the foundation of Lord Derby's stud just as Perdita II
did for King Edward VII. It was in 1906 that Keystone II

repeated the victory in the Oaks for the sixteenth Earl of Derby, and these were his only Classic triumphs in the 15 years of his racing-career.

The seventeenth Lord Derby won 20 Classic races in 40 years. He won the One Thousand Guineas with Canyon (1916), Ferry (1918), Tranquil (1923), Fair Isle (1930), Tide-Way (1936), Herringbone (1943), and Sun Stream (1945). He won the Derby three times, with Sansovino (1924), Hyperion (1933), and Watling Street (1942); the Two Thousand Guineas twice, with Colorado (1926) and Garden Path (1944), also the Oaks with Toboggan (1928) and Sunstream (1945); six times the St. Leger, with Swynford (1910), Keysoe (1919), Tranquil (1923), Fairway (1928), Hyperion (1933), and Herringbone (1943).

Lord Derby headed the list of Winning Owners on seven occasions, his 1,000-odd winners crediting him with stake money exceeding £800,000. His Lordship also raced with conspicuous success in France, where, following the First World War, he was Ambassador to Paris in 1920 and in that year won three races. He raced in partnership with Mr. Ogden Mills and his daughter, Lady Granard, winning the Grand Prix de Paris with Cri de Guerre and the Prix de l'Arc de Triomphe with Kanter. At the time of his death, there were 13 brood-mares at the Stanley House Stud, including Aurora, the dam of Alycidon, who put British bloodstock back on its former pedestal by winning the Gold Cup at Ascot (1949) in the style of the greatest stayer we have had for years. Alycidon carried the famous black-and-white colours which have been handed down to the deceased sportsman's heir, the present Lord Derby, who will be carrying on the best traditions of this illustrious family. Besides Alycidon, the present Earl owns another courageous colt in Swallow Tail, who, with more luck in running, might easily have won the 1949 Derby. He made some atonement for that defeat by winning in splendid style at Ascot.

At his home meeting at Aintree the late Lord Derby has won eight Liverpool Spring Cups and six Autumn Cups, and many other handicaps. One of the most important of them was the Ebor, with March Along (1921). Of all the good brood-mares he owned from time to time, I should say Scapa Flow and Selene were the greatest of them. The progeny of the former won £85,000 in stakes. No breeder had a better collection of stallions. They included Swynford, Chaucer, Phalaris, Fairway, Hyperion, Borealis, and Bobsleigh.

His Highness the Aga Khan has, like the late Lord Derby, made a tremendous and valuable contribution to Turf history, though he has not been racing for anything like the same number of years. It was not until the early part of 1900 that the Aga Khan decided to embark on the hazardous sea of ownership. It was

at the late Lord Wavertree's suggestion that he commenced to
race and, very wisely, he sought the co-operation of the late Hon.
George Lambton to select his first batch of yearlings. These
he sent to Whatcombe to be trained by R. C. Dawson. The latter
prepared for him his first Derby winner, Blenheim (1930), which
had been bought from Lord Carnarvon. The Aga Khan won
two other Derbys, with Bahram and Mahmoud, in successive
years (1935 and 1936), the former winning the Triple Crown.
Bahram was his second winner of the St. Leger, his first being
Firdaussi (1932), and in that year the Aga Khan had the unique
experience of also owning the second, fourth, and fifth in the race.

It was in 1931 that Frank Butters became trainer for the Aga
Khan, and the following year he won the Oaks with Udaipur.
In 1934, Felicitation, with Gordon Richards in the saddle, won
the Ascot Gold Cup and also the Churchill Stakes at the same
meeting. Other good horses that Frank Butters trained for this
owner, were Umidar and Tehran. The Aga Khan headed the
list of Winning Owners on 10 occasions, which, as a matter of
fact, beat Lord Derby's record by three. A victory which must
have given him and his painstaking trainer the greatest satisfaction, was that of Migoli in the Prix de l'Arc de Triomphe, which
contributed to the restoration of the prestige of British bloodstock which had received something of a setback by the successes
of so many French horses in this country the two previous years.
M. Marcel Boussac, among other notable successes at Ascot and
Newmarket, won our Gold Cup two years running.

Another owner who has been in the forefront as a staunch
patron of racing is Lord Rosebery, who headed the list of Winning
Owners in 1939, his 14 winners producing £38,464. That was
the year that Blue Peter won the Derby and other important
events. His Lordship also won the substitute Derby (1944) with
Ocean Swell, who also credited him with the Ascot Gold Cup.
Blue Peter has already made his mark at the stud, and Ocean
Swell should be equally successful when his stock begin to race
over longer distances than a mile as he is bred on the lines to
get stayers. Lord Rosebery won the St. Leger in 1931 with
Sandwich, a son of Sansovino-Waffles, and the Eclipse Stakes
with Miracle when he was senior Steward of the Jockey Club.
Lord Rosebery, with his up-to-date methods and profound knowledge of racing, has done much to bring about reforms and
generally to effect improvements in many directions.

Another who has figured prominently in racing-circles the last
20 years or more is Viscount Astor, whose mare Conjure, bought
for £100 with an idea of riding him with his University Drag,
turned out to be a wonderful winner-producer for his Lordship.
Lord Astor had no more luck in his efforts to win the Derby than

has Gordon Richards to ride one : Blink (1918), Buchan (1919), Craig an Eran (1921), Tamar (1922), and St. Germans (1924), all finished second in the Epsom Classic. Better fortune has attended him where the Oaks has been concerned, as he has won the "lady's" Classic on five occasions, with Sunny Jane (1917), Pogrom (1922), Saucy Sue (1925), Short Story (1926), and Pennycomequick (1929). Craig an Eran also won him the Eclipse (1921), as did Buchan (1919 and 1920), Saltash (1923), and Rhodes Scholar (1936). He won the St. Leger with Booklaw (1927), a remarkable horse that more recently carried these famous colours conspicuously on a race-course is High Stakes, a gelding who since 1944 won 27 races and was 11 times placed.

When first I remembered the late Lord Woolavington, he raced as Mr. Kincaid and then Mr. Buchanan, and I remember one of his first winners was Epsom Lad, who won a race at Sandown Park with the South American rider, Toterolo, finishing bare-back with his saddle in his right hand, after it had slipped from under him. Lord Woolavington raced with varying success under both codes, having many good National Hunt performers with the late Bob Gore. His Lordship, later in life, raced on a higher scale and found the Derby one of his lucky races, winning first with Captain Cuttle (1922) and then Coronach (1926), two of the biggest horses to win the Epsom Classic. This fine sporting owner, who—like the late Lord Derby and Lord Astor— betted but little, if at all, also won the St. Leger with Coronach and Hurry On (1916). In the opinion of his trainer, Fred Darling, Hurry On, the sire of Coronach, was the best horse he ever had under his charge. Lord Woolavington's daughter, the Hon. Mrs. MacDonald-Buchanan, won the wartime Derby with Owen Tudor (1941), also the Gold Cup when it was run at Newmarket (1942). Owen Tudor was the sire of Tudor Minstrel, the winner of the Two Thousand Guineas (1947) but who failed to stay the Derby distance after starting a very hot favourite. Mr. MacDonald-Buchanan owns Abernant, second in the Two Thousand Guineas and probably the fastest three-year-old in training judging by the way he won at Ascot, Newmarket, and Goodwood. The same owner has Royal Forest, who, like Tudor Minstrel, was favourite for the Derby (1949) but did not perform as well as his owner and trainer had hoped. The late Lord Woolavington headed the list of Winning Owners in 1922 and 1926.

The death of Lord Glanely was a serious blow to racing, as his Lordship was not only a breeder on an extensive scale but an intrepid bidder at all the yearling sales. In fact, he gave what were then record prices for both Westward Ho and Blue Ensign. Neither, however, fulfilled expectations. Lord Glanely previously raced as "Mr. W. Tatem", but had few good horses until first

TATTENHAM CORNER, EPSOM

THE PEARLY KING, QUEEN AND FAMILY

[Facing page 148

THE SCENE JUST AFTER MISS DAVISON IN SUFFRAGIST COLOURS, HAD THROWN HERSELF IN FRONT OF THE KING'S HORSE AT TATTENHAM CORNER IN THE 1913 DERBY. MISS DAVISON WAS KILLED, THE HORSE, ANMER, AND H. JONES, THE JOCKEY, WERE UNINJURED

the late Frank Barling and then the late Tom Hogg trained for him. He then won the Derby with Grand Parade (1919), ridden by Fred Templeman; the Oaks with Rose of England (1930); the St. Leger with Singapore (1930) and Chumleigh (1937); the One Thousand Guineas with Dancing Time (1941), and the Colts' Guineas with Colombo (1934), who finished third in the Derby, won by Windsor Lad, although heavily supported by his connections for that race.

The late Lord Dewar was another to own a number of good horses, including Forfarshire, but he never came near to winning the Derby. When he died he left his fortune, his race-horses, and stud to his nephew, Mr. J. A. Dewar. Among his horses in training then was Cameronian, whose nomination would, in the ordinary course of events, have been void on the death of his owner. The late Edgar Wallace fought a test-case which led to the abolition of that ruling and, not only did Cameronian run in, but won, the Derby (1931). Mr. Dewar also won the wartime Oaks (1941) with Commotion, which has done well at the stud since, being the dam of Combat and Faux Tirage, both of whom were unbeaten as 2 yr. olds. Mr. Dewar breeds his own horses at East Grinstead and seldom buys yearlings at public auction.

The late Sir Abe Bailey liked nothing better than supporting horses he ran, and the South African magnate brought off many big coups in his long association with the Turf. He won the Oaks with Lovely Rosa (1936) and the Ascot Gold Cup with Foxlaw (1927) and Tiberius (1935). There is an oil-painting in the Cape Town Museum of these two stayers and their sire, Son-in-Law. The latter proved a prolific sire of stayers and lived to a great age under the care of his trainer, Reginald Day. Son-in-Law was third in the list of Winning Stallions, to Buchan and Phalaris, in 1941 and fourth to Hurry On, Solario (whom Reg Day also trained), and Blandford in 1944. Solario also lived to a great age and I was present at Epsom when his owner turned down the big offer of £100,000 for Solario, who turned out a conspicuous success at the stud, his mares, especially, leaving his mark in the English Stud Book.

One of the biggest gambles of my time was brought off when Sir Abe Bailey won the Royal Hunt Cup in 1909 with Dark Ronald, ridden by an unknown jockey in W. Williams and backed down from outside rates to 4 to 1. Foxlaw also won Sir Abe the Northumberland Plate in 1926.

The late Sir Hugo Cunliffe-Owen, owner of that good sprinter King Sol, began his racing-career when his horses were trained by the late Harry Batho. In after years, he trained with the late Captain " Ossie " Bell, who prepared Felstead for him when that horse won the Derby (1928). Sir Hugo also won the One Thousand

Guineas and Oaks with Rockfel(1938) and the wartime Gold Cup at Newmarket with Finis. Filator was owned by him when he won the Cesarewitch in 1941. He never got near the list of Winning Owners, nor was he ever made a member of the Jockey Club.

Lord Milford, who has a number of useful animals in Jack Jarvis' stables—animals he bred himself—won the Two Thousand Guineas with Flamingo (1928), the Ascot Gold Cup with Flyon (1939), and the Champion Stakes with Honeway, who is now at the stud. His Lordship is a member of the Jockey Club.

Mr. James V. Rank won the St. Leger (1938) and the Coronation Cup with Scottish Union, the Oaks with Why Hurry (1934), and the Goodwood and Doncaster Cups with Epigram, who is by Son-in-Law. Both Scottish Union and Epigram are proving themselves successful stallions. Mr. Rank, who patronises both branches of the national sport, owns that good 'chaser Prince Regent, generally considered unlucky not to have won the Grand National. This son of My Prince was thought by many to be one of the best 'chasers since Manifesto and Golden Miller. Mr. James V. Rank takes a great personal interest in the Salisbury race-meetings, of which he is an acting-Steward.

The Honourable Miss Dorothy Paget had more horses in training, the last few years, than any other owner of any knowledge. Including horses in training, broodmares, foals and yearlings in England and Ireland, she is reputed to possess some 500 horses. Her most important success to date was winning the Derby with Straight Deal (1943), a son of Solario who is now getting winners. Her horses were then trained by Walter Nightingall, but G. Johnson Houghton and the Jelliss's, father and son, had charge of Miss Paget's flat-race horses in 1949, while her National Hunt horses are with Fulke Walwyn at Lambourn. She owned the Grand National winner Golden Miller.

Lieut.-Colonel Giles Loder, related to the owner of that great mare Pretty Polly and who now trains at Beckhampton with Noel Murless, won the Derby with Spion Kop (1920) and the One Thousand Guineas with Cresta Run (1927). He owned that good-looking weight-carrier The Cobbler, winner of the Royal Hunt Cup with top weight and who was sold to an Irish syndicate for £25,000 following his Ascot victory.

In 1908, 1913 and 1914 Mr. Jack Joel headed the list of winning owners and was one of the most successful owners of that period. His son, Mr. J. H. Joel, is carrying on the stud and has a few useful horses but none of outstanding ability. His trainer is Jack Watts, who trained Call Boy for the late Mr. Frank Curzon when that horse won the Derby (1927). The late Mr. Sol Joel won a lot of handicaps, including the Lincoln and Royal Hunt Cup with Long Set (1912), the City and Suburban with

Maiden Erlegh (1914). Mr. Sol Joel's son, Mr. Stanhope Joel, won the St. Leger with Chamossaire (1945) and his close friend, Mr. J. G. Ferguson, the Derby and St. Leger with Airborne (1946).

It is only of recent years that the Maharaja Gaekwar of Baroda has joined the ranks of owners in England, though he raced with marked success in India. After having a few horses in training with F. Armstrong, he launched out and gave the record price of £28,000 for Sayajirao with whom he won the St. Leger (1947). He won the Two Thousand Guineas with My Babu (1948), but that good-looking colt, for whom he also paid a big price, did not do as well as expected in the Derby and joined his owner's stud in Ireland. Sayajirao is a brother to Dante with whom Sir Eric Ohlson won the Derby (1945), and this horse's first crop of two-year-olds performed with distinction on the track. Baroda's horses were transferred from Newmarket to Epsom in June, 1949, where they were trained by T. Carey, while C. Smirke succeeded E. Britt as jockey.

It was in 1938 that Mr. William Woodward won the Ascot Gold Cup with his American-bred Flares, and each year he has sent over some of his best yearlings for Captain Boyd-Rochfort to train ; with Brown Betty he won the One Thousand Guineas (1933), while Boswell won him the Eclipse (1937), and the St. Leger (1936). Black Tarquin also won the last-named event (1948) and was favourite to beat Alycidon in the Gold Cup (1949), but was no match for the latter, who clearly out-galloped and outstayed the American, much to the satisfaction of all those who have British bloodstock at heart. Following Black Tarquin's poor display in the Princess of Wales Stakes, he was returned to his owner in America.

Sir Alfred Butt has, what he terms, only a small stud, but year after year he has turned out a number of good winners. He won the Oaks with Steady Aim (1946) and the Victoria Cup with Petition (1948), and the latter, who also won the Eclipse the same year, is expected to make a name for himself at the stud.

One of the leading sires now at the stud is the Italian horse (though possessed of an English pedigree) Nearco, who in 1947 headed the list of Winning Stallions. For this horse Mr. Harry Benson paid £65,000, after he had parted with Windsor Lad (who won him the St. Leger in 1934). Nearco has got many top-class track performers, but not all of them stay as well as he did when he won 14 races of all distances in Italy and France before coming to this country.

A reliable indication of the fluctuations of fortune experienced by prominent breeders of the English thoroughbred is furnished by the following record of Lord Astor's racing successes since the establishment of his stud at Cliveden.

	Horses to run.	Races Run.	Races Won.	Times pl. 2nd & 3rd.	Stks. w (ex pl. money) £.	Position among Winning Owners.
1906	4	8	—	2	—	—
1907	4	—	—	—	—	—
1908	4	6	2	3	882	145
1909	4	31	9	8	4,245	22
1910	5	27	9	10	12,959	8
1911	5	16	2	3	1,165	98
1912	5	8	2	4	581	166
1913	6	24	4	9	4,030	34
1914	6	30	10	10	16,617	2
1915	7	12	1	—	185*	169
1916	9	29	3	4	1,103*	29
1917	3	9	3	3	1,408*	17
1918	5	12	5	4	4,734*	6
1919	5	19	6	8	8,120*	10
1920	8	21	6	8	8,928*	12
1921	9	48	15	17	22,822	2
1922	9	21	$5\frac{1}{2}$	8	14,302	6
1923	10	44	15	12	23,444	3
1924	9	37	17	9	16,611	6
1925	17	81	20	19	35,723	1
1926	13	66	14	27	24,187	3
1927	15	50	10	10	29,975	2
1928	22	84	12	17	7,484	20
1929	22	73	7	15	13,263	9
1930	19	83	10	17	5,778	17
1931	17	80	19	22	26,959	3
1932	17	56	12	17	11,824	7
1933	20	81	15†	20	17,546	4
1934	21	56	11	16	8,518	11
1935	25	108	11	33	11,358	5
1936	27	110	19	29	38,131	1
1937	12	63	11	16	10,025	11
1938	17	62	8	12	9,507	12
1939	22	82	11	16	8,107*	11
1940	16	50	6	12	1,678*	14
1941	11	36	7	6	1,817*	19
1942	11	44	$3\frac{1}{2}$	12	820*	48
1943	7	22	4	6	1,110*	28
1944	10	33	6	7	1,958*	19
1945	14	63	$25\frac{1}{2}$	14	17,647*	2
1946	22	88	14†	21	9,023	14
1947	12	67	36	16	22,003	5
1948	15	47	15	14	7,270	21
Total	—	1,987	$421\frac{1}{2}$	516	—	—

The horses trained in 1906 and 1907 were bought. Subsequently practically all the horses were bred at Cliveden.

* Value of races reduced through war.
† Incl. 2 dead-heats counted as 1 race.

Summary of Results :

Horses Bred	352
Average Runners Each Season	12
Total Winners	184
Total Top Class as Winners or Producers .. (Classic, Cup, etc.).	53
Races Run	1,987
Total Winnings	£463,837

Place in Winning Owners :

In first dozen	24	times
Placed 2nd or 3rd	7	,,
1st	2	,,

The number of horses to have run on English courses in the last 50 years are as follows :

Year.	2.Y.O.	3.Y.O.	4.Y.O.	Five and Upwards.	Total.
1899	1,438	1,059	558	698	3,753
1904	1,154	884	456	525	3,019
1909	1,420	1,002	631	797	3,850
1914	1,434	1,074	627	771	3,906
1919	1,293	816	457	703	3,269
1924	1,561	1,191	709	1,125	4,586
1929	1,562	1,295	752	993	4,602
1934	1,619	1,194	764	983	4,560
1939	1,483	1,145	583	782	3,993
1944	797	570	161	98	1,626
1948	1,678	1,454	612	700	4,444

During the last 50 years, I have seen a large number of innovations, including the starting-gate, number-cloths for the identification of horses walking round before their races, the Totalisator and, with it, the broadcast of runners, jockeys, and the draw. Before the allotment of places, the inside position at the start was taken by the jockey who arrived at the post first, and inexperienced riders had, even then, to give way to their seniors who "jockeyed" them out of the most favoured

positions. It was no uncommon thing before the " gate " was
introduced, for delays of 10, 15, and sometimes 20 minutes
before they took their place when fractious horses refused to
come into line.

The first starting-gate had but one strand of webbing. This
was frequently broken, then three strands were introduced and,
finally, five. It is seldom that the stout strands now in use are broken.
The present system is admirable and discourages a jockey from
attempting to take undue advantages. Within the last year or
two the names of horses, in addition to the number, are printed
on number-cloths in most big races, visitors thus being able to
identify the horses without looking at their race-cards. At one
time, horses were paraded in front of the stands in nearly all big
races, but in more recent years such parades have only taken place
in the Derby and one or two of the big races at Ascot, as the
authorities came to the conclusion that it was apt to excite nervous horses. This decision was probably influenced by the
objection of the owners and trainers, not by the paying
public.

I have seen and reported on many famous animals, thrilling
races, splendid exhibitions of horsemanship, and a good many
incidents. I have witnessed every Derby for 53 years, but not
quite as many St. Legers and Grand Nationals, and I have always
contended that Flying Fox was the best horse to win the Derby,
but some present-day critics may vote Blue Peter or Bahram in
that category. I am not crossing swords with them in their belief,
all three being great horses. I have seen Derbys in all descrip-
tions of weather, the worst being when St. Amant won in the
terrific thunderstorm of 1904, and I recollect lending his owner,
Mr. Leopold de Rothschild, my umbrella from the Press Stand
when he proceeded to lead in his gallant winner. Sansovino had
to plough through mud and slush when he won the 1924 race
for the late Lord Derby. The two gamest horses to win the
Epsom Classic were unquestionably Sunstar (1911) and Humorist
(1921). That pocket-hercules George Stern got the last ounce
out of the first-named.

Long before St. Amant's Derby, I interviewed his owner as
to what he thought of the institution of the starting-gate. He
was strongly opposed to it and expressed the opinion that it was
bound to be a failure. On the contrary, it has proved the most
progressive move the Jockey Club had made up to that time.

Tod Sloan revolutionised race-riding in this country by his
short stirrup, forward seat, and great judgment of pace. He came
to this country a year or two after the dark-skinned Sims arrived,
also from America. Before the advent of Sloan in 1899,
Mornington Cannon was the leading jockey of the period, but

whereas other jockeys pulled-up their leathers, following the example set by Sloan, Mornington Cannon did not change his style of riding.

I have no hesitation in naming Swynford (1910) as the best St. Leger winner within my memory. The late Lord Derby's horse was as handsome as he was big and powerful. His trainer, George Lambton, shared a similar opinion and often referred to him, when we discussed the merits of various winners, as the best horse he ever trained.

No winner of the Oaks captured the imagination of the racing-public to such an extent as Sceptre, owned by the Prince of Gamblers, the late Bob Sievier. Sceptre and Pretty Polly won their respective Oaks by exactly the same distance—three lengths. Bert Randall, who started his riding career as an amateur and was a member of the firm of boot manufacturers, rode Sceptre and W. Lane rode Major Eustace Loder's great filly. Not since these two famous mares, has there been one to compare with them in looks or racing-ability. Curiously, neither became as famous as stud-matrons as race-course performers. It is strange that so many Oaks-winners failed to produce offspring capable of emu- lating their brilliance on a race-course. Neither Signorinetta, dual Epsom winner in 1908, nor Tagalie, the One Thousand Guineas and Derby winner in 1912, have been successful broodmares. Rockfel was another good mare, but she could not be compared with the fillies mentioned in the matter of looks.

Unquestionably, the best Oaks winner of recent years was the King's leased Sun Chariot (1942). Her jockey, Gordon Richards, has expressed the opinion that he has never ridden a better, but that was before he commenced riding Pambidian. Quashed, a great mare in many respects, won the Gold Cup in 1936 after winning the Oaks of 1935. She provided another instance of a good race-mare turning out a failure at the stud. There is, how- ever, one exception that I can recall. Reference is made to Keystone II, a daughter of Persimmon, who won the Oaks in 1906 ridden by that great jockey Danny Maher, the finest and most artistic finisher I ever saw. After winning the Champagne Stakes as a two-year-old, Keystone II, the following year, won the Oaks in a canter and then gained an easy victory in the Coronation Stakes. She did not meet with the best of luck in the St. Leger, in which she was fourth to Troutbeck, Prince William, and Beppo. Later the same year at Sandown Park, in the Produce Stakes of £5,000, she beat Prince William who had beaten her in the St. Leger. It was the fact that this good mare trained off as a four-year-old that influenced Lord Derby to retire all his best fillies at the end of their three-year-old careers : a policy which has paid handsome dividends. At the stud, Keystone II bred

Archaic, who was second in the Derby (1920), and Keysoe, the winner of the St. Leger (1919).

It was during the last few years of his period as a trainer that I became acquainted with John Porter. Although the great Ormonde was racing a year or so before my time, I have a distinct recollection of La Fleche, probably the best mare ever trained at Kingsclere. Ormonde, known as "the Ormonde of the age", bred Orme, and the latter became the sire of Flying Fox, whom I saw win the Derby for the late Duke of Westminster.

Such great horses as Nearco, Nasrullah, Black Tarquin, The Phœnix, Colombo, Blue Peter, Dante, Fair Copy and a whole host of others are descendants of Ormonde, while, in France, Flying Fox became the sire of Ajax who sired many good performers in France, including Teddy, Sir Gallahad and Asterus, and the last-named figures in the pedigree of many of M. Boussac's splendid stayers.

The horses trained by John Porter can thus be said to have left their indelible mark on both English and French thoroughbreds of the present day.

Other good horses he trained, included Throstle, Sainfoin, Common, Blue Gown, Isonomy, Hawfinch, Geheimmis, Candlemas, Matchbox, La Voir, and St. Blaise.

In 1899 he headed the list of Winning Trainers, with 42 races to the value of £56,546. In all, he prepared horses to win over a thousand races and over £720,000 in stake-money. Horses trained by him won seven Derbys and six St. Legers : truly a wonderful record. John Porter, who served his apprenticeship with a member of the Day family, an ancestor of mine, retired from training in 1905, then devoted his remaining years to the successful development of Newbury Race-course.

Alec Taylor, whom one will always associate with the training triumphs of Manton, headed the list of Winning Trainers seven years in succession, from 1917 to 1923. He also achieved similar distinction in 1907, 1909, 1910 and in 1914 and, when he accomplished this feat in 1925 his 25 winners won £56,570 in stake-money, which was his record and exceeded the amount won by John Porter.

Alec Taylor, who succeeded his father (who prepared Teddington to win the Derby and Ascot Gold Cup for Sir Joseph Hawley) at Manton, was so successful in training stayers, that he earned for himself the soubriquet of the "Wizard of Manton" though, in after years, he won so many races with his second string when running two horses in a race that the "Manton neglected" became notorious. He died a rich man, leaving over £300,000. He made successful deals with adjoining farms before and after Lord Manton had acquired the property. Alec Taylor never gambled on his horses ; in fact, he was the smallest of backers, his investments seldom exceeding the " pony " (£25) line of business.

Two of the best horses he trained were Bayardo and Gainsborough. The latter, owned by Lady James Douglas, won the Triple Crown for Manton. Alec Taylor won the Oaks seven times—on four occasions for Lord Astor—but never succeeded in winning the Derby for this popular owner, though he saddled horses that were second on five occasions. Bayardo was owned by Mr. Faerie Cox, who also owned that good horse Gay Crusader, who won the Two Thousand Guineas, the Derby and St. Leger in 1917, but good as this Triple Crown hero was, he was not a success at the stud ; nor was Lemberg (the 1910 Derby winner) a success as a stallion. Gainsborough, on the other hand, made a great name for himself at the stud and in 1932 and 1933 headed the list of Winning Sires. In all, Alec Taylor trained the winners of five St. Legers, including two at Newmarket (1917 and 1918).

He first made his name as a trainer when, in 1896, he trained Love Wisely to win the Ascot Gold Cup, a race which he subsequently won with the White Knight (1908), Bayardo (1910), and Aleppo (1914), and again with Gay Crusader and Gainsborough in 1917 and 1918 when the race was at Newmarket during the war years. Alec Taylor was never so successful in the One Thousand Guineas as he was in the Oaks, his only victory in the One Thousand being with Lord Astor's Saucy Sue in 1925. The Ascot Stakes was another favourite race of his, as he won it with Pradella (1906), Torpoint (1907), Haki (1919), Juniso (1923), and the Duke of Buckingham (1927). He trained Grey Tick (1903) and Air Raid (1918) to win the Cesarewitch. The latter was ridden by Otto Madden, who was his jockey for a number of years afterwards. Frank Bullock and Victor Smyth rode many horses for him, the latter being retained by Lord Astor, who had such useful horses as Buchan, Pogrom, Saucy Sue, Craig-an-Eran, Short Story and Book-Law. Like John Porter, during his brilliant career as a trainer, Alec Taylor turned out over 1,000 winners, who won over £500,000 in stakes.

The name of Peter Purcell Gilpin has gone down to history as the trainer of Pretty Polly, who was probably the outstanding filly of my Turf experience. Longer odds were laid on this filly for the One Thousand Guineas and the Oaks than ever before, 100 to 8 being laid on her when she cantered away with the Epsom Classic in 1904, and she won the St. Leger (still with W. Lane riding) at 5–2 on. Gilpin also prepared Spearmint and Spion Kop when they won the Derby in the respective years of 1906 and 1920, and when the former won he had Pretty Polly to put

in a gallop.   Perhaps the most remarkable horse Purcell Gilpin
ever trained was Comrade, for whom he paid only 25 gns. as a
yearling, as this horse might have won our Classics had he been
entered.   As it was, he went to France and won both the Grand
Prix de Paris and the Prix de L'Arc de Triomphe for his owner,
M. St. Alary.   In 1922, Gilpin won the Two Thousand Guineas
with Lord Queenborough's St. Louis.   Pretty Polly was not the
only filly to win him the One Thousand Guineas, as he won it
in subsequent years with Mr. L. Neumann's Electra and Lieut.-
Colonel Loder's Cresta Run in 1909 and 1927.   Other good races
Gilpin won for his clients, were the Ascot Gold Cup with Throwaway (1904), and the Eclipse Stakes with Llangibby (1906), while
the best staying mare I can remember him training was Hammerkop, who in 1905 won the Cesarewitch with the useful weight
of 8 st. 9 lbs.   Gilpin was unlucky not to have won the Cambridgeshire, but that is another tale.   He won the Manchester
November Handicap twice, with Baltinglass (1907) and King
John (1919).

Few men have been more fitted to train for Royalty than
Richard Marsh, who was immaculate in his attire and thorough
in his stable-methods.   Moreover, few trainers have prepared
their horses looking more worthy to carry the colours of reigning
monarchs.   Before mentioning the deeds of the horses he trained
for King Edward and King George, let me state that, in three
of the four years 1897 to the end of 1900, Richard Marsh turned
out close on 150 winners of the value of over £100,000 and,
after his racing-days ended, King Edward's Persimmon headed
the list of Winning Sires in 1902, 1906, 1908 and 1912.   Besides
the Two Thousand Guineas he won with Diamond Jubilee, he
won it with Gorgos (1906), and the One Thousand Guineas with
the King's Thais (1896).   "Dick" Marsh trained the winners of
the Goodwood Cup three years in succession, with Fortunatus
(1901), Perseus (1902), and Rabelais (1903), and again in 1905
with Red Robe.   It was in 1900 that King Edward, then Prince
of Wales, headed the list of Winning Owners, his horses winning
in nine races £29,585 in stakes.   It was, of course, Diamond
Jubilee's year.

Richard Marsh always expressed the opinion that, good horse
as Diamond Jubilee was, the best horse he ever had the good
fortune to train was Persimmon.   Of the nine races in which
he ran, he won seven big events, inclusive of the Derby, St.
Leger and Gold Cup.   As a two-year-old, Persimmon, though
starting favourite, failed to win the Middle Park Plate, in which
he was third to St. Frusquin and Orlandina.   The following year,
he took ample revenge by beating Mr. Leopold de Rothschild's
colt in the Derby, in which race St. Frusquin started at odds on.

In 1895 Marsh trained Florizell II for Persimmon's owner, and the latter's own brother won the Prince of Wales Plate at Epsom, the Princes Handicap at Gatwick, the Gold Vase at Ascot, the Goodwood Cup, the Manchester Cup, and the Jockey Club Cup. Perdita, the dam of Persimmon, Diamond Jubilee and Florizel II, was bought for the Prince of Wales by John Porter for 900 gns. and went down in Turf history as being as great a success at the stud, as sire of Conjure for Lord Astor and Canterbury Pilgrim and Scapa Flow for the late Lord Derby. In all, the progeny of Perdita won 26 races for the splendid aggregate of £72,912. These figures do not take into account the £30,000 for which Diamond Jubilee was sold to the Argentine. Besides the great deeds of Persimmon on the race-course, he was a great success at the stud. Among other good animals he sired was the illustrious Sceptre.

From 1886 to 1909 Dick Marsh won King Edward £146,128 in stakes. The stallions, including Persimmon, Diamond Jubilee and Florizel II, earned over £200,000 in stud-fees, and the sale of His Majesty's horses realized £77,000, figures that were given in the book written by Marsh.

Another horse of which Marsh had the highest opinion was Friar Marcus, the fastest horse, no doubt, he ever had to handle. This horse was by Cicero out of the Persimmon mare Prim Nun. Friar Marcus, after a successful career on the Turf, afterwards went to the stud at Sandringham and was the sire of a great number of winners; from 1918 to 1938 his progeny won 36 races, to the value of £143,672. Among them was Friar's Daughter, dam of the unbeaten Bahram.

Although King George V did not have many good horses under Marsh's charge from 1911 to 1924, he won close on 100 races. One of the first horses to win for him was Dorando, named after the wonderful little Marathon-runner in the Olympic Games of 1908. Weathervane won him the Greenham Stakes at Newbury, just as Minoru did for King Edward. Weathervane also won the Royal Hunt Cup (1923). London Cry won the Goodwood Stakes in the presence of the King and Queen in 1924. That was Marsh's last year of training and, on his retiring, Willie Jarvis took over the King's horses at Egerton House.

There were not many better amateur riders in his day than the Hon. George Lambton, who, during his successful riding-career, admitted having broken every bone in his body. The legacy of those accidents left him with a slight limp. His exploits in the saddle were told in his most readable book under the title of *Men and Horses I have Known*. For many years, he was trainer to Lord Derby and gained instant success. Such high-class horses as Swynford (perhaps the most handsome horse he ever turned

out), Sansovino, Tranquil, Colorado, Phalaris and Hyperion were
numbered among his great winners.

His three most successful years as a trainer were in 1906, 1911,
and 1912, in each of which he headed the list of Winning
Trainers. The amount in stakes his charges won during those
years amounted to over £100,000. One of the smallest horses
he trained was Hyperion, winner of the Derby and St. Leger of
1933, and the little chestnut, in after life, headed the list of
sires on five occasions. The Stanley House master won the
Eclipse twice, with Swynford and Caerleon ; the Northumberland Plate three times, with Reminiscence, Princess Florizel and
The Tylt, and the Ebor Handicap, with March Along. He
achieved handicap successes, with Eos in the Cambridgeshire ;
Dorigen in the Lincolnshire Handicap ; Glacis, Spithead and
Damascus in the Chester Cup, and Donnithorne and March
Along in the Manchester Cup. His successes in the Liverpool
Summer Cup were gained with : Canterbury Pilgrim (1896),
who became the foundation of Lord Derby's famous stud ;
Glasalt (1902), Chaucer (1905 and 1906) ; Swynford (1910) ;
Redhead (1920) ; Pharos (1924), and Zane Grey (1932). The
Hon. George Lambton also turned out six winners of the
Liverpool Autumn Cup at Lord Derby's home meeting. One of
the best mares he ever trained was Diadem, with whom Steve
Donoghue got on so well and on whom he won many valuable
races. A truly remarkable man was the Hon. George and one
of the most popular trainers of his day. There has been no more
knowledgeable man in Turf-matters in my time.

Succeeding the Hon. George Lambton in 1926 as Lord Derby's
trainer, Frank Butters gained instant success with such splendid
performers as Fairway and Toboggan, with whom he won the
St. Leger, the Eclipse, and the Oaks. Before Toboggan's success,
he won the Oaks for Lord Durham with Beam, a triumph he
repeated in 1932 with the Aga Khan's Udaipur, having trained
for this owner since 1931. Frank Butters headed the list of
Winning Trainers on eight occasions and, in 1934, won 79 races
worth £88,844. In 1932 he won 62 races of the value of £72,436.
In 1949 he won 20 races, with £71,721—a record of which he is
entitled to be proud. He has won the Oaks six times with Beam
(1927), Toboggan (1928), Light Brocade (1934), Udaipur (1932),
Steady Aim (1946), and Masaka (1948), and the Derby twice,
with Mahmoud (1936) and Bahram (1935). The latter was the
best of his Classic winners.

The year after he started to train for the Aga Khan, he won
the Oaks with Udaipur and the St. Leger with Firdaussi (1932),
and the Doncaster win of the latter must have given him the
greatest satisfaction, his four runners in the race finishing first,

second, fourth and fifth. In 1934 he turned out nine winners
in the four days at Ascot, including Felicitation with whom he
won the Churchill Stakes and the Gold Cup the following day.
Other good stayers he has trained were Bosworth and Umidad.
He trained Petition for Sir Alfred Butt and won the Victoria Cup
and the Eclipse with him. Migoli's win in the Prix de L'Arc de
Triomphe will probably remain longest in his memory, for the
gallant grey helped to put the British thoroughbred on its pedestal
again. Owing to the accident with which he met in the Autumn
of 1949, Frank Butters has retired from training and has handed
the Aga Khan's horses over to Marcus Marsh, a son of Richard
Marsh. Frank Butters has every reason to review his many great
racing triumphs with a deal of satisfaction, for there is only one living trainer who has had more Classic winners through his
hands.

No modern trainer has turned out more Classic winners than
Fred Darling from the time he stepped into his father's shoes
and started training at Beckhampton. His father, Sam Darling,
trained two Derby winners for Mr. Gubbins—Galtee More and
Ard Patrick—and when, after retiring from riding, he under-
studied his father he could not have had a finer tutor. He first
topped the list of Winning Trainers in 1926, the year that
Coronach (who died in November, 1949, in America at a great
age) won the Derby. This was not Beckhampton's first winner
of the Derby, as Lord Woolavington won with Captain Cuttle
in 1922. Steve Donoghue rode both these great horses, as he
did Manna in the same race in 1925, but Freddie Fox rode
Cameronian for Mr. J. Dewar in 1931. That was the year when
the "void nominations through death" was quashed. Other
Derby winners he trained were Bois Roussel, Pont l'Eveque (which
was his personal property), and Owen Tudor. Not until 1941
and 1942 did Fred Darling succeed in training a winner of the
Oaks. Successes in the fillies race came with Commotion (1941)
and Sun Chariot when, during the war-years, the Classic races
were run on the July Course at Newmarket. Gordon Richards
has always contended that Sun Chariot was the best filly he has
ever ridden.

Fred Darling won the St. Leger three times: in 1916 with
Hurry On (whom he regards as the best horse he ever trained),
Coronach (1926), and Sun Chariot (1942). Two great fillies he
trained were Tiffin and Myrobella and he also prepared Pasch,
winner of the Two Thousand Guineas and Eclipse (1938), and
Big Game, who won the Two Thousand Guineas for the King
in 1942. Had not illness curtailed his activities and compelled
him to turn his stable over to Noel Murless (who in his first
season, 1948, headed the list of Winning Trainers with 63 won,

to the value of £66,542), no doubt Fred Darling would be adding other Classics to his already remarkable score.

R. C. (" Dick ") Dawson gave up training so as to have health to enjoy his retirement. He is one of the oldest, if not *the* oldest, of living trainers. Bob Armstrong, if not " Atty " Persee, may be able to concede him a year or two, but I doubt it. At the stables at Whatcombe, Dawson turned out such Classic winners as Diophon, Blenheim and Salmon Trout. The inner history of the St. Leger win of the latter horse has never been written and I doubt if it ever will be. The true facts would make sensational reading, but R. C. Dawson's confidence in his charge winning can be said to have been justified. Blenheim was bred by Lord Carnarvon, who sold him to the Aga Khan : he won the 1930 Derby with him and subsequently sold him to America, where he has turned out a stud-success. R. C. Dawson, besides training Mumtaz Mahal (probably the fastest filly of all time, for she still holds the time-record for a sprint at Newmarket), also trained Trigo, who won both the Derby and the St. Leger of 1929 for Mr. Barnett. R. C. Dawson, no doubt, had his love for racing engendered by having won the Grand National with Drogheda as far back as 1898, but he did not come to England from Ireland to train until many years later.

Another good horse he trained for Trigo's owner was Athford, with whom he won the Jubilee in 1929. For several years, R. C. Dawson trained for Sir Edward Hulton, the newspaper-proprietor. He won the 1916 (war) Derby at Newmarket with Fifinella, who won the Oaks of the same year ; but this filly, when at the stud, never threw anything as good as herself. Of R. C. Dawson's Handicap wins, Charley's Mount was the easiest to remember, in the Cesarewitch of 1924, when he started at 100 to 1. Dawson also won the same race for the Aga Khan with Ut Majeur in 1930. He also won the Cambridgeshire in 1915 with Sir Edward Hulton's Silver Tag, the Liverpool Autumn Cup of 1926 with Doushka. R. C. Dawson was at the top of the list of Winning Trainers : in 1916 with 32 races of the value of £16,386 ; in 1924 with 26 races to his credit of the value of £48,857, and in 1929 with 58 races of the value of £74,754.

When Alec Taylor retired, Joe Lawson took over the reins of office at Manton. Lord Astor, among other owners, left horses with him and he won the Two Thousand Guineas for this patron with Court Martial, and the Oaks with Pennycomequick. Joe Lawson holds the record of having won more money in stakes in one season than any previous trainer. This was in 1931, when he won 69 races of the value of £93,899. In that year, he won the Ascot Gold Cup with Trimdon, who won the same race the following year, as did Tiberius in 1935. His Classic successes were gained with Orwell, Pay Up, Kingsway, and Court Martial. With Dancing Time he won the One Thousand Guineas, and the latter event and the Oaks with Exhibitionist and Galatea II. He also trained Rhodes Scholar to win the Eclipse. When Joe Lawson left Manton in 1947 George Todd took over the establishment and Lawson went to Newmarket to train, and has kept up his good average of winners.

Captain Cecil Boyd-Rochfort, the Freemason Lodge trainer, enjoyed two particularly successful seasons in 1937 and 1938 when, each year, he " headed the list " with just on 90 races won of the value of over £100,000. He trains those horses bred by the King at Sandringham, and in 1946 he won the One Thousand Guineas for His Majesty with Hypericum, and the Oaks of 1944 with Hycilla. Before this, he won the One Thousand Guineas with Brown Betty, one of the most beautiful little fillies in the matter of looks in my time. He subsequently trained Rising Light, who won the Jockey Club Stakes in the Royal colours. Kingstone was another good horse he trained for the King. One of his lucky races has been the Jubilee, which he has won four times.

For the American sportsman, Mr. William Woodward, he has trained four Classic winners, as well as the Eclipse winner, Royal Minstrel, who also credited him with the Victoria Cup. Other Eclipse winners he has trained have been Loaningdale and Boswell and also the Ascot Gold Cup winners Precipitation and Flares. Another good horse with which he did well was Persian Gulf who is now at the stud—not forgetting that he won the St. Leger with Black Tarquin, also the property of Mr. William Woodward.

During the comparatively few years Fred (" Sam ") Armstrong trained for the Maharajah Gaekwar of Baroda, he won races of the stake value of over £172,000, and his wins for this Indian owner included the St. Leger of 1947 with Sayajirao. One of the best-trained Classic winners of my recollection was My Babu, winner of the Two Thousand Guineas (1948). Armstrong did well with moderate horses when he trained at Middleham, but he has done even better since taking up his training-quarters at Newmarket in March, 1946. Since then, he has turned out 223 winners.

Jack Jarvis, the Park Lodge trainer, has had horses to prepare for Lord Rosebery for a good many years now. He turned out Classic winners in Ellangowan and Plack for the Earl's father. He won the Derby with Blue Peter and Ocean Swell (1939 and 1944) and the St. Leger with Sandwich (1931). The best stayer he has trained, so far, was Golden Myth, with whom he won the Ascot Gold Cup in 1922 ; he again won the race in 1933 with

Foxhunter and in 1939 with Fly On. Jack Jarvis has also found
the Eclipse his lucky race, as he has carried off the rich stake
three times, with Golden Myth, Miracle and Blue Peter, the last-
named pair the property of Lord Rosebery, his chief patron. He
has also done well for Lord Milford with Honeyway and other
useful horses, as he did with Flamenco with whom he won the
Lincolnshire Handicap in 1935. It was in 1939 that he headed
the list of Winning Trainers, winning 34 races of the value of
£56,219.

It was in 1908 that Charles Morton, training for Mr. Jack Joel,
came out on top of the leading trainers of the year with 20 races
won of the value of £26,431. Prior to that, the Berkshire trainer
had trained Glass Doll to win the Oaks and, three years subsequently, he won the Derby for his chief patron with the game
Sunstar, whom the French jockey, George Stern, rode to victory.
C. Morton also won his first Oaks with Our Lassie as far back
as 1903. One of the most popular handicappers to carry Mr.
Joel's colours was Dean Swift, who won the City and Suburban
twice. It was also in 1908 that Morton won the St. Leger with
Your Majesty, that race placing him at the top of the tree of trainers for that year. Morton also won the St. Leger with Black Jester,
who also won the City and Suburban. Among owners for whom
C. Morton trained were Abington Baird, the amateur rider of that
time, "Boss" Croker, of Tammany Hall fame, and Lily Langtry,
who afterwards became Lady de Bathe. A great little man was
Charles Morton and a very able trainer. If he had a fault it was
his gambling propensities, which more than once got him into
financial trouble, as he related in his book.

There was no more severe trainer than George Blackwell, who
trained Rock Sand when that horse won the Derby of 1903. He
was early to appreciate the merits of Danny Maher, the American
jockey, who rode for him whenever available. One of Blackwell's
finest training-performances was the winning of the Cesarewitch
of 1898 with Chaleureux, a horse that was bred by Mr. Elliott
Hutchison, " Special Commissioner " of the *Sporting Life* at that
time. Blackwell bought Chaleureux out of a selling-race, for a
small figure and landed a big gamble with him in the Cesarewitch,
the horse starting a comparatively short-priced favourite, 75 to 20.

H. S. Persse ("Atty" as he has always been known to a whole
host of friends, both in Ireland—land of his birth—and in
England), when he was at the zenith of his fame as a trainer, had
such horses as The Tetrarch, Tetratema and Mr. Jinks under his
charge for Major Dermot McCalmont, who rode as an amateur
in this country from 1909 to 1913. "Atty" Persse was a very
fine horseman and I remember seeing him ride Aunt May when
that mare was third to Ascetic Silver and Red Lad in the Grand

SIR HUGO CUNLIFFE OWEN.
Ascot, 1924.

LORD DERBY. Ascot, 1926.

LORD ASTOR LEADING IN SAUCY SUE,
F. BULLOCK UP. Oaks, 1925

[Facing page 164

MR. "BOB" SIEVIER   MR. SOLLY JOEL

MR. AND MRS. J. A. DEWAR.   Ascot, 1935.

National of 1906. Not only has he been a great trainer, but he
is an authority on all matters connected with the Horse and has
written a treatise on training. He still trains for Major McCalmont
and among his patrons is Lord Sefton, for whom he has won a
large number of races. Persse will go down to posterity as having trained The Tetrarch, a horse—because of his curious grey
markings—known as the " Spotted Wonder ", and who was
probably the fastest two-year-old of all time. Unfortunately, he
broke down at the end of his first season on the Turf and never
ran as a three-year-old.

Richard Wootton, an Australian, was the greatest trainer of
moderate-class horses of the period under discussion. He trained
for Sir Edward Hulton, but, though he fancied Lomond, Storn-
away and Shogun in their respective years, success dodged him
in the Classics. His sons, Frank and Stanley, were great jockeys.
Fine a rider as Frank Wootton was, he never rode the winner of
a Classic. It was in 1913 that " Dick " Wootton headed the list
of Winning Trainers, with 66 races of the value of £28,284.

When the Hon. George Lambton gave up training for Lord
Derby and College Leader (who succeeded him) died, Walter
Earl (the former jockey) was installed trainer at Stanley House,
and he soon made good in that capacity. He won all the five
war-substitute Classic races for his chief patron, the Two Thousand Guineas with Garden Path, the One Thousand Guineas with
Herringbone and Sun Stream, the Derby with Watling Street
(now at the stud), and he also prepared Gulf Stream to win his
Lordship the Eclipse Stakes. Half-way through the 1949 season,
Walter Earl was taken seriously ill and was compelled to take a
rest, but he resumed training in the spring of 1950.

Like his father, William Nightingall, Walter Nightingall has
done remarkably well in his profession and in 1943 he headed
the list of Winning Trainers. He was then training for Miss
Dorothy Paget, for whom he won the Derby with Straight Deal,
who was ridden in that race by T. Carey, who is now training.
In 1949 Walter Nightingall trained that good filly Pambidian
for Mr. Claude Harper and that three-year-old proved herself
the best filly of her year up to a mile. Few trainers turn out
winners more consistently than the South Hatch (Epsom) trainer.
In 1949 he won 46 races of the value of £26,364.

The Druids Lodge trainer, Noel Cannon, is regarded as one
of our " leading trainers ". With the horses he trains privately
for Mr. James V. Rank, he turned out 33 winners to the value
of £22,188 in 1949. His best winner was Jock Scot, the winner
of the Liverpool Autumn Cup under top-weight. Noel Cannon
trained Scottish Union to win the St. Leger (1938), and this
Classic winner has made a name for himself at the stud.

M

Marcus Marsh (son of the former Egerton House trainer, Richard Marsh), is worthy of inclusion in this list, for did he not train Windsor Lad, the winner of the Derby and the St. Leger in 1934. He is now training for the Aga Khan, on the retirement of Frank Butters.

Reg Day worthily enters this list of leading trainers by virtue of what he accomplished with that good St. Leger and Ascot Gold Cup winner, Solario, to say nothing of Son-in-Law and Bracket, both of whom he trained to win the Cesarewitch. Donnetta was another good animal he trained. I knew Reg Day's father "Bushranger" Day well and know how unlucky he was, not to have won the Cambridgeshire with Malua. Still, his father never had such good horses as Son-in-Law and Solario to train and these two horses were indeed great winners for the Terrace House trainer.

CHAPTER XI

ADVANCES IN VETERINARY PRACTICE

By Dr. John A. Burkhardt, M.A., Ph.D., M.R.C.V.S.

DURING the past fifty years veterinary practice among thoroughbreds has undergone many changes. Most of these have occurred coincident with the advances of medical veterinary surgery in general and there are few techniques in use to-day which can be described as peculiar to thoroughbred or, indeed, to horse practice.

As in every other department of medicine, so in thoroughbred practice new treatments are tried for the limited number of complaints which are commonly met with. They frequently become somewhat fashionable—are excessively used and found out by the acid tests of time and experience. Some of them survive their teething troubles and eventually take their place in the practitioner's repertoire. It is, perhaps, fortunate that economics play such an important part in veterinary surgery for many treatments which have only been discarded in human practice after a too-prolonged trial are simply found " not worth the expense " in the sister profession.

On the other hand there can be no doubt that this very factor " expense " has held up progress in many forms of research in bloodstock. Experimental animals are expensive and facilities up to now have been greatly restricted. It is with a view to improving this position that The Equine Research Station at Balaton Lodge, Newmarket, has been established and maintained through the support of many bodies in this country and overseas connected with the thoroughbred industry and also through the generosity of a large number of private individuals.

It may be of interest to take stock of the situation in the veterinary field of the thoroughbred as it was in 1850 and to consider some of the more radical changes which have occurred since the beginning of the present century.

Examination for soundness has been made more precise by the use of instruments. The ophthalmoscope has made the detection of cataract more acute and allows of better definition of the eye. The improvements in modern stethoscopes permit a clearer picture in examining the heart—while the electrocardiograph, whose potentialities are as yet scarcely considered in thoroughbreds, will record photographically some of the more obscure cardiac disorders such as partial or complete heart block.

The advent of reliable anaesthetics and improvement in the technique of nerve blocking has made the diagnosis of obscure lameness more accurate and considerably easier for the practitioner. X-ray photographs of the lower limbs confirm the diagnosis of fractured pastern, pedal bone and sesamoids, although experienced practitioners find these conditions fairly simple to detect from long association with the symptoms.

The treatments for lameness have remained substantially the same over a long period of time.

Applications of heat or cold in various forms remain the only method of relieving pain while the former is essential in improving blood supply to the affected part. However, there is now evidence that diathermy may serve a very useful purpose in supplying this increased heat evenly over an inflamed area and that sprained tendons, ligaments and sore shins may be successfully treated by this method without having recourse to blistering, with its long enforced rest period, before work can be recommenced. When firing must be resorted to, and there are still cases which remain obdurate to any other form of treatment, the Deckery auto-cautery—a French type of firing iron in which the head of the instrument is heated by vapourising ether has proved a great advance over the old type irons where constant reheating is required throughout the operation. Moreover these instruments allow a very neat work in pin firing with a much more pleasant post-operative appearance.

The administration of medicine has been revolutionized by the invention of the stomach tube. Gone forever are the bad old days of standing on an upturned stable bucket while a very reluctant patient, backed into a corner of the box, dribbled the contents of a quart bottle down the sleeves and other garments of the luckless veterinarian and his assistant. These stomach tubes, made of rubber, or more recently of smooth-finished plastic, are made in three sizes, for foals, yearlings and adult horses. They can be passed through the nose into the stomach of any horse and whatever medicine is to be given can then be poured down the tube by way of a funnel or pumped in the case of large quantities from a bucket. The method is safe in skilled hands and has proved of inestimable value in all horse practices.

As regards operative surgery, the advances made in this field are relatively few. The number of specific operations has not greatly increased but the general technique of operations has benefited from experience in the human field. A better range of suturing materials with the development of sterile catgut and nylon, more careful aseptic precautions before, during and after operations; respiratory stimulants and anti-shock treatments such as the intravenous injection of glucose saline; and the use of penicillin and sulpha drugs to prevent and combat operative infection, have all combined to reduce the casualty rate and encourage the practitioner to increase his surgical work.

New operations for individual complaints are few in number. Among the more successful may be mentioned : (1) Forsell's operation for cribbiting ; (2) stripping the ventricles of the larynx in horses which " make a noise " ; (3) operation for ruptured bladder in the foal ; (4) operation for the treatment of recto vaginal fistula in the mare ; (5) Caslick's operation for suture of the vulva in the mare.

The horse is not a suitable subject for abdominal operation, nor are there many indications for opening into the abdominal cavity. A point to remember is that the introduction of tetanus anti-toxin has reduced the incidence of tetanus as a post-operative complication to a minimum and it is now a golden rule in thoroughbred practice that anti-tetanus injections are given after any surgical interference, no matter how trivial. Castration cannot, of course, be listed as a new operation being amongst the oldest surgical techniques in the world, but the instrument devised by Messrs. Haussemann and Dunn, of Chicago, is worthy of mention. This, by cutting the fibrous tissue of the cord and crushing the blood vessels contained therein at the same time, allows castration to be done on colts in the standing position preferred by owners with the minimum of risk from hæmorrhage.

Anæsthetics in horse practice have not made the progress comparable with human practice and small animal surgery. Chloroform remains the most popular and, perhaps, the most convenient of the general anæsthetics although chloral hydrate given intravenously has, in my opinion, considerably more to recommend it. A new type of anæsthetic being developed by Imperial Chemical Industries may become a general choice for operations of short duration.

Spinal anæsthesia in the horse, though not nearly so simple to administer as in cattle, has considerable practical use and is invaluable for difficult foaling cases where straining on the part of the mare must be eliminated before a malplaced foal can be brought into position for delivery.

For pre-medication or quietening a patient before a general anæsthetic, chloral hydrate given by stomach tube is to be preferred above any of the morphine derivaties which are most irregular in their action on horses in general and thoroughbreds in particular.

As regards the breeding side of the bloodstock industry, progress has been considerably more rapid during the past decade. One of the most important steps has been to establish closer contact between stud-grooms and veterinary surgeons.

This has been made possible to a large degree by the establishment of courses for stud-men which are held annually at
Newmarket under the auspices of the Animal Health Trust. The
courses are held in the spring and autumn and aim at allowing
the training of young selected men in modern methods of
breeding management and hygiene, and in allowing them an
insight into practitioners' methods. The bad old days of secrecy
on both sides are being outmoded, and it is felt that nothing but
good can result from these courses which are open to all members
of the Thoroughbred Breeders' Association to send a representative. It is only by training the young generation along
scientific lines that the veterinarians can hope to achieve best
results in those studs which he attends.

Classes on these courses deal with the subjects of stud routine
from foaling mares to the building of boxes on up-to-date lines
and visits are made to the best run studs in the Newmarket
district with a view to seeing all aspects of the business and
hearing first hand from their managers the good or bad points of
the various units in each.

Together with this increased knowledge among the lay staffs,
practitioners have been given vastly more powerful weapons
with which to fight disease on the stud. In the past, disease of
new born foals comprised an important factor in economic
losses. This problem has always been associated to some extent
with foaling in boxes in consequence of which the Australians
have taken advantage of their milder spring climate, and foal all
mares down in small paddocks which can be flood-lit by night in
case the mare is in need of assistance. Such measures are
obviously impractical in Great Britain and though joint ill has
become extremely rare thanks to better hygiene, foals are still
subject to certain post-natal infections.

Among these may be mentioned navel or joint ill which,
though nowadays, fortunately of rare occurrence, can be generally
controlled if taken in its early stages by penicillin injections.
This must be administered at frequent intervals as in human
medicine but is fortunately capable of controlling most of the
more common bacteriological infections, particularly those
caused by the groups of streptococci and staphylococci which
comprise the largest families of dangerous bacilli known to-day.

The sleepy foal disease while not responsive to penicillin is
curable with streptomycin. This disease, which is characterised
by a small weakly foal unable to rise and suck its dam, was until
the advent of streptomycin invariably fatal to those which
became infected.

The infectious diarrhœas or scours in young foals can be
very largely controlled without much loss of condition by

members of the sulpha-group of drugs which, though somewhat eclipsed from public notice by penicillin and streptomycin, form a most important group of medicines at the hand of the veterinary and medical practitioner.

Lastly, research at present in progress to control the incidence of the fatal hæmolytic jaundice in foals through incompatibility of blood groups between sire and dam leads us to hope that this problem may also be overcome in the near future.

But the greatest advances in this field of veterinary medicine have been on the subject of infertility. These advances have been made possible through the clinical investigation of Messrs. Caslick and Dimock in the United States. This country owes a great debt of gratitude to these men as well as Dr. John Hammond of Cambridge University, who, though not a veterinarian, has applied himself and his workers to investigate breeding problems in horses as in the other domestic animals.

Thanks to these men the reproductive cycle in the mare has been the subject of intensive study during the past fifteen years and results have been gratifying to breeders.

Since the breeding of racehorses is very largely an artificial business—the demand for early foals being largely contrary to nature, but essential for early two-year-olds—the problem of mares not coming into season loomed large. This problem was accentuated during the war years by the lack and poor quality of foodstuffs. Veterinarians have now two methods of treating mares for this phenomenon and nowadays it is extremely rare for a mare to return from a public stud without having been covered. The release of the egg from the ovary can be very largely controlled by an appropriate hormone injection which not only ensures " ovulation " in a high percentage of those mares treated but also can be used to reduce the number of services given by the stallion.

Infections of the genital tract can be treated with a good measure of success by Caslick's operation, and the mare's recovery can be accelerated if the operation is delayed until the beginning of the covering season by the use of penicillin. The appropriate time for this operation, and indeed for the examination of all barren mares, is during the months of September and October, when plans can be made for the next season's matings and treatments can be carried out with adequate time for recovery.

Pregnancy diagnosis can be made at an early date by those experienced in this branch though the accuracy of such diagnosis will, of course, depend on the skill of the individual. This early diagnosis is useful for mares covered during the first half of the breeding season, which have not shown to the teaser since their last service. Diagnosis is generally made at six weeks although a few mares may require a second examination after a fortnight. It is possible to give a definite diagnosis when required at four weeks after service in many maiden and barren mares, but this should only be undertaken in extreme cases as for example at the end of the season where another week's delay would rule out the question of the mare being covered again.

Treatment of ovarian cysts has very largely gone out of fashion since Caslick reported that these " cysts " were quite normal in both pregnant and non-pregnant mares. It was extensively practised but without any real success as a cure for infertility, but nowadays examination of the ovaries can be so precise that most workers in this field realise the truth of Caslick's finding. Certain types of mares still baffle the clinician but most of these behave normally the following season while those which are really bad stud propositions can be detected in very large numbers at a reasonably early stage.

From this article it will be seen that the veterinary practitioner of to-day has an easier time than his predecessor of fifty years ago. The chemist has done much to help him by the introduction of specific drugs to treat bacterial infections which killed many foals and older animals. Improved methods of administration of these drugs have rendered treatment safer both for veterinary surgeon and patient. The most important step forward, however, has been the marked improvement in relations between the practitioners and those in charge of bloodstock so that with very few exceptions both parties now treat each other as a friend and confidant.

CHAPTER XII

SOME WOMEN IN RACING

By The Hon. Mrs. George Lambton

WHEN I first went racing many years ago, the female-element formed a very small minority of regular race-goers and was confined largely to what would have been known as the leisured class. On all race-courses, there were a far greater number of men than women, more especially in the cheaper enclosures, but now the reverse is the case and there is no doubt that during the last 20 years racing has become tremend-ously popular among women of all classes and stations in life. They know, or think they know, quite a lot about it ; they study form and follow horses and often bet quite as keenly, and more frequently, than their male friends and relations, and there are many who own horses whereas, not so long ago, women-owners were rather exceptional.

I came of a family with no interest or connection with the Turf and, until I married " into racing ", an occasional visit to an Ascot meeting on the Gold Cup day had been about the limit of my experience. But one of the curious memories of my child-hood is the fact that my father, a Somersetshire squire, could tell you without hesitation the name of any Derby winner in any particular year, going back for 100 years. So I suppose there must have been some remote influence in the past history of my family, some ancestor who, perhaps, went racing long ago, but I would think it most unlikely that it was a woman !

The so-called " racing set " of those early days that I remember and into whose exclusive precincts I " gate-crashed " timidly and rather romantically, was the most select group of Edwardian society imaginable. Headed by the King, who loved racing and was never so happy as when at Newmarket, it was composed of men and women of picturesque and outstanding personality ; they went racing all the Summer, many of them hunted all the Winter and were known on the race-course as " The Regulars ".

My first introduction to them took place at a Lincoln meet-ing, and I so well remember arriving with my husband (I think on the horse-special, a way in which we often travelled), and being introduced to Mrs. Featherstonehaugh who, with Lord Cholmondeley, was walking up the course. Mrs. Featherstone-haugh, whose husband later managed King George V's stable for many years, was an inveterate race-goer and a good judge of

form. She still rarely misses a big meeting, and is always to be
seen in the Jockey Club Stand at Newmarket taking as keen an
interest as ever in the horses.

To go for a moment further into the past, and here I can only
speak from what I have been told, one of the most outstanding
personalities among women on the Turf was Caroline Duchess
of Montrose, and, I would think, one of the first big women-
owners who raced and managed a large number of horses of her
own. In those days, it was not the custom for women to race
in their own names and " Mr. Manton " was her *nom de plume*
on the Turf. She owned many good horses and had a big stud-
farm at Newmarket, where the Stanley House stables and Lord
Derby's stud-farm are now situated. On her death, her stud was
dispersed and many good horses sold, including Pilgrimage
(carrying Jeddah, 100-to-1 winner of the 1898 Derby), and her
daughter Canterbury Pilgrim, then a yearling, who became the
foundation mare of Lord Derby's stud, winning the Oaks (1896)
and being the dam of Chaucer and Swynford. To quote the
words of Mr. George Lambton when writing of the Duchess,
in *Men and Horses I have Known* :

> " She owned some of the best blood in England and she
> bred and raced many good horses, but their management
> left much to be desired and her success was not what it
> should have been. She led her trainers an anxious life and
> was capricious and changeable with regard to her jockeys,
> a failing not unusual in her sex; but with all her peculiarities,
> the Duchess was a great lady and a good sportswoman. She
> loved her horses and was a good judge of racing, and a
> great figure on the Turf."

Another woman-owner of those days, whom I remember, was
" Mr. Jersey ", the assumed name of Lily Langtry, one of the
most famous beauties of all time. When I knew her it was towards the end of her life and she had married Sir Hugo de Bathe
and lived at Regal Lodge, Kentford, just outside Newmarket.
It was a charming house with a lovely garden and she had a few
horses nearby, with Fred Darling as her trainer. He was a very
young man at the beginning of his great career and he won the
Cesarewitch for her in 1908 with Yentoi, ridden by Freddie Fox.
Before the time of which I am writing, she had owned a good
horse in Merman, who also won her the Cesarewitch (1897), the
Goodwood Cup (1899), and the Jockey Club Cup and the Ascot
Gold Cup (1900), and her colours—turquoise and fawn hoops and
turquoise cap—were very well-known to race-goers.

A very rich woman of those times, Lady Meux, widow of Sir
Henry Meux, raced under the name of " Mr. Theobalds ". She

was an eccentric and extraordinary character and I only remember
seeing her once, when she was a very old woman, at Brighton.
When she died, she left her fortune to my brother-in-law Admiral
of the Fleet Sir Hedworth Lambton, who afterwards took her
name. She bred and owned Volodyovski, by Florizel II, out of
La Reine by Rosicrucian (winner of the Derby in 1901), but she
leased the horse to an American owner, Mr. W. C. Whitney,
and he won in his name and colours. He must have been a
good horse, for the field was a very representative one and the
Duke of Portland's William the Third was second, beaten three-
quarters of a length. Lester Reiff rode Volodyovski and M.
Cannon was on William the Third.

Soon afterwards, they met again, in a mile-and-a-half race at
Hurst Park, and Volodyovski, giving 3 lbs., was beaten a short
head. In the St. Leger, with the odds of 6 to 5 laid on him, he
was beaten a neck by Mr. Leopold de Rothschild's Doricles, also
by Florizel II, out of Rosalie, a Rosicrucian mare. Volodyovski
afterwards stood at the stud at Theobald's Park, his owner's place
close to London.

A woman-owner whom I knew well and who was a character
of considerable interest, was Mrs. Arthur James. When my husband trained for the late Lord Derby, Arthur James had a few
horses in the Stanley House stable. He had been a great friend
of King Edward VII and had previously trained with him at
Egerton House. When Arthur died, his widow, to everyone's
great surprise, decided to carry on his racing-activities. Up till
then, I think, she had been more interested in the social side of
racing and entertained many house-parties for Goodwood and
Warwick, which was her home meeting, but she took over his
small stud at Coton, near Rugby, and, with George Lambton's
help and advice, bred a number of winners and met with considerable success. I think the best mare she owned was Stony Ford, by
Swynford, out of Gneiss by Rocksand, but her career was unlucky
and marred by a really tragic incident. Stony Ford was being
trained for the Oaks in 1918, towards the end of the war, when
racing was confined to Newmarket and the Classic races that year
were run on the July Course.

Lord Derby's Ferry had won the One Thousand Guineas rather
unexpectedly, starting at 50 to 1. Stony Ford did not run in that
race but proved herself much the better mare at home when training
for the Oaks, and it was decided that she should be the "selected"
from the stable and that Carslake, then the stable-jockey, should
ride her, Lord Derby giving up his prior claim. About a fortnight, or less, before the race, she hit herself and went lame and
it looked very doubtful if she would be able to run. Plans were
then changed and it was decided to start Ferry also and, naturally,

Carslake was claimed for her. Stony Ford, who was fortunately very forward in her preparation, was given long trotting exercise on the roads prior to the race and improved so much that she eventually got to the post and " Skeets " Martin, who rode a good deal for the stable in those days, was given the mount.

The favourite (6 to 4) was Mr. Faerie Cox's My Dear (by Beppo), a good mare trained by Alec Taylor and ridden by Steve Donoghue. Coming out of the dip and rising the hill, Stony Ford was nearly three lengths in front and she won the race in a canter, but half-way up the straight her rider did not keep a straight course and came across on to the near rails. Why he did this he never knew himself, but " Steve ", on the favourite, lodged an objection for bumping and boring. Actually, the bump was supposed to have taken place a long way down the course, in the early stages of the race, but the Stewards were influenced by the fact that the mare was not three lengths clear when she came across and, after a very long enquiry, felt bound to disqualify her. It was in the nature of a tragedy for her connections, because she could have won by a far bigger margin and it made not the slightest difference to the true result for she was definitely the winner on merit. Poor Martin was terribly upset, and I well remember Mr. Faerie Cox, the owner of My Dear, disappearing into the Plantation until after the excitement had died down. Mrs. James took the sad business extremely well : she had plenty of courage and was in many ways a gallant woman. Stony Ford went to the stud and bred a useful horse in Sunstone and a good one in Salmon Leap by Salmon Trout.

Salmon Leap was a big, overgrown horse and was given plenty of time to mature. He did not run as a two-year-old, and at three years he came out for the first time in August. After running twice unplaced, he finished the season with three races to his credit and £1,500 in stakes. At four years, he won the Newbury Summer Cup (1931), was third to Trimdon and Singapore in the Ascot Gold Cup (1931), won the Bibury Cup, the Dullingham Stakes at Newmarket, and the Goodwood Cup. He was kept in training when he was five years and then came the best race of his career, when he defeated Goyescas and Cameronian half-a-length and a short head in the Coronation Cup at Epsom (1932). It was a most exciting race and he was ridden as in almost all his races by Tommy Weston who, light as he was in those days, had an amazing faculty for riding big horses. After that, Salmon Leap ran in the Ascot Gold Cup, where he was second to Trimdon with a field of good horses behind him, beaten two lengths, and he was then retired to the stud. He stood at his owner's place near Rugby, but he did not really have the success he merited. Perhaps he lacked that all-important

quality of speed, but, at the same time, his victory in the Coronation Cup was a brilliant performance.

Mrs. James also won the Victoria Cup at Hurst Park in two
consecutive years with the own brothers, Phalaros and Herbalist,
both of them by Phalaris out of Picardel, by Picton out of
Fascination, who was out of Charm.   Phalaros was, I think, the
better of the two : he carried 8 st. 3 lbs. and won by four lengths
from Capture Him.   He afterwards dead-heated for the Salford
Borough Handicap at Manchester, and for the July Cup at Newmarket with Diomedes.   He was a very good-looking brown
horse and was sold to go to the U.S.A.   Herbalist, a very good-
looking, chestnut colt, carried 7 st. 3 lbs. and was ridden by
Weston, beating a useful field of horses.   Afterwards, he won
the Voltigeur Handicap at York and, later on, the Town Moor
Handicap at Doncaster and was sold to go to France.

Another son of Picardel that I must mention, was Pricket,
bred by Mrs. James from Twelve Pointer.   He won the Duke of
York Handicap as a three-year-old in 1931, remained in training
until he was 10 years old, winning innumerable races and becoming quite a hero with the racing-public.   He was a sweet little
horse of great character and finished his life ridden as a hack by
my children.

The lilac jacket of the James's family is still happily to be seen
on the race-course, for Mrs. James' great nephew, Colonel Burns,
inherited her bloodstock and is keenly interested in racing.

During the years after the 1914–18 War, racing came into
its own again and was tremendously popular, more people
than ever crowded the race-courses, rather in the same way
as we have seen of late years.   Harry Cottrill had a large stable
of horses at Seven Barrows, Lambourn, and Mrs. Sofer
Whitburn was one of his principal patrons.   She and her
husband, Colonel Whitburn, owned a number of horses in
partnership : they ran for a long time entirely in her name,
and her colours, blue and white hoops were very often in
front.   Seven Barrows was a delightful establishment on
the Lambourn Downs and I think the gallops in those days
were some of the best in England ; it was certainly the most
lovely place to train horses.   The master of it, Harry Cottrill,
was a very fine stableman and turned out a great number
of winners.   He had that great asset, the most wonderful and
irrepressible spirits, was a confirmed optimist and, no matter what
happened, if you trained with him you must have had a great
deal of fun.   " This *will* win " was one of his great expressions
and, whether it did or not, Harry always came up smiling and
had another " certainty " for his friends ; but he was really a
very shrewd and clever trainer, and turned out a great number

of winners, and when his money was " on " it was worth following. It was a great loss to racing-people when he gave up
training after the war and turned his attention to farming in a
big way. I believe he is just as enthusiastic now about his Jersey
cattle as he was about his race-horses.

Lincoln and Chester were, in particular, happy hunting-grounds
for the Whitburns and Mrs. Whitburn won the Chester Cup two
years in succession with Chivalrous (1922 and 1923). She raced
under the assumed name of " Mr. C. Burn " when winning the
Great Metropolitan with Annecy in 1914. Annecy had won the
race in 1913, but not in her ownership, and he was trained by
Atty Persse ; but in 1922, when Chivalrous won the Chester Cup
he ran in her own name. Carrying 7 st. 5 lbs., he was ridden
by an Australian lightweight jockey, G. Smith, who put up 4 lbs.
overweight and, making the whole of the running, he won by
four lengths " hard held ". Happy Man ran in the race, but had
a bad accident in it which kept him off the race-course until the
following year. Chivalrous afterwards won the King Coal Stakes
at Manchester, beating Golden Myth, the winner of the Ascot
Cup, by four lengths, and at the end of that year Mrs. Whitburn
was fifth in the list of Winning Owners, with £16,214 in stakes.

In 1923 Chivalrous again won the Chester Cup (carrying 8 st.
11 lbs.) and, ridden by Michael Beary, again led from start to
finish. This is an unusual thing for a horse to do over two and
a-quarter miles, but the Chester course is a law unto itself,
and when Damascus (1935) won the Cup for my husband,
Humphrey Foster, who rode him, had the same orders and won
in the same way.

Chivalrous then ran in the Ascot Cup (1923), where he was
fourth to Happy Man and Silurian. He came into the straight
leading, but went slightly lame in the race and ran no more. He
won £7,340 in stakes, not to mention two large Cheshire cheese.
By Amadis, out of Courtesy by Isinglass, he was bought for
500 gns. from Mr. Donald Fraser, who had given 100 gns. for
him as a foal.

I think the woman who, perhaps, had most influence on the
Turf in the years of which I write was Lady James Douglas,
although she was probably a less well-known figure to the general
public than some others. She had the distinction of being the
first woman to win the Derby, but was primarily a breeder and
more interested in selling yearlings than in racing them. She
won four Classic races : the Oaks with Bayuda in 1919 ; Gainsborough was a Triple Crown winner for her in 1918, at the time
when racing was confined to Newmarket. She also bred Rose
of England who won the Oaks (1930) for Lord Glanely.

Lady James Douglas had the great advantage of Alec Taylor's

help and advice in her racing-activities and, had it not been for him, I believe she might have parted with Gainsborough as a yearling. When the horse came up for sale as a yearling in 1916, Alec Taylor had a great fancy for him and Lady James asked him what reserve she should put on him. He begged her not to take less than 2,000 gns., which was quite a high price in those days of rather precarious wartime racing, and when the colt was passed out of the ring at that figure, the owner asked Alec Taylor to train him at Manton. Before he got there, however, she was offered 2,000 gns. and then 2,500 gns., but her trainer advised her to keep him, and that is how Gainsborough went to Manton and repaid so brilliantly the confidence of his owner and trainer. He sired many good horses. Perhaps his best son was Hyperion, winner of the Derby and St. Leger in 1933 and the sire of several outstanding fillies.

Bayuda won the Oaks for Lady James in the following year, when it was run at Epsom for the first time after the war. She beat Roseway, winner of the One Thousand Guineas and to whom she had been fourth in that race, and there is no doubt that it was her superior stamina that caused the reversal of form. She was retired to her owner's stud, but her record was rather disappointing, although her first foal, by Hurry On, fetched 4,000 gns. From the year 1920 to 1938, 107 yearlings were sold from the Harwood Stud averaging 1,500 gns.: a remarkable achievement and surely a record.

No account of these years would be complete without mention of Lady Barbara Smith, a delightful character and an enthusiast where horses of all sorts were concerned. Daughter of Lord Coventry, she was brought up in Worcestershire with horses and hounds. When I first knew her she was no longer a young woman and she and her husband, Gerald Smith, lived in a charming house at Newmarket where, in the old days, Matthew Dawson had his stables. They were the kindest and most hospitable couple and greatly liked by everyone who came into contact with them. Lord Coventry owned a good mare in Verdict, which he bred, who won the Cambridgeshire (1923) for him, beating Epinard a neck, and the Coronation Cup (1924) as a four-year-old. She was not in the Stud Book, being by Shogun ex Finale, but in addition to being a very good race-mare, she bred a number of good winners, including Quashed, described by Mr. Somerville Tattersall as " the gamest mare of all time ".

Lady Barbara inherited her father's stud and leased the progeny of Verdict : first, Versicle, who won four races as a two-year-old, was second in the Queen Mary Stakes, and won the Ribblesdale Stakes at three years, and then Quashed, to Lord Stanley, the eldest son of the late Lord Derby. For him, Quashed won the

Oaks in 1935 and the following year the Ascot Gold Cup after a great race in which she beat the American champion Omaha a short head and earned Mr. Tattersall's description of her. In all, she won nine and a-half races and £18,997 in stakes. Lady Barbara sold the yearlings from her small stud for a number of years for very big prices, but somehow the blood has not quite fulfilled its early promise.

When a now-famous trainer, Cecil Boyd Rochfort, started at Newmarket as a young man, one of his first patrons was Florence, Lady Nunburnholme, and he won many races for her. I think one of his first big successes was the victory of Perhaps So in the Stewards Cup at Goodwood in 1926. Perhaps So was a very good-looking mare by Hapsburg, out of Pert by Eager, and was five years old at the time. She had been bought as a foal by Captain Rochfort, who gave only 150 gns. for her, and she had won at two, three and four years previously. She started in the Stewards Cup at the remunerative price of 100 to 6 against and her connections were reputed to have won a good deal of money. She was bought at the end of that year by Mr. George Lambton for an American client.

In the previous year, Lady Nunburnholme had won the Great Jubilee Handicap with Amethystine, a race which she again won with Racedale (1931), the latter being bred by her from Perfection, who was also the dam of Loaningdale, winner of the Eclipse Stakes in 1933, the year after her death. " Lady Nun ", as her friends called her, was a personality and a woman of great character, a very good friend to those she liked. She must have been very good-looking as a young woman, but when I knew her she was well over middle-age and the widow of a very rich shipowner in the North. Warter Priory, her beautiful home in Yorkshire, was a centre of entertaining and famous for its wonderful shooting and exceptionally beautiful gardens. We used to stay there for York races, and very pleasant it was, for she was a wonderful hostess, giving her guests delightful company and the best of everything. I often remember hoping so much I would be asked there.

Another patron of Captain Boyd Rochfort's stable, very prominent among women owners, is Lady Zia Wernher. Daughter of the Grand Duke Michael of Russia, she has lived all her life in England and she and her husband, Sir Harold Wernher, have been very successful in breeding and racing their own horses. They own the Someries Stud at Newmarket and, as you enter the gates, facing you is a memorial-stone to Double Life, the foundation mare of their stud. By Bachelor's Double, that great sire of brood mares, out of St. Joan, she won six races and over £5,600 in stakes, including the Perkins Memorial, the Chesterfield

MRS. M. GLENISTER LEADING IN NIMBUS, E. C. ELLIOTT UP. Derby, 1949.

LADY JAMES DOUGLAS HOLDING GAINSBOROUGH, J. CHILDS UP.

MRS. G. H. MILLER LEADING IN MID-DAY SUN, M. BEARY UP. Derby, 1937

THE DUCHESS OF NORFOLK AND LADY IRWIN

Cup, the Duke of York Stakes, and the Cambridgeshire (1929) —carrying a penalty and beating Vatout a neck. She was bought by Captain Rochfort for 600 gns. and her stud-career was a great one, for she bred Precipitation (winner of the Ascot Cup), Casanova, Hollywell, and Persian Gulf. Both Precipitation and Persian Gulf stand at the Someries Stud, and Precipitation has sired many winners, including Airborne, winner of the Derby in 1946. He is a grand-looking chestnut horse of great substance and quality, with the best of limbs, while Persian Gulf resembles his sire Bahram in that he is a horse of very beautiful quality. In his first season, he is the sire of Abadan, said to be the best two-year-old in Ireland. I think he has a great future and will bring more success to the Someries Stud.

My memory is now turning back again to the years 1914–18 of the previous war, when many people connected with racing and training migrated to Newmarket from the country owing to the fact that racing was more or less centralized there. Among them came Sir Robert Wilmot with a small string of horses and, with him, his two daughters. They were, I think, almost the first girls to ride and " do " their own horses, certainly the first I had ever seen, and I well remember the small sensation they created when they first rode out on Newmarket Heath in very neat breeches and tweed coats like a couple of boys, a sight not so familiar in those days as it is now. They were both very good riders and had been schooled and trained by their father until they were certainly in the top class.

Kathleen, the elder, married after the war and for some time ran a horse-dealing business with her husband in Leicestershire, but Miss Norah Wilmot carried on her father's stable and still lives and trains in her old home at Binfield Grove. I remember Sir Robert's great wish was for her to be allowed to take out a trainer's licence, and if ever a woman was well qualified to do so it would be her. A fine rider, with all the knowledge of stable-management acquired from practical experience, she is certainly the equal of many men in the profession. But the Jockey Club have always been adamant over this question, and I must say I think rightly so : once the door was open and women allowed into the sacred precincts of the weighing-room on the official footing as trainers, what is to stop them from becoming jockeys too ? No doubt many in these days have that ambition, but although there are plenty of embryo " National Velvets " in the making, I think it will be a very long time before feminism asserts itself to this extent ; in fact, the Turf will remain a last ditch !

However, do not let me decry the women who have in many instances really made it a profession and with the greatest success. Many trainers during the last war could not have kept their

stables going without the assistance of their wives, and how many
women carried on the business most gallantly for those away—in
times made more difficult by wartime conditions. And, apart from
the war, women are able to be of the greatest assistance, both in
and out of the stable : entries and book-keeping are an important
part of the business, and an intimate acquaintance with the form-
book is an advantage that cannot be overestimated.

Miss Marjorie Nightingall has been assistant to her brother,
Walter Nightingall, for many years and is as good a judge of both
'chasing and the flat as any man and has made her life in racing.
Mrs. Victor Tabor will be remembered by many readers as a very
well-known figure at Epsom, where her husband trained for many
years and where she took a most active part in everything to do
with his stable. She was extremely popular and greatly liked by
everyone who came into contact with her. A brilliant personality
in the steeplechasing world was Mrs. Fulke Walwyn. She kept
her husband's small stable going during the war and, when it
afterwards became one of the largest and most influential of the
jumping-establishments, she played a very great part in its success
and her recent tragic death was a cruel blow to everyone who
knew and loved her.

Writing of Fulke Walwyn's stable brings me to Miss Dorothy
Paget, for whom he trains a large number of steeplechase horses.
I do not remember in what year Miss Paget first came into racing,
but I think it was in 1930 that she first registered her colours.
She was the daughter of Lord Queenborough and she and her
sister inherited a great deal of money from their American mother,
Pauline Whitney. She must also have inherited her great love
of racing from both sides of her family, for the Whitneys have
always been big supporters of the Turf and their colours were
very popular when the Americans first came racing over here.

Miss Paget's first big success as an owner was with Golden Miller,
one of the best and most beautiful steeplechase horses of our time.
She then trained with Basil Briscoe, who as a young man started
training a small string of jumpers at his home, Longstowe, in
Cambridgeshire. He soon made his name, for he had great ability
—in fact, brilliance—and came to Newmarket, where he trained
at Beechwood Exning, mainly for Miss Paget. Golden Miller's
story is full of romance. Bought as a yearling at the Dublin
Sales for 100 gns., Briscoe paid £500 for him and as a three-year-
old hunted him in the Fitzwilliam country. I believe he was a
very indifferent hunter, but he re-sold him to a patron, Mr.
Philip Carr, for £1,000 after he had won over hurdles and been
beaten a head in his first steeplechase. Later on, Miss Paget
expressed a wish to buy a young horse likely to develop into a
high-class steeplechaser, and she gave £6,000 for Golden Miller

in the Winter of 1931. She was well repaid for, not only did he win the Grand National, but his five victories in the Cheltenham Gold Cup are a Turf record that is unbeaten. She must, indeed, have experienced the fulfilment of a supreme ambition.

I was lucky enough to see the race for the Gold Cup at Cheltenham between Golden Miller and Thomond in 1935 : it was one which no one could forget, but in one way a tragedy, as the National was only 14 days ahead. I believe Thomond was thought to be unlikely to run in the race, which would then have been easy for Golden Miller and part of his preparation, but, as it was, both horses ran the race of their careers and I think it probably lost Golden Miller his second National although that can never be proved. From the turn into the straight at Cheltenham, the two horses came away from the rest of the field and raced neck and neck, jumping each fence together at a terrific pace, ridden by two great artists in their profession, Wilson and Speck. They came over the last fence side by side and had a terrific struggle in the run in, Golden Miller winning by three-quarters of a length with Kellsborough Jack five lengths away third. Thomond, although he ran third in the National soon afterwards, never, I think, got over the race. He was rather a delicate horse and never won again, but Golden Miller went on to win another Gold Cup the following year. It was undoubtedly one of the finest and gamest performances on the part of both horses that has ever been seen, and one that will live for ever in Steeplechasing history.

Those years were memorable for Miss Paget for, not only did she own Golden Miller, but also Insurance, the best hurdle-race horse of the day. He was also bought from Mr. Philip Carr by Basil Briscoe at the same time as Golden Miller, and he won the Champion Hurdle at Cheltenham two years in succession on the same day as his stable companion triumphed in the Gold Cup —what a wonderful record for an owner and trainer. Since those days, Miss Paget has had many more successes and has well deserved them, for no doubt her one absorbing interest is her horses.

She has also raced very extensively on the flat, and in 1933 she laid herself out to buy the best brood-mares that she could and, at the December Sales that winter, she gave 21,000 gns. for three mares. They were Dorigen, winner of the Lincoln Handicap carrying 9 st. 1 lb. ; Salome, winner of the Atlanta Stakes and the Newmarket Oaks, and Speckle, winner of the Atlanta Stakes and covered by Blandford, but Good Deal, the mare which bred her the Derby winner Straight Deal, was bought in 1936 for 1,800 gns. Straight Deal, by Solario, was bred at his owner's stud at Elsenham, near Bishop's Stortford, and was sent to Walter

Nightingall as a yearling in 1941. He won the wartime Derby on the July Course in 1943. It was a thrilling race in which, ridden by T. Carey, he beat Umidad a head with Nasrullah half-a-length away and a good field of horses behind him, including Persian Gulf (who was fourth), Pink Flower, Kingsway, and Way In. That same year, Miss Paget had a good two-year-old in Orestes, who ran four times and was unbeaten, winning at Salisbury and Ascot previous to his successes in The Coventry Stakes and the Middle Park Plate, but his three-year-old career did not fulfil his early promise and he was sold at the end of it for 5,100 gns. to go to the stud.

I remember Mrs. J. V. Rank, before the war, first appearing on a race-course and making a sensation by her very pretty face and rather exciting tilts against the Ring. Since then, she has become a very serious and interested owner and, although her husband has a large private stable at Druid's Lodge, she has a few horses of her own which are trained by Jack Leach at Newmarket. She is a good judge, and a determined bidder if she fancies a yearling.

The Duke and Duchess of Norfolk's Arundel Stable has been very much to the fore this year and has enjoyed its best season since it was started by the Duchess in 1942. The stable has won 41 races with 20 horses, and £19,701 in stakes: a great achievement and one of which the Duchess may well be proud, for it was under her management and organization that it was started during the war, and she has carried it on most successfully in later years. She and the Duke trained previously at Michel Grove with Victor Gilpin and, when he joined the Army at the beginning of the war, the Duchess volunteered to carry on the stable and train the horses with the head-lad holding the licence. This she did at Michel Grove for two years, under considerable difficulties, for it must have been very hard work going over from Arundel every morning in all weathers to superintend the work of the horses—which she never failed to do—and at the same time carry on the many other duties that fell to her share during the war.

When the training-grounds at Michel Grove became impossible owing to the encroachments of the Army, the Duchess moved the whole establishment to Arundel, where gallops had to be made in the Park and everything reorganized. It was a most brilliant effort and has met with well-deserved reward, for the stable has become one of the most important in the South. Among the women who go racing to-day, she is certainly an outstanding figure, with a great knowledge of horses and a delightful and infectious enthusiasm for anything to do with them. I remember her as a very little girl following her step-father Lord Rosebery fearlessly over the biggest fences in the

Whaddon Chase country, on a wonderful thoroughbred pony which eventually came into the possession of my own children.

I think one of the horses she liked best was a sweet little chestnut mare, Honest Penny by Fair Trial, whom she leased from the breeder and who won her a number of races during the war, and was seldom out of the first three. Banco, another horse of hers, was a big-race hero, for he won the City and Suburban in 1947, and this year his full brother Suivi has done good service, winning four races and never being out of the first three in seven attempts. W. Smyth trains for the Duke and Duchess and, with T. Burn riding for them, the combination of owners, trainer, and jockey is a very happy one.

Mrs. Glenister, who was the fortunate owner of the Derby winner of 1949, is to be congratulated on a very good and game horse. Nearco's son Nimbus is to take up his duties at the stud this season and I was much impressed with him when I saw him at the Hamilton Stud. He is undoubtedly a very beautiful horse of great quality and substance and has all the necessary attributes which go to make a successful stallion. It was a thousand pities that his career was cut short at three years and that he could not represent this country in the Prix de L'Arc de Triomphe, which was originally the very sporting intention of his owner.

And now I must refer to the latest recruit to the ranks of women-owners, for the whole Racing world has lately acclaimed with delight the success of Princess Elizabeth. That she and the Queen should have entered into partnership in a steeplechase horse has given intense satisfaction to all National Hunt enthusiasts and that the horse is a good one and has already won an important race is all that could be desired. When Mr. Cazalet and Lord Mildmay bought Monaveen for her, they made a lucky and judicious purchase. He is a bay gelding by Landscape Hill out of Great Double by Stefan the Great. Landscape Hill is the sire of several good jumpers and is a very well-bred horse, his third dam being Stella, the dam of Gleneski and Flying Orb, and from her also descend Trigo and Athford and many other good horses. Monaveen's victory at Hurst Park was really a triumph for all concerned and the pleasure and enthusiasm of the Princess were delightful to behold. May there be many more victories for her, both on the flat and over fences. What could be better than one day to see her lead in the winner of the Derby.

CHAPTER XIII

JOCKEYS AND JOCKEYSHIP

By A. J. Dickinson

WHEN a man reaches the age at which his friends begin to regard him as an "old-timer", it can be assumed they are either envious of his experience or have pity for his greying hairs.

I realise that, when trying to do justice to a subject covering fifty years, there are two things I must avoid lest the impression is created that I am older than is actually the case : I must not laud the past at the expense of the present and I must not allow old friendships to affect my judgment.

To accomplish this has not been easy. I saw my first Classic race in 1906, and my first Derby a few years later. During such a long time one is apt to develop a few fixed ideas but, perhaps, as one peruses my contribution it will be conceded that I have not permitted myself to suffer from prejudices.

To write of fifty years of jockeyship in England means that one must plunge in immediately to mention of an American horseman, one Todhunter Sloan. He had a tremendous, almost revolutionary, influence on race-riding in this country as it was practised at the turn of the century.

"Tod", as he was universally known, arrived with a cigar in his rather loud mouth and a bunch of ideas in his crafty brain. If he did not actually invent the short leather, the crouching seat (almost on his mount's neck) and the waiting in front style of riding, he perfected these methods and compelled our native jockeys to copy his tactics. Otherwise they soon found they just could not compete with the man from across the Atlantic.

Before Tod came here (it was the famous Lord William Beresford who introduced him in 1897) the fashion was for our jockeys to ride long, to sit at least halfway down their horses' backs, to dawdle (almost walk sometimes) in the earlier stages of a race, and then come with as fast a swoop as they could contrive in, say, the last half furlong. Shades of Sam Chifney, George Fordham and Fred Archer still haunted our racecourses, and, anyway, had not these legendary figures won thousands of races between them ? It seemed good enough.

Mr. Todhunter Sloan proceeded to alter all that. He rode with his knees higher than we had hitherto seen and got so near his horse's neck that the famous "monkey-up-a-stick" song is said to have been inspired by the sight of him in action. He always tried to anticipate the starter, sometimes so successfully that he was halfway home before other jockeys in the race realised proceedings had begun.

It was all so new that not at once did Tod's rivals realise they would have to copy his methods or else suffer to take rearward watching briefs whenever the newcomer was riding.

English jockeys were never slow on the uptake, and before long Sloan was not having everything his own way. Some of the pupils even began to beat the master at his own game. Not, however, in so short a time as this takes to write, and meanwhile Tod had become the vogue. Owners clamoured for him to ride their horses, and he was even persuaded to get up on occasion for King Edward VII (then Prince of Wales).

In one season Sloan had 43 winners and 21 seconds with no more than a total of 98 mounts. Just think of it : First or second 64 times and fewer than a hundred rides. It was an almost incredible percentage.

Then came a season when his 345 mounts yielded 108 winners. He was the first jockey to succeed five times at Newmarket in one day, and in two consecutive afternoons, also at Turf Headquarters, he rode 12 winners out of 16 mounts.

Much as we have to admire a jockey who could so stamp his individuality on the English Turf, I fear we can pay no homage to Sloan the man. I was only a child when Sloan was in his heyday ; in later years I learned from his contemporaries that he was a bumptious braggart, that his vices were many and varied, and that he worshipped at the shrine of King Midas. By no means a lovable character, it would appear.

Yet because Sloan had so much to do with the " architecture " of race-riding in England I must say a little more about his career. At the height of his fame he proved that he could not " stand corn ". He became overbearingly heady ; many " friends " of the wrong type gathered around and were made welcome, and to put it kindly Tod developed into " a very naughty boy ". Wagering by the Sloan school became fearsome in its proportions, and it is said that the jockey himself stood to win £100,000 had Codoman (100 to 7 against) won the Cambridgeshire in 1900 instead of being second to the Irish trained Berrill (20 to 1).

Naturally this could not be allowed to go on, and at the end of that season it was intimated to Sloan that it would be inadvisable to apply for a renewal of his licence.

Tod rode for a spell in France before returning to his native America, where he ran an unsuccessful tipping business and then became the main attraction at a billiards saloon. He died penniless in 1933 at the early age of 59, and there in brief is the story of the man who had as much to do as anybody with fashioning English race-riding as we now know it. He had developed a new and brilliant technique, and had proved what sharp wits could do towards exploiting a situation as he found it. It seems a pity that the straight and narrow path did not attract him !

If Sloan had taught how races *could* be won, he had also shown his disciples how to act when they decided that races *had* to be won. And as some of his methods were not too scrupulous, it will be realised that the legacy he bequeathed was two-edged. The malevolent side of his influence remained, and there were, unhappily, others who were eager enough to carry on the win-at-any-price tradition.

It is to be feared that things had been getting a little out of hand, and before they had time to readjust themselves there descended upon England from several parts of the world a set of villainous, gangster-type riders. Not all came from America, for the Continent yielded some who knew all the less reputable tricks of the trade. These gentry did not last long ere being warned off to seek what security they could find elsewhere.

But there remained a feeling of, at least, " recklessness " in the air, and if some of the tactics employed had a touch of self-defence about them, they are not to be condoned. Which raises the question whether a jockey is right in retaliating should he find himself likely to be put over the rails.

The American brothers, Lester and Johnny Reiff, have some-times been described as master tacticians. They were certainly " fearless ", and that word can be unkind sometimes when applied to a jockey. So was Charlie Trigg, who earned for himself the name of " Hell-fire-Jack ". The Reiffs were American ; but Trigg was an Englishman, and though he came rather later on I feel that he must have known all about the far too merry Sloan period.

However, despite all they had to suffer at times, we still had English jockeys who could show the criss-crossing jostlers the nearest way to the winning post. I have in mind such delightful artists as Mornington and Kempton Cannon, Otto Madden, Sam and Tom Loates, Willie Lane, Elijah Wheatley and Billy Higgs, to mention only a few.

Gradually these horsemen, backed up by many lesser lights, restored English jockeyship to the peak from which it had temporarily lost its grip. We never lose the last battle, do we?

Otto Madden will live long in my memory. Top of the list of winning jockeys in 1898, 1901, 1903 and 1904, he made a dramatic comeback in 1918 when, on Air Raid (25 to 1) he won the Cesarewitch, a race in which he had last been successful in

1898, when Chaleureux (75 to 20) won. Thus, the slim, dark-haired jockey I had admired so long ago, emerged from retirement to give at least one war-worn soldier a big thrill when the news came through of another Cesarewitch success twenty years later.

But, much as I dislike expressing the opinion, I doubt if any influence the Englishmen I have named had on race-riding was as potent as that exercised by Tod Sloan. And, curiously enough, neither of the next two leaders of race-riding fashion was English. Danny Maher was an American and Frank Wootton an Australian.

Readers of this story will not wish to be bored by too many figures ; rather will they prefer to know about men and methods. Yet to emphasise my point I must give a small table to show how my next " jockeys of influence "—Maher and Wootton—imposed themselves.

For half a dozen years they were supreme among the jockeys riding in England during their regime as the following comparative table testifies :—

		MAHER		WOOTTON	
Year		Mounts	Wins	Mounts	Wins
1908	..	491	*139	602	129
1909	..	423	116	777	*165
1910	..	460	127	630	*137
1911	..	436	99	747	*187
1912	..	443	109	438	*118
1913	..	427	*115	329	91

* Indicates leader winning jockeys' list.

Rivalry between the pair was terrific, and if the two jockeys did not make it a matter of personal enmity you can rest assured that their partisans did, and many are the savage rows I have seen between the two factions, both on and off a racecourse.

Ten times Maher topped the century in a season and on another occasion reached 99, whilst Wootton exceeded three figures five times—four in a row and in that run he was leading jockey every time.

In the classics of 1903 Maher was never out of the first three, and he won the Derby and St. Leger on Rock Sand. In 1906 he pulled off the Derby and Oaks double with Spearmint and Keystone II. In a rather extraordinary race for the Leger of 1909 Danny, on Bayardo, beat Frank on Valens, by a length and a half. At Doncaster the following year Frank secured revenge when he won on Swynford, with Danny, on the odds-on favourite, Lemberg (who had won the Derby for Bernard Dillon) only third.

Well, there was not much in it between the pair on performances. Otherwise there was a lot. Just as Tod Sloan had got himself disliked by the best people, so did Maher do much towards putting our affection for American riders back on the map. He was photographed with what was then known as Society, and with those people his manner was just as quiet as it seemed to be when he was riding. But in a race there was plenty of fire under that apparent calmness. His rivals realised that !

Some years after he had reached his zenith, and had retired from the saddle, Danny Maher was persuaded to try a " come back ". It was not successful, for, alas, he was even then in the grip of the lung disease which caused his early death. Frank Wootton also passed over some years ago—in Australia.

Frank was a different type from Danny. He was all dash and would seek an opening where even an angel would fear to tread. Shogun in the Derby was a case in point, and often remembered by old-timers. But this is not a history of past-run races, but rather a " look-back " at jockeys who have done something towards shaping race-riding as the reader looks at it now.

Maher and Wootton surely had their share in this. The brighter or mercurial type of boy moulded himself on the Wootton dash, and the steadier and less vivacious lad, in stables, perhaps, and determined to get on, took Maher as his example. I shall always think of Frank as a forerunner of jet-propulsion and of Danny as a sturdier and steadier sort of machine who got there just the same. (Please forgive the aircraft analogy ; but I served in the Royal Air Force for some years.)

Perhaps I should add that Frank Wootton later on found fame as a rider over hurdles. In that rôle he was apt to try (and pull off) things which nearly made bald people's hair curl.

It is all wrong really to write about the influence of Frank Wootton, though doubtless many a young ambitionist modelled his methods on those of the handsome and successful boy who had made his English home at Epsom. If only they had known, they were getting their tuition at second-hand from the greatest teacher of horsemanship there has been since the senior Chifney and John Osborne's father.

I refer, of course to Richard Wootton, the Australian master who came over here with two boys and a few hundred ideas. The boys were Stanley and Frank and the ideas of riding, tactics and other things which were a bit secret were there for development. I have written about Frank ; many people will tell you, however, and I rather think I agree, that son Stanley was the better pupil of Father Richard. Stanley's weight, increasing all the time, did not allow of a long career in the saddle. Stanley now trains, is a coach, too, and is also Lord of the Manor at Epsom.

Richard Wootton's ideas embraced not only horsemanship and jockeyship (two very different things) but ways and means about winning races which did not always bring his students eye to eye with the authorities.

Yet Richard Wootton had set his personal seal on English methods of jockeyship, which was now, by and large, ready for shaping, just as it was when the notorious Tod Sloan appeared on the scene.

Happily there came along a man capable of taking matters into his own hands, though with no conscious effort, and to give the keynote to English jockeyship as we know it to-day. I refer to the inimitable Steve Donoghue.

But before we start to write about Donoghue, a word, please, for Richard Wootton : " Thank you very much ! " And, as we shall see a little later, Stanley Wootton well and faithfully carried on the family tradition.

The reign of " King Stephen " was long, happy and victorious. To record that he was champion jockey from 1914 to 1923 (though Charlie Elliott shared the title with him in the last-named year) says a lot but hardly anything really about Steve's quiet mastership. He did more than rule the roost ; he set an example of everything which was as it should be. Once on a racecourse, he was a jockey and nothing else. And how did the people try to tempt him to be otherwise !

The story of how he tramped in clogs from his native Warrington to Dobson Peacock's place at Middleham, almost made good, and then decided to desert because of a " snooper " is past history. He went to France and then to Ireland, and it was when in Erin's Isle that he gained the experience (a bit rough in those days I have been led to understand) that made him the wide-awake man he was when I first knew and came to love him in England.

In my opinion Steve had everything. Hands were his, and so was a seat. The way in which he could "kid" a "green" two-year-old or "rough-ride" a savage had to be seen to be believed.

It was after Steve had won the Irish Derby on Land of Song in 1914 (he had also won it the previous year on Bachelor's Wedding) that I first knew him. Thereafter, for many years, we remained friends, and it was at Nottingham in 1941 that I last saw " the little man ". He was then training and had just turned out a 10 to 1 winner and I was in uniform. I congratulated him and then, with tears falling, he told me he had just heard the news that " young Steve " was dead. Apple of his father's eye, the younger Steve was never in racing.

Just one more personal reminiscence, please. The night before Steve rode his last race—it was at the Manchester November meeting on November 27, 1937—I asked him if I could send a photographer round to get a picture of him. " Whatever you like " said Steve, " and you'd better be in it ". Well, I was, and that photograph has an honoured place in my home to this day.

Many jockeys stole their methods from earlier masters of the art. Not so Steve. To borrow a line from a once popular song, it was, with Steve, " doing what comes nach'rally ".

He had that knack of getting on with a horse which is, perhaps, a sixth sense and granted to few people in a generation. When he got up on a horse, and this particularly applied to timid youngsters, he would say to them " You're a nice little thing. Let's get on with it and see if we can't beat these other nothings ". If he did not use those actual words he conveyed the meaning, and that was ofttimes good enough.

Yet when Steve was a boy Tod Sloan was his hero !

Steve told me that when he was first required to get up on The Tetrarch he was not particularly impressed. But once he had the " feel " in his hands and between his legs he knew he was on " something ". Steve insisted The Tetrarch was " a phenomenon and a freak ". Moreover " he was the fastest horse I ever rode " and even such a man as Steve once said " He certainly had been on this earth before ".

But then Steve always thought that some horses were nearly human. Apart from The Tetrarch, I believe his favourites were Diadem and Brown Jack. Yet Steve also said that Gay Crusader was " the greatest horse I ever rode ". Steve was ever a man of immense affections, and from what he has told me I think Brown Jack was his big love.

It is necessary to go back to The Tetrarch for a few lines because I am trying to illustrate the influence jockeys have had on jockeyship. Steve's handling of The Tetrarch was always such a masterpiece that it had younger riders not only agog with envy but also with the spirit of emulation. That was all to the good.

Just to show Steve's humanity I propose to quote from his own autobiography. It was in the big two-year-old race at Sandown Park, and this is what Steve wrote of the Tetrarch.

" He jumped off to a false start . . . got the tapes caught in his mouth . . . and came down on his knees. I was nearly heartbroken . . . here we were enmeshed in the tapes and the field rapidly disappearing out of sight . . . I had little hopes of catching them as they were at the two furlongs post when I got the great horse balanced . . . I knew that to . . . impose my will on him would be disastrous. He went after the field like a swallow and won the race by a neck on the post ".

Steve goes on to record that, in a thick mist, neither the general public nor the horse's trainer, Mr. " Atty " Persse, ever realised what had happened that day—though Mr. Persse did later. Steve says : " I was sorry for the great horse. It was not the distance he had to make up, it was the disappointment of being caught in the tapes ".

Can you think of anything finer than that from a thought-to-be heartless professional jockey ? Steve was sad when The Tetrarch had to be scratched from the Derby through an injury. But he has left on record : " Mark you, he could have won the Stewards' Cup as a two-year-old with top-weight ".

Steve, as a man and jockey, was idolised and copied by almost every other man or boy who put on silk and boots, in the hope they might be a worthy disciple of their master.

I must mention Steve's association with Brown Jack, if only to point out what a partnership the pair built up. Once after they had won at Ascot I, rather needlessly, in my excitement just after the race, said to Steve " How did he go ? " Steve was not annoyed, for he answered : " If you'd been on your honeymoon you couldn't have had a happier time ".

Six years in succession Steve won the Queen Alexandra Stakes at Ascot (the longest race in the " Calendar ") on Brown Jack. Once he rode him home with a broken wrist, but that was nothing to a man who had ridden a Derby winner with a writ in his pocket ! Steve says that nobody except his doctor *and Brown Jack* knew about the injury. Perhaps the jockey told the horse about his injury ; anyway " he gave me not the slightest trouble but won his race like the gentleman he always was ".

Steve maintained that the day Brown Jack " won for me " my sixth Queen Alexandra Stakes was the " happiest day of my life ". Then, surviving from celebrations, Steve won a race on the Saturday at Windsor, and after an aeroplane flight to France, won the Grand Prix de Paris on Admiral Drake, and only " Steve " could tell you what it felt like to race in such circumstances.

I had previously seen Steve win the Grand Prix on Kefalin. He beat Ramus that day and the following season it was on Ramus, at Goodwood, that Donoghue gave the finest exhibition of sitting on a buck-jumper that I can remember.

So there you have Steve—great artist in the saddle, grand pal out of the saddle and, in or out of the saddle, one of the finest sportsmen it has ever been my privilege to meet.

Steve would never have acknowledged the fact, if one had ever suggested it to him, that he was the man upon whom future generations of riders on the English Turf were to mould themselves. It is none the less true.

We have seen that men like Tod Sloan, Richard Wootton (through his pupils), Danny Maher, the Cannons (and others during their time), and lastly Stephen Donoghue, had all exerted a great influence on jockeyship in England during the first quarter of the present century. But before everything was " ironed out " into the shape of things as we see them now, there were others, not so far mentioned, whose example was sufficiently magnetic to attract imitators.

The people I have in mind can be divided for convenience into two groups ; the " Colonial " and the " Continental " schools. Mostly, the Colonials were Australians, whereas the Continentals were jockeys of different nationalities who had done the bulk of their riding in France.

Many of the Colonials whom I recall were big and strong ; all of them were tough in a finish and some of them could find a delicate touch when occasion arose. And how they excelled in a match or in a race which became a struggle between two horses ! They would try to " kid " each other in the most delightful fashion and they got as much enjoyment as any spectator from these battles of wits. There is a robust inheritance from these chaps which has exercised a beneficial influence upon modern race-riding.

Two typical and outstanding examples of the Colonial school were Frank Bullock and Bernard (" Brownie ") Carslake. Few present-day jockeys can equal this pair for all-round ability.

One match in which they " brought the house down ", I shall never forget. It was on Cesarewitch day at Newmarket in 1924, and the event was the Select Stakes, run over the famous Rowley Mile. " Brownie " was on Twelve Pointer and Frank on Caravel. Twelve Pointer, a four-year-old, had to concede 10 lbs. to the three-year-old Caravel, which is 3 lbs. more than the weight-for-age scale demands. The betting was guineas to pounds ; that is, 21 to 20 on Twelve Pointer.

Bare facts are that the pair raced together for 6 furlongs and then Frank Bullock took a slight lead on Caravel. The two jockeys were watching each other like hawks and both still had plenty upon which to call. So far, neither had moved, and it was in a tense silence that the crowd awaited the finish. Then, in the Dip, Carslake feinted to make an effort on the inside, and, as Bullock prepared to counter that move, Twelve Pointer's attack was switched to the outside and, in a flash, he had gained a lead on to which he hung like grim death to win by a short head. It was so close that the Judge would certainly have asked for the camera's evidence had the photo-finish been operating then.

Naturally, the crowd had been roaring as the pair swept up the Hill to the finish; but when the numbers went up, pandemonium seemed to break loose. Nobody but the Judge knew with certainty which horse had won, and this had been a fierce-betting race. Returning to scale, Frank Bullock's face was as inscrutable as ever, but "Brownie" permitted himself a brief smile as he acknowledged the congratulations showered upon him.

My pen may not have made this picture anything like so dramatic as it was in fact; but my memory of that wonderful race is still vivid after more than 25 years, so you can guess what an impression it must have made. Just another job of work, perhaps, to two great artists. But the thrill of a racing lifetime to those privileged to see it.

Twelve Pointer went on to win the Cambridgeshire that year, Carslake again riding; the following year, he again won the Select Stakes, this time by half-a-dozen lengths.

One of many other races in which Bullock and Carslake were opposed was the Rous Memorial Stakes at Ascot in 1925. Here, Frank was on his old favourite Caravel, and "Brownie" was riding Diophon, who had won the Two Thousand Guineas the previous year with George Hulme up. Caravel received 10 lbs. and beat Diophon a short head. Thus, revenge came Frank's way, but there were not quite the same thrills attaching to this race as there had been in the famous Twelve Pointer-Caravel struggle the previous season.

Those who never saw these two great horsemen in action missed many a treat. I have written enough, I hope, to explain why they left a lasting impression on English jockeyship.

Before leaving the Colonial school, mention must be made of the Dutch-South African, Isaac Strydom. In all my experience, I have never seen a jockey with such powerful strength. Built like a weight-lifter, Strydom had enormous shoulders and chest-development, and if his homely features have been described as "ugly", well, all jockeys can't look like matinee idols. Strydom did not stay long over here, for he was homesick for his native land. Nor, perhaps, did he wield any vast influence on younger horsemen. At the same time, this Hercules cannot possibly be left out of any chapter purporting to tell of Colonial jockeys. Bullock and Carslake were, of course, resident here for many years.

A Continental within this category was Ed Haynes, who was attached to "Gene" Leigh's stable when that famous American trainer had the mighty Epinard in his charge. Haynes showed how races *should* be won when easily winning the Stewards' Cup at Goodwood in 1923 on Epinard, and then, on the same horse in the same year, showing how it should *not* be done when losing the Cambridgeshire by a neck to Verdict.

No doubt, Haynes was a good jockey, and just as clearly, he has been overblamed for losing the Cambridgeshire on Epinard. It has been said that he wandered like a lost sheep on Newmarket's vast course, and certainly he did not keep a dead straight line. In any case, he took a leading part in providing one of the most stirring finishes I can remember in a race which is noteworthy for many a close struggle. In my opinion the critics who was severe in their comments on Haynes's race-riding ability overlooked the fact that he was on a three-year-old carrying the hefty burden of 9 st. 2 lbs., and was being asked to give 18 lbs. to a filly of proved ability, well handicapped, and beautifully ridden by Michael Beary. [This Verdict-Epinard duel has always been a classic within my memory and revealed Michael Beary at the peak of his brilliance.—THE EDITOR.]

On actual achievement, I suppose George Stern was about the best of the Continental school. He was contemporary with Frank Wootton and Danny Maher. He won the Derby (1911) on Sunstar and was thrice placed in that race, the most memorable of these occasions being when, on Louviers, he was beaten a short head by Herbert Jones, riding King Edward VII's Minoru. Stern's only victory in the St. Leger was on the Duke of Westminster's Troutbeck (1906), who beat Prince William by a head, and one of his two successes in the Two Thousand Guineas, that on Sir J. Thursby's Kennymore (1914), was gained by a short head from Corcyra.

Jockey on Corcyra that day was Frank O'Neill, who was another glittering ornament of the Continental school. In 1911 O'Neill, riding Mr. T. Pilkington's Prince Palatine, beat Stern, on Lycaon, in the St. Leger, while Stern also had to be content with second place in the Doncaster Classic when he was beaten by G. Bellhouse, whose mount, Tracery, easily got the better of Maiden Erlegh. Bellhouse, another of the " head boys " in the Continental school, rode Archaic into second place behind O'Neill in that memorable Derby won by Spion Kop—when the pace broke Tetratema's heart and Steve Donoghue took a terrible-looking toss on Abbot's Trace.

Frank O'Neill was one of the Continental riders to take part in that extraordinary race for the Ascot Gold Cup in which French horses filled three of the first four places, Massine (A. Sharp) beating the almost-white Filibert de Savoie (J. Jennings) a short head with Le Capucin (Bartholomew) fourth. The jockeys from the Continent rode as a real " team " that day, and if the " wrong " horse won (the second was 4-to-1 favourite and the winner at 100 to 8), here was a striking example of combined brainwork. Incidentally, this sort of thing has often happened when an English horse runs in France, and our only jockeys who have

GORDON RICHARDS   STEVE DONOGHUE

[*Facing page* 196

M. CANNON

D. MAHER

B. CARSLAKE

F. WOOTTON

seemed able to hold their own over there in comparatively recent times, have been " Steve ", Charlie Smirke, and, of course, Charles Elliott. Anyway, the last-named is as much at home in France as in his own country.

Rae (" Togo ") Johnstone is, I suppose, the best example of the Continental School now riding regularly in England. On Colombo, he is supposed to have ridden a bad race in the Derby won by Windsor Lad (1934). But I think he would have needed wings to get home that day. Just for once, our home jockeys did not wish a " foreigner " to win. Or am I wrong ?

In recent years, native French jockeys have seemed to shine in this country on occasion, yet that has been due to the superiority of their mounts rather than to any great merit on the part of the horseman concerned. In the same way, the Italian jockey, Enrico Carniel, looked good when winning a couple of races—at Ascot and Goodwood respectively — on Tenerani, from his own country.

The Continental jockeys referred to in the preceding paragraph have, however, left but a fleeting memory and no traceable impression on English riding-methods.

When the first of the major wars of our time ceased, there was a kind of hiatus in English jockeyship, just as there was in most other things. All seemed to be poised, or hanging in the balance, and one could sense a temporary lack of leadership. Some jockeys found momentary fame, and if it was then that Steve Donoghue began to wear the mantle that he was destined to carry with renown for some years to come, it has to be remembered that he had first worn the crown in 1914.

I award Donoghue the highest marks, for the reason that he had to cope with such fierce competition. Look at the people he had to meet.

Steve's rivals were many, ambitious and strong. They included such men as Carslake and Bullock, about whom I have already written. Then there was Vic Smyth, " Snowy " Whalley, Fred Fox, Fred Templeman (still a great force on the course and now a clever and successful trainer), Joe Childs, Michael Beary, and a host of others : such as Charles Elliott, Tommy Weston, and the amazing Gordon Richards, the last-named of whom will get special mention later on.

First to wrest the championship outright from Steve was Charles Elliott. Then, as now, Charles was a well-dressed figure with always a head coiffeured in a way that friends admired and ladies could not resist. As far as I know, Charles is the only present-riding Newmarket-born jockey to achieve real fame. There have, of course, been many in the past, and even now there is Flatman Street in Newmarket which perpetuates the name of

one of the finest jockeys ever. Flatman won the Derby on
Colonel Peel's Orlando, who, in 1844, was awarded the race on
the disqualification of Running Rein, who had run as a four-
year-old. But to return to Charles Elliott. His wide experience
as a rider for M. Marcel Boussac has enabled him to meet all the
cracks in Europe, and to beat them too. His superb judgment
is his biggest asset. It has driven him into a position second
to none and I regard him as the best jockey riding in 1949.

He excels over Newmarket Heath, which is only fair and
proper; elsewhere, he shows that regard for his chosen profession which makes him a master among men. He has a
" knack " with horses which many others envy.

I place Vic Smyth (now turning out many winners from Epsom)
pretty high among those who were challenging for supremacy
in the early 1920's. Always inclined to be on the big side, Vic
showed a mastery over his mounts which many less able men failed
to copy. I was glad that he realized increasing weight was beating him and retired from the saddle to the stable-yard and
training-ground.

Any reader of these pages is challenged to tell me the name
of a better rider of horses over a distance than Joe Childs. He
may not be the only man I have seen " lift " a beaten horse first
past the post, but he is one of the few men I have seen nurse
a horse so skilfully as to come again and win when victory seemed
impossible. And he did it time and again.

Joe rode so many good horses for so many good owners and
trainers (he was never very talkative) that, try as I would, I could
never get him to tell me what he thought was the best he ever
rode. He did once open-up so far as to say that " Solario was a
nice one the day I won the St. Leger on him (1925)." I remember
that day very well. Joe was in the dressing-room when a message
was sent to him that Princess Mary (now Princess Royal) would
like to speak to him. Out went Joe, half-dressed under a
voluminous great coat, and I regret that it was only a muttered
" Thank you very much " in return to the " Congratulations,
Childs ; well done " and a handshake from the Princess. Joe
was then, of course, riding all His Majesty's horses on which he
could do the weight.

At the time of which I am writing, not a great deal had been
heard of Tommy Weston, whose main activities had been confined to the North Country. Then he burst from bud into leaf
by distinguishing himself in a number of handicaps, and ere long
blossomed into first jockey for Lord Derby. Perhaps the dirtiest
Derby Day I can remember from a weather point of view, was
that on which Tommy won the great race on Sansovino (1924).
He wore white gloves to prevent his hands slipping on the reins;

but I think it would have required a squadron of tanks to keep Tommy from slipping first past the post on Sansovino that day. He won by six lengths, with the others floundering.

In 1933, Weston won the Derby again, this time on Hyperion, owned by Lord Derby and trained by Mr. Lambton, just as Sansovino had been. Here Tommy won by four lengths as against the six he had in hand previously. He never cut it fine if he could help it, though he was always prone to lose his cap in the process of winning. Tommy had a distinguished career in the Royal Navy during World War II.

Harry Wragg was a most distinguished member of a Sheffield family which also produced brother jockeys in Sam and Arthur. The story of how I once bathed Arthur's baby is neither here nor there; how Harry won the Derby on Felstead (1928) is another matter altogether.

For it was on this occasion that Harry Wragg first adopted those tactics—coming from behind with a long finishing run—which later earned him the nickname of the " Head Waiter ". The previous year he had been second on Hot Night to Charlie Elliott on Call Boy (Mr. Frank Curzon was just well enough, before he died, to lead in that winner). In 1930, Harry rode his second Derby winner, this time the Aga Khan's Blenheim. In following years, he was twice third and once second, yet he did not win the Derby again.

This was the sort of opposition Steve had to meet before, during and after his own great Derby triumphs. These facts may help one to appreciate the sort of men by whom he was opposed. Other jockeys in the limelight about this period, apart from those I have mentioned, were George Hulme, who was a master in his day but a bit of a problem to his friends and probably to himself; Fred Slade, of the sloe-eyes; Fred Lane, who rode one of the best races of all when he won the Derby on the late Tom Wall's April the Fifth (1932); Bobby Jones, little more than a tiny boy when he won the St. Leger on Royal Lancer (1922); Dick Perryman, ever quiet, kind and effective in his handling of horses, and the ever-buoyant " cheeky cheery " Charlie Smirke.

Charlie's " effervescence " (shall we say) in the saddle caused him to be " stood down " by the Stewards of the Jockey Club for quite a long spell—I believe their sentence had extended to five years before application for a renewal of licence to ride was granted. Then what a come-back he made! In the space of three seasons, he twice won the Derby—Windsor Lad and Mahmoud (1934 and 1936)—and won the St. Leger twice—Windsor Lad and Bahram (1935). Charles has also won the Grand Prix de Paris, as well as other races at Longchamp, where the cry of

" Smeerk " was once as familiar to happy English ears as that of " Donoggo ".

It may not be an opinion shared by many race-goers, but I declare that, next to Elliott, Smirke is the best jockey we now have. He is one of the many brilliant products of the Wootton academy : for remember that Stanley Wootton has turned out some grand jockeys, just as his father had done before him. I need mention only Sirett, Gethin and Caldwell in addition to Smirke.

When first I saw Charlie Smirke, after the Second World War, he was still in khaki following a spell of hard service in the Near East. We had halted in our respective cars on the road to either Fontwell or Plumpton—anyway, one of those places so cheerily presided over by Bob Wigney—when I heard a voice say, " What'll you have ? I've not seen you for a long time ". Charles carefully bought himself a lemonade ; I had something else.

I have not overlooked Gordon Richards as will be seen later. What I have been trying to show, is that English jockeyship was just about at its peak in the late 1920's and early 1930's. A personal opinion, perhaps, but it is why I reiterate that " Steve " was certainly up against something during the period he was "Daddy" of them all. For sheer skill, can you name half-a-dozen to match these race-riders at the present time ? I very much doubt it.

Now to pay homage to that incalculable piler-up of records, the Shropshire lad, Gordon Richards. Since Gordon first hit the top in 1925, he has maintained that proud position except on three occasions—on two of them because of ill-health or injury, and once when he was nosed out of the championship by Fred Fox, who pipped him by one point in 1930.

I have called Richards " incalculable ", because nobody, spectator or opponent, knows what he is going to do next. His methods are frequently unorthodox ; but if he breaks all the known rules of race-riding, he also breaks riding-records, and, after all, the acid test of successful jockeyship is the ability to ride winners.

Gordon has ridden more winners than any other Englishman; has topped the century 19 times, which is another record ; has more wins to his credit in one season than any other jockey, and once rode the winners of 12 consecutive races, a feat never accomplished in this country before or since. And although he has now been riding for almost 30 years, he is as fit as ever, with the word " retirement " not in his vocabulary !

Gordon has won every big race we have in the English Racing Calendar, with the exception of the Epsom Derby. It is surely a safe bet to prophesy that this prize will fall to him ere he is much older.

What is the secret of this amazing man ? I feel he must have one, though expert lookers-on have failed to discern it. He has a marvellous sense of balance and fine hands ; so has Michael Beary. He can be quick from the gate and he can ride a storming finish. So can Charles Elliott. People will tell you that he is able to pick and choose his mounts ; so could other jockeys at the zenith of their powers. But they did not smash records in the Gordon manner. There must be something else behind it all.

If you tell me that Gordon lacks style, I will retort by asking what you mean by style. In my opinion, what passes for style in race-riding is often nothing more nor less than mere showman-ship. There are no frills about Gordon. Sometimes, in fact, he looks positively " untidy ", with arms and legs appearing to work overtime and his reins hanging slack—in short, doing everything wrong from the viewpoint of the purists.

Yet by his very successes, this man Richards tends to disarm criticism. Therein may lie part, at least, of his secret. I suggest that it is his instant appreciation of a situation which allows him to supply the requisite methods for the moment and bring victory in train. His hair-trigger brain works quickly and the message for appropriate action is transmitted so fast that the response seems almost instinctive. That is a considered opinion and no mere flight of fancy.

Another reason why Gordon wins so many races is that he has made a profound study of the peculiarities of our many and varied race-courses. Watch him force the pace down the hill in races on the round course at Lingfield Park, for instance ; see how he always strives to get that essentially good place turning into the straight at Sandown Park ; recall the judgment bred from know-ledge, of his challenges at places like Bath and Salisbury and you will realize what I mean.

Gordon, the modest family man, has interests other than racing. Association Football, of which he was once no mean exponent, used to be his first love, but nowadays he seems to tend more towards his racing-pigeons and his Winter-sports in Switzerland. He has no weight troubles, riding a normal 8 st., and though he usually starts the season at a pound or so more than that, he can get below it should need arise.

During many of Gordon's years at the top of the tree, his most persistent and consistent challengers have been the brothers Eph and Douglas Smith. Nowadays, it is Douglas who tends to be the more fashionable of this pair of riders who have many characteristics in common. Both, for example, seem to exert power and control in excess of what could be expected from their slight physique, and they get more out of their mounts than many heavier jockeys. Both, too, excel in judgment of a finish.

Michael Beary is the Peter Pan of present-day jockeys. Sometimes he appears to ride with almost uncanny judgment, and I have seen him win races in circumstances which would have proved too much for many another horseman. Michael, who, incidentally, is an expert judge of horseflesh and a familiar figure around the sales-rings, has been riding better than ever during the past few seasons.

Billy Nevett, Lancashire born and now "naturalized" Yorkshireman, has been the outstanding jockey in the North Country for the past 20 years or so. That he is fully capable of taking on the Southern cracks on their "home" ground is proved by three victories in the Derby, when war necessitated the running of that race at Newmarket, and a success in the Epsom Oaks. Billy is a fearless and confident race-rider with some exceptional feats to his credit. He likes a hearty battle and makes no secret of his pleasure when he has emerged from a keen tussle with credit.

Edgar Britt, the Australian who came here from India to ride for the Maharaja of Baroda, I regard as something of an enigma. His quiet style is completely different from the typical methods of the Colonial school to which I have previously referred. In more than one close finish, he had appeared to be getting less out of his mount than some of the other riders concerned, but that is because there is nothing of the "whirlwind" about him. He has as nice a seat as any man now in the front rank, and he rarely fails to find an advantageous position for his horse when tactical handling is called for. He probably wins more races before "the distance" is reached than any other jockey.

Perhaps the King's jockey, Harry Carr, does not get as much credit as is his due for his thoughtful race-riding. He is a jockey well worthy to wear the Royal silks. A man for whom I have much admiration is Ken Gethin, ever to be relied upon when the heat of the battle is fierce. There are other clever horsemen who are capable of doing little that is wrong and much that is right when they have the mount on a worthwhile animal ; but those I have named appear to be outstanding among Gordon's present most serious challengers.

Many riders of good and gallant races have, perforce, to accept the mount on inferior horses when the "cream" is offered to men with more-famous names. I think I could safely mention at least 10 jockeys who would win many more races if only they were given the right material. Apropos, let us spare a kind thought for the men who have to get up on horses who are not properly fit, who are in need of a race, or who have no hope of winning but run just because the owner wants to see his colours carried at, say, his local meeting. These are the riders who are unfortunate enough to be second jockey to a stable. When the sort of horse I have mentioned is really fit and fancied, it is almost a certainty that a man with a more fashionable name will get the ride.

It is inevitable that the dozen or so top riders of 1949 cannot go on for ever. Where are the youngsters who will step one day into their places ? Happily, there are a number of budding " cracks " on whom the mantle of Richards, Elliott and Smirke will fall with dignity when the time comes.

Not many trainers nowadays seem willing to spare the time to teach their apprentices so patiently as Richard Wootton did in the past. Stanley Wootton has produced lads of merit to carry on the tradition of the family, and I have noticed that Billy Stephenson and Ernest Davey can usually send out boys of ability. Some other trainers seem to neglect chances. After all, a capable apprentice is a gold mine, and it should be worth while telling a lad how to comport himself on the course.

I attach some importance to this teaching. We have seen lads get up on horses, even at Newmarket, when they had not the slightest justification for so doing. I know a lad has to start sometime or other ; but spare me the sight of a frightened kid on a big horse who is nearly a good thing to run away with him. There have been cases like this.

Many lads, of course, are never lucky enough to make the grade. One who will do so, without any doubt, is Ron Reader, a 21-year-old, Sussex-born boy who is with Walter Nightingall. This boy rode some nice races last season, when he could comfortably manage 6 st. 5 lb. His master thinks a lot of Ron.

Billy Snaith is out of his time. Leading apprentice of 1949, he now has to ride without the allowance. A Newcastle boy, he was with Fred Armstrong. He rode the Northumberland Plate winner, on his native Tyneside, on Fol Ami. And that day, the Geordies cheered almost as much as on that memorable day when another Northumbrian, Adam Scott, led in Jazz Band.

Manchester lad Frank Barlow is out of his time with Henri Jelliss and is now with Michael Blackmore. Weight is a problem with this fast-growing boy who could do hardly less than 7 st. 8 lbs. last season. He may get bigger still, yet I have an idea that Frank will win a good many races before he is much older.

Tommy Gosling is only 24, yet this Scots lad is another who is troubled by increasing weight. Not less than 8 st. can he manage, but he is very good on horses who want pushing along.

Dennis Buckle, tutored by Ernie Davey, is out of his time with his mentor. The Stewards once told Dennis not to use his whip so heartily. He has learned from that reproof and, now that he is riding as a free lance, I consider he has a promising future.

" Manny " Mercer is a West-Riding boy who has a brother

apprenticed to Major Sneyd. "Manny" rode Jockey Treble when that horse won the Lincolnshire Handicap at 100 to 1 in 1947. It is not unlikely that Mercer will ride winners of other big races.

From South to North went Ron Sheather to gain all that Ernie Davey could tell him, and Tony Holloway went from Nottinghamshire to Hednesford before he showed promise of making good.

Born at Warrington, birthplace of the illustrious Steve Donoghue, Walter Cox is destined to be a "big noise" of the future. In fact, if I had to give a prophecy at the moment, I would tip Cox and Reader to be the main stars who are now going into bloom.

Another boy with a big future is the quiet-mannered Joe Sime. A Liverpool lad who now lives at Doncaster, Joe is one of the few boys who went from apprenticeship to jockeyship without a turn of the hair. When he lost his apprentice-allowance, he proceeded to ride winners.

There are many promising lads whose names I may have omitted. I must, however, mention Lester Piggott, who is, I am told, still at school. His father, Keith Piggott, was a good jockey; his grandfather, Ernie Piggott, was one of the best horsemen I have seen riding in jumping-races. Lester will hit the highlights, if only he will listen to what dad and grandad have to tell him. I hope they will not be mum!

I have tried to look at English jockeyship in times both sad and gay. As we see race-riding now, I suggest it has been built up over a period of many years from the style and manner of a number of vivid personalities of several nationalities. And why not? After all, the English language and the English folk themselves are the fruit of Roman, Saxon, Norse and Norman influences. But, as in other things, we have come out on top in jockeyship. May it ever be thus!

CHAPTER XIV

BETTING THROUGHOUT THE CENTURIES

By Frank Harvey

THE early history of horse-racing has been a troublesome subject for many historians and those diligent in research, but the attendant matter of betting has rarely been treated as other than a practice affecting the sport on broad lines. A lack of reliable data regarding racing and betting in the earliest times is regrettable, but individual chroniclers and fervid students have established many reliable links with the past and it is possible, therefore, to visualize to some extent the ways and means by which the " Sport of Kings " came to perfection, as we know it to-day.

A Royal Commission on Betting, Lotteries and Gaming has sought to probe the problems of wagering in the terms of modern interpretation. The mere fact somewhat upset my original ideas when the Editor invited me to cover the same field sportingly rather than technically, but I quickly realized that Royal Commissions rarely " carry the day " in any connection, and at once decided to pursue my own road without resort to minutes of evidence and other complicated memoranda. In good time, the findings and recommendations of the 1949–50 Royal Commission will be promulgated and, of course, widely discussed : yet, to the man in the street, they will have little meaning—unless by any chance they further restrict his liberty and independence. One never knows !

Many years ago a sporting-writer who had to deal with racing and betting, as he knew it then, made some observations which are applicable even to-day. " This universal amusement did not spring up of a sudden to share the fate of many other habits and customs, and to be almost as quickly flung aside, but it has been the steady growth of centuries—gradually rooting itself in our character till firmly and permanently established."

A century has passed since these words were written. Nothing has happened to disprove their weight, their truth, or their sincerity. Indeed, one can only stress the fundamental sentiment which actuated their author, for it would entail but the addition of another short sentence to bring the whole thing up to date.

The Turf is an institution—soundly and solidly based and happily accepted—in all parts of the world. From the earliest times, it had to contend with the political troubles of the period.

Even to-day problems occur and recur ; but the inclination of the people to indulge their favourite pastime cannot, and never will, be eradicated. Extraneous aspects of wagering, as laid before Royal Commissions ought really not to be confused with the honest-to-goodness betting which devotees of horse-racing know so well. Government supervision may be deemed right and proper in certain directions, but if we except the Totalisator —in which the Home Secretary is of necessity interested—I think we can argue that our wagering on the race-course is entirely our own affair.

Supervision and control of betting-off-the-course might have advantages. In any case, the activating spirit behind the operation would not be quashed by red-taped officialdom. Nor would any form of " interference " quell the ardour of the far-flung army of sportsmen who wager because they desire to do so and will for ever persist in doing so. That is an admitted fact which no government, tribunal, commission, or court of justice, can turn aside or ignore. As well think of closing the Stock Exchange, or disrupting insurance companies, as talk of wiping-out betting and gambling. Life is a gamble, anyway !

In the year 1654, Cromwellian England had cultivated the racing bug to such an extent that the Lord Protector issued a Proclamation banning the use of race-courses in England and Wales for a period of six months. " The evil use made thereof by ill-disposed persons " can be interpreted as you please, but, to me, the significance of the words is perfectly clear. Anyhow, within 10 years, Newmarket Heath was " back on the map " again, and, if history truly depicts the situation, England revelled in an orgy of betting on cards, dice, cock-fighting, coursing, horse-racing and countless other pastimes. King Charles II (like James I), and afterwards Queen Anne, were " pillars of the Turf " who unquestionably gave the Sport of Kings their blessing.

Early in the eighteenth century the established, endowed, and well-patronized race-meeting had come into existence. Parliament pondered the matter and decided that racing for small prizes here and there had " contributed very much to the encouragement of idleness, to the impoverishment of many of the meaner sort of subjects, while the breed of strong and useful horses hath been much prejudiced thereby ". Acts were accordingly passed to raise the status of the Turf by divers means ; and so we pass on to 1786, when " the sport had almost reached its pinnacle in practice and popularity ". The Prince of Wales, as the outstanding patron of racing of the era, had played a tremendous part in thus establishing the pastime, which had, in fact, become an industry of considerable importance.

Nevertheless, it was a horse owned by the Prince of Wales

that (in 1791) caused the sporting-public, and particularly those actively engaged in ownership and betting, to sit up and take notice.   The Jockey Club questioned the running of Escape in two races and the unfortunate incidents quickly developed into what is known as a " scandal ", in consequence of which the jockey, Chifney, fell from grace and esteem.   The Prince of Wales partly retired from racing, but from first to last, and as England's monarch, his ruling passion was the thoroughbred.   Royal patronage of the Turf was withheld for many years after the death of George IV, yet on all sides the pursuit of racing spread enormously.   By 1853 the rulers of the country were once again disturbed about the wide increase in betting and by the " opening of places called betting-houses or offices ", where speculation on horse-races had become rife.   Steps were taken to curb the " malady ".

Epsom, Chester, York, Doncaster, Ripon, Newmarket, Lincoln, Paisley and other race-meetings in various parts of the country were the " battlegrounds " on which the masses first saw thoroughbreds in action and betted on them to win or lose. " Going racing " 200 years ago was something more than an adventure ; as witness the experience of a sportsman returning from Epsom.   He was attacked by a single highwayman, who robbed him of nearly £20 and his watch.   The " gentlemen of the road " appear to have their counterparts even now, for many contend that this is an age of "robbery without violence" in many matters connected with sport.

Hardships met in journeying to and from races in olden times are related in countless stories and so, too, are the details of strange bets unfolded with fitting gusto.

How, one wonders, were the results of races made known in distant parts in the era before railroad and telegraph had been thought of ?   We learn that in 1836 the result of the Doncaster St. Leger was sent by " special messenger " to Manchester, where it arrived in just under $2\frac{1}{2}$ hours.   The distance travelled was 58 miles, and the horseman had to walk about 2 miles when one of his nags gave out.

That same day, the St. Leger result was known in Birmingham (94 miles), thanks to the kindly offices of a tavern-keeper who also contrived a special courier.   A certificate of the Leger result, signed by the judge, was handed to the messenger, who had five horses at his disposal along the route.   " Quick work " they called it then—and quite rightly !

An advertisement by a York coffeehouse-keeper in 1837 informed the sporting public that his customers could have " The bettings, per first post, twice a week from Tattersalls, and the different meetings in the country ".   By such means, were the sportsmen of England—and backers, in particular—enabled to keep in touch with the events of the moment. There were also in existence daily and weekly papers exclusively devoted to racing and kindred sports, but the means of circulating them were limited and slow.

The *Racing Calendar* was first published in 1727 on a semi-official basis. Its price was 7s. 6d., and early subscribers included dukes, peers, baronets and a large proportion of the landed nobility and country squires. Mr. John Cheny, of Arundel, founded the venture but, for obvious reasons, had to contend with many difficulties.

With the formation of the Jockey Club in the middle of the eighteenth century, an even wider interest was aroused in racing. The ruling body quickly got to grips with the complexities of a much maligned and unbridled pastime and very soon " law and order " was established as regards the actual conduct of the sport. Not, perhaps, the law and order, rules, regulations, and principles in force to-day, but, at any rate, the planting of an acorn from which the big oak was to grow. Not long after the inception of the Jockey Club, there came into being newspapers which promised their readers "authoritative and warranted intelligence on all matters pertaining to racing throughout the land ". By this means, events like the Derby, Oaks and St. Leger soon became universal topics of conversation, and were betted upon by all and sundry.

At the outset, the " Rules and Orders of the Jockey Club " were applicable only to meetings held at Newmarket. It was years later before they were extended to embrace the 66 meetings regularly taking place at other centres. By general consent, these were eventually brought " into the fold " and subjected to " Rules concerning horse-racing in general ". As proof of the expansion of racing since the Jockey Club took over orthodox control, I adduce the following statistics, taken from semi-official records :

Year	Races Run	Stakes
1762 ..	.. 261	£61,440
1862 ..	.. 2,171	£280,406
1948 ..	.. 2,205	£1,511,822

Whether betting has correspondingly expanded is problematical. Time was when sweepstakes were in operation all over England and they had such a tremendous vogue that the minions of the law called for their suppression. Every kind of sporting event served a purpose when sweepstakes were mooted, and none clamoured for lotteries more than the humble worker who, even then, nurtured those "money-for-nothing" theories which still persist in the "best circles". I may not be far wrong in saying that the sweepstake of old has its near counterpart in the rich football-pool dividends which are so coveted nowadays. But a point worth stressing is one relating to taxation. Old-time governments received nothing from sweepstakes or any other form of betting. Now it is all so different.

If the stirring story of *Ben Hur* were positively factual, we would know that something akin to ferocious wagering took place among the Romans. Possibly it did. Their chariot-racing must have been awe-inspiring, and betting was no doubt an important feature of it. We have no positive picture of the betting scene on English race-courses in the earliest times, when the annual gatherings at such places as I have already named were in the nature of riotous country-fairs, whereat many forms of gambling —and no little roguery—were practised. Bookmakers, as such, were non-existent, and the betting that took place involved, principally, the owners of the horses taking part in matches, or races run in heats. Fields of present-day size were then unknown.

Match-making was the first step towards horse-racing as conducted now. They were the means by which supremacy was settled as between two horses, athletes, gamecocks, or any active disputants in whom interest was general. Whenever thoroughbreds were matched, vast numbers invariably attended and " one of the greatest crowds ever assembled at Newmarket " is reputed to have watched Hambletonian and Diamond engage in a " needle " contest on March 25, 1799. Expert jockeys—Buckle and Fitzpatrick—were employed and a sensational race over four miles (most matches were run over that distance) ended in favour of Hambletonian by a head.

" Large sums fell to be paid and received over this event, the betting having ruled high. Yorkshire, to a man, supported Hambletonian and all the Newmarket people backed Diamond."

One can better understand the animation of such a hard-fought match when we are told that " evens " was to be had against either horse. Bets, of course, were just exchanges between individuals, and " margins " for bookmakers were unknown. Cockfighter and Sir Solomon were matched for 500 gns. at Doncaster in 1801, but £50,000 changed hands as a result of the encounter. One of the most noteworthy matches ever decided drew more than 100,000 people to York's Knavesmire in August, 1804, when Mrs. Thornton, on Vingarillo, rode her horse against a Mr. Flint's Thornville, for 1,000 gns. Wagers exceeding £200,000 were at stake on this affair and, although Vingarillo started favourite, his fair owner had the mortification of letting all Yorkshire down. Mrs. Thornton, however, won other matches that proved her to be a splendid rider and a sterling judge of horseflesh.

The Flying Dutchman-Voltigeur match at York (May 13, 1851), was one of the great events of that time. The two horses were among the best ever seen on the Turf up to that period. Lord Eglinton owned the Dutchman and Voltigeur belonged to Lord Zetland. The match, which aroused more interest than any previous contest, was regarded as " the race of the century " and resulted in a hard-won victory for The Flying Dutchman. That was not the only time they met.

Gradually, as the years progressed, matches began to lose their appeal. Sportsmen wanted larger fields, greater excitement, and a wider range of activity for betting. " Laying odds on or taking even money is unpalatable work to the great majority of those who attend race-meetings ", wrote a scribe, who further asserted that, 10 times in 12, the real merit of a race-horse was not revealed in matches.

I ought, perhaps, to have mentioned before now the mighty Eclipse, easily the most famous and revered race-horse of all time. He was foaled on April 1, 1764—on which date there was an eclipse of the sun—and ran his first race in 1769, as the property of a prolific gambler, Colonel O'Kelly, concerning whom fabulous stories have been related. O'Kelly ran Eclipse in 18 races and the horse never suffered defeat. None ever knew the amount O'Kelly amassed as winnings over Eclipse, but the world knows that the immortal hero founded the line of thoroughbreds to which practically every race-horse living is linked, directly or indirectly.

No dependable data exist as to how and when the professional bookmaker came into being, and this point is stressed because I came across the following observation in a book written in the reign of Queen Victoria : "A history of the rise and progress of betting would be fraught with great interest ".

There, you see, is a lament which could rightly be repeated to-day. Furthermore, if I fall back upon the old-time author for more views and inspiration it must be accepted that one is driven to do so from sheer necessity.

" It takes two, and occasionally more than two, persons to make a bet, and in the earlier days of horse-racing the amounts betted on both sides were usually deposited or, in racing parlance, the money in dispute was ' staked ', in the hands of a third party till the event betted upon could be decided.

" While no evidence is available in regard to the origin of the bookmaker, it may be taken for granted that the ' penciller ' was not evolved at once. The system grew by means of what it fed on—originating doubtless in the practice adopted by certain gentlemen who, having made a series of bets, were anxious to get ' round ', as the process of hedging is called. In other words, they sought to be in a position not to lose their money, or at least to have a fair chance of winning something and not losing all.

"At the beginning of racing and for a considerable time thereafter, what betting occurred took place chiefly on the race-course. As time elapsed, certain men distinguished themselves, or at least became notorious, as ' betting men ', both giving and taking the odds all round, and accepting the odium of sometimes being called ' legs ' (blacklegs) by such persons as only made single bets and resented the wholesale modes of betting which were coming into fashion.

"As betting increased in magnitude, the ' bookmaker ', or professional betting man, became a necessity and, as always, demand soon created a supply.

" It used to be the fashion to bet on one horse ' against the field ', and that mode of speculation was long prevalent : in fact, it did not change into the present, more-extended way of doing business until the nineteenth century was well advanced. Such betting was mainly indulged in by the owners of race-horses, their humour finding a vent chiefly in arranging matches between their respective animals for sums of money, ranging from £50 to £5,000 or even more.

" The ' professional ' bookmakers who first took the field in opposition to the aforesaid ' legs ' were not, in the matter of education and manners, particularly bright. But in consideration of their being prompt to pay when they lost, their shortcomings were overlooked.

" Many gentlemen who owned horses had discovered that the mere winning of a stake by means of any particular race, however large the sum run for might be, did not reimburse them for their many outlays: hence, the horse became an instrument of gambling and still remains so."

Lotteries, sweepstakes, and draws were extensively patronized all over the country at a period when racing-news spread with greater rapidity. They eventually grew to such an extent that the strong arm of the law enforced their suppression, whereupon came the era of " list " betting, which became so popular and widespread that " degradation and demoralization " followed.

It was estimated at one time, that close on a thousand " lists " were open in London alone—most of them placed in hotels and public houses. By the persistent display of the " lists ", betting extended among all classes—as little as 6d. being accepted in the majority of places.

It should be explained that a " list " was a written or printed document containing the name of horses engaged in the particular race to be betted upon, with a price affixed against the chance possessed by each animal. Such " lists ", in fact, have their counterparts in those used by the bookmakers on all race-courses nowadays.

Previous to the institution of the lists, we are told, the great body of people had been well contented with a ticket in a Derby or some other sweepstake, of which a great number—at prices ranging from pence to pounds—were regularly drawn in London and many towns in the provinces. All the principal handicaps and the Classic races were embraced in the sweepstakes craze and thousands of pounds changed hands almost daily.

History records how a butler in one of the most famous Pall Mall clubs in London drew the winner of the Chester Cup in one rich sweepstake. He promptly became the lessee of a public house in a little street in the City and proceeded to do well, for his customers were all " sports " and much enjoyed his taste for the Turf. The house soon became a rendezvous for those who were fond of a bet.

One evil day, a frequenter of the place introduced a friend who expressed a wish to start a betting-list and, with an eye to business, the landlord assented. For a while, all went well : custom increased, money was made, and betting-claims punctually met.

But at length came the frowning of Dame Fortune, and with it an altogether different story.

The " list "-keeper was a keen backer and more than once jeopardized " the book " (as so many have done since) by having all his money on a horse he thought " sure to win ". He paid for his foolishness when the horse he had backed for a big handicap ran unplaced, whereas most of his punters were on the winner. Unable to come up to scratch over the winning animal and aware that he could not meet his liabilities, the unhappy man absconded, leaving the landlord in a state of terror, because he feared and dreaded he would in some way be held responsible for the default of the runaway " list "-keeper.

His forebodings were more than realized when an incensed mob all but wrecked his premises, and finally he lost his licence.

The outcome was that the unfortunate victim turned tipster and, as " a retired club steward ", made good at that always precarious business. It may surprise my readers to know that " tipping " and tipsters flourished long before professional bookmakers and authentic racing " information " had come into being. Indeed, the guile and artifice of the earliest tipsters compared well with anything the modern exponent can conspire or produce. A certain Mrs. Adelaide Merryweather achieved enormous fame and notoriety as a result of her " knowledgeable advices ", and it is to her credit that she not only satisfied the " knowing ones "

F. FOX

T. WESTON

E. C. ELLIOTT

W. NEVETT

W. H. CARR

E. SMITH

D. SMITH

E. BRITT

of the Turf, but also succeeded in marrying one of her most generous clients !

As a tipster, Mrs. Merryweather resorted to various devices when soliciting patronage. Her masterpiece was, perhaps, contained in a circular worded as follows : "A jockey's wife, her husband being unable to ride now in consequence of having sustained a paralytic shock of the lower limbs, does not ask for charity : but, being anxious for the sake of her small children to earn a living, will be glad to hear from gentlemen who take an interest in racing. Her husband, having been a noted trial rider, knows well the form of all the horses now running." Address, etc., etc.

This "human document" made a very wide appeal and its author was rewarded handsomely when the tips she gave were successful.

A little research has disclosed that 100 years ago wagering on the Chester Cup and other events began in the previous December. This naturally suited the growing army of tipsters and furthered the operations of the " list " men, who were always anxious to bet on any future event. We are told that a horse could be backed to win upwards of £50,000 in one hand, and at a fair price, for such handicaps as the Chester Cup, and certain it is that, soon after its inception in 1839, the Cesarewitch provided a market so rich and profligate that any runner might have been supported to win £100,000. The owner of Weathergage, winner of the Cesarewitch in 1852, won £40,000, after having landed the Goodwood Stakes and £20,000 with the same horse a few months earlier. Weathergage was only a three-year-old at the time and, having won Mr. Parr a fortune, that gentleman sold him for £2,500.

When another three-year-old, Lecturer, won the Cesarewitch of 1866, one backer alone collected £80,000 from the ring, though in the fullness of time this great gambler died " broke " !

Where and whence came the men who by reason of their fabulous successes and failures on the Turf are still remembered so long after their passing? Crockford, Gully, Ridsdale, Swindell, and Davis " the Leviathan " are names which occur over and over again in the majority of volumes dedicated to the Sport of Kings, whilst the extravagant or reckless careers of such "sprigs of nobility" as the Marquis of Hastings, Colonel Mellish, George Payne and countless others are part and parcel of racing lore and accredited history. It is not possible, within the limits of this cursory review, to outline the careers of the persons mentioned, so they must perforce be dealt with briefly.

The Marquis of Hastings flourished at a time when it was believed that the race of plungers would never become extinct.

P

His brief, meteoric career on the Turf is, even to this day, recalled with pathos, mixed with some measure of admiration. In his youthful heyday, the Marquis had many admirers who thought there was something heroic in the way he staked hundreds of thousands of pounds and lost them.

Before he attained his majority, " Harry Hastings " had developed a passion for racing. Ackworth won for him the Cambridgeshire of 1864, and The Duke captured the Goodwood Cup two years later. The noble owner was then in his early twenties and an idea of his keenness can be gathered from the fact that in 1864 his horses won £10,000 in stakes, £13,000 in 1866, and £30,000 in 1867.

Yet it was as a backer of his own and other people's horses that the Marquis gained notoriety. The ring which had cheered him as a comparative youth, hooted him as a defaulter at the Derby of 1868. One year earlier the Marquis, by laying persistently and bitterly against The Hermit, lost upwards of £100,000. He left the course on that occasion with a party of friends—and in the gayest humour he later sat down to dine. " Harry Hastings " parted with his Scottish estate to meet racing-debts of over £100,000.

The shattered, ruined Marquis died at the age of 26, and from that day to this, the precise manner of his downfall has remained a problem. Was it due to his racing-losses, or were cards and extravagance in other directions the contributory causes ?

Henry Chaplin, owner of the Derby winner Hermit, raced in the same era as the Marquis of Hastings and, for reasons unconnected with the Turf, they were to all intents and purposes ever at arms length. Chaplin was an outstanding figure of high-mindedness and political ambition, while his sporting instincts —racing, hunting, deerstalking and other diversions—were the passion of his life. His triumph with Hermit was but one achievement on the Turf and it so chanced that the Marquis of Hastings by opposing Henry Chaplin's Classic winner reduced his dwindling fortunes considerably. The world knew that the young gambler lost more than £100,000 over the success of Hermit, and it also knew that he had to impoverish himself to raise the money. Chaplin, never rapacious, did insist, with all good grace, that a debt of honour must be paid.

Lord George Bentinck, by his commanding personality, became a veritable " King of the Turf " and is treated as such in all old-time volumes of historical value. As a son of the Duke of Portland, he quite naturally cultivated an early liking for all forms of sport and was a very good amateur rider. His first important victory as an owner (when racing as Lord Lichfield) came with the St. Leger of 1836, when Elis won after being conveyed from the South to Doncaster in a horsedrawn van, specially designed for the purpose.

The " Bentinck era " really began in 1841, when he was maintaining a huge string of race-horses and a large stud. His betting was correspondingly high and this can be instanced by the fact that he supported Gaper to win £150,000 in the Derby of 1843, in which the colt ran unplaced.

Nevertheless, Lord George did not overlook the winner, Cotherstone : in fact, by the success of this horse, he was enabled to show a profit of £30,000 on the race. His estimated betting winnings in 1845 were £100,000, with colossal expenses as a set-off. The best of all his winners was Crucifix, a filly who took the One Thousand Guineas and the Two Thousand Guineas and also the Oaks in 1840. Her owner landed £20,000 when she won the Epsom race, and that despite her starting an odds-on chance.

When he was at the zenith of his fame, Lord George Bentinck amazed the sporting world by selling his horses, lock, stock and barrel. The transaction was completed almost within the hour, so to speak, and among the horses so quickly and cheaply disposed of was Surplice, winner of the Derby and St. Leger of 1848.

A week after that St. Leger, the great Lord George was found dead in a meadow on his father's estate. A spasm of the heart ended his meteoric career. He died with the character of being the beau-ideal of an English nobleman. Furthermore, his beneficial work on behalf of the Turf—its advancement and reform—gave him a strong and lasting claim to remembrance as a monument to racing.

George Payne and Lord George Bentinck were contemporaries, and their Turf ventures are therefore co-related to some extent. Payne had an income of £80,000 per annum on attaining his majority, but, even before that, had staggered the sporting world by reason of his wagering. There was a little matter of £33,000 lost over the St. Leger of 1824, for instance, and the remark, " It's a pleasure to lose, by jove ! "

The youthful gambler had taken the liberty of laying against the winner—Jerry—in the belief that the horse was infirm. He had to resort to a moneylender in order to settle. Payne owned race-horses from 1840 to 1878, but never had a really great colt or filly, and his solitary Classic winner was Clementina (One Thousand Guineas, 1847). Apart from his racing extravagances, Payne played cards regularly and it was said that, over a period of 50 years, he spent more nights at play than any man who ever cut a pack of cards. The result of all these devotions to the " Goddess of Chance " can best be imagined. When he died, George Payne had dissipated practically the whole of his fortune and patrimony. Yet he left a reputation for chivalry and honour which few have exceeded or equalled.

Perhaps, in the annals of racing, there are few of the nobility whose Turf successes compared with those of Sir Joseph Hawley. His colours were carried by such " giants " as Teddington, Beadsman, Musjid, Blue Gown, Aphrodite, Mendicant, and others. The " cherry and black cap " silks were first registered in 1844, and three years afterwards Miami bore them to victory in the Oaks. In 1851 Teddington won the Derby for Sir Joseph and his " partner ", Mr. J. M. Stanley, who by then had become recognized as " darlings of the Gods ". Their good fortune can be illustrated in one sentence. Mendicant, for whom they paid 3,000 gns., produced Beadsman, who in 1858 won the Derby and enabled the owners to win much more than £100,000 in wagers alone.

When he died in 1875, it was agreed that the Turf could ill-afford to lose such a princely supporter. Nearly every big race had, at some time or other, fallen to a horse carrying his colours, and tremendous sums of money were invariably at stake in the way of bets.

And here, perhaps, is the moment to mention the " Leviathans of the Ring " who played such important parts in the scheme of things and made the golden days of that gambling era a topic for all time.

I have mentioned Davis " the Leviathan ", John Gully, and Crockford. Their names are indelibly written in the chronicles of the Turf because of their prodigious manner of wagering and the influence they wielded in the very best circles.

Gully made early fame as a prizefighter. Crockford began as a fishmonger, and Davis earned his first wages as a carpenter. Yet they became prominent in Turf affairs and were trusted by the highest in the land. " Their mere word is better than other men's bonds ", said a baronet who raced in their time.

From " nothing ", as it were, Davis rocketed to the heights. His original small " bank " was increased when he backed the Two Thousand Guineas' winner (Sir Tatton Sykes, 1846), and cleverly laid all the losers. From then onwards, Davis expanded and became famous in the betting-houses of London for his generous prices and bold offers. Ready-money speculations were his speciality. " The horse which wins ", he would say, " brings you nothing. All the others do." Modest in manner, invariably polite and civil, astute and nimble at figures, Davis speedily made his name and fame—and a fortune—to become the first of the Leviathans. He was both an operator and a patron of the " lists ", but definitely not the originator of them. When Lord Zetland's Voltigeur won the Derby (1850) Davis had to pay £40,000 on his " list "-accounts, apart from his responsibilities on the race-course. By now, Davis was laying the odds to fabulous amounts, and the success of Teddington at Epsom took more than £100,000 out of his book. On many races, he cleared correspondingly large sums.

Davis eventually retired and lived in Brighton. When he died, he left £150,000. That was £10,000 more than the amount bequeathed by Frederick Swindell when he passed on. This gentleman left the North to take up business in London, where his first venture was a public house, whereat betting was the vogue. Swindell thrived as a bookmaker and as a commissioner and in due time reached the top flight in both capacities. His betting was carried on in the grand manner and, when entrusted with a commission, he took the most extraordinary steps in order to ensure secrecy of movement. He once laid Sir Joseph Hawley £18,000 to £1,000 against a winner on the instant. Thereupon, Swindell proceeded to back the horse to win himself a goodly fortune.

John Gully (the pugilist) and his friend, John Ridsdale, became far-famed on account of their multifarious betting transactions. They were outstanding among the racing adventurers of their time and, being of humble origin, had to fight the hard way. Gully actually became a Member of Parliament, after graduating as a butcher, prizefighter, publican, and bookmaker. Ridsdale, his long companion, began life in a livery-stable.

It was while in business as a publican that Gully sensed the way to fortune in the betting-arena. Like others before him, he early discovered that " backing " horses was a precarious undertaking and he at once decided to " lay " them.

In the process, he and Ridsdale had many viscissitudes, but they were a brave pair and slowly but surely attained eminence in the right circles. Gully had made an attempt to win the St. Leger with Mameluke before he joined up with Ridsdale and it was only later that the partnership actually began to thrive and flourish. St. Giles, owned by Mr. Ridsdale, winner of the Derby of 1832, is reputed to have won Gully and Ridsdale £100,000. The same season, when Mr. Gully's Margrave won the St. Leger, the confederacy cleared another huge " packet ". Ridsdale, as a matter of fact, questioned his share of the spoils and Gully assaulted him—and the upshot was a trial at York Assizes.

Gully's own horse, Pyrrhus the First, won the 1846 Derby and enriched him enormously. His winnings were increased by the success of his filly Mendicant in the Oaks the same year.

William Crockford was a product of Billingsgate Market. He early acquired a taste for gambling, however, and seems to have been singularly successful at cards, dice and other table pastimes. He introduced a roulette-table on the race-course and enjoyed a reputation for his jolly establishments in London. Although interested in racing as a means to gambling, Crockford, while from time to time an owner of race-horses, had no love for the Turf. He started " houses " in Newmarket and London and his name lives to this day.

I think we can now turn our attention to modern-day betting, as we see it practised at the moment and during the past 30 or 40 years.

The days of the " Leviathans " have gone, the " lists " and the gambling-houses are forgotten, race-course villainy is no more —rectitude prevails everywhere. Credit betting has taken the place of surreptitious wagering, most of the bookmakers we see on the race-courses are members of accredited organizations, the rings are under the supervision of the Jockey Club, the Totalisator functions at all meetings—and still betting is illegal. We have, as I said at the beginning, a Royal Commission probing the methods and principles of Betting and Gambling. Its object is to find out by what means pools, totalisators, bookmakers and so on can be brought even nearer to the law and contribute to the Exchequer.

Betting of a sort is indulged in by millions of our citizens, but the amounts staked by individuals are modest if not meagre, and outright gambling is confined to the race-course. To suggest that untold thousands are staked would be ridiculous, since there are not the bookmakers to provide the facilities, and anything " old-fashioned " in a betting sense is unthinkable. Any man now desiring to back a horse substantially must needs resort to the utmost cleverness, because the " market " all over England is sensitive to a degree and any investment of a few hundred pounds can quickly be traced to source. Countless measures to " protect " the bookmakers have been in operation for a long time and the telephone, " blower ", tape-machine and such inventions have given the layers a tremendous advantage.

The first and foremost factor relating to modern betting is undoubtedly the Totalisator, which has an annual turnover of approximately £25,000,000. This money is neither lost nor won, since it represents naught but the aggregate passed through the Tote in a full year of racing. From 1930 to 1950, the Tote handled approximately £110,000,000, but it must not be thought that this vast sum has been taken from the pockets of punters and irre-trievably lost by them. It stands for a capital sum which the Tote has received and disbursed in its capacity as a " bank " and the one sure winner is the Tote itself, because of the over-all deduc-tion it makes from all monies handled. From time to time the percentage accruing to the Tote has varied, but the deduction is now stabilized at roundabout 12½ per cent. By this means, very substantial sums are allotted annually for the benefit of racing. Details of the Tote's operations are published season by season and are first submitted to the Home Secretary.

Not long after the Totalisator was introduced on race-courses, the devotees of Greyhound-racing clamoured for the "machine" on similar lines and in due course their demands were satisfied. On the greyhound-tracks spread over the country, the Tote handles far more money than the race-course counterpart, but it was some time before the Government realized that a rich source of income had been overlooked. Now, of course, the yield to the Exchequer is the despair of greyhound-track (and tote) proprietors.

In the great scheme of gambling, the Tote plays an insignificant part, because the money it handles is in the nature of a casual transaction. Small investors contribute to the turnover only when they are able to attend a race-meeting and, but for the investments made through an off-the-course agency, the daily pools would be much smaller. They would, in fact, be practically halved, which goes to prove that the amount of ready-money available for betting is in reality limited, whereas "credit"-betting with bookmakers is beyond estimate.

I suppose there are 30,000 bookmakers to whom backers can resort by one means or another. The amount of capital involved is, however, not assessable and to what extent the "market" might be drained is debatable. On certain outstanding races, the large firms handle tremendous sums, but rarely is a great risk undertaken, since "cover" can easily be arranged almost when the horses are about to run. Facilities to this end have been perfected as betting expanded, and the bookmaker is "protected" by the most extraordinary means. He can, for instance, invest through the "Blower" hundreds or thousands of pounds at a moment when the runners are at the starting-post. Alternatively, by means of special private telephone-lines to fellow-bookmakers, he can make last-minute bets which assure his own safety. One great point about modern-day betting is that much of it takes place among bookmakers themselves, and this applies to wagering on the course, as well as in offices.

The "Blower" remains something of a mystery to many backers of horses who have no intimate knowledge of the methods adopted by bookmakers in the conduct of their business. Therefore I will try to explain exactly how the "Blower" came about and what its functions are from day to day.

Betting has spread by reason of the wider publicity enjoyed by racing over the years. Results that were once conveyed by devious means, received an impetus when the telegraph was invented. Then came the telephone and still-faster despatch. Tape-machines brought, and still bring, immediate results to towns and cities everywhere. What happens on the race-course is known in sporting circles minute by minute, even if the man in the street is dependent upon the newspapers for his information.

The " Blower " service is purely a telephonic arrangement invented and evolved for the benefit of bookmakers, on and off the course. It started as an " information " channel, by means of which starting-price bookmakers were made aware of the odds offered on the course. A man subscribed to the service and thus became linked with the actual race-course scene. By the knowledge gained, he could adjust his commitments race by race to the utmost satisfaction. Mr. Fred Howard—one-time Mayor of Holborn, London—was the recognized founder of the " Blower ", and his earliest experiments were remarkable. His task from the outset was quickly to establish telephonic contact where no telephone existed, and this entailed unique and novel methods, in which various tic-tac men were employed. The difficulties were enormous and official help was not always forthcoming, yet Howard established his system and founded a prosperous business. Nowadays, the " Blower " is not a one-man affair, as several agencies are interested in the dissemination of news and other matters principally affecting betting.

By mutual arrangement, a bookmaker can now invest through the good offices of the " Blower " any amount of money on a horse and, by so doing, greatly affect the wagering on the course, which is the place where the starting-prices are determined. " Blower " money is usually " insurance " money and, as such, does not always define winners.

You will ask how the big bets of to-day are transacted and seek enlightenment as to their magnitude, especially in comparison with old-time wagers. I shall say at once that the " Leviathans " of the ring are nowadays given the title purely by courtesy. Their transactions have a smash-and-grab flavour which is all part of the new age. There are, perhaps, a dozen well-known characters who bet boldly, winter and summer. They engage in a sustained tussle with the bookmakers meeting by meeting and, if their method of approach varies, the " professional " touch is always apparent. In no respect do the operations of the best-known betting-men compare with the spectacular methods employed by erstwhile celebrities whose names are still remembered. Nor are the layers of to-day noted for their bold responses, unless they have definitely been licensed to deal in " dead meat ", as the saying goes.

The present century dawned when money flowed freely, especially on the Turf. Owners of good horses backed them fearlessly and accommodating bookmakers were out to encourage them.

King Edward VII, as the "first gentleman of Europe", was then the figurehead of the Turf. His followers included Royalty, peers, squires and commoners, and one glance at the owners whose horses then thrilled the populace must convince the observer that we now live in times of austerity and littleness. Into the early-century picture came the immortal Sceptre to win four of the five Classics and thus make history. The bets of her owner, Mr. "Bob" Sievier, were on a grand scale and, if the thousands he won soon melted into thin air, it has to be admitted that few braver gamblers have emerged in the meantime. When very short of funds, Sievier backed Sceptre to win the Lincolnshire Handicap for £40,000 and when he saw her beaten by inches treated it as a mere matter of luck. Ten years later when Warlingham won him the Cesarewitch, the genial "Bob" landed a £30,000 gamble and the bookmakers to whom he did not happen to owe money were pleased to pay.

But by this time, racing had become a "commercialized" industry up to the point that the patrician owners—the true pillars of the Turf—were slowly but surely passing out, and newcomers intent on "making the game pay" were creeping in and running their horses with one avowed object. One reflects on the sterling qualities of the owners who were contemporary with King Edward VII and at the same time attempts to compare "the ring" of that era with the ring of to-day. Lord Lonsdale, Lord Falmouth, Mr. Leopold de Rothschild, Sir Abe Bailey and men of that quality illuminated the Turf in their day and there were bookmakers equally famous for the part they played in concreting the Sport of Kings. That the character of racing has changed is beyond dispute and, while there is still "big money" in the game, there are no gamblers of any account, for with bookmakers it is mostly a case of dog-eat-dog. That the names of once famous "Leviathans" are still used for trade-purposes, partly substantiates my arguments.

To my knowledge, £40,000 to £1,000, and £10,000 to £1,000 a place, was laid against a horse in the Derby a few years ago. The stable-commission for another Derby candidate (which won) was £25,000 to £3,000. The late Mr. "Daddy" Clayton was laid £100,000 to £100 against his horses (he had several in each race) winning the Cesarewitch and Cambridgeshire not so many years ago. Heathorn, the layer, got a rare shock when Clayton's horse won the "first leg", but was content when the other suffered a narrow defeat. Possibly the last owner to land a prodigiously lucrative double, was Mr. A. Macomber, with

Forseti, and Masked Marvel when they won in 1925. In the matter of single-handed bets, it may be supposed that, among living owners, Mr. James de Rothschild, Sir William Cooke, Mr. Stanley Wootton, Mr. T. Westhead and a few others have tasted the sweets of victory more often than most. But in no sense have the exploits of these gentlemen bordered on the sensational. Quite the reverse, in fact.

It was not uncommon to see Mr. James de Rothschild move from one end of the rails to the other backing one of his long-priced horses freely and openly. His bets were always substantial enough to carry weight and the very fact that he executed them himself caused him to be talked about. Slowburn, Pickersgill, Hibbert, Bayliss, Steele and other well-remembered bookmakers were ever ready to satisfy the demand of the reckless backers of their time and it was their withdrawal from the field that marked the beginning of other methods.

That betting is more widespread than ever before cannot be denied, yet the money involved is distributed over a big area and, in the aggregate, would not represent a large sum. The 30,000 bookmakers to whom reference has been made are for ever engaged in keen competition and I do not think it out of place to say that most of the really " big " money is in a few hands. The market as we know it is governed by the richer layers.

Once upon a time, a Derby candidate was supported months beforehand to win £270,000. If this could be done nowadays, I am unable to explain the process, since the advertised odds of certain reputable firms are only laid to the tune of a " tenner ", or a " pony " (£25) at the most. Any genuine investment on a genuine horse means an " inspired move " all over the country, and within 24 hours the odds are clipped many points. How, then, can a straightforward, honest-to-goodness commission be " worked " or put into motion? The enforced method is to approach a responsive bookmaker and get him to lay a fair price for the full investment. Thereafter, he must be allowed to skim the " market " in his own way, and if he can contrive to do this without his brethren " smelling a rat ", all the better. Sad to relate, many modern bookmakers on the course frequently have " one to lay " and that is a part of the great game which I deplore.

If a " small " backer can, by any chance, find the winners of " double-event " races, such as the Lincoln and National or the Cesarewitch and Cambridgeshire, he will have no difficulty in collecting £10,000 or £50,000, provided his wagers are wisely distributed. The money is there, but the " Bank " is a fortress which is protected in every conceivable way. A regular supply of " mug money " serves to keep the " ring " affluent and, at the same time, enrich the few who are fortunate enough to wager heavily on their winners.   One could name the lucky few on the fingers of one hand.   Gone are the plungers like " Harry " Hastings, Abington Baird, the " Jubilee Juggins ", and all the young aristocrats with fortunes to dissipate.   The loss of £50,000 would, to-day, make any man notorious and there are few on the Turf to whom credit to that extent would be granted.   There are, of course, disillusioned backers in existence, to whom, £50,000 once appeared a lowly sum.   While they were on the flood tide and the luck held good, what was money worth anyway ?   In the fullness of time, they got to know all the answers.   And it was long ago established that, in the end, betting on horses is a sure way to ruin.   Once in a while, certain owners, trainers and their friends, acting as a confederacy, contrive to " beat the books " for big sums of money.   This has been done and can still be done in face of all difficulties.   But, with the " Market " primed and sensitive—alert to every move on the board—one does not hesitate to say that those who succeed in draining it will need to be skilful and cunning.   It all makes one think that the days of " lists ", betting-shops, delayed-results, and so on, were indeed the good old days of the Turf.

CHAPTER XV

RACE BROADCASTING

By Raymond Glendenning

IT is only roughly 25 years ago that the microphone officially found its way on to the race-course. Before that, I'm sure there were broadcasts, just as there are to-day, but they were localized and heard only by the people around at the time they were spoken. Jump-by-jump and furlong-by-furlong commentaries, for the use of the Press agencies and the " blower ", have been carried out for years, and even the enthusiast reading a race to his friends who were without binoculars must have been a regular figure long ago. But when I talk about " broadcasting " I mean broadcasting as we mean it to-day—through a microphone to listeners spread far and wide, up and down the country, and in all parts of the world.

Racing broadcasting is nearly as old as Outside broadcasting, which, as its name implies, covers everything from an opera or a variety show happening in a theatre to the Boat Race or the F.A. Cup Final. In point of fact, it was not until January 8, 1923, that the first Outside broadcast (or, as we at the B.B.C. affectionately term them, " O.B.'s "), took place. And then, indeed, it was an opera—a broadcast of one of the Acts of " The Magic Flute " from Covent Garden. Strangely enough, it was not until about three months after, that the first " sports talk " took place from a " studio " and not until nearly six months after —June 6, to be exact—that the first eyewitness account was given of a sporting event that had previously taken place that afternoon.

Racing first came into the picture on Derby Day, 1926. A " daring experiment ", as it was then styled, took place when a microphone was installed to broadcast " the crowds at Tattenham Corner ", was connected by telephone-line to the old 2 LO studio and, from there, listeners at home, clamping their earphones hard to their ears, " heard " the Derby. Amidst a background of tipsters and bookies, Laurence Anderson, Vera Lennox and R. E. Jeffrey carried on a conversation as they looked around them. Actually, the 1925 Derby was to have been the first Epsom Outside Broadcast, but the negotiations broke down and nothing transpired. This was the year of Steve Donoghue's last Derby victory, when, despite last-minute rumours that he was to ride the King's Runnymede, he rode the horse for which he had been originally engaged—Mr. H. E. Morriss's Manna to score his sixth Derby win.

The 1926 broadcast was hardly hailed by the critics as a success and, though the unseen mass of listeners got a terrific thrill from the concerted shout of "They're off", their entertainment was thereafter restricted to the murmur of the crowd and something of this sort as the horses flashed round Tattenham Corner : " Here they come—now they're getting down to it — he's drawing ahead — it's sure to be Lex—No, Harpagon ", and then a somewhat distant voice, I gather, read from his race-card : " It looks like 9—5—1". Without even translating the numbers into horses, a voice from the studio then announced the end of the broadcast. Coronach (J. Childs) won the 1926 Derby for Lord Woolavington. However, the idea of sporting running-commentaries, and racing ones in particular, had begun to capture the public imagination. My old friend, Harold Abrahams, went as far in February, 1927, as to herald the " dawn of a new sporting era", though he is reported as saying that broadcasting will never be " quite the same as seeing the event on the spot ". The dawn of the new racing era quite definitely came in the following March, and Programme Records for 2 LO and Daventry 5 XX show that the first racing-broadcast was staged between 2.30 p.m. and 3.32 p.m. on that day, from Aintree, when Meyrick Good and George Allison first described the Grand National. As early as February in that year, it had been officially announced that the B.B.C. were considering " a Turf experiment, but there were many difficulties on the technical side to be overcome ". A little later, it was confirmed that listeners would be introduced for the first time to a " new and thrilling kind of broadcast description", although, as the B.B.C. cautiously added, " it must be treated purely as an experiment, because we have no previous experience to go on."

What is interesting about this first racing-broadcast, is that it involved the use of five microphones. One in the Private Stand, from which Meyrick Good described the progress of the race, and one hanging down in front of him to pick up the cheers of the crowd and the noises from Tattersall's ring. A third one was overlooking the Paddock, from which some of the preliminaries were described by George Allison ; a fourth one, over the Unsaddling Enclosure, brought in the cheers for the winner, whilst a fifth fulfilled its purpose when Ted Leader, who had ridden Sprig to victory, was heard—if somewhat breathlessly—to say : " Good afternoon everyone. I'm very proud and very happy. Sprig gave me a wonderful ride." And after Ted, came Mr. T. R. Leader, the trainer of the winner, who admitted to thousands who had never seen him that he had realized the ambition of his life in training a Grand National winner which his son had ridden.

Yes, that microphone certainly did its stuff. The main part of the broadcast was hailed as a great step forward, although, since the commentators were stationed on the Grand Stand, it was obvious they couldn't be asked to describe falls happening round by the Canal Turn, and, unfortunately, the roar of cheering as the winner passed the post completely drowned the commentator, so that listeners had to wait until the official result was announced to find out which horse had won. But it was a great achievement and the B.B.C. engineers tackled manfully this job of trying to bring the background-atmosphere to the listeners without interfering with the reception of the commentator.

In June, 1927, came the first running-commentary of the Derby. Geoffrey Gilbey and George Allison were the men behind the microphone on that occasion. It was a rather long broadcast, judged by our standards, for it went on from 2.30 p.m. to 3.26 p.m. and, if a lot of the pre-race atmosphere (with its interviews with the crowds on the Downs and selections from an itinerant band) failed to satisfy the critics, at least the listeners had the thrill of hearing, at the very second that it happened, Charlie Elliott riding Call Boy comfortably to victory.

Then followed the St. Leger, 1927, with Geoffrey Gilbey, assisted by his brother Quintin, describing how Lord Astor's Book Law (7-to-4 favourite) justified the great public faith in him. It was here that the " desensitized " microphone was first tried out, the object being that the voice of one person speaking close up could be heard without any background noise and that a separate microphone which could be faded-down to a lower level was introduced to give atmosphere.

Again, the B.B.C. engineers were cautious in their verdict: "A certain measure of success was achieved," they are reported as having said, " but the voice of the commentator had not 100-per cent. quality." So much progress had been made in the matter of relaying a " live " event to a listening public that it was quite obvious race-broadcasting had come to stay, though it is interesting to note that evening newspapers, selling, as they said, " copies " where before they had sold " hundreds ", began to regard broadcasting as a menace. One incident recounted then, was of a 500 crowd which had listened to the race through a loudspeaker and had dispersed before the newsagent had stamped even one copy with the official result.

In turn, came the 1928 Grand National. Does the name Tipperary Tim convey anything special to you? Let me refresh your memory. The official winner was Tipperary Tim (100–1), ridden by Mr. W. Dutton; second was Billy Barton; there was no third—and that out of a field which had numbered 42. Perhaps it was fortunate for the commentators, Geoffrey Gilbey and H. W. Hobbiss, that the field thinned-out, for with the mud, fog and rain it must have been a terrible job to see the competitors, even from the top of the Aintree Stands.

But still, the listeners got that great final thrill—" They're coming on the race-course—Billy Barton's in the lead—Great Span's running beside him—Great Span's down—it's Billy Barton and Tipperary Tim—and Billy Barton's down and Tipperary Tim's coming home alone." Billy Barton was remounted to finish second.

Listeners were growing in number. As evidence, the story can be told of a couple of police-officers in a big city, who, being worried about the hold-up in traffic occurring because of the avid listeners crowding round a doorway above which there was a loudspeaker, remonstrated with a shopkeeper. I am happy to record, however, that they were human enough to wait until the instrument had diffused the news of Tipperary Tim's victory before hurriedly emerging and dispersing the crowd with the voice of authority.

On June 6, 1928, came the Derby again. This time, the broadcast had been cut to half-an-hour ; the preliminaries had been ruthlessly pruned. The commentator, the late R. C. (" Bob ") Lyle, as the horses were parading in front of the Epsom stands, referred to Felstead and remarked that, although he was a Felstead boy, he hadn't a penny on it. He must have been a saddened man as he described the finish. Fairway, the favourite, was not too well away and, as the race neared its climax, it was a duel between Felstead and Flamingo which ended in Harry Wragg riding Sir Hugo Cunliffe-Owen's 33–1 Felstead past the post for the premier honours.

Race-broadcasting in those days was still something of a mystery, if not a miracle, and it caused a tremendous stir when passengers aboard the Flying Scot, passing through Newcastle on its trip to Edinburgh, heard R. C. Lyle announce Trigo as the 1929 Derby winner at the very moment at which it passed the post. Two wireless-engineers had a set on the train, and even Americans on board were amazed on receiving, a couple of moments later, a printed card bearing the result although the train must have been a good 300 miles from the scene of the race. Nineteen twenty-nine is important because the Berlin Radio station first broadcast an English race, with quick interjections in German by a commentator sitting in the studio over there.

In the 1930's, race-broadcasting continued on pretty much the same lines, though technical improvements were constantly being made, but it wasn't until 1937 that Geoffrey Gilbey and Quintin gave the initial broadcast of the Oaks. Later that June, came the first-ever Ascot commentary with its description of the Gold Cup and the (at that time) sensational addition of a woman's voice to describe to the unseen listeners, who had multiplied in their thousands, a mouth-watering description of the enchanting fashion-parade. In the October of that year came the first broadcast of the Cesarewitch.

In April, 1938, the microphone went to Newmarket for the first broadcast of the Two Thousand Guineas. The commentator was Thomas Woodroffe and it was about that period the B.B.C. started to evolve the technique of having an experienced " microphone speaker ", coupled with an expert " race-reader ", to paint the picture in even fuller detail than had been possible previously. As far as I can trace, it was in this year, too, that the Northumberland Plate was first broadcast. It was in the Cesarewitch of 1938 that I had my first link with English race-broadcasting, and a link it was in very truth, for the position allotted to me was at the very end of Devil's Dyke, as it is popularly known, or, as that peculiar long ridge of earth is more correctly called by the locals, " the Ditch ". The Cesarewitch course, as regular race-goers know, is roughly " V " shaped and, for the first time, my description of the first mile and a-quarter was sent back to a control-point at the Grandstand by means of a mobile-transmitter: the " radio link ", in other words !

I had been broadcasting races in Northern Ireland since 1936. I remember my first commentary extremely well, though I was only acting as " Number Two " at a point-to-point race in the far North of Ulster. As my duties were only to set the scene, I had not bothered to memorize the race-card with any serious intent, but whilst the horses were on parade and the racing-expert had taken over, I did, out of idle curiosity, " mug up " the colours which distinguished the various animals to see whether I could follow the race. About half-way through the race—I think from " nerves ", for, able rider though he was, this was his first broadcast—the expert dried up and I hurriedly stepped into the breach and had to describe the rest of the race. Was I thankful that I had even *thought* of committing to memory the jockeys' distinguishing jerseys and caps ? After that, I had plenty of experience in describing races in Northern Ireland, including those at the Maze for the Ulster Derby and at Downpatrick for the Ulster Grand National.

In 1939 I was transferred to London and, from then on, frequently renewed my acquaintanceship with English race-courses (both " jump " and " flat ") in a broadcasting capacity. The sport, of course, was limited and regionalized and the races were, on many occasions, " substitutes " for pre-war events, but, with the advent of the Light Programme, the scope of race-broadcasting was gradually enlarged until, towards the end of the war, the B.B.C. were covering nearly all the main races, though it was not until May, 1946, that the One Thousand Guineas was first put over the air. Since then, I have described literally hundreds of races, yet I must confess I get the same " kick " out of that climax which listeners tell me still leaves them gripping the arms of their chairs or riding the winner home at the expense of the drawing-room furniture.

What is a commentator's job? In my view, frankly to pass on the thrill of that moment to someone who, had it not been for illness or business reasons, would have been there to see for himself or herself. The commentator must be accurate and co-herent and must convey only genuine excitement. For this, the test is : does the pace and pitch of his delivery match the vari-ation in the background of the the roar of the crowd on the rails? If so, he is being truthful. Impartiality is essential. Hundreds of people with their " bobs " on outsiders want to know what is happening to their fancy and must be told, but it is impossible to keep mentioning every animal and, therefore, those most heavily supported get a certain priority. The leaders, of course, always get most mention. So does the way they change about, and that is why the ultimate winner coming through a ruck of horses as he usually does " at the distance " only seems to arrive on the scene at the last minute. Rarely does a horse win " from in front " in a flat race. If he did, more often, the commen-tator's job would be much easier. A natural obstacle is bad visibility, about which you never know until the last minute, and although race-course executives are most co-operative in help-ing in the choice of our " pitch ", we are often, because of the lay-out of the course, up against difficulties not appreciated by the man at the other end of the loudspeaker. The commentator really turns himself into a human movie-camera, fitting each bit of action into its proper and recognizable place in the word-picture he is painting. Therefore, his creation must be, not only accurate, but well-designed. Here an orderly setting of the scene and a neat description of the course before the race is most im-portant. Contrasts and conflicts between different nations, various parts of the country, rival stables and riders bring out the highlights of each particular event. Then comes the most difficult part of his task. The (roughly) 300-word-a-minute des-cription of how the race is working-out in relation to the signposts he has already planted. " The finish " naturally pro-vides the greatest task of all! Unfortunately, the construction of most of our race-courses does not often allow for a microphone-point to be placed " dead on the finishing-line " and, having to decide between two fast-moving thoroughbreds travelling at top speed across an invisible line at an angle to you is not an easy job.

Especially difficult is this when the horses come more-or-less thundering straight at you as at Newmarket. A " split-second " recognition of the multitudinous variations of basic colours worn by the riders is of vital importance, and that is why I still carry on a practice I started way back in Ulster when I started in 1936. It is a little system I devised to make sure I can recognize instantaneously any horse in a race. When the acceptance come out, I paint the colours of the owners onto a set of cards—rather like playing-cards. At odd moments, then, for the few days before the race I shuffle the pack and deal them out rapidly, tagging on to each colour the name of the horse concerned, until I know each one backwards. But, however much homework a commentator may do, one pair of eyes cannot really take in all that happens in a race. For that reason beside me on the course is what we call a " race-reader ". He is usually a professional man who spends his life reading and reporting races. Listeners hear only one voice, thanks to the small directional microphone which the commentator holds right up to his mouth. It is the modern, improved counterpart of the " desensitized " mike they tried out way back in 1928.

Nowadays, as the commentator describes what he sees happening, the race-reader spots anything that he thinks his colleague has missed or with which he may be unfamiliar and " speaks his thoughts " in short, crisp sentences. The art of weaving into a rapidly moving picture this additional information and still keep talking cohesively is not an easy technique to master, but it is the best method discovered to date and does enable one to give the fullest possible sound-picture. The listener must not be aware of anything that breaks the easy, smooth flow of the voice he is hearing and, never obtruding yet never failing, my excellent collaborators always do a grand job of work.

Now the second half-century stretches out before us ! Television, which brings a visual picture right to the viewers' eyes hundreds of miles away and which made its debut before the war, is now firmly established and threatens to revolutionize, if not to put into the shade completely, the technique of to-day's sound-broadcasting. The new medium is being confronted with problems and difficulties as peculiar to itself as were those of pioneers of broadcasting in 1927. I am sure it will rise to equal heights and that anyone writing in the year 2000 will have, if not as thrilling, at least as interesting a story to tell as this one I have briefly tried to set on paper.

CHAPTER XVI

GREAT HORSES BRED IN FRANCE

By Baron Jacques Noirot-Nerin

ALTHOUGH there are so many connections between the English and the French Turf that the majority of the French stakes are reasonably familiar to English sportsmen, I think, perhaps, in order to make this review comprehensive, it might be advantageous to recall the chief events of our Classic record. We don't pay much attention to the races for two-year-olds ; it happened several times that our biggest winners did not run in their first season. The chief clashes for two-year-olds, however, are the Prix Robert Papin (former Omnium De Deux Ans), run at 6 furlongs at Maison-Laffitte at the end of July ; the Prix Morny (6 furlongs), at Deauville, three weeks later, and the Grand Critérium (1 mile), at Longchamp in the middle of October ; such are the three jewels of the " Triple Crown " for juveniles. Other interesting stakes are the 5-furlong Poule de 2 Ans in June ; Prix la Rochette in July ; Poule des Foals in August ; Biennal de Maison-Laffitte (against older horses) in September ; Prix d'Arenberg in October, and the longer stakes, Critérium de Maisons-Laffitte (7 furlongs), Prix de Condé and Critérium de St. Cloud (10 furlongs).

Three-year-old Classic colts used to compete in various " Poules de Produits ", from $1\frac{1}{4}$ to $1\frac{1}{2}$ miles, leading them to the Classics ; they are the Prix Greffulhe, Hocquart, Daru, Noailles, and Lupin, with other important races as the Prix Juigné (horses which had not run previously), Jean Prat, Matchem, La Rochette, Pénélope (for fillies), etc. The equivalents of the Guineas, the Pouldes d'Essai, have not the same importance as in England. The Prix de Diane (French Oaks), Prix de Jockey Club (French Derby), and Grand Prix de Paris, at 1 mile 7 furlongs, are contested in June. Later, three-year-olds may run in the 10-furlong Prix Eugène Adam, Prix de Minerve (fillies), then compete at the Deauville meeting in the Prix Jacques le Marois, Kergorlay, etc. In September, the Prix Royal Oak and the French St. Leger are decided and the fillies may contest the important Prix Vermeille. Good opportunities of meeting the older horses are provided by the Grand Prix de Saint Cloud, former Prix du Président de la République, in July, the Vichy and Deauville Grand Prix during the Summer, then the Coupe de Maisons-Laffitte, the Prix de l'Arc de Triomphe and du Conseil Municipal in October.

There is practically no Cup programme for old horses : they used to make their reappearance in the 10-furlong Prix des Sablons in April ; if they gave evidence of possessing stamina, they may run in the 2½-mile Prix de Cadran in May ; if not, they clash with the three-year-olds in the aforementioned events. The Prix de l'Arc de Triomphe is a weight-for-age event, but experience showed that only a true champion was able to win it against a good three-year-old. The 7-furlong Prix de la Forêt is for two-year-olds and upwards. Handicaps in France are of no value and contested only by second-class animals.

The nineteenth century had gone with a racing tragedy at Epsom : I am thinking of Flying Fox's Derby ; the French challenger Holocauste had him beaten when he broke a leg. How curious is fate ! The leading French owner and breeder of the time, M. Edmond Blanc, bought Flying Fox, which was the pride of England, for a fabulous price, thus creating one of the stoutest French strains. The loss of the best son of the famous stallion (Holocauste), Le Sancy, was to be irremediable for the French stock, and how could the success of Roi Herode have been foreseen at that time ?

Le Sancy died in 1900, the year when he had been represented on the Turf by a great filly, the Baron A. de Shickler's Semendria. She won her two races as a juvenile in 1899, and, having cantered to victory in the Poule d'Essai des Pouliches, it was a surprise to see her beaten in the Prix Lupin. She returned to winning form, however, in the Prix de Diane, the Grand Prix de Paris and the Prix Vermeille (giving 8 lb.), but suffered a setback in her last outing in 1900, being unsuccessful in her attempt to concede 9 lb. and the sex allowance to the majority of her opponents. The race was won by Codoman, who, too, was a good horse, subsequent winner of the Prix des Sablons and other races. Semendria did not show the same form as a four-year-old, but scored in the Prix Hédouville, de la Jonchère, and Grand Prix de Bade. The first glimpse of her career at the stud suggests she was a failure, but her granddaughter, La Bidouze, was to breed Biribi.

It is curious to note that the first three great thoroughbreds of the present century in France were fillies : after Semendria, came M. A. Abeille's La Camargo, and then M. E. de Saint Alary's Kizil Kourgan. La Camargo traced to St. Simon through her sire, Childwick, a son of the famous Plaisanterie, by which she returned to the type of Monarque. Like Semendria, she scored as a two-year-old in the Prix de la Forêt, then went on to register an easy victory in the Poule d'Essai and the Prix de Diane, having meanwhile been beaten a neck in the Prix Lupin by the subsequent Derby winner Saxon. In the Autumn, she won the Prix Vermeille but could not give the weight in the Prix de Flore and du Conseil Municipal.

Her subsequent record differed from Semendria's since she showed her true form in her fourth and fifth years. She was second to Codoman in the Prix des Sablons ; she was also second to the good stayer Amer Picon in the 3¼-mile Prix Rainbow, but failed in the Ascot Gold Cup. She stayed well, however, a fact reflected by her seven wins recorded at this age. In addition to her victories in the Prix du Cadran and La Rochette, she won the Prix Biennal, Grand Prix de Bade, du Prince d'Orange, du Conseil Municipal and du Pin ; in the Prix du Conseil Municipal, she carried the biggest weight permissible in that race.

The same thing happened the following year, in which La Camargo defeated all her opponents ! She scored ten times out of twelve, chiefly in the Prix des Sablons, Bolard, de Meudon ; her two setbacks were at Bade, owing to bad riding tactics. At last, this wonderful mare won all her four races as a six-year-old, but was robbed of one of them, her jockey having forgotten to be weighed ! La Camargo was one of the very great fillies of the French Turf : she was purchased by M. E. Blanc, but failed to breed her equal ; however, her daughter Mauri was the subsequent dam of the great Massine.

Kazil Kourgan was a daughter of the famous Omnium II which had passed, the same year as Le Sancy. She was a true example of whole French origin and was as backward as stout ; she ran but once as a juvenile, when second in the Prix de la Forêt. The following year she won the Poule d'Essai, Prix Lupin, Prix de Diane, and Grand Prix de Paris in a row. Her wins were not brilliant, since her great quality was her gameness : her jockey used to say that " she would have battled against an ass ". She often scored by very narrow margins ; in the Grand Prix de Paris, in which the great Sceptre ran badly, she won only by a short head over the Derby winner Retz and dead-heated with the subsequent Gold Cup conqueror Maximum. After this great achievement, the filly ran but once, in the Prix de Flore, in which she could not give 8 lb. to her runner-up of the Prix de Diane. Retired to the stud in 1903, she had to wait 15 years to foal the grand crack Ksar, one of the greatest among French horses.

The year 1903 was not a great one from the Classic standard : there was no real champion in it, the best performers being Ex Voto (Prix du Jockey Club) and three colts belonging to M. E. Blanc—Quo Vadis, Caius, and Vinicius, who achieved the record of securing the first three places in the Grand Prix de Paris !

Flying Fox's first crop reached its third year in 1904 : it was at once a big success. As a matter of fact, M. E. Blanc's Ajax and Gouvernant gained for him the major portion of the big

stakes of the year. Ajax retired unbeaten, after having scored as
a two-year-old (Prix de St. Firmin) and four times next season :
in the Prix Noailles, Lupin, du Jockey Club, and Grand Prix de
Paris. He was certainly a stout horse, but I would hesitate to
grade him as a real champion, since he had great difficulty to
beat Turenne in the Grand Prix and was retired soon after. However, he gained further credit when siring the great Teddy, his
chief success at stud. It is well known that, had he been better-
tempered, Gouvernant would have proved superior to Ajax ; he
would have beaten anyone in his good days. He won the Poule
d'Essai, Prix du Président de la République, Prix du Cadran,
Grand Prix de Bade, and many other stakes. In the same year,
M. E. Blanc won the Prix de Diane with Profane. An extraordinary thing happened in the Prix du Conseil Municipal when,
in heavy going, Pretty Polly was beaten by Presto II. Such are
the surprises of racing !

Edmond Blanc had another great year in 1905 : in fact, he then
owned the best horse he ever bred, Jardy, another son of Flying
Fox. Unbeaten in his first season in four races, his victories including the Middle Park Stakes at Newmarket. As a three-year-
old, he scored in storming manner in the Prix Noailles and Daru
and was sent to Epsom for the 1905 Derby. There was then a
coughing epidemic in his stable, but his owner took the risk of
running him in spite of the strange aspect of his health. Jardy
ran with a strong fever, finished second to Cicero, and fell danger-
ously ill, with the symptoms of typhoid. That was why he was
not kept as a sire for the stud of which he bore the name; he was
sold in South America, where his blood is found in many pedigrees.

His stablemate, Val D'Or, another son of Flying Fox, had been
unbeaten as a two-year-old, winning the Grand Critérium and
Prix Morny. Next season, he lacked stamina and failed in the
Grand Prix, but scored in the Poule d'Essai, Prix La Rochette,
Prix Monarque, and Eclipse Stakes. In the latter event (1905),
he avenged Jardy when easily beating Cicero, and in the previous
one he had beaten Finasseur, a colt bred by E. Blanc, whom
he unfortunately sold, since he won the Prix du Jockey Club,
Grand Prix de Paris, and Prix du Président de la République in
a row.

Edmond Blanc's era was followed by the success of the American owner W. K. Vanderbilt with two exceptionally good colts
in the same year, Prestige and Maintenon. W. K. Vanderbilt was
the precursor of the big American " invasion " which came later,
with Belmont, Duryea, Macomber, Widener, etc. The unbeaten
Prestige had not been entered in the big events. He easily
won all of his 16 races, including the " Triple Crown " for two-
year-olds, the Prix de la Forêt, Lagrange, Eugène, Adam, etc.,

beating the older horses as convincingly as his own contemporaries. The famous trainer W. Duke used to say that Prestige was
the best horse he ever trained. Well, Prestige was by a dark horse
named Le Pompon, but there are serious presumptions that he
was really sired by Flying Fox, a fact that would explain why
Prestige's son, Sardanapale, so strongly resembled Flying Fox.
There are, however, no certain proofs of this origin. The fact
remains that Prestige was really a great horse who, unfortunately,
went lame in his early years.

Maintenon was a grandson of Le Sancy through Le Sagittaire ;
he was a tall horse and a backward one. He did not run as a
two-year-old, but won for the first time in the Prix Hocquart ;
he was beaten in the Poule d'Essai and Prix Daru, then scored
in the Prix Lupin and du Jockey Club. It was a pity he suffered
from a tendinous inflammation when contesting the Grand Prix
de Paris, since it has been wondered if he would not have beaten
Spearmint, so much superior was he to Brisecoeur who finished
a good second. After a rest, he was unbeaten to the end of the
season, winning the Prix du Président de la République, Grand
Prix de Deauville, Royal Oak, Coupe d'or de Maisons Laffitte,
Prix du Conseil Municipal, etc. He had begun a similar record
at four years, when he broke down. The best achievement of
Mr. Vanderbilt's two champions at stud was when a daughter
of Prestige, mated to Maintenon, foaled a filly, Brumelli, the
winner of the war Classics Poule d'Essai, Prix de Diane, du Jockey
Club, and Grand Prix de Paris, a wonderful record !

Other famous horses of this time were the " père Lieux's "
Punta Gorda and Moulins La Marche ; their owner used to race
them without any interruption for years ! The mare, Punta
Gorda, later sold to Mr. Vanderbilt, ran 73 races and won 25
from two to five years, for an amount of nearly 500.000 fr., then
a big sum ; she had won the Grand Prix de Deauville. Moulins
La Marche remained in training to his eighth year, contesting 120
races and winning 41 times, including the Prix des Sablons, de
la Forêt, etc., more than 550,000 fr. !

The 1907 Grand Prix winner, the Baron Ed. de Rothschild's
Sans Souci II, a top-class horse, became a great sire at his owner's
stud of Meautry. Then the Vanderbilt horses again proved
superior to those of Ed. Blanc's. In 1908 he won the Prix du
Jockey Club (dead-heat) and du Président de la République with
Sea Sick, and the Grand Prix de Paris with Northeast. The former developed into a good stayer, but was prevented, by an
accident, from running in the Grand Prix. M. E. Blanc took his
revenge in the Autumn with his filly Medeah, winner of the Prix
de Diane over the good Sauge Pourpree, and went on to score
in the Prix Royal Oak and Vermeille. Her name is in many

American pedigrees, chiefly Omaha's and Flares. The same year, Bindou was able to give 18 lbs. and a beating to Radium in the Prix du Conseil Municipal.

E. Blanc won again in 1909 with a good filly, Union, but his American rival was lucky enough to win his third Derby in four years with the outsider Negofol, while his best horse, Oversight, was third, beaten a head by Union; the fourth was the Baron M. de Rothschild's Classic winner Verdun, which went on to score in the Grand Prix du Président. He was sold as a stallion to South America, where he was most successful. Really, it was not a great crop, but it was better than the following year, in which we may mention Mrs. Cheremeteff's Nuage, winner of the Grand Prix over the English candidates Lemberg and Charles O'Malley, unplaced in a sea of mud. There were, however, two good fillies, Basse Pointe and La Francaise, but they did not reveal their best form until they were four years old: the former then won the Prix du Conseil Municipal, Grand Prix de Deauville, and the Prix Gladiateur over La Francaise, which, however, improved into a very fine stayer.

The two best colts of 1911 were both sons of Perth, which had taken the place of the unlucky Holocauste at the head of his own crop. One was the Baron M. de Rothschild's Faucheur, who ran promisingly in the Spring, then fell lame and had to be retired. The Baron G. de Rothschild's Alcantara II was a very racing-like colt who found his true form the day when he was allowed to make his own pace: he then cantered to victory in the Prix Lupin and du Jockey Club. In the Grand Prix, he made the mistake of fighting against a second-class horse for the lead 7 furlongs from home and was beaten before entering the straight. The winner was the Marquis de Ganay's As d'Atout, a grandson of Le Sancy through Le Sagittaire.

After the very bad crop which ran in 1912, we had two interesting colts the following year. Without any hesitation, I give first place to M. A. Aumont's Nimbus, a son of Elf which would have won Craganour's Derby (1913) but for the incident at Tattenham Corner, and later scored in the Coupe de Maisons-Laffitte and Prix du Conseil Municipal under big weights, before showing his class and stamina as a four-year-old. However, and in spite of the fact that he sired Le Capucin, he was overshadowed by the Grand Prix and Royal Oak winner, M. de St. Alary's Bruleur, owing to the sensational success of the latter at stud, where he sired four Derby winners, one of them being the great Ksar. Three other good colts in the same crop were: Isard II, Dagor, and Ecouen.

But for the war, 1914 would have been a great racing year. First of all, we, at last, won the English Derby with Durbar II;

it was the first time since Gladiateur's days, owing to the mishaps of Holocauste, Jardy, and Nimbus. Mr. H. Duryea's colt, however, was only the third of his crop, behind two Rothschild representatives : the Baron Edouard's La Farina, by Sans Souci II, had beaten the Baron Maurice's Prestige colt Sardanapale in the Prix Daru and Lupin, but the latter had scored in several stakes, including the Prix Hocquart and the Prix du Jockey Club (in which La Farina did not run). In the Grand Prix de Paris, La Farina set a very hard pace and entered first in the straight in front of Sardanapale ; a terrific struggle ensued between the two horses and their famous jockeys, O'Neill and G. Stern, and Sardanapale got up on the post to win by a neck ; Durbar II was third, three lengths away. In spite of La Farina's subsequent failure in the Prix du Président won by Sardanapale, and owing to the much harder race he sustained, I wonder if he were not the better of the pair. Anyway, he was a better prospect at stud than his rival.

Then came the war. There was no racing in 1915, and in the following years only on a very modest scale, for the *preuves de sélection*. Nineteen-sixteen revealed the famous Teddy, who became so grand a sire, in Europe and in America. In 1917, it was the turn of the aforementioned Brumelli, then, in 1918, of a colt named Montmartin. The war was a big blow for our stock and we had nothing worthy to oppose the English Galloper Light in the 1919 Grand Prix. In 1920, there were fans of the easy Prix du Jockey Club winner Sourbier ; they affirm he ought to have won the Grand Prix de Paris, had he been ridden with other tactics. It is true he had then reached the peak of his form, but I really doubt he was superior to the English-bred and French-owned Comrade, which went on to score in the first Prix de l'Arc de Triomphe. On the other hand, Lemonora should not have won the 1921 Grand Prix, since we then had one of our greatest cracks, Ksar.

The first of Bruleur's Derby winners, Ksar, out of the famous mare Kizil Kourgan ; both his sire and dam had won the Grand Prix. He was bred by M. E. de Saint-Alary and purchased as a yearling by M. E. Blanc ; the latter, however, died before the colt's success ; his widow kept him under the famous orange-and-blue silks. Rather backward, Ksar was seen only twice as a two-year-old, winning one event and being second in the other. The following season, he scored successively in the Prix Hocquart, Lupin, and du Jockey Club. In the third event, he displayed a wonderful superiority, cantering with a stride impossible to be forgotten once seen. He was then made a strong favourite for the Grand Prix. The great jockey G. Stern rode him and it was a pity he chose this race to make the poorest show of his career !

He fought for the lead in the hard slope of the *petit bois* and his horse was beaten before entering the straight!

Ksar, however, proved he was not deficient in stamina when he won the Prix Royal Oak (same distance) very easily from the Grand Prix second, Flechois, in front of whom he cantered again in the Prix de l'Arc de Triomphe. Ksar ended his year with a surprising dead-heat with the moderate Vatel in the Prix Edgard Gillois. As a four-year-old, Ksar gained easy successes in the Prix des Sablons and du Cadran. In the Prix du Président de la République, he was ridden by J. Childs, whose inexperience of the horse may have contributed to the short-head victory of Kircubbin. Ksar cantered home in the Prix du Prince d'Orange and, again, in the Prix de l'Arc de Triomphe. His connections were imprudent to risk him in the Prix Gladiateur (3 miles 7 furlongs) against that true incarnation of stamina, Flechois, who beat him for the first time (he was, in fact, the second of his crop and had scored, too, in the Prix du Conseil Municipal). To sum up this subject, Ksar, who was closely inbred to Omnium II, was without doubt the best of his crop, and he was, too, superior to those which followed. He was a big success at stud.

His fourth year overshadowed the Classic results of 1922 : M. Marcel Boussac, then a newcomer to the Turf, won his first Derby with Ramus (he had been second the year before with Grazing); the latter was the Grand Prix runner-up. However, I shall give preference to his grand mare Zariba, who was to become much more famous at stud, in spite of her good record on the Turf, having bred Goyescas, Corrida, Abjer, and Goyer!

And now I arrive at what is called " the famous 1920 crop "; the chief elements of which were Massine, Sir Gallahad III, Epinard, Le Capucin, Filibert De Savoie, Checkmate, and Niceas. The best and most accomplished was Mr. Ternynck's Massine, by Console out of Mauri, a daughter of La Camargo. The winning two-year-old of the Prix de Villiers, St. Roman, and de Condé, he was beaten, on his reappearance, by Mackenzie (a very good horse who disappeared too early), then scored in the easiest manner in the Prix Hocquart and Lupin. It was a pity he fell after that, being thus deprived of the opportunity of competing for the Derby and Grand Prix trophies. He came back in the Prix de l'Arc de Triomphe, but was not fit enough and was caught on the post by Parth, winner by a short head. He ended his season with very easy successes in the Prix Edgard Gillois and Delamarre. Massine was even greater as a four-year-old, in spite of the fact that he was beaten by Filibert de Savoie and Le Capucin in the Prix du Cadran, owing to his jockey's nervousness, and in the Grand International d'Ostende (short head) by Le Capucin in very heavy going. (Pharos did not run, owing to the severe conditions.) Massine won at various distances in the Prix Edgard Gillois, des Sablons, Biennal, Ascot Gold Cup, and Prix de l'Arc de Triomphe : he was really one of the greatest and became a very good sire.

Another to earn fame at stud was Mr. J. D. Cohn's Sir Gallahad III, by Teddy out of Plucky Liege. He was rather a miler, and, after three wins as a juvenile, he scored in the Prix Edgard de la Charme, Daphnis, and Poule d'Essai ; but after his success at Deauville in the Prix Jacques le Marois, he failed in his other attempts as a three-year-old, though gaining places in such events as the Prix du Jockey Club (two necks) and Royal Oak. He continued his successful career in 1924, when winning the Lincoln-shire Handicap, the Prix Boïard, Daphnis, and a match against Epinard, who was giving him 10 lb. His owner had, the same year, in addition to a good filly, Anna Bolena, the dam of Mary Tudor, another Classic colt in Checkmate, a son of Teddy. The latter would have been the champion of a normal crop as he was second in most of the great events and the winner of such as the Prix Greffulhe, Eugène Adam, Grand Prix de Vichy, etc.

Le Capucin, a son of Nimbus, had the distinction of being the Derby winner of such an exceptional crop and of beating Massine twice. He was rather a stayer, whereas Filibert De Savoie, by Isard II, proved to be the best in the Grand Prix, Royal Oak, and Prix du Cadran, losing only by a head to Massine in the Ascot Gold Cup (1924). Mr. Wertheimer's Epinard was the incarnation of speed : he used to take several lengths at the start and maintain them to the post. He was unbeaten as a two-year-old, as he won easily on every occasion with the exception of the Prix Morny, in which he was left at the start. His chief successes were the Critérium de Maisons-Laffitte, the Grand Critérium, and the Prix de la Forét. In his next season, he was kept to short distances, winning the five first, including the Stewards' Cup at Goodwood (1923), and being beaten a neck by Verdict in the Cambridgeshire after a great race. It is known now that only Sayani (1926) was able to show a more gallant effort in the Cambridgeshire. It would have been better had Epinard been sent then to the stud ; his subsequent failures as a four-year-old, though honourable, in France as well as in America, added nothing to his glory. He became a good sire of sprinters, but none of them, even Rodosto, showed the same class.

Niceas, a son of Sundridge, was also a sprinter, and suffered setbacks over distances longer than a mile ; over shorter trips, he was unlucky, too, in encountering Epinard and Sir Gallahad III, but he managed to score in many good events and was able for example, to give 4 lbs. to the three-year-old Tapin and 30 lbs. to the two-year-old Belfonds and Ptolemy in the 1924 Prix de la Porêt. He was the first good winner in France for the Aga

Khan, who won his first Derby in 1924 with the Bruleur colt, Pot Au Feu. It was a moderate crop and the Grand Prix went to a big outsider, Transvaal. The best horse of the year was the Baron E. de Rothschild's Cadum, but he did not show his best until his fourth year, when he won seven of his eight races; his wins included the Prix des Sablons, du Cadran, du Président de la République, and de l'Arc de Triomphe: in this last event, however, an objection having been lodged by the second, the race was given to Priori, by Bruleur.

There were but few good individuals in the 1922 crop; M. E. Martinez de Hoz won his first Derby in 1925, with Belfonds, but the Grand Prix went again to an outsider, the filly Reine Lumiere. A third one, Take My Tip, scored in 1926 in record time! The Prix du Jockey Club had been won by Madrigal; the three best horses of the crop, however, were Asterus, Biribi, and Nino. I liked very much M. Boussac's Asterus, a son of Teddy, though his record on the Turf suffered from several setbacks. He was at his best from 1 to $1\frac{1}{4}$ miles, and this enabled him to win the Prix Greffulhe, Poule d'Essai, Royal Hunt Cup (1927), and Champion Stakes (defeating Colorado). Asterus became a grand sire and his influence on French breeding, chiefly through his daughters, was tremendous, in spite of his premature death.

There was more regularity in Biribi's performances: he gained places in the Prix Juigné, Greffulhe, du Jockey Club, Grand Prix le Paris, du Président de la République and Grand International d'Ostende; he was the winner of the Prix Noailles, Lupin, Royal Oak, and de l'Arc de Triomphe. In his fourth year, he won the Prix des Sablons and became a useful stallion and sired Le Pacha. A very serious individual was M. Moulines' Nino, by Clarissimus: he had but few occasions to score as a three-year-old, but became the best of his age at four years and is the only horse to have won the Prix du Président de la République twice. He was as honest at the Stud and was still alive in 1949. Other good representatives from the 1923 crop who did not show their best until they reached their fourth year were the Aga Khan's Dark Japan and Mr. Wittouck's Bois Josselyn, who developed into fine stayers.

In 1927 Mon Talisman and Fiterari were outstanding from the Classic point of view. M. Martinez de Hoz's Mon Talisman, by Craig an Eran, was certainly a grand horse; he did not run as a juvenile and just cantered home in his races as a three-year-old— the Prix Juigné, Daru, Lupin, and du Jockey Club. Meanwhile, M. Moulines' Fiterari, by Sardanapale, won the Poule d'Essai after three failures as a two-year-old, and finished second in the Prix du Jockey Club. In the Grand Prix, however, the thrilling speed of Mon Talisman was unable to prevail against the powerful

rush of Fiterari, and the same happened in the Prix Royal Oak.
It seems, however, that Fiterari surpassed himself on the former
occasion and that Mon Talisman was not quite fit on the second.
There was more class in him, and in the Prix de l'Arc de Triomphe
he just cantered again, as well as in his only outing at four years
—the Prix du Président de la République. Frank Carter considered him to be the best horse he ever trained, not excepting
his own son, the unbeaten Clairvoyant.

Nineteen twenty-eight was similar to 1926, inasmuch as the
Jockey Club and Grand Prix went to rather moderate horses,
Le Correge and Cri De Guerre. The latter belonged to Mr.
Ogden Mills, who had a much better horse in Kantar, of which
Dick Carver told me not very long ago that he would have given
20 lbs. to the other! Unbeaten as a two-year-old (Prix Morny,
Grand Critérium, etc.), Kantar was unlucky to lose the Derby of
his year, but he had an easy win in the Prix de l'Arc de Triomphe,
in which he was narrowly beaten by Ortello the following year.
By Alcantara II, Kantar became the sire of Victrix. Another
Alcantara colt in the same year was Pinceau, the Grand Prix
runner-up, which later sired Verso II. Bubbles and Palais Royal,
the latter a successful " invader " in England, stood at the top
of their year, close behind Kantar. The ungraceful and backward
Motrico won the Prix du Conseil Municipal at four years ; his
first Prix de l'Arc de Triomphe was won at five years and the
second at seven years ! The history of the Turf is full of these
gallant old horses who reach their peak after the Classic-time,
as, for instance, Rialto, Frolic, and others.

Though he won the Prix Hocquart, Lupin, du Jockey Club,
and Grand Prix in 1929, I don't consider M. Esmond's Hotweed
to have been a great horse : he had a lot of class, but did not
know how to use it. Vatout was much more interesting ; he
won five races as a three-year-old, including the Poule d'Essai,
and gained many places (second in the Prix du Président de la
République, Cambridgeshire, etc.), and he became a great stallion
—the sire of Bois Roussel, Vatellor, etc.

In 1930 M. Henriquet's grey filly, Commanderie, showed her-
self as a new Semendria when trouncing the Derby winner
Chateau Bouscaut in the Grand Prix de Paris. She also won the
Prix Vermeille, but was subsequently a failure on the turf and
at stud. She showed merit, however, when beating Chateau
Bouscaut, who was a very consistent performer, winning the Prix
Robert Papin, Morny, de la Forêt, Noailles, du Jockey Club, du
Cadran, etc. At stud, Chateau Bouscaut sired many good horses,
among them Chanteur.

Nineteen twenty-eight produced the best crop of thoroughbreds since 1920. It included Tourbillon, Pearl Cap, Barneveldt,

Deiri, Bruledur, Celerina, Confidence, etc.   The best individual
was the filly Pearl Cap, by Le Capucin, one of the greatest we have
had in France.   Had she not allowed her stable-mate, Indus, to
win the Grand Critérium, she would have been unbeaten as a
juvenile in six races, including the Prix Robert Papin and Morny.
In her next season, she won every good race for the fillies in
France, also the Prix Jacques le Marois and the Prix de l'Arc de
Triomphe against the colts.   She had but one setback, when
second to Prince Rose in the Grand International d'Ostende.
Unfortunately, she awaited her sixteenth year to breed the English
Derby winner, Pearl Diver (1947), who was far from being a
real champion.   Pearl Cap was so good, that the Oaks winner
Brulette, the Grand Prix de Deauville successive winners Celerina
and Confidence, who were excellent fillies, had no chance against
her.   She proved also to be superior to the colts.

The best of the colts was M. Boussac's Tourbillon, by Ksar
from Durban, who, after a good juvenile record, scored successively in the Prix Greffulhe, Hocquart, Lupin, and du Jockey Club
in grand style, a rare sequence.   Barneveldt, the winner of the
Prix Miss Gladiator, and Daru, beat Tourbillon in the Grand
Prix de Paris and, a week later, in the Prix du Président.   Tourbillon, Deiri, and Barneveldt were most successful at stud, and
Tourbillon ranks as the most famous sire in France of this century.
Tourbillon, by the way, was not the lone top horse in his stable,
since M. Boussac owned Goyescas, the first foal of Zariba, by
Gainsborough.   He ran in England as a two- three- and four-
year-old and, since he beat Sandwich, Orpen, Cameronian, Firdaussi, Singapore, and others, I think he was unlucky not to have
won a Classic.   He was second in the Two Thousand Guineas
(1931) and Eclipse Stakes (twice), 1931 and 1932 ; fourth in the
Derby, and won the Champion Stakes and Hardwicke Stakes.
When he returned to France, he affirmed incontestable supremacy
as a four-year-old, but unfortunately broke a pastern in the Prix
du Président de la République in 1933 and had to be destroyed.

The latter event was won by M. Jean Prat's Macaroni, who
had scored in the previous Prix de Conseil Municipal (1932).   It
was a pity he lacked Classic engagements, since he was superior
to the moderate Strip The Willow who, however, won both the
Jockey Club and the Grand Prix in that year.   In 1933, the situation was not much better : M. Boussac took his third Derby
with his Ksar colt, Thor II, but this one was beaten by Lady
Granard's Cappiello in the Grand Prix; third, another neck away,
was Assuerus.   Cappiello rested on his laurels.   Thor failed in
his subsequent attempts.   He was, however, a good stayer, winning the Prix du Cadran as a four-year-old and finishing second
in the Gold Cup at Ascot between Felicitation and Hyperion.

Assuerus was versatile: he ran a long time, gaining numerous places in great events, but winning few (Prix du Conseil Municipal, du Président de la République, etc.).   In these conditions, there was no serious opposition for the Italian colt Crapom in the Prix de l'Arc de Triomphe of 1933: he won easily.   In the beaten field was the Princesse de Faucigny Lucinge's Epinard colt, Rodosto, who won the Two Thousand Guineas at Newmarket the same year.

One of the great French champions, the Baron Ed. de Rothschild's Brantome was the hero of 1934.   The previous year, as a juvenile, he had scored in his four races, including the youngsters' Triple Crown.   He had taken as easily, in his next season, the Prix de Sevres, Poule d'Essai and Lupin when, like Massine, he was prevented from competing for the big trophies of the Jockey Club and Grand Prix, owing to coughing.   These two races went, therefore, to the moderate Duplex and the lucky Admiral Drake, half-brother of Sir Galahad III (and subsequently of Bois Roussel), who demonstrated more class at stud than on the Turf, but I consider him to have been inferior to Brantome and to Easton and Maravedis.   Brantome came back in the Royal Oak and, though bumped, he finished so strongly that he won. The Prix de l'Arc de Triomphe was a true apotheosis since the game Brantome just cantered in front of Assuerus, Felicitation, and ten others, including Admiral Drake, Duplex, Astrophel, Maravedis, etc.   The champion filly, Mary Tudor, and her conqueror in the Prix de Diana Adargatis, who became great broodmares, were not in the field.

Brantome, in his four-year-old days, cantered in the Prix du Cadran and Edgard Gillois and was then unbeaten in 11 attempts. But, having escaped in the Chantilly Forest, he had to be submitted to an antitetanic prick and then lost all his form.   He finished last but one in the Ascot Gold Cup and, after a last win in September in the Prix du Prince d'Orange, he failed in the Prix de l'Arc de Triomphe, behind the three-year-old fillies, Samos, Peniche, and Corrida.   Brantome had sired Pensbury when he was taken by the Germans; he is now back in France.

The Classic crop in 1935 was a very bad one; the Princess de Faucigny-Lucinge's Louqsor and Ping Pong are the only colts worthy of mention.   In fact, it was a year of fillies, as it appeared in the Prix de l'Arc de Triomphe after the win of a half-sister to Brantome, Crudite, in the Grand Prix de Paris.   The best of all, however, was M. Boussac's famous Corrida, by Coranach out Zariba.   She won the Prix Morny as a two-year-old, the Marseilles Grand Prix the next year, and found her true form as a four-year-old, winning then the Hardwicke Stakes, Grand International d'Ostende, Prix du Président de la République and de l'Arc de Triomphe, etc. At five years, she took, among other trophies, the Grand Prix de la Capitale du Reich, and, again, the Grand International d'Ostende and Prix de l'Arc de Triomphe. She was a worthy daughter of La Camargo and, had she not shown versatility, her record would have been ever greater, since she contested without success the One Thousand Guineas and the Oaks. Annexed by the Germans, Corrida left but one colt, but he proved capable of winning the French Derby of 1945—Coaraze !

Corrida's great success slightly overshadowed the Classic results of 1936 and 1937. In the former year, a Massine colt, Mieuxce, established his superiority when cleverly winning the Prix Hocquart, Lupin, du Jockey Club and Grand Prix. An accident caused his early retirement, and he was sold to England, where his daughters have succeeded more than his sons. Mieuxce proved superior to M. Volterra's Vatellor, who, in spite of numerous wins, including the Prix du Président de la République 1937, did not seem destined to become such a famous stallion. There was a good filly, too, in the same crop, Mistressford, in which M. Esmond had nearly a new Pearl Cap.

Nineteen thirty-seven was the year of Clairvoyant, the best son of Mon Talisman. He won the Prix Hocquart, Lupin, du Jockey Club, and Grand Prix. In the last-named event, he trounced the Italian champion Donatello II, previously unbeaten. Clairvoyant was trained by Frank Carter (who died the same year), who also won the Two Thousand Guineas at Newmarket with Le Ksar. Victrix, whom he also trained, did not show his true form until Clairvoyant had retired, winning then the Prix Royal Oak, and as a four-year-old the Prix des Sablons, du Président de la République, Grand International d'Ostende, etc. Several fillies gained good credentials in this crop, especially Lady Granard's En Fraude (Prix de Diane) and Baron Ed. de Rothschild's Tonnelle, runner-up to Corrida by a head in the Prix de l'Arc de Triomphe after having won the Prix Vermeille.

Let us not forget that one of the best representatives of the 1934 French crop was in England—Goya II, half-brother to Goyascas, Corrida, and Adjer. Goya II, trained by the Hon. George Lambton, won the Gimcrack Stakes, was second to Fair Copy in the Middle Park Stakes, to Le Ksar in the Two Thousand Guineas, and Flares in the Champion Stakes. In 1936, Goya II returned to France as a four-year-old in 1938 and was in top form for another two years, winning the Prix des Sablons (twice), the " Deutsche Braunes Band ", the Prix des 3 Ans et au dessus (wartime Arc de Triomphe, 1940). At stud, he gained distinction by siring Nirgal, Goyama, Sandjar, Corteira, and Good Luck before being exported to the U.S.A.

M. LEON VOLTERRA

BARON G. DE WALDNER LEADING IN PEARL DIVER,
G. BRIDGLAND UP. Derby, 1947

[Facing page 244

M. MARCEL BOUSSAC LEADING IN SANDJAR, R. POINCELET UP
French Derby, 1947

MY LOVE WINNING THE 1948 DERBY; SECOND, ROYAL DRAKE;
THIRD, NOOR

Goya II was the first great son of Tourbillon ; Cillas was the second and in 1938 gave M. Boussac his fourth Derby winner. Unfortunately, probably owing to close breeding, Goya II was excessively nervous and could only reveal his class at Chantilly, where he was trained. In the Grand Prix de Paris, he could make no impression on the unbeaten Italian crack, Nearco, who won from Canot ; Bois Roussell, whom the Hon. P. Beatty had purchased from M. Volterra, was third, and then proceeded to provide the third French Epsom Derby winner. It must be recalled that Nearco and Bois Roussel became great sires, while Canot, who bred Imprudence and Cillas, had few opportunities owing to his early demise. In the Autumn, a new star arose in Eclair Au Chocolat, who won the Royal Oak and the Arc de Triomphe, beating Antonym, a Vatout colt who had gained success in Belgium and Germany, and who won the Kempton Park Great Jubilee in 1939.

In the Spring of this memorable year, several colts had shown quality, the best of them being, probably, Hunter's Moon IV (who won the 1940 Cesarewitch under top weight, 9 st. 5 lbs., and was sold in the U.S.A.). Then a phenomenon, Pharis II appeared on May 21, in the Prix Noailles : he did not understand what was expected of him until the last furlong, then won in a canter in front of the excellent Galerien. He was then made favourite for the Jockey Club and, though he entered the straight last but one after a violent bump that nearly threw him upon his knees, he just made hacks of his opponents, Galerien again being the best of them. Then came the Grand Prix and so great was the fame of this wonderful Pharis II that he started at evens. Numerous race-goers had the opportunity of seeing the most sensational finish within their experience. A furlong from home, Tricameron (the unlucky winner of the White Rose Stakes, subsequently given to Hunter's Moon), running on strongly in the manner of a true stayer, was cantering three lengths ahead of the field in the midst of which the favourite was unable to find an opening. Suddenly, 100 yards from the post, a gap appeared and Pharis II slipped in and produced such a tremendous burst of speed that, in a few strides he had joined Tricameron, then had him beaten, and, eased, passed the post some four lengths ahead ! The oldest sportsmen did not remember having seen such a finish and it was a big disappointment that the war prevented him from meeting Blue Peter in the St. Leger : since I consider Pharis II to have been the equal of an Ormonde, a St. Simon, or a Gladiateur, I feel sure he would have won ; no horse in the world would have beaten him. At stud, he sired three champions in his first crop, Ardan, Priam, and Palencia, then was purloined by the Germans. He is back now and should again have good Classic representatives in 1950.

R

It is a hard task to select the successor to a Pharis II! However, the following crop had again a true champion in Djebel, by Tourbillon from Loika. He, too, was owned by M. Boussac, and he invaded England to score in the Middle Park Stakes and Two Thousand Guineas; so easy were his wins, that he would surely have taken the Derby, had he not been prevented from competing by the German invasion. He lost his form and was not quite himself as a four-year-old when he was beaten twice by his contemporary Mauvepas and once by his cadets Le Pacha and Nepenthe. But he fully recovered in his next and was unbeaten in seven attempts, including the Prix des Sablons, Grand Prix de St. Cloud, and Prix de l'Arc de Triomphe, twice beating Le Pacha, the 1941 winner of the Grand Prix and Derby. With his stablemates, Adaris, Jock, and Horatius, he began the big Boussac era. In the absence of Pharis II, Djebel took his place at stud and became, at once, a great stallion, having sired Arbar, Sjelal, Montenica, My Babu, Djeddah, Coronation, etc., in his first produce.

His younger rival, Le Pacha, by Biribi, was the hero of the 1941 campaign, in which he was unbeaten, winning in a row the Prix Greffulhe, Hocquart, Lupin, du Jockey Club, Grand Prix, Royal Oak, and de l'Arc de Triomphe. His very powerful stride enabled him to take an early lead, but twice he beat Lord Derby's Nepenthe only by a short head; the latter was the only other good horse of the year. As a four-year-old, Le Pacha won two of his four races, but was caught by Djebel in a sensational finish in the Grand Prix de St. Cloud, and he met with an accident in the Prix de l'Arc de Triomphe. His early career at stud did not realise expectations.

The Classic crop running in 1942 was moderate and the Viscountess Vigier's Magister was a bad colt, in spite of his lucky wins in the Prix du Jockey Club and Grand Prix. Lord Derby's Arcot had bad legs and had often to be put on the easy-list. Tornado, a Tourbillon colt, was the most consistent, though he was sometimes beaten by the Boussac colts, Tifinar and Hierocles. The same owner had a very good Tourbillon filly in Esmeralda, whom I consider to have been the best individual of the crop: she was unbeaten as a juvenile, won the Poule d'Essai, and gave grand performances when four and five years old in the Prix de l'Arc de Triomphe, Grand Prix de St. Cloud, de Deauville, and de Marseille; unfortunately, she was only really herself in the Autumn. Coronation was her first foal.

The crop born in 1940 was a very good one. Grandson of Epinard through his sire Rodosto, M. Couturié's Dogat was an exceptional miler and proved superior to the Epinard colt, Fanatique, who also was very speedy. The third contender in this category was the Boussac filly Caravelle, by Abjer, the winner of the Grand Critérium, but she proved more than a sprinter, since she won the Poule d'Essai, Prix de Diane, Prix de la Forêt (twice), and was a top-class filly. Mr. R. B. Strassburger owned a good pair in Pensbury (by Brantome) and Norseman (by Umidwar). As a two-year-old, the former won the Critérium de Maisons-Laffitte, but failed in the Grand Critérium; the latter had won the Prix Robert Papin. It was a pity that Norseman, after his win in the Prix Daru, was generally used as pacemaker to his stablemate, since I wonder if he were not the better of the two. Pensbury, however, won the Prix Greffulhe and Lupin, then he met, in the Prix du Jockey Club, the Comte de Chambure's Pinceau colt, Verso II, the winner of the Prix Hocquart. The race produced a thrilling finish in which Verso II beat Pensbury a short head. The latter, however, took his revenge in the Grand Prix, after which he lost and had to be destroyed the following Spring, having broken a leg.

Verso II, then, remained the champion of the year, since he beat Marsyas II in the Royal Oak as well as Emeralda and Norseman in the Arc de Triomphe. In 1944, Norseman showed himself the best over 1¼ miles and Marsyas II began his career as a grand stayer, winning his first Prix du Cadran and the Prix Gladiateur by 15 lengths. It may not be necessary to recall what a wonderful Cup horse he became in England, and how he won three other times the Prix du Cadran, trouncing Souverain in 1947. It was a pity he was unable to contest the Gold Cup that year, as he would probably have had his name enrolled as winner between his two brothers, Caracalla II (1946) and Arbar (1948).

Nineteen forty-four was notable for the introduction of Pharis stock, especially Ardan. Before dealing with this great horse, I shall recall the career of the filly Palencia, which was so good that she had made hacks of her elders, Dogat and Fanatique, over 5 furlongs as a two-year-old; she had cantered in the Poule d'Essai, but split a pastern three days before the Prix de Diane. Priam II, too, beat Fanatique and Caravelle, at three years; he had won the Grand Critérium the previous season, but had been ill during the Winter. After many successes, he was the first French horse to run in England after the war and, in 1945, nearly dead-heated with Court Martial in the Champion Stakes at Newmarket. He won the Hardwicke Stakes the following season.

M. Boussac, however, had an even better one in Ardan, the best horse bred in France since his sire, Pharis II; I consider him to have been unlucky not to have been unbeaten. The winner of the Prix Robert Papin, he was second to his stablemate, Priam II (first choice) in the Grand Ctitérium, at three years, and but for two short heads in the Royal Oak, he would have been unbeaten. He scored successively in the Prix Greffulhe, Hocquart, Lupin, du Jockey Club and Grand Prix, always making all the running, at a very fast pace. In the last event, however, which he had won in record time, he was placed third after an objection. Ardan was an easy winner of the Arc de Triomphe, and in 1945 was narrowly beaten in the same event when not at his best ; then he won the Coronation Cup at Epsom in 1946, as a five-year-old. He was really a grand horse and I am sorry he left France for the U.S.A.

In 1945, after the complete failure of Chanteur II against his elders, Ardan, Priam II, and Samaritain, I thought that the Classic crop was moderate, but changed my mind since : apart from the unbeaten Caracalla II, there were Chanteur II, Basileus, Coaraze, Mistral, Nikellora, Le Paillon, Kerlor, etc. M. Volterra's Mistral had shown great superiority during the Spring, Basileus and Chanteur II seeming the best after him, but M. Boussac's Coaraze beat all of them in the Jockey Club and the same owner's Caracalla revealed his class in the Grand Prix and the Royal Oak. Mistral disappeared, Basileus won the Grand Prix de Deauville, then the Prix du Conseil Municipal, under big weights ; meanwhile, he had been beaten, with Chanteur II and Coaraze, by the top filly, Nikellora : a surprising result, since Ardan, too, was beaten. At four years, Coaraze showed supremacy over intermediate distances and won the Grand Prix de St. Cloud, while Chanteur II and Basileus, beating each other, remained inferior to Caracalla II, winner of the Ascot Gold Cup (1946) and the Arc de Triomphe. Kerlor and Le Paillon became great hurdlers, but both won the Grand Prix de Deauville (1946–47) and the latter ended his career by winning the Arc de Triomphe (1947). Chanteur II became a big winner in England.

Unbeaten as a two-year-old and winner of the juvenile Triple Crown, Nirgal seemed the best prospect for 1946, but he fell ill and could not recover his form until his fourth year. He and his stable-mate Goyama became very good winners in France and in England in 1947–48–49, taking between them the Prix des Sablons (twice), the Coronation Cup, the Winston Churchill Stakes (twice), the Grand Prix de St. Cloud, the Prix du Conseil Municipal, etc., etc. Their common failure at three years left the place of honour to Prince Chevalier, whose superiority remained undisputed until a new star arose in the Grand Prix with Souverain : and Prince Chevalier never won again, though beaten only a head in the Arc de Triomphe. Souverain developed into a grand stayer, winning the Royal Oak, King George VI Stakes, and Ascot Gold Cup (1947). Quite different was Sayani, whose victory in the 1946 Cambridgeshire will not be readily forgotten !

Yong Lo and Vandale were other very good colts from the same crop.

M. Boussac dominated French racing in 1947 with Sandjar (Jockey Club), Djelal (Lupin), Giafar (Noailles), Timor (Matchem), and, finally, the best of them, Arbar (King George VI Stakes), beaten a short head by Sayajirao in the St. Leger. Sandjar, Giafar, and Timor soon disappeared owing to accidents, but Djelal turned into a fine sprinter and Arban proved to be one of the greatest horses of the century when cantering in the Gold Cup (1948). The Baron de Waldner's pair, Tourment (Royal Oak, second—a head—in the Jockey Club) and Pearl Diver (Derby), lost their form very quickly.

France again won the Derby in 1948, with My Love, owned in partnership by M. Volterra and the Aga Khan; this colt went on to score in the Grand Prix de Paris, but failed in the St. Leger. It was a very bad crop and neither the Spring star Rigolo, nor the Prix du Jockey Club winner Bey, the big stakes runner-up Flush Royal, Tanagrello, or Royal Drake sustained their earlier form. Estoc might have proved useful, but he broke down early; his stablemate Djeddah, half-brother to Priam, found his form at four years and won the Eclipse Stakes.

Nineteen forty-nine was distinguished by the good perform- ances of the fillies Coronation and Bagheera, and of the colts Ambiorix and Amour Drake (the former being bought for a big price as a stallion for America). In spite of the high standard of their stock, American breeders still look for the best strains of French blood—the best tribute paid to our breeding.

CHAPTER XVII

BREEDING AND RACING IN EIRE

By Thomas E. Healey

WITH the exception of one dull period some years after World War I had finished, Irish horsebreeding and racing have, during the past half-century, enjoyed a measure of prosperity eclipsing that which had characterised the industry in its previous most brilliant era. There is no present sign of interruption of prosperity, though we are warned that seven lean years will follow seven years of plenty.

The golden age of Irish racing was claimed by an older generation of chroniclers to have been from about 1850 until about 1875, but their claim cannot be maintained against that which is made for racing in the past 50 years. For one thing, highest total of stake money competed for in any one year during the period 1850–75 was £33,617, as against £269,222 in 1948 ; and, for another thing, racing which used to be the sport of the few has long since become the sport of the many ; whilst, yet again, horsebreeding which was carried on in a more or less haphazard way and a sort of sideline has developed as an industry and is no longer looked upon, as once it was, as a more or less interesting hobby. Dr. O'Higgins, Minister for Defence in the Irish Government, said in a speech during 1949, that the export of horses was worth £6,000,000 annually to Ireland.

Just one further reference, by way of comparison between the two periods mentioned, before discussing other matters. Highest total of races decided in any one year between 1850 and 1875 was 442, in 1872 ; but since 1900 we have not had in a single year a smaller number of races than 532 (in 1918), and in 1932 980 were run. (I should, perhaps, mention that the word, " races ", is not used solely to denote flat races, but applies also to hurdling and 'chasing, for these run side by side with flat racing, during the season appointed for flat racing, March 17–November 22 ; and jumping is continuous.)

Introduction of three innovations has hoisted racing to a higher pinnacle of success, and kept it there, than could have been imagined even by a super-optimist at the close of the 90's, when admittedly, " there was a boom on " ; and these innovations were the provision of the Tote, the rule requiring horses to be declared the day before running, and the levy (first of 5 per cent., now of 2½ per cent.), on a backer's stake on a race-course. Not

everyone wanted the Tote, for not everyone understood its working, nor took forethought of its possibilities. Indeed, in certain
quarters, there was the prevalent notion that " backers " would
' break the Tote ' " ! " How much money has the Tote ? " asked
a certain trainer. "About £30,000," he was told. His comment
was : " The backers will get that in next to no time ! "

Certain vested interests were opposed to the introduction of
" the declaration rule ", but it came in spite of strong opposition, and it is there to stay ; for the public desires to know the
horses which will run next day ; and though there was fear expressed (I doubt the fear was very deep seated !) that the goose
that laid the golden egg would be killed when the levy became
operative, the goose has not been killed, nor are the golden eggs
fewer than before. The fund accumulated from the levy and
from Tote profits is allocated to provide increased stake-money
(at reduced entry-charges and forfeits), to financing carriage of
horses free-of-cost to owners, and to make available for race-
executives grants wherewith to improve their courses and carry
out other necessary works. Outstanding success of Irish racing
has not " just happened "—it was been the outcome of hard
work.

First important event in the world of sport in 1900 was, as
Irishmen asserted, the victory of the Prince of Wales's Ambush II
in the Liverpool Grand National. He was Curragh trained and
started second favourite. Except that he was Irish bred and
trained in Ireland, every other association with him was English.
His Royal Highness (afterwards Edward VII) entrusted his
management to Mr. G. W. Lushington (the son of a London
police-court magistrate resident in Ireland, where he owned
horses, trained and rode them), and his jockey was "Algy "
Anthony, who had served an apprenticeship with Sam Darling
at Beckhampton. It is a fact worth notice that many English
sportsmen have played, and play, a leading part in furthering the
fortunes of the Irish horse industry in its many phases ; breeding, owning, training, buying, riding, and so on.

I must not, of course, be taken as asserting that, until the
opening of the twentieth century, Irish horsebreeding had not
held a foremost place : for such assertion would betray a woeful
ignorance of one's subject. Irish horses have been famous for
many centuries, so much so that one untruthful historian, writing
in the Middle Ages, recorded that, " Ireland produces nothing
worthy of mention but corn and excellent horses, which the in-
habitants term urbinos ! "

Not long after Henry Lindé had died (his name will crop up
again in these notes), Major (or, as he was, Captain) Loder bought
Eyrefield Lodge, near the Curragh, where Lindé had trained and

bred horses to carry his colours, and also trained for other owners. He was in a big way of business. Captain Loder carried on Eyrefield Lodge as a breeding-racing establishment, as it had been, until the breeding side became so important that there was no longer room to accommodate the two " departments ", and he sent his horses into Joseph Hunter's stable at Conyngham Lodge, Curragh, over which establishment Mr. Lushington presided as manager.

Major Loder had not long to await " a dividend " on his Irish investment, for in 1901 was foaled the peerless Pretty Polly, who was beaten only twice in a busy career, once in France, and once at Ascot (by her " compatriot ", Bachelor's Button). Pretty Polly was not raced in Ireland at any stage of her career, and was one of the charges at Clarehaven Lodge, Newmarket, of Peter Purcell Gilpin, a Co. Kildare-born sportsman, who had been a patron of the Irish Turf before he went across to Langton House, Blandford, and, as gossip of the time said, won a small fortune by the victory of his mare Clarehaven in the 1900 Cesarewitch, the proceeds enabling him to set up his establishment at Newmarket. Major Loder bred many other notable winners, but none greater than Petty Polly, whose winnings of £37,297 were accumulated by her successes in the Champagne Stakes, Middle Park Plate, One Thousand Guineas, Oaks, St. Leger (1904), Coronation Stakes at Ascot, two Coronation Cups at Epsom, Champion Stakes, Jockey Club Cup, and so forth. Pretty Polly did not herself breed a Classic winner, but from her descendants have come many British, Irish, and Italian Classic heroes and heroines ; and, perhaps, there have been such winners in other countries, too. Pretty Polly established a dynasty which is flourishing. The highly successful Italian-bred sire, Donatello II, is in fourth generation from Pretty Polly.

Major Loder's Hammerkop was another game and good mare. She was one year senior to Pretty Polly, and was also in Peter Purcell Gilpin's stable. She was a great stayer and included two Ascot Alexandra Plates, the Cesarewitch (1905), Yorkshire Oaks, Great Yorkshire Handicap at Doncaster and many other races in her triumphs. She ran once in Ireland when eight years old, but was past her best and we had not the pleasure of seeing her achieve success almost within stone's throw of the stud in which she was born. Hammerkop, Pretty Polly, and other high-grade mares passed to Lieut.-Colonel Giles Loder, as he is to-day, on the death of Major Eustace Loder, who was his uncle. Although Pretty Polly did not breed a Classic winner, Hammerkop bred Spion Kop, who won the Derby at Epson in 1920. The " luck of the Loder's " was proverbial, especially so in the case of Major Eustace Loder ; and an instance was that Spearmint, whom he purchased for 300 gns., won the Derby (1906) and Grand Prix de Paris for him; and Spearmint carried on the good work by siring Spion Kop. One hears that " it is better to be born lucky than rich ", but better, is it not, to be born both lucky and rich?

Major Loder's stud gave to the American stud the champion stallion up to his own time, and there have not been many greater since in America. This was Star Shoot, a weakling as a foal and kept alive only by treatment of the utmost tenderness. He was kept wrapped in blankets in front of the fire during his prolonged weakness. Yet, despite this early delicacy, he was five times top of the sires' table, second three times, and third twice : whilst seven times he was leading sire of two-year-old winners, and in 1916 his juveniles set up a world-record (it still is, so far as I know), when 27 won. Add that six times from 1925 to 1929 (both years inclusive) he was champion sire of brood-mares and the story of his mighty career is told in brief.

Major Loder was a patron of the Irish Turf before his purchase of Eyrefield Lodge (he had been racing in England previously). He was in the 12th Lancers and when his regiment went to Ireland he brought Admiration (to become Pretty Polly's dam) with him. She was very moderate and, having run without winning at two years of age, her first bracket was gained in the following season in a £50 race at Baldoyle. She had one other flat-race success, in a £120 race at Leopardstown, and wound up her career as a 'chaser at Punchestown! A very coveted Punchestown prize by the British military in Ireland was the Irish Grand Military Steeplechase and Major (he was then Captain) Loder had high hopes of landing it with Admiration, who had the assistance of that brilliant horseman Major Hughes-Onslow. She started favourite but was only third. Who could have foreseen that day in 1897 that this moderate mare (whose dam had been used as a hack after producing two moderate winners !) would produce one of the greatest mares in the history of breeding? Major Loder greatly extended his horsebreeding enterprise some few years after purchase of Eyrefield Lodge by the acquisition of the Old Connell property two or three miles distant from " the Lodge "; and his nephew continues to maintain these two establishments on the same liberal lines as those of their founder.

When Diomed, winner of the first Derby, reached America, his American importers gleefully proclaimed that " a million dollars struck American soil as he came charging down the gangplank ". That was just a way of saying that Diomed was a most successful stallion. But, in more sober language, what is the answer to the question : " What was the worth to Irish breeding in cash and prestige of the setting up of Tully Stud by Col. W. Hall Walker ? " He founded it in 1900. During his tenure and that of the British Government, the stud (known as "the National Stud" whilst the British Government controlled it) produced 10 winners of 14 British Classic races—an almost unbelieveable achievement! Here is the score:

	No. of classics.
Minoru—2,000 Guineas and Derby	2
Prince Palatine—St. Leger	1
The Panther—2,000 Guineas	1
Night Hawk—St. Leger	1
Royal Lancer—St. Leger	1
Big Game—2,000 Guineas	1
Chamoissaire—St. Leger	1
Cherry Lass—1,000 Guineas and Oaks	2
Sun Chariot—1,000 Guineas, Oaks and St. Leger	3
Witch Elm—1,000 Guineas	1
	14

Col. Hall Walker (later Lord Wavertree) planned to breed and race extensively in Ireland and, as to the racing end of his scheme, he had constructed at Tully a very fine training-ground. But the stud's requirements grew and training, which had been in charge of John Smith, was discontinued, and, instead, when Smith set up as public trainer at Rossmore Lodge, Curragh (present quarters of the successful young trainer Paddy Prendergast), Colonel Hall Walker sent him horses which did not go to England. The best of those which Colonel Hall Walker raced in Ireland was Jean's Folly, a brilliant two-year-old, unbeaten in five races. She was sent over to W. T. Robinson at Foxhill when three years old and gave further proof of her quality by adding the Chippenham Plate at Newmarket to her earlier gains, but did not train on, and went to the stud when four years old. She more than justified her existence, for she bred ten winners, one of them the St. Leger hero, Night Hawk (1913).

A number of great winners came from the Tully Stud, but omission of Blandford's name would be a serious lapse. Lieut.-Colonel MacCabe (who trained Orby for " Boss " Croker to win the Derby, 1907, Irish Derby, etc.), went to the Newmarket December Sales in 1920 to buy the brown yearling colt by Swynford out of Blanche, by White Eagle, at a figure which he estimated was well within the colt's valuation, but his friend, R. C. Dawson, the Whatcombe trainer, outbid him at 730 gns.and so Colonel MacCabe lost, and Dick Dawson obtained, a good race-horse and a record-breaking stallion. Blandford sired four Derby winners—unbeaten, triple-crowned Bahram, Blenheim, Trigo (winner also of St. Leger and Irish St. Leger), and Windsor Lad

(he took the St. Leger, too).   Moreover, he surpassed in 1934
Stockwell's achievement of siring winners of £61,391 in 1866,
with a total of £75,707.   Nearest aggregate to Stockwell's best-
on-record had been £59,109 to the credit of Hurry On in 1926 ;
but Blandford's considerable accumulation put all other totals in
the shade.

Tully Stud was re-named The National Stud when the British
Government took it over, and its management was committed
to Sir Henry Greer, with the title, " Director of the Stud ".
Under his ægis Blandford was bred.   The stud passed to the
British Government through Colonel Hall Walker's presentation
to the British nation of two stallions, 30 brood-mares, 10 year-
lings, 20 foals, and eight horses in training, valued by Sir Henry
Greer (he was Captain Greer at the time) at £74,000 ; and as
against that gift, the British Government paid Colonel Hall
Walker £65,625 for Tully and Russley farms.   The Government
of the Republic of Ireland, with admirable foresight, has realised
the importance of Tully and, on receiving the property from the
British Government, formed The Irish National Stud Company,
Ltd., which has pursued an active policy in thoroughbred-horse
production.

Colonel Hall Walker was raised to the peerage as Lord
Wavertree for his gift of bloodstock.   He has been criticised that,
" no trainer could please him ", and that, " his horsebreeding
was done by ' reading the stars ' ".   Lord Wavertree was an
astrologer and claimed to have foretold important events, but one
pauses before accepting the theory that he " bred horses ' by the
stars ' ".   His consistent production of " star performers " was
because he knew the value of the bloodlines he mated and reared
his young stock on limestone land, having the stock properly
handled.   He had many trainers in England after he began breeding at Tully ; but in Ireland he had, I think, only one trainer,
John Smith.   Lord Wavertree may not have been easily " got
on with ", and his frequent change of trainers gave occasion to
a wag to name him " Whimsical Walker ".

He had been a patron of Irish horses long before he formed
Tully Stud.   He had won the 1896 Liverpool Grand National
with the half-bred The Soarer, whose breeder, the late Pat Doyle
of Hollywood, Co. Wicklow, never indulged the ambition of
breeding a Grand National winner, but did desire to breed the
winner of the local farmers' race at Punchestown !   He never did,
I believe, breed the winner of that race, but instead obtained
world-wide publicity as breeder of the winner of the greatest
steeplechase.   Such was the vagary of Fortune !

At Tully is the picturesque garden (called The Japanese Garden), designed and executed by a Japanese landscape gardener

brought from Japan by Lord Wavertree (though he was not en-
nobled when he had this work done) ; and the garden is so laid
out as to tell symbolically the history of Adam and Eve in the
Garden of Eden. Spare a short time from the horses to see the
garden, if you should visit Tully, for it is a gem of its kind. Mr.
J. Reid Walker, following the example of his brother, also came
to Ireland early in the present century to found the Joristown
Stud in Co. Westmeath. Results were not comparable with those
forthcoming from Tully, but, none the less, the Joristown enterprise was not by any manner of means barren of a measure of
success. Its proprietor was not such an extensive patron of the
Irish Turf as his brother had been.

The century was still young when an unexpected—and wholly
unforeseeable—incident gave Ireland a further big lift in the
bloodstock world. It all came about in this way : " Boss "
Croker, ex-Tammany Hall Chieftain, had amassed a fortune in
New York politics, and had come to England to enjoy his retirement. He had been racing in America, and transferred his horses
to England. They were trained at Wantage, but Newmarket was
Croker's ideal, and at Doncaster Sales in 1904 he bought three
fillies which, he proposed, should be trained by the Australian
J. E. Brewer at Heath House, Newmarket. He paid 8,800 gns.
for the trio—3,600 gns. for one Gallinule filly, 3,100 for a second
Gallinule, and 2,100 gns. for a St. Simon. Permission was refused
by the Jockey Club for the fillies to be trained at Newmarket !

Croker was not one to kiss the rod. He was Irish-born (but
had not been to Ireland, except perhaps on a flying visit, since
he had left it as a lad of seven years with his parents), but he had
had no intention when quitting New York politics of residing in
Ireland, although he had run his crack sprinter Americus in the
Pegasus Cup at Cork Park in 1900, Mr. J. C. Sullivan's Berrill
beating him after a strenuous contest.

The Jockey Club's action in excluding Croker's fillies from
Newmarket was said to have been taken because of the unsavoury
history of Tammany Hall politics. The ex-" Boss " made a
quick decision, decided to make his home in Ireland, breeding
and racing horses as a hobby. He purchased Glencairn estate in
Co. Dublin, spending about £60,000 on alterations and improvements. He re-sold, for about 3,000 gns. less than he had paid,
his three Doncaster purchases and brought to Ireland (at first to
French House Stud, Curragh, until Glencairn was ready for occupation) his American-bred mare Rhoda B., and American-bred
stallions Americus and Dobbins. Croker's chagrin can well be
imagined when his plans were not only obstructed but he was
publicly humiliated. Did he vow vengeance and, if so, what form
of vengeance did he conceive possible ? He had his revenge, but

his conception that it would take the form it did could not be possible. He could not penetrate the future. He bred the winners of three Classics, himself owning two of the winners (Orby, the Derby; Rhodora, One Thousand Guineas at Newmarket, 1908), and the third Grand Parade (Lord Glanely's property) when winning the 1919 Derby, he sold for 470 gns. when a foal! Croker is said to have " gloated" over these triumphs, but I question whether that was his attitude. He was not one to " gloat"; rather, I should say, he accepted the results with icy cynicism.

He had several trainers in Ireland. His first trainer was J. J. (afterwards, Senator) Parkinson: Croker had a lengthy string with him at the Curragh; but when Croker arranged the training of his horses at his Dublin home, he put Colonel MacCabe in charge; later, James Allen came in (he had been Colonel MacCabe's right-hand man), followed by C. Prendergast, F. Grundy, and others; whilst "Atty" Persse and the late Paddy Hartigan had a few of his horses in England. Croker was not, I think, fond of change for change sake, and if he tired of breeding and racing a couple of times, his interest reawakened.

Once, at a Leopardstown meeting, when he was tiring of racing, he was moving about with characteristic deliberateness, hands in pockets, smoking the inevitable cigar, a lonely, detached figure, seemingly dead to all that was transpiring, when Dan Leahy, the bookmaker, called out to him from " the rails " : "Aren't you going to have a bet on ' yours ', Mr. Croker ? " " No; I guess I won't buy any more motor-cars for book- makers." Pure and simple fortuity threw Croker into Eire's arms. He had great good fortune in the country, for he topped the Owners' list in 1905, 1906 and 1911; was second in 1907 (Orby won the Derby and the Irish Derby that year), and third in 1910. Orby was the first, and remains the only, Irish-trained English Derby winner; and Rhodora is in like case in the One Thousand Guineas. So, Croker's colt and filly were record- makers.

Mr. Joseph McGrath purchased the long-established Curragh- side stud, Brownstown, not so many years ago, and made a mag- nificent sucess of it. There is, perhaps, no need to refresh the memories of readers of this book that at Brownstown was bred the famous Birdcatcher, whose blood runs in the veins of every British and Irish-bred thoroughbred entered in the pages of Weatherby's *General Stud Book ;* nor to write that Birdcatcher was " a cornerstone " in the tail male descent of Bend Or, whose paternal line is dominant in these islands. Mr. McGrath bought for his stud the highest-priced brood-mare ever brought into an Irish establishment; she was Carpet Slipper, at 14,000 guineas.

Her son, Windsor Slipper, was the second Irish Triple Crown winner of Irish 2,000 Guineas, Irish Derby and Irish St. Leger. First Triple Crown winner in Ireland was Sir Victor Sassoon's Museum, in 1935 : he was trained by that unsurpassed trainer, the late J. T. Rogers. Windsor Slipper was unbeaten, and his stock includes many winners of high-class races.

Brownstown Stud may be the oldest in Great Britain and Ireland. It was running long before 1833 and may have been running in the last decade of the eighteenth century. Its history would make a book in itself, but, in passing, it may be noted that Birdcatcher was, at least, twice leading stallion in Great Britain and Ireland (in 1852 and 1856), and that his own brother Faugh a Ballagh (also a Brownstown Stud product) included amongst his winnings a St. Leger and Cesarewitch.

A few years after Mr. McGrath had bought Brownstown, he added another area of land at Kildare, a few miles distant from Brownstown, and Trimblestown Stud to his possession. Trimblestown is in Co. Meath and was formed as a stud farm-training centre by Mr. Frank Barbour, who had a big stake in the linen industry in the North of Ireland. He and his nieces owned many high-class winners, especially jumpers, Blancona, Easter Hero, Koko, and several more of their standard, or near it. With Windsor Slipper at Brownstown Stud, stands Nasrullah, acquired from the Aga Khan ; and that no mistake was made in obtaining him was proven by his having sired the Irish Derby winner, Nathoo, in his first season, whilst the dual Classic-winning filly, Musidora (One Thousand Guineas and Oaks) came from Nasrullah's second covering season.

Brownstown Stud is situated in that most famous horse-breeding area in Co. Kildare wherein also are found Sheshoon Stud, Irish National Stud, Gilltown Stud, Eyrefield Lodge Stud, and—not so very far away—Ballymany Stud, Old Connell Stud, and the Maharaja of Baroda's establishment which is the home of Sayajirao. Aggregate acreage of Brownstown (where are the graves of Birdcatcher and of his wonderful son, Gallinule, who also made history), Kildare and Trimblestown is about 660.

Another present-century introduction was Palmerstown Stud, also in Co Kildare, but several miles away from the Curragh. A strictly accurate statement would be that it was a *re-introduction*, for during the second half of the nineteenth century, Lord Mayo of the period, bred horses fairly extensively there, and I think the Palmerstown Stud of his time was the first stud-company formed in Ireland. It enjoyed a fair, but not outstanding measure of prosperity as such. Mr. W. J. Kelly—who owns The Solicitor (for which he paid £10,000)—owns Palmerstown, and conducts it as a stud-farm and training establishment.

Fort Union Stud, Adare, Co. Limerick, is of long standing, for it was founded by a previous Lord Dunraven (and amongst his stallions was the successful Desmond) ; and Lord Adare, now its owner, also possesses a leading sire in Panorama, who endows his offspring with the great dash which he himself possessed. There, also, is located His Highness, owned by a syndicate, and whose son Beau Sabreur was claimed by Irish sportsmen to be the equal of any other crack four-year-old in Europe.

Nothing succeeds like success, and there was no reason for surprise, with numbers of big winners coming out of Ireland, that the Aga Khan chose that country for his stud-farm, though later he had a second stud-farm in Normandy whence came his Derby winner Mahmoud. He established Sheshoon Stud on the borders of the Curragh in Co. Kildare, afterwards enlarging it by founding another stud at Ballymany, on the opposite side of the Curragh ; and, if I am not mistaken, he had a partnership interest with his son, Prince Aly Khan, in Gilltown Stud in Co. Kildare (where the late Lord Furness bred a host of winners), Eyrefield House, also in Co. Kildare, and Ongar in Co. Dublin. A volume, not a chapter in a book, would be required to recount all His Highness's winners of great races, for Sheshoon Stud has been a brilliantly successful nursery throughout its career. It is, and always has been, solely a brood-mare stud-farm, a stallion not being kept. Bahram is Sheshoon's champion-to-date.

Other notable breeders with studs in Ireland include Mr. James McVey, jun. (whose studs are at Wood Park, in Co. Meath, and Confey, in Co. Dublin), Maharaja of Baroda, Don Ferdinando d'Ardia (" The Island Estates ", Waterford), Mr. A. L. Hawkins (who acquired Flier Stud, near the Curragh, from Mrs. Parkinson), Prince Aly Khan (who is interested in several properties), Sir Percy Loraine (whose bloodstock are reared and whose stallions are kept at Kildangan Stud in Co. Kildare by Mr. R. More O'Ferrall), Duke of Westminster (who years ago owned the Ballymany Stud, now forming portion of the Aga Khan's studs : appropriately, the Duke's first winner from Ballymany bore the name Ballymany), Mr. and Mrs. Evan Williams (whose Knockany Stud was the birthplace of the Classic-winning half-brothers, Ard Patrick and Galtee More, and of, at least, one Liverpool Grand National winner, etc.), Mrs. Bloomfield (who has a splendid property in Co. Kildare), Mrs. Luke Lillingston, who is in occupancy of Mount Coote Stud in Co. Limerick, long the home of the sporting Russell family, and, for a time, maintained by Sir Gilbert Greenall, long before he was raised to the peerage as Lord Daresbury.

The last decade of the nineteenth century was nearing its close when the brothers George Edwardes and Major Edwards (they

spelled their names differently) established Ballykisteen Stud
in Co. Tipperary. It was, I think, the first foundation in Ireland,
by non-residents, of a large-scale farm for race-horse production.
George Edwardes, as is generally known, was the theatrical magnate whose many promotions captivated the musical-comedy-
loving world; his brother, who had been training in England
(and later in Ireland), was a retired army veterinary surgeon.
Ballykisteen Stud was, I believe, George Edwardes' sole property,
his brother being associated with it only until he had set up his
own establishment (where also he trained) at Rathduff, near
Cashel, also in Co. Tipperary. Major Edwards bred the Liverpool
Grand National winner Shaun Goilin. First manager of Ballykisteen Stud was the late Mr. J. W. A. Harris, and his son is
present-day manager of the property. A Classic winner has not
been produced from Ballykisteen yet, but the fact is especially
interesting that the late Lord Derby's wonderfully successful
brood-mare Anchora (who had been a good winner) was bred
at Ballykisteen. Numbered among descendants, in the second
generation from her, are Pharos and Fairway, names with which
to conjure.

Other leading breeders, some in the late '90's and well into the
1900's, and their younger colleagues, who began horse-breeding
in the twentieth century, will be named, but space does not permit an exhaustive list. The late Mr. Edward Kennedy, of Straffan
Station Stud in Co. Kildare, filled a prominent place in the Breeders' table with production of such notabilities as The Tetrarch,
Delaunay, and Dark Ronald (who, before going to Germany sired
famous Son-in-Law). The late Mr. J. J. Maher (first a breeder
of 'chasers before he went in for yearling production) bred at
Confey Stud the Classic winners Caligula, St. Louis, Manna, and
Sandwich, in addition to handicap winners of high grade. Mr.
Maher was one of Ireland's " biggest men " in the bloodstock
world. The late Mr. T. K. Laidlaw, a Scotsman who settled in
Ireland, did not attempt anything ambitious as a horse-breeder,
but he produced the Derby winner Aboyeur (even though he was
winner only on disqualification of Craganour); and the late Mr.
Dan Sullivan bred the hardy, staying Windsor Lad in Co. Dublin.
The late Mr. W. Barnett gained Classic honours in the Derby and
St. Leger with Trigo, of his own breeding: and the Irish St.
Leger was another prize he captured. One of the few studs which
have been disbanded following a profitable time was that maintained by Mr. W. B. Purefoy at Greenfield, in Co. Tipperary. His
confederates were Mr. A. P. Cunliffe and Mr. J. H. H. Peard, and
the trio, with one or two others, were racing-associates in the
Netheravon stable when John Fallon first had charge of it, Tom
Lewis succeeding him. Charlebelle was an Oaks winner (1920)

GOING UP THE HILL, HALF A MILE FROM THE START, STEVE DONOGHUE ON THE RAILS. 1934 Derby.

MRS. V. GRAY
CONGRATULATING
H. BERRY ON RIDING
HIS NINE HUNDREDTH
WINNER

THE GREYVILLE COURSE, DURBAN

from the Greenfield paddocks, and supporting her achievements were those in handicaps by other stock raised at Greenfield.

Newmarket trainer Peter Purcell Gilpin had his stud-farm at Dollanstown, Kilcock, Co. Kildare, and it was a profitable venture, rendered the more so by Mr. Ludwig Neumann's horses (which Gilpin trained) having been bred there. Sir Gilbert Greenall (afterwards Lord Daresbury) maintained a particularly fine stud at Mount Coote, for several years; he bred the Oaks winner Love in Idleness (1921).

References to breeding and breeders would not be complete without mention of that somewhat extraordinary race-horse, but stud failure, The White Knight (1903), bred by the late Col. T. Y. L. Kirkwood in Co. Roscommon. Scarcely any weight was too much, or distance too far, for him. He won Ascot Gold Vase, two Ascot Gold Cups, two Coronation Cups (1907 and 1908), a Goodwood Cup, etc.; and when carrying 9 st. 12 lbs., failed by only three-quarters of a length to give his fellow four-year-old Demure 45 lb. in the 1907 Cesarewitch! Colonel Kirkwood sold a half-share in him to Mr. W. R. Wyndham for £10,000, and on Colonel Kirkwood's death his brother inherited the deceased's half-share. M. Blanc came along with an offer of 32,000 gns., which Mr. Wyndham declined to accept and bought out his partner's share for £16,000. The Hungarian Government desired possession of the stallion, and tendered 40,000 gns., which Mr. Wyndham would have accepted if an undertaking were given that the horse would not leave the British Isles. That guarantee was not forthcoming. Colonel Kirkwood had won the Liverpool Grand National with Woodbrook, long before The White Knight had appeared on the scene " to witch the (racing) world " with his artistry.

Who among bygone generations was Ireland's greatest trainer ? The senior generation will promptly and unhesitatingly answer " Lindé ". His name has already been before us. He died a few years ere the 1890's had run their course. His charges won at home and abroad. They won Liverpool Grand Nationals and most other outstanding 'chases in England (the Lancashire Handicap Steeplechase, and so forth); they won Paris Hurdle Races and Paris Steeplechases and other French jumping races; and they won in Ireland almost every flat race and jumping race worth winning. Lindé put many of his own, and many of his patrons' horses, capable of winning high-class flat races, to jumping.

I suppose judgment by results is the only standard of comparison we can adopt in endeavouring to " number off " our trainers. Yet that method is not quite fair, for a trainer with only a few horses in his stables (he may desire only a few) may do more with them than a trainer with a huge " string ". However, we

S

must take things as we find them, and judge by results. I suppose
that, during the present century, our greatest *home* trainers (not
taking into account those now practising) were Senator Parkinson
and Michael Dawson, both of whom controlled big stables of
horses at the Curragh. I have to italicise the word *home*, because
I must not be unmindful that Peter Purcell Gilpin, "Atty"
Persse, R. C. Dawson, the late J. C. Sullivan, Captain Dewhurst,
P. F. Hartigan, (no doubt others, also), trained in Ireland before
migrating to England : and that they all had prosperous innings
here before seeking "fresh woods and pastures new". They
have also prospered among "the fresh woods" and in the "new
pastures". On the other hand, Hubert Hartigan, who has a
flourishing stable at Melitta Lodge, Curragh, returned to Erin
after successful training in England.

Senator Parkinson, who trained at Maddenstown Lodge,
Curragh, was a veterinary surgeon (graduate of London Veterinary College) and passed through his stables winners of high
degree, notably Orby (which he trained in his two-year-old
season), Glenesky (a very fast, weight-carrying sprinter), Americus
Girl (probably the fastest filly in her day), First Flier (an Irish
Derby winner, and a winner of important races in India), May-
fowl (one of the best horses in India), Trepida (Duke of York
Stakes winner, etc.), Illinois (a notable winning two-year-old,
owned by "Boss" Croker; yet Orby was 21 lbs. better than
him), Irish Fun (one of the best mares raced exclusively in Ireland), The Gunner (a 'chaser of merit, beaten a neck for second
place in Liverpool Grand National (1904).

But I shall always think that Michael Dawson—who had been
a professional jockey in the first flight of riders—had, on the
whole, greater horses in his boxes at Rathbride Manor, Curragh,
than had Parkinson in his. I name some of those which I recall
off-hand : Bachelor's Button (only conqueror of Pretty Polly in
England), Winkfield's Pride (Cambridgeshire, Lincolnshire, Prix
due Conseil Municipal, Doncaster Cup, etc.), Bachelor's Double
(City & Suburban, Royal Hunt Cup, etc.), Jerry M (one of the
greatest 'chasers that carried saddle), St. Brendan (an Irish Derby
winner, and fancied for Sceptre's St. Leger, though he was at his
best at a mile or under), Great Surprise (a champion sprinter;
he ran 5 furlongs at Epsom in 55⅜ secs., carrying 10 st. 3 lbs.),
Hornet's Beauty (topmost 6-furlong horse in his day), Ebor (he
was first named Oisin : Kempton Park Jubilee, etc.), Ayn Hali
(best two-year-old of her season ; winner of five races consecutively), and so forth. Of course, Michael Dawson did not train
every one of these horses for the races after their names, but he
trained them before their purchase, or removal to other quarters.
Michael Dawson was the first trainer in Ireland with winnings

reaching five figures in one season's campaign. This he accomplished in 1908 with £11,205. From 1906 until his death, his year-by-year record in the Winning Trainers' list was impressive, as will be seen from the following figures :

> First—1906, 1907, 1908, 1909, 1910, 1912, 1913, 1922, 1924, 1925.
> Second—1911, 1914, 1915, 1918, 1923, 1926.
> Fifth—1916, 1919, 1921.
> Sixth—1917.
> Eighth—1920

Michael Dawson's total-money record remained unbeaten until 1923, when Parkinson's charges beat it with £12,150, and this trainer's annual achievements were very noteworthy, too. I give them up to 1939 :

> First—1914, 1917, 1919, 1923, 1926.
> Second—1906, 1907, 1908, 1909, 1910, 1912, 1913, 1925.
> Third—1911, 1915, 1916, 1918, 1920, 1924, 1927, 1936, 1939.
> Fourth—1928, 1929, 1935, 1937, 1938.
> Fifth—1931, 1934.
> Sixth—1922, 1930.

Jos Hunter (alive and well), the late J. T. Rogers, Cecil Brabazon (whose stable is prospering and includes the Irish champion four-year-old, Beau Sabreur), James Canty (Joe Canty's brother), the late " Philly " Behan (who got exceptionally good results with two-year-olds), A. J. Blake, Harry Ussher, and others have disputed the issue in several seasons with Dawson and Parkinson, but the last-named pair, as may be seen, were main contenders for first honours.

Hubert Hartigan has been accomplishing deeds of importance, for when he topped the Trainers' table in 1937 his total of £12,372 beat Parkinson's figures set up in 1923 ; and in 1948 Hubert Hartigan went one better by surpassing his previous total, establishing the Irish Trainers' record at £12,654. He has one of the most influential stables in the country. He was a fine horseman when younger, and the majority of readers will recall that he was not in the heyday of his youth when he took the leg-up on Old Tay Bridge (trained by his brother Frank Hartigan) in the 1924 Liverpool Grand National—exactly a quarter of a century ago. Of course, " the Hartigans " are bred to be horsemen, because of their inheritance on both sides of their pedigree, but more especially so through their mother, née Miss Moore, daughter of John Hubert Moore, who was of immense stature, both physically and mentally ; and a trainer of mark.

Then, also, " the Hartigans " are nephews of those gallant fellows Willie Moore, who trained at Burbage, and Garrett Moore,

accomplished Corinthian rider.   Garrett won the Liverpool
Grand National on The Liberator (1879), which he owned in
part, and he had to fight a battle in the Law Courts before he
could run the horse, for the other partner desired not to run him
and sought an injunction to prevent him from running.   The
law is not always " the h'ass " it is said to be, and the presiding
Judge ruled that the business of a steeplechase-horse was to run
in steeplechases and that, accordingly, Garrett Moore had full
right to start the horse in the Grand National.   How very appropriate that he won !   He started second favourite, winning in a
canter by 10 lengths.

Captain Darby Rogers, M. N. Walker (son of " Reggie "
Walker, accomplished amateur horseman in his day, with a splendid training record), Harry Ussher (another skilful amateur rider
who also topped the Trainers' table), Paddy Sleator, Charlie
Rogers (who has a big " string " of Miss Dorothy Paget's horses
in his boxes), Paddy Beary (Michael Beary's brother), A. J. Blake
(who has been champion trainer), James Canty (also champion
trainer some years ago), M. C. Collins (who has a fine team of
horses, including Ascot winner, Solonaway), Tom Dreaper (who
has won a lot of races for Mr. Rank with Prince Regent and
others), R. Fetherstonhaugh (who has been top of the Trainers'
tables, and whose charge, Circus Lady, well may be the best filly
in the world, judging her merits on the easy defeat she administered Coronation V in the Irish Oaks), Henry Harty, M. Hurley,
Tim Hyde (Prince Regent's jockey), H. Freeman Jackson (who
owned, trained and rode Result, winner in 1949 of the coveted
Galway Plate), John Kirwan, Paddy Lenehan Seamus McGrath
(who trains his father's (Mr. Joe McGrath) horses in Glencairn
stables, where once the Classic winners, Orby and Rhodora were
located, Dan Moore (fearless horseman and expert trainer), F. S.
Myerscough (who owned the highest-priced European syndicated
stallion, The Phœnix, at £160,000), " Barny " Nugent (who has a
stable of flat racers, 'chasers and hurdlers, with which he obtains
most gratifying results, M. V. (" Vincent ") O'Brien (who has
probably won more important races in Ireland and England, Irish
and English Classic races excepted, in a shorter time than any
other Irish trainer ; champion hurdler Hatton's Grace, and
champion 'chaser Cottage Rake are amongst those he trains), Jos
Osborne (who sends out many winners), Johnny Oxx (who wins
his proportion of races with splendidly turned out charges),
Paddy Prendergast (another of the younger generation of trainers
who has quickly come to the front), E. M. Quirke (training
successfully, following many profitable years as a professional
jockey), and there are dozens of others, all of whom are prospering.

From very remote days, when Irish law laid down that, " none but a noble's son might ride in a race ", until the present day, the standard of Irish horsemanship has been good.   This observation applies alike to Corinthians and professionals.   The twentieth century has been prolific in output of Corinthians of the highest calibre, worthy successors to the McDonoghs, the Beasleys, the Moores, the Nugents, the Cullens and hosts of others of first ranking ;   whilst of professionals of high skill there have been, and are, many ;   but not a few of the unpaid and the paid brethren go away from us to England, and even further abroad, and Irish Racing is poorer as a consequence.   One of the most dashing short-distance jockeys we have had in the present century was the late John Thompson, who served as an apprentice with J. J. Parkinson and, throughout his career, was attached to his stable.

It would be misuse of language to write that Thompson was " unbeatable in sprints ", but he came as near being " unbeatable " as anyone could on a fancied animal.   Most regrettably, he was killed when schooling over hurdles.   He was the first Irish-born jockey, riding in Ireland, to adopt the modern style of short stirrups ;   and this he did against the grain, at the suggestion of his master ;   and Parkinson, as a Corinthian, was the pioneer in Ireland of what we used to term, " the American style ", when it burst upon notice.   Thompson was chosen by that wonderfully good judge, the late J. C. Sullivan, to ride his Cambridgeshire winner Berrill in 1900.   Thompson was then an apprentice.   The data available are sufficient to indicate his high competency, for from 1904–07 (both years inclusive) he was champion, and he repeated that achievement in 1910, 1911, and 1912, his fatal accident occurring in the last-named year.

Another highly promising jockey who met his death in the same year as Thompson was David Condon, whose name will not be so familiar to the younger generation but was known to their seniors.   Competent judges spoke of him as one of the brainiest jockeys Ireland produced.   The Doyle family has been producing capable jockeys for three or four, or more, generations; and without making comparison between members of the family, I shall expect agreement with the opinion that the late John Doyle (father of the present James, Joseph, John and their brothers) was unsurpassed in his period.   That he was a long way out of the common run, even when very youthful, is evidenced by that shrewd judge of men and horses, Captain Machell, bringing him to England for a season to ride the lightweights in the stable which he managed.   Doyle's health failed some years before he died. He had been training since relinquishing the saddle.   Mention of names is unnecessary, but a certain jockey (distinguished alike on the flat and over jumps) said to a friend of the writer after Doyle had beaten him by a very narrow margin in an important Irish race : " Doyle made a monkey of me ! " Doyle, when a lightweight, won the 1892 Cesarewitch on Burnaby, who started favourite.

"Algy " Anthony rode for the Prince of Wales (afterwards King Edward VII) in Ireland. He was a perfect picture in the saddle, and had not a compeer, especially over hurdles and fences. He fared well as a trainer. As a jumping jockey, his proudest win was on the Prince of Wales's Ambush II in the 1900 Liverpool Grand National.

Peter Hughes, who died only a few years ago, was a plucky and highly competent jockey, whose merits were never fully recognized : but he got plenty of riding ; Fred Hunter, another of Parkinson's apprentices, was a stylist. He was in the first flight among the lightweights, and as he increased in weight his services continued in demand. He rode with particularly sound judgment, and on Grey Tick he won the 1903 Cesarewitch. The aged gelding had only 6 st. 9 lbs. and was a 20-to-1 chance.

Mr. J. C. Sullivan brought W. Higgs to Ireland on trial, and Higgs at once went ahead ; so much so that when Mr. Sullivan cast his lines in England, Higgs went with him. He was even more successful in England than he had been in Ireland, and it was said of him that he " was the best ' horse ' in Sullivan's stable ". The partnership was a long and profitable one, and Mr. Sullivan, whom I knew intimately, never tired of telling of Higgs' loyalty and skill. The ever-youthful Michael Beary was in the leading rank when riding in Ireland, and in England he has retained his eminence to the present day. A fine horseman, a very strong finisher—and he never tires.

The Beasley brothers—Paddy (" Rufus "), Harry, and Willie— were horsemen from the cradle, and if they hadn't been so gifted, there would be a sad lapse in heredity, for their father, Mr. " Harry " Beasley was one of the greatest amateurs who graced the saddle, and his brother, Mr. " Tommy " Beasley was superexcellent, if I may use that term, for among his victories was the defeat of Fred Archer at the Curragh, with Archer on a hot favourite. There were other brothers (all uncles of the present Beasley generation) who also were celebrities. Paddy (" Rufus ") is a successful Malton trainer and Harry is assistant trainer to C. A. Rogers, who has Miss Paget's Irish team in his Curragh stable.

The riding of W. (" Bill ") Barrett always impressed discerning judges. He was a resolute finisher (probably stronger than most of his contemporaries), and seldom was the verdict against him a " near thing ". I could name an Irish Derby which he won, but should have lost ! His power and endurance were too much for his rival, capable though that rival was.

Joe Westlake, who died in 1948, began his career as a light-weight and so terminated it. A cool, sound judge of racing, and a highly competent horseman. M. Wing is riding as well as ever he did. " Never leave Wing out in a sprint ", said the late S. C. Jeffery, who trained at the Heath, in Queen's County, to me, and Wing's unequalled dash justified that appraisement. He has been champion jockey so often that I daresay he forgets the count himself.

Joe Canty, another of the senior generation, was beloved of the crowd. Opportunity was ever sought by the crowd to cheer him, as we have seen on the occasion of his fleeting successes now-adays, for he rides but seldom. Time was when he was, perhaps the busiest of his brethren. He is the perfect horseman : and, " a horseman ", we are told, " is one who *knows how* to ride a horse : ' a jockey ', one who rides a horse." His mount was always balanced. I am sure it is correct to write that, in his hey-day, he knew no superior, particularly in a long-distance race. None excelled him at " waiting ", and his run at the finish was almost irresistible. Another thing : he could tell more about the merits of a race than any other rider I know. I always sought his opinion when in doubt. He set the Irish riding record at 117 wins (with the wonderful average of 34.51) in 1925, and it has never been in danger of being eclipsed.

Tommy Burns, sound judge of pace, was in the first flight, too, though, like Joe Canty, he does not ride so often as heretofore. Short-distance races and long-distance races were alike to him. He was a masterful finisher, and could win with a deal in hand by a very slight margin and few onlookers could penetrate his artistry.

A middle-weight who was doing better than ever in 1949, was Herbert Holmes, who showed in the Irish Oaks (1949) what a splendid mare Circus Lady was : for he held her up till 2 furlongs from home, when she responded to his call to go for her race by putting in a spurt that surely would have won a 5-furlong sprint! Among the younger generation, there are several riders especially talented, Martin Molony (equally as good on the flat as over jumps), Aubrey Brabazon (who makes no distinction between hurdles and fences and the flat), P. F. Conlon (best of the apprentices), and so on ; but I must not write a litany of names.

We have not so many brilliant Corinthians as in former years, say, in the days when the Beasley brothers (Tommy, Willie, Harry, John, and Jimmy), and others of their grade were riding: and, still later, when " Reggie " Walker, Joe Manley, Cecil (who is training numerous winners) and Leslie Brabazon, Harry Ussher (another successful trainer), Frank Tuthill (who is Senior Judge of races to-day), Harry Nuttall (who beat Danny Maher at

Leopardstown), Harry Poe, J. C. Kelly (who has told me that he has never ridden another horse the equal of Jerry M), Hubert Hartigan, and Willie Parkinson, who topped the Amateurs' table first season he rode, and who had not thrown a leg across a horse until a few weeks before he took his first mount, for he was intended for engineering, not for the Turf—all these, and many others, were all " brilliants ".

Ireland is not without accomplished Corinthians, but there may be quantity at the expense of quality. I should not place another pair in front of Mr. J. R. M. Cox, M.R.C.V.S., and Mr. P. P. Hogan. Both have perfect style and, though substantially framed (Mr. Cox especially), they are light in the saddle, good judges of pace, and expert at the end of a race : finished horsemen. Mr. P. J. Lenehan has for many years been a leading light, but he does not take so many mounts as formerly, devoting most of his time to his training-stable.

CHAPTER XVIII

RACING IN AUSTRALIA

BY ALLAN DEXTER

AUSTRALIAN racehorses to-day gallop five seconds faster at a mile, eight seconds faster at two miles, than they did 50 years ago. But are they better horses? Or is it merely that tracks have improved, riding methods are more streamlined, racing plates are lighter?

James Scobie, probably the most capable and best-known Australian trainer to have patted a horse on the rump and sent him out fit to race for his life, wrote in his autobiography:

" Horses are harder to train now than they were in my youth. I am referring to young thoroughbreds whose physical powers need to be developed. I maintain that the present-day thoroughbred doesn't last nearly as long as those which I trained years ago."

Yet Neil McKenna, secretary of the New South Wales Owners' and Trainers' Association, with a background not so illustrious but quite as extensive as that of Scobie, contends:

" It is my considered opinion that racehorses to-day are better than they were 50 years ago.

" There was not the intensive study of ' nicks ', nor the modern selectiveness in mating. A man would import a stallion from England, and then put it in a paddock with station mares.

" Carbine was a wonderful horse in his day, but I think he'd be only fair if racing to-day.

" I often hear it said that races years ago were not run truly from start to finish. I rode my first winner in 1885 and have seen a lot of racing in my life. Throughout my experiences, practically all races were run fast. Jockeys didn't keep a firm hold on their mounts, didn't hold them back for a sprint home."

Unquestionably, the Australian racehorse has become progressively less rugged. He cannot run the long journeys, sometimes twice a day, often four times a week, which his predecessors did. The distances of his gallops are cut short until in 1949, only three flat races in Australia are beyond two miles. Australian racing has become speed racing, admittedly.

But when the modern Australian horse has to run his 2 miles, he runs them at a speed which the old-timers reserved only for sprints. The day of the slow stayer has gone.

It is hard to conceive that nothing has been gained by the exchange of haphazard method for selective breeding. Surely the millions of pounds which have been put into the Australian thoroughbred industry have not been wasted. For nearly fifty years now, Australian breeders wisely have turned to England for blood lines.

Australia has magnificent breeding grounds. The Hunter Valley in New South Wales, the Darling Downs in Queensland, the Goulburn Valley in Victoria are natural lime districts which help develop strong, flat bone and, for thoroughbred rearing, are perfect in climate and contour. Yet there is something in Australia which, from a bloodhorse viewpoint, is enervating. The Australian racehorse needs a constant infusion of English blood, otherwise quality fades and finally disappears.

Of course, there have been Australian sires of great worth and success. Wallace, Maltster, Heroic, Spearfelt, all have given champions to the Australian turf. But the Australian breeder of this century will continue to favour English stallions. To-day, he is infusing into Australian blood like that of Hyperion, Blandford, Bahram, Nearco, Felicitation, Sir Cosmo, Big Game. And, through the grey Nizami, The Tetrarch strain already has produced a Melbourne Cup winner, Hiraji.

But there is one drawback which, in future years, could affect the standard and standing of the Australian racehorse. While the bloodlines of recently-imported English stallions are excellent when printed in stud book and brochure, the individuals themselves sometimes lack quality and often have very meagre race performances. Leading Australian breeders see the danger. They admit they would like to secure the best English stayers, but they cannot afford to pay the huge prices, ranging over £100,000, for such animals.

The solution, on paper, would be Australian syndicates, to share a high-priced stallion proportionately. But human natures are too uncertain, self-interest too strong, and few breeders are optimistic enough to believe that such syndicates could function amicably. A few Australian studmasters still prefer local race-horse champions to the moderately-performed, though highly-bred, English horse. They argue that, when given real chances at the bigger studs, Australian sires have been successful.

Maltster, a Derby winner sired late in the nineteenth century by Bill of Portland, was leading Australian stallion in five successive years before 1915.

Wallace, by Carbine, sired winners of five Victoria Derbys,

six VRC Oaks, two Melbourne Cups, two Australian Cups and a Sydney Cup.

Heroic, by Valais, was retired to the stud after winning £38,062, and until his death in 1939, exercised a vast influence on Australian breeding. He was leading sire for seven successive seasons from 1932. His progeny won £300,000 and his sons, Ajax, Hall Mark, Nuffield, Hua, The Marne and Royal Step have been good sires. The Australian thoroughbred to-day, though he may lack top English quality, is no longer the poor chimney-sweep of the world's racing.

Shannon brought to the United States a realisation that an Australian racehorse can be good. Bernborough's stock already has sold highly in America. The intensive student will advance many reasons for Australia's improved horseflesh, but most vital, perhaps, was the importation into Australia, at the end of World War 1, of English horses, Valais and Magpie.

Valais introduced a sire line and a strain of brilliance which still is coursing through the veins of Australia's best gallopers and stud stock. It has given Australia such champions as Heroic, Hall Mark, Hua, Flight, Manfred and Fuji San. Valais had been a good racehorse in England. He had won up to a mile and 7 furlongs and had finished fourth in the 1916 Derby won by Fifinella at Newmarket. Through both his sire, Cicero, and his dam, Lily of the Valley, he was a member of the successful Bend Or line and of a great sire line descended from Beeswing. Bought in England for 3,500 gns., Valais produced winners of £250,000 and was sold in Australia, by his original purchasers, for 14,400 gns.

Magpie, by Dark Ronald from Popinjay, raced in Australia before Percy Miller, of Kia Ora Stud, New South Wales, paid 5,000 gns. for him. The blood of Magpie will leave as lasting an impression on Australian staying lines as did that of Carbine. Steve Donoghue wrote in his autobiography : " Magpie never liked it better than when the whips were cracking ". Magpie's greatest son, Windbag, inherited the gameness, and although Magpie has been dead 15 years, his blood influences the result of most long distance handicaps to-day. His daughter Idle Words, too, is the dam of Shannon.

When Sol Green, after making a fortune at bookmaking, imported the Persimmon horse, Comedy King, to Australia 40 years ago, he won the 1910 Melbourne Cup for himself and gave Australia another successful sire of stayers. From Comedy King's loins came Melbourne Cup winners, Artilleryman and King Ingoda, and a dual Derby winner, Biplane. His progeny ran long distances, and with Magpie and, perhaps, The Buzzard, did most to bolster up the flagging stamina of Australian horses.

The Buzzard raced in England as The Bastard. But, with that queer Australian twist of mind which permits a man to call a spade a So-and-So shovel with one breath, but closes his mouth over a perfectly normal English word, racing authorities ordered a change of name. The Buzzard, standing at Lyndhurt Stud in the lush Darling Downs of Queensland, gets common-looking stock which, because they lack lustre, polish and precocity, often sell below value as yearlings.

Few colts and fillies by The Buzzard sprint fast, although there have been exceptions. But most of his progeny stay well. They have won £350,000 in stakes and among them have been Melbourne Cup winners, Old Rowley and Rainbird. The Buzzard is a direct descendant of Carbine, whose blood still dominates the historic breeding establishment of Hobartville more than 35 years after his death at Welbeck Abbey.

Percy Reynolds, 92 years old in 1949, built his breeding fortunes upon a Carbine foundation when, in 1900, he undertook the ownership and stewardship of Hobartville, 40 miles from Sydney. For what other horse, he asked himself, had had such an influence on Australian racing? What other horse could impart to Australian strains the courage, stamina, and great-heartedness needed to win classics and rich handicaps?

So, through the years, the Carbine tradition has dominated Hobartville. At one time, when only 11 mares by Carbine remained in Australia, Percy Reynolds possessed four of them. The Carbine strain remains in the brood mares and, to give a double dose of the blood, the only sire now at Hobartville is Felcrag, a male descendant of Carbine through Felstead, Spion Kop, and Spearmint (All English Derby winners).

Although one of his sons, Moorland, won the AJC Derby in 1943, Felcrag has not imparted to his stock the stamina of his famous forbear. The Felcrag horses have gone fast, but not far ; still, they have had their influence upon the sprinting standards of Australia.

Four generations of one Thompson family have cared for Widden's 5,500 acres in the Hunter Valley. In 1949 the master was Frank W. Thompson, president of the New South Wales Breeders' Association, still under 40 years, and destined to become a commanding figure in Australian racing.

Widden's lucerne and grass paddocks, timbered slopes, modern boxes and yards are different from the valley as the first Thompson saw it 83 years ago. Back in 1866, William Barbour Thompson and his son, John, direct from Leeds and with pack horses laden with household effects, made a slow, perilous journey across the mountains in search of a new home. For much of the way, they clambered over precipitous trails, down steep gorges.   Ahead and behind were forbidding mountains. Then, from the Widden Spurs, branch of the Great Dividing Range of New South Wales, they came to the beautiful Widden Valley, partly wooded by wild-apple trees, stretching for miles before them.   Clearing the apple trees and founding magnificent grazing lands, the Thompsons raised cattle, then Clydesdales, and during the last 50 years, some of Australia's finest racehorses.

Widden's first thoroughbred sire was The Gem.   Russley and Dorchester followed, but the fame of Widden was established firmly by Maltster and the English stallion, Linacre.   Their progeny won a total of more than £600,000.   Not even Heroic, in later years, was more famous as an Australian-bred sire than Maltster, whose skeleton was exhumed from Widden in 1932, and now is exhibited at the Institute of Anatomy, Canberra. To-day, the Widden sires are Brueghel, bought in Italy from Signor Tessio, the man who sold Nearco to England ; Al Wassat, by Hyperion ; Whirlaway, by Bahram ; and, standing his first season, Valognes.

In the centre of rich limestone country of the Hunter Valley is the 2,650 acres Kia Ora Stud, where Shannon first nibbled grass.   Kia Ora, for two years, was a sheep and cattle run until 1915, when Percy Miller, prominent in the meat industry of New South Wales, absorbed an idea to breed bloodstock.   In the 34 years of its existence, 3,500 foals have been dropped and reared at Kia Ora.   The stud costs £12,000 a year to maintain, but the 44 colts and fillies it offered at auction in 1949 aggregated £55,710.   The old home of Magpie, Kia Ora proudly shelters Midstream (by Blandford) most successful sire in 1947–48, and the progenitor of Shannon.

Only a fence divides Kia Ora from Segenhoe, where some of the stone stables and fodder barns built by convicts in 1820 still stand.   Segenhoe's original 12,000 acres, granted to early settler Potter McQueen, have been carved and subdivided until only 1,500 acres remain.   On the ashes of McQueen's domain arose a breeding ground, established by the Honourable James White, of Belltrees and now modernised by Lionel Israel.   New Zealand-bred High Caste, equine lord of Segenhoe, has as his companions the Nearco horse, Nilo, bred by the Aga Khan, and Al Dakhil (by Hyperion), for whom the Aga Khan paid 12,500 gns. as a yearling.

St. Alban's Stud, at Geelong, 50 miles from Melbourne, was founded by James Wilson during a depression in the 1870's, produced good racehorses in the early 1900's, but later was a dairy farm until Victoria Racing Club committeeman, Guy Raymond, and H. B. Ranken bought it 20 years ago.   Gay Lothario, by Gay Crusader, was St. Alban's main stallion until

he died in 1944, and his progeny won more than £300,000 in
stakes. First stallion at St. Alban's in 1949 was the English horse
Enfield, still young but already the sire of two Melbourne Cup
winners, Sirius and Rimfire. Enfield imparts to his progeny
six lines each of St. Simon, Sterling and Springfield.

Helios, who suffered an accident when in full training at
Flemington and now has one foreleg, from fetlock joint down,
turned back to front, was the most successful sire in Australia
in 1948. With Dhoti, who was to have been raced in Australia
by the Duke of Kent, Helios stands at Warlaby, close to
Melbourne, where another VRC committeeman, E. A.
Underwood, puts into practical operation his vast knowledge of
thoroughbred breeding.

Further back in the last 50 years of Australian racing was the
Melton Stud, Victoria, owned by Ernest Clarke, where The
Welkin sired Gloaming and where Cyklon got Trivalve, a
Melbourne Cup and dual Derby winner (1927).

Comedy King, when sold by Sol Green for 7,300 gns., went to
another famous Victorian breeding-ground, Noorilim, owned
by Norman Falkiner. On Noorilim's rich and spacious paddocks,
30 years ago, roamed the most valuable collection of mares in
Australia ; and there, too, the Spearmint horse, Spearhead, sired
Spearfelt, a Melbourne Cup winner (1926) and later one of
Australia's most successful stallions.

Bearded, grim-visaged coal millionaire, John Brown, early
this century bred more horses at Wills Gully, in the Hunter
Valley, than he really could count. He raced many himself,
sold a few, but allowed hundreds to run loose and untried in the
stud paddocks. Brown was a queer, unfriendly man who
believed that what he did was his own business. Once he paid
2,600 gns. (a big price then) for a yearling by Valais from
Shepherd Princess, and did not bother to race the colt. John
Brown was successful as an owner. With Prince Foote, in 1909
and 1910, he won the Melbourne Cup, the Victoria and AJC
Derbys, and the VRC and AJC Legers. He won the Victoria
Derby, too, with Richmond Main (1919) and his estate with
Balloon King in 1930. Prince Viridis won for him the VRC St.
Leger (1918), Duke Foote the AJC Metropolitan (1912), Sir
Foote the AJC Doncaster Handicap (1902) and Prince Charles
the Sydney Cup (1922).

John Brown's counterpart to-day, in the number of his horses,
is wool and shipping magnate, F. W. Hughes. He turned to
racing in 1934, when his doctor advised him to adopt a hobby.
He set out mildly, bought a few moderate animals, and then let
his racing interests spread as quickly as a rabbit plague. He
established a modern stud at Kooba, in central New South

Wales, later extended it to Coleman, in the Riverina district of NSW. On his combined properties, Hughes has 300 mares, eight or nine stallions, and a big collection of yearlings and foals.

Hughes prefers to keep his most promising young horses for himself, sends a few comparatively cheap lots to the annual yearling sales in Sydney each year, and will not part with any of Nizami's stock. Tired of waiting for his own stallions and mares to provide him with a Derby winner, which is his racing ambition, Hughes, in 1949, delved into the yearling market as a buyer, and paid 17,650 gns. for nine promising youngsters.

Wherever racing is staged, it is a rich man's sport. Only an optimist takes up ownership with hope of profit. Costs are too heavy, good horses too few. Yet there have been rich men in the last 50 years of Australian racing history who, like Ernest Clarke, of Victoria, have found gold on the racecourse.

Clarke's first big winner was Emir, who won the AJC St. Leger and weight-for-age races in 1904 and his trainer, James Scobie, expressed the opinion that Emir would have been as great as Carbine, but for a physical disability. In the years until Trivalve won him the Melbourne Cup in 1927, Clarke's horses won 146 races and total prize money of £128,935.

Charles B. Kellow, a motor industry executive in Melbourne, ushered in the big-money era for thoroughbreds when he paid 16,000 gns. at auction for Heroic, in 1924. Forced into the sale-ring through the disqualification of his owners, Heroic was first " sold " to Martin Wencke. The Victoria Racing Club, however, would not recognise the sale and Heroic was re-offered. Kellow had no reason to regret his bid. Heroic was a great racehorse and in 1933, Kellow won the AJC and Victoria Derbys and the Melbourne Cup with Heroic's son, Hall Mark, and the two Derbys with another son, Nuffield (1938).

E. M. Pearce, a newcomer to racing, raised eyebrows in 1926 when he bid 5,500 gns., then a record, for a yearling by Valais from Courante. The colt, named Avant Coureur, had speed but lacked courage. Still, he was as good a racehorse as Dominant who, in 1928 was sold as a yearling for the still record figure, 6,750 gns.

No Australian owner in 50 years, however, has splashed— and lost—money like Alan E. Cooper from 1936 to 1939. He paid £19,000 for Talking after that colt had won the AJC Derby in 1936. He paid £7,000 for Mala and £10,000 for Gold Salute, and from the trio had a disappointing return. Cooper, on the other hand, lost two good horses cheaply. In a fit of pique, he sold St. Constant for £1 and saw the horse win more than £10,000 in stakes. He leased Main Topic (one of Talking's first progeny) with a £500 purchase option, which was exercised against him immediately after Main Topic had won the AJC Derby in 1942.

O. R. Porter, a boot manufacturer in Melbourne, paid more than £50,000 for horses between 1941 and 1949 and, probably has shown a profit. An affable, hearty little man, who is unchanged whatever his current racing fortunes, Porter ignores the yearling ringside, will buy only proved or promising horses. His greatest success, St. Fairy, was winner of the 1945 Caulfield Cup and £25,000 in stakes.

Men like E. J. Watt, L. K. S. Mackinnon (a chairman of the Victoria Racing Club), P. H. Osborne, and Agar Wynne have owned extensively, but mainly for enjoyment and to the exclusion of betting.

Edward Moss, E. A. Connolly and Darcy Eccles were racing professionals, owning good horses and many poor ones. Connolly, with a reputation as the shrewdest man of his day, finally left an estate of less than £10,000. Eccles has had his reverses, but has not delved deeply into ownership since The Trump won the Caulfield and Melbourne Cup double in 1937.

Moss, who rose from small beginnings, invested large sums of money where it could not be affected by his racecourse plunges, and died a rich man.

George Badman, who has had outstanding success with Royal Gem (sold to America), Beau Gem, Crown Gem, and Regal Gem, all from the one mare, French Gem, bets heavily on his own horses. Azzalin Romano, proprietor of a Sydney night club and restaurant, won heavily on Bernborough. Romano bought Bernborough in Sydney for 2,600 gns. and later sold him to America for an amount said to be £93,000, but more likely 93,000 dollars.

W. J. Smith, the man who bought Shannon at auction for 25,000 gns. and later sold him to America, is a millionaire who seldom invests more than £5 on a horse. He first took up racing in 1929, when he and F. P. Cruttenden formed the successful " Smithden " partnership. Smith later acquired the St. Aubins Stud at Scone, transformed it from a dilapidated dairy farm into a show establishment, and there installed Manitoba and, before he was sold recently to the U.S., Ajax.

To what extent Shannon's successes in America proved the value of the Australian horse, or to what extent they demonstrated a temporary weakness in American race standard, is a matter of opinion. I believe that Shannon had passed beyond his peak when W. J. Smith sold him to the United States. Had Shannon gone to America about the time he ran his mile in 1 min. 34½ secs. at Randwick in 1936, few American horses, no matter how good, could have held him at 8 or 10 furlongs.

MR. F. W. HUGHES

AERIAL VIEW OF RANDWICK RACECOURSE, AUSTRALIA

[Facing page 276

J. E. PIKE

D. MUNRO ON SHANNON

W. COOK

W. JOHNSTONE ON COLOMBO

Shannon up to 1949 was Australia's greatest stake-winner. It is an unfair honour, as the bulk of his winnings came from inflated prizes in California. In Australia, he won less than £20,000. As an individual, Shannon was natty but not big. He lacked the proportions of his rival, Bernborough, whom, unfortunately, he was destined not to meet.

Bernborough was good, there is no mistaking that, though whether his world rating was as high as his owner and trainer believed, is a different argument. A slow beginner, Bernborough had an unusual ability to gain speed on turns, which he rounded like an expert cyclist.

Bernborough and Shannon each had a lowly breeding background. Bernborough was bred from a 20-years-old mare, Bern Maid, apparently of little account when put to the newly-imported English horse, Emborough, by Gainsborough. Shannon was sired by the Blandford horse, Midstream, but his dam, Idle Words, had been bought at auction for 75 gns., and had produced one race failure and had missed once, before dropping Shannon.

Neither Shannon nor Bernborough was as great a racehorse as Phar Lap, who, in 1932, won the Agua Caliente Handicap at his only American start and died of colic at Menlo Park, California. Phar Lap, a tall gelding with a 27 feet stride, became a national hero. But not, apparently, to the money-worshippers. An attempt was made to shoot him before the 1930 Melbourne Cup, for which he was odds-on, and armed police guarded and escorted him on to the very race-track on Cup Day.

As geldings, Beauford and Gloaming (actually a New Zealand horse in ownership and racing) have left nothing to the turf except memories—but memories of two brilliant horses, not stayers in the real sense, but whose extreme speed carried them to the end of 1½ miles.

Beauford, the son of a cheap stallion, Beau Soult, and a mare Bleuford (who could buckjump better than she could gallop) won only £17,186 in stake money. He is far down the list of Australia's stake-winners. But of him, Dr. W. H. Lang, handicapper to the Victoria Racing Club and one of the most knowledgeable thoroughbred judges in the land, said: " Beauford is the greatest galloper I have seen. He is St. Simon over again ".

Breeding experts, expecting champions to come only from the mating of proved mares with high-credentialled stallions, looked askance at Beauford's bloodlines. They condemned him not only for the apparent lowliness of his parents but because one of his ancestors, Free Trader, won a Liverpool Grand National (1856). No real champion ever springs from a jumping family, they assured themselves.

But when the New South Wales breeder, W. H. Mackay, sent
Blueford to Beau Soult, he was adhering to a family strain
similar to that which produced The Tetrarch. Beauford, like
The Tetrarch, was inbred to No. 2 family, of which he had five
crosses, and of which Bruce Lowe said was the most successful
and most important in world racing history.

Beauford and Gloaming ran four memorable races in Sydney
in the spring of 1922. The score was even—and when they
gather in sporting or club corners, racing men still argue
concerning their respective merits.

More brilliant horses have skimmed the short-cropped grass
tracks of Australia. Perhaps greater stayers have won the
famous Melbourne Cup, but Windbag, greatest son of Magpie,
probably is the most versatile Australian champion in 50 years.
He won £35,939 in stakes. Earnings alone do not make a
champion. Comparative nonentities, racing when standards are
low, have built up astounding prize-winnings.

Windbag, however, raced when every state of Australia could
claim good horses. He won the 1925 Melbourne Cup with
9 st. 2 lb. against Manfred, one of the most remarkable three-
year-olds Australia has produced. He won from 6 furlongs to
2 miles, and possessed a speed and stamina he passed to many of
his offspring.

Yet this Windbag, this horse of all distances, grew from a
puny yearling who was turned down, at second glance, by a New
Zealander, Ian Duncan, after he had bid 150 gns. for him at
auction. Inspecting Windbag after purchase, Duncan shuddered
at his lack of size and ignoble appearance, re-sold him for 125 gns.
to Robert Miller, brother of breeder Percy Miller, and so made
one of the most astounding mistakes of the Australian turf.

Manfred, the three-year-old whom Windbag outstayed by half
a length in the 1925 Cup, was an amazing colt who might have
been Australia's most famous thoroughbred had he not inherited
from his sire, Valais, a hot-headed, fiery nature which left him
unpredictable at the start of his races. Yet for all Manfred's
vice, and allowing that a jockey's opinion is not always reliable,
his rider, William Duncan, says : " I don't care what horses
they argue about—Carbine, Gloaming, Beauford, Phar Lap,
Windbag or Ajax—Manfred would have beaten them all up to a
mile and a quarter."

Manfred, by Valais from Otford, by Tressady, could carry
weight and run long distances when his strangely-working brain
told him to gallop. He won the 1926 Caulfield Cup with 9 st. 6 lb.,
6 lb. above weight-for-age. He won the AJC Derby in 1925
after having given the field 100 yards start. But the day he really
decided to stand at the barrier—which he did often—Manfred

stood as firm as Gibraltar. Frank Dempsey, well-known in England, averred that " only a stick of dynamite could have moved Manfred when he took it into his head not to race ".

Since world-famous Carbine won with 10 st. 5 lb. in 1890, only one horse, Poitrel (1920), has won the Melbourne Cup with 10 st. or more. Poitrel, bred from an English stallion, St. Alwyne, and an Australian mare, Poinard, barely topped 15 hands 3 inches. He was not powerfully built and, adding to his troubles, he had shelly feet which necessitated long hours of standing in patches of moist clay. But he had heart, the staying heart of which Dr. Stewart Mackay formulated a theory, and there was never an inch of any race at which Poitrel did not try his hardest.

Australia, in its last 50 years, has had other good horses. Wakeful, whom the long-beards of Australian racing declare was the best mare to have raced in this country, was not trained seriously until she was four years. She was the heroine of the first few years after the turn of the century ; beat—and habitually beat—the best performers of her day at all distances, and yet, in most races, was horribly ridden. Dunn, her jockey, was an indifferent horseman, but Wakeful's owner, Leslie McDonald, preferred his honesty to the brilliance of his rivals.

Forty years later, Flight, by a Heroic horse, Royal Step, arose to challenge Wakeful's memory as Australia's greatest mare. Flight, bought for 60 gns. in 1942, when the Japanese were threatening Australia's shores and racing was likely to fade out, won an Australian record for a mare, £30,627. She was brilliant and a great fighter, but she may not have been another Wakeful.

Wakeful always has been classed as a failure as a matron. She certainly did not produce anything of her own class, but her son, Night Watch, won the Melbourne Cup in 1929. Flight, only recently retired to the stud, has a yearling son by Dhoti, a filly foal by Helios. How good they will be, only the years will tell.

Wherever he has gone in the world, the Australian jockey has been successful. Frank Wootton (although he did not ride in Australia), Frank Bullock, Brownie Carslake, W. H. McLachlan senior and junior, James Munro, Rae Johnstone, Edgar Britt, and Bill Cook have gained the heights either in England, on the Continent or in India.

The Australian jockey has been criticised for his exaggerated crouch. Perhaps he does buckle his leathers a hole or two too high. Perhaps, too, his monkey-on-a-stick attitude prevents him from exercising complete control over a horse. But he is quick-thinking, dashing, and his very crouch minimises wind resistance in a race.

It is claimed in Australia that a " local lad ", Tot Flood, introduced the crouch seat years before Tod Sloan, from America, shocked English racegoers by his riding style and his successes. In the early 1900's, however, Australia's foremost jockeys compromised with a saddle seat somewhere between that of Tod Sloan and the straight-backed school.

James Barden, one of the first to break away and really bend over a horse's neck, enjoyed outstanding success, but not solely because he reduced wind resistance and allowed a horse to carry his weight on its withers. Barden was a horseman. He had balance and hands, judgment and a cool, clear head. When the race became desperate, when an extra ounce meant victory, Barden, too, could ride with demoniac finishing strength.

Bob Lewis, conversely, gave the long-stirrup school a lifelong argument. He rode more important winners than any other Australian jockey, and he lasted longer. Lewis was an old man when he won the 1927 Melbourne Cup on Trivalve, yet, from the time he first vaulted into the saddle as a boy, he did not materially shorten his stirrup lengths. Head clearly above the other riders, Lewis was conspicuous during a race. To modern standards, his style may not have been attractive, but he knew where he was going, and his mounts quickly knew, too, what was expected of them.

Lewis and the G.O.M. of Australian trainers, James Scobie, commenced an association in 1895 which remained unbroken for 40 years, except for a short period when Lewis was in England with J. E. Brewer. Lewis won four Melbourne Cups, eight Victoria Derbys, four AJC Derbys. He fully deserved Scobie's final praise of him : " A good servant, absolutely honourable and straight ".

W. H. McLachlan, in the years up to 1920 and a little beyond, was a fine rider, and in the next decade, Frank Dempsey, William Duncan, and Jack Toohey rode with great judgment and ability. Dempsey did not continue long after his return from riding in England, and now officiates as starter on many courses in Melbourne.

Parochial outlooks can distort judgment, but, to my viewpoint, Australia's two finest jockeys in the last 30 years, at least, have been James E. Pike and James Munro. They sat close to their horses, were tacticians both in handicaps and at weight-for-age, and could judge to a fraction the capabilities of their mounts.

Pike, as an apprentice, went to England with his master, William Kelso, but remained only a short while, and subsequently refused several offers to ride outside Australia. Munro had several successful seasons in India, and later accepted a retainer to ride in Germany for Baron de Rothschild.

His brother, David Hugh, as popularly known to Australian crowds as " Darby " as is " Gordon " to English racegoers, is a different type of rider, but has had equal success. Darby Munro uses his head, his hands, and his eyes during a race but, perhaps, an even greater attribute is his strong left arm, with which he can whip a horse with real force, and with which he often has snatched seemingly impossible victory.   A. Breasley, Munro's rival among the older jockeys in Australia to-day, is a rails rider who, by patience, has gained miraculously clear runs to success.

Younger men, J. Thompson, Neville Sellwood, and J. Purtell have yet to attain the fully-fledged ability of the men before them, but they ride well and sensibly.   And, just as important, they are clean-living, family men, who are helping to dispel the old social prejudices against " the little men in silk ".

There are possible criticisms of Australian racing to-day. Progress is progress, and even the staid adherent must knuckle under to the innovations of science.   But, in some ways, the sport is growing too mechanical.

Although Melbourne has scrapped all systems of starting stalls and races are run from the open barrier, most Sydney courses (Randwick is an exception) are using the American apparatus, with glass doors replacing barrier strands, and a bell ringing discordantly when the doors fly open.

The camera has displaced the human judge (although that official still is a figure-head in the box) on all major courses, and many clubs, particularly the Australian Jockey Club, have introduced regular tests for doping.

Australian racing, too, is a betting sport.   Admiration for a horse, as a horse, is infinitesimal.   If one can gallop faster than the others—and if you back him—so much money in the pocket. Pound notes are cheap on Australian racecourses, and in one season (1948-49), a Sydney bookmaker, Ken Ranger, handled £2,250,000 in bets.   That figure is accurate, not so much romance, because bookmakers have to lodge with the Treasury an exact accounting of all their wagers.

But then, lest anyone believe this big-betting craze is strictly modern, Sol Green laid £100,000 to £1,000 against Poseidon and Apologue, winners of the Caulfield and Melbourne Cups in 1907 and next morning, paid the full amount in cash at the Victorian Club, Melbourne !

CHAPTER XIX

RACING AND BREEDING IN SOUTH AFRICA

By A. L. Robertson

THE dawn of the present century found South Africa in the grip of the unhappy conflict between Briton and Boer, which disrupted many other things besides racing and the breeding of the Thoroughbred horse. During this troubled period there was a good deal of racing at the Cape where large British military forces were assembled, but the breeding districts in the Northern Cape and in the Orange Free State fell within the sphere of military operations, and breeding was severely impeded and in a good many instances completely suspended.

When the war ended in 1902 and the British occupied the Transvaal, racing was quickly revived, and The Johannesburg Turf Club, the premier Transvaal racing club, staged a three-day meeting on the 26th and 27th of December, 1902, and the 1st of January, 1903. The feature event was the Johannesburg Summer Handicap over a distance of one mile and worth £1,500. During the guerilla period of the Anglo-Boer War there were importations of horses from the British Isles, the Argentine and from Australia, so when the time came to race again in earnest, a very good field went to the post for the important Summer Handicap. Twenty-five horses bred in England, Ireland, Australia, Argentina and South Africa were in the field. The English bred filly Love Match by Matchmaker started favourite and won for her owner, Mr. (later Sir) Abe Bailey, with Mr. Henry Nourse's South African bred filly Ocean Gem by Pearl Diver in second place and Sir Abe Bailey's Australian bred horse Chesney third. The winner was ridden by Ray and trained by Trundley.

The betting on this first big race on the Rand after an interval of four years, must have been very heavy, for the writer was told by the late Sir Abe Bailey, who knew how and when to bet, that he won more over Love Match's victory in this race than over any other in his long association with the British and South African turf. His next biggest win was over Dark Ronald's Royal Hunt Cup at Ascot in 1909.

The bigger centres like Cape Town, Port Elizabeth, Durban, Pietermaritzburg and Kimberley all staged important meetings, and all over the country there were race meetings of various sorts. Some of them gave quite respectable stakes, but the majority were of the gymkhana type and confined to enthusiastic amateurs. The chief winning owner in that first year of racing after the war was Mr. Henry Nourse who won 35 races worth £6,705, mostly with animals bred by Mr. Charles Southey at the Culmstock Stud in the Middelburg district and sired by Pearl Diver, one of the most successful stud sires ever domiciled in South Africa. Messrs. Willie & Julius Meyer also kept a big string of horses and won a lot of races, and Mr. Abe Bailey, as he then was, had some good imported horses and won several of the best races. Other owners who were prominent at that time were Mr. F. W. Blood, Mr. W. E. Earle, Mr. J. Hershensohn, Mr. F. Katzenstein, Mr. D. S. Lategan, Mr. Jim Piccione, Mr. Ted Sieveright and Mr. F. White.

The horse-breeding industry was seriously dislocated by the war, though prior to the outbreak there were only really four studs that had much influence on the South African Turf. Three of these were in the Cape Province, or Cape Colony as it was then styled. They were the Culmstock Stud of Mr. Charles Southey in the Middelburg district, the Halesowen Stud of Mr. H. Hilton Barber in the Cradock district and the Stormfontein Stud of Mr. Alex Robertson in the Colesberg district, while in the Orange Free State Mr. Frans Schimper had a well-known stud, Bresler Flats in the Winburg district. The only studs to escape the ravages of war were Culmstock and Halesowen.

Soon after peace settled on the land two more important studs were founded. Mr. Henry Nourse bought Dwarsvlei near Middelburg (Cape) and built up a stud which was to have a great influence in the country, and Sir Abe Bailey started the Arundel Stud in the Colesberg district and later transferred to Grootfontein in the same district, where his son carries on the Clewer Estate Stud at the time of writing. Mr. Nourse started with his Pearl Diver mares bought from the Culmstock Stud, and had phenomenal success with them, aided by the purchase from the Duke of Portland of Greatorex, a son of the mighty Australian horse Carbine, and the English Oaks winner Mrs. Butterwick by the greatest Thoroughbred of all time, St. Simon. From the combination of Greatorex on his Pearl Diver mares, Mr. Nourse dominated the breeding scene and it was only when his stud grew to unwieldy dimensions that the glory of Dwarsvlei faded, until at the time of Mr. Nourse's death, his tremendous studs of Thoroughbreds, numbering about a thousand head, had become more of a menace than an asset to the Turf and its attendant horse-breeding industry. Every filly bred at the Nourse studs was retained for breeding purposes with the inevitable result that there was rapid deterioration, though many of the great lines of blood developed by Mr. Nourse live on and have enriched other studs.

The aftermath of the Anglo-Boer war, as of every other war, was a slump, which in these more enlightened days is called a recession in prices. Racing and breeding were, of course, affected, and by 1904–5 the total amount distributed in stakes in what was to become the Union of South Africa, plus Southern Rhodesia, totalled only £122,815 as against the £961,005 given in 1947–8. About 1,600 horses raced during the year of which about 15 per cent. were eligible for registration in the Stud Book, and yet we find " Old Timers " who still claim that better horses were bred then than now. It is and ever will be so in this and every other country. The lowest amount distributed in stake monies since the end of the Anglo-Boer War was £102,498 in 1907–8.

Mr. Henry Nourse, Sir Abe Bailey, and Mr. Jim Piccione were still among the leading owners of race-horses, and another to come to the fore was the Australian Mr. Richard Wootton, who later settled in England and attained great success as a trainer. His son, Frank, became champion jockey after serving his apprenticeship with his father in Johannesburg, and another son, Stanley, also rode winners in England and was a successful trainer with a particular flare for turning out good jockeys. About this time Mr. J. Piccione imported a number of horses from Argentina, who did him good service on the South African turf, among them the good racehorses Chinois, Ramenti, Baluarte and Cordon Rouge. Actually the best of all was the Argentine Derby winner Pippermint who did not strike form here and was repatriated to his native land to make a considerable name for himself as a sire of good winners. Another good Argentinian was Charcot who later went to England where he won races carrying big weights. The best sprinters of the period just after the war were the Argentine bred Charcot and Regia and the South African bred Camp Fire, who later raced in England with distinction as Camp Fire II.

Camp Fire II was sent to England by Sir Abe Bailey as a five-year-old. He was bred by Mr. Charles Southey at the Culmstock Stud and got by the great sire Pearl Diver (son of Master Kildare), out of Wallflower by imported Whackum from imported Wild May by Wild Oats. In his first season in England he won over 5 furlongs at Newmarket, where races usually take a bit of winning. He was also beaten a head in the Great Surrey Handicap at Epsom and was third in three races including the Portland Plate at Doncaster in which he was conceding the winner 25 lbs. As a seven-year-old he started in ten races, winning the Great Surrey Handicap from a very good field ; the

Windsor Castle Handicap, beating the great sprinter Melayr and eight others; the King's Stand Stakes at Royal Ascot with 10 st. 2 lbs., giving the second horse over 3 st.; and the Soham Plate at Newmarket with 10 st. 9 lbs. in the saddle and conceding 1 st. 6 lbs. to 4 st. to each of the other runners. He was also placed three times and then retired to stud. He sired some winners but nothing of much class and was eventually brought back to South Africa to take up stud duties at a small stud where he got very few chances to distinguish himself. Camp Fire II did prove himself in the very top class as a sprinter in England. The only other South African bred horse to win in England before that was Pearl Rover who was bred at the same stud as Camp Fire II and by the same sire. He won over 6 furlongs at Newmarket and over five at Sandown Park. Forty years elapsed before the next South African bred horse won in England, of which more anon.

In the decade which elapsed between the end of the Anglo-Boer war and the outbreak of the first World War, racing and breeding jogged along at what looked like a settled pace. The highest stakes disbursed during this period was the £147,794 in 1908-9, and strangely enough the lowest was the £102,498 of the previous year and this was followed by the next lowest in 1909-10 when £105,798 was allocated to stake monies. These monies refer only to racing under Jockey Club rules. At this time unregistered racing was flourishing on the Rand where the Auckland Park Racing Club raced every Saturday until a Transvaal Provincial Ordinance laid down that no Racing Club should race for more than fifteen days in a year. This allocation was inadequate to keep the sole unregistered Club going, so Auckland Park came into the Jockey Club fold and has remained there ever since. Unregistered racing has been frowned on by the various Provincial Administrations, under whose jurisdiction racing falls, until the Orange Free State Provincial Executive granted a licence to an unregistered club to race at night. This licence was granted about the middle of 1949 and racing was expected to start before the end of the year. If this type of racing catches on, it will be a serious blow to legitimate racing and to the Thoroughbred horse-breeding industry, and might even destroy the production of Thoroughbreds altogether.

To revert to the period under review, that between the Anglo-Boer War and the first World War, there was a steady increase in the number of breeders and several studs made their mark, chief among them the Prospect Stud of Mr. D. J. de Wet in the Robertson district; the revived Leeuwpoort Stud of Mr. T. Everard in the Carolina district; Messrs. P. A. de Lange and C. E. Todd who had their respective studs in the East Griqualand area ; Mr. L. G. Bland in the Dordrecht district, where Mr. E. V. Birch started the Vogelvlei Stud which was designed to play such a very important rôle in the production of South Africa's best Thoroughbreds.

The dominating thoroughbred sire in this period was Mr. Henry Nourse's imported Greatorex by Carbine out of Mrs. Butterwick by St. Simon. He headed the list of Winning Sires ten times between 1910 and 1922 and was twice second. Other sires to attain premier honours during those years were Pearl Diver, then coming to the end of his great career ; Greenlawn by Kendal, who sired a lot of South African winners before being imported by an East Griqualand breeder to end his days in South Africa. Campanajo by Isobar also topped the list, chiefly through the many good ponies and galloways sired by him. The New Zealand bred Uniform by Hotchkiss who stood at Mr. Alex Robertson's Stormfontein Stud also headed the list as did the very speedy Quickmarch by Saraband, the property of Mr. C. E. Todd. Among other successful sires at this time were Minor Forfeit by Minting ; Leisure Hour by St. Simon ; Sir Daniel by Winkfield ; Dundonald by Carbine ; Catrail by St. Frusquin and King's Favourite by Morganatic.

Among horses racing then, the most distinguished included Sir Daniel, an imported son of Winkfield, who won two Johannesburg Handicaps before attaining to considerable fame as a sire during his short stud career. The South American bred Baluarte by St. Mirin was another very good horse, who was later exported to England to do well there on the Turf before returning to South African for stud duty, with moderate success. The imported gelding Lombard by Veronese won a Johannesburg Handicap and a Durban July Handicap and was rated by his great trainer Fred Murray as about the best horse he ever had through his hands. Pamphlet, a big massive imported son of William Rufus, gained fame by reason of his weight carrying efforts, his victories including two Durban July Handicaps and many other important events. At stud he failed lamentably. Gondolier, bred in the United States and imported by Sir George Farrer, was a good racehorse but, like Pamphlet, a sorry failure at stud. About the best stayers between wars were the mare Marcristine by Marco and Wavy by Wavelet's Pride, the latter proving quite a good sire. The South African bred Tiger by Simonwick, bred by Mr. H. C. van Zyl at the Hanglip Stud where some of the best early South African bred thoroughbreds were reared, was also a good stayer and in addition could go fast as his win in the Johannesburg Summer Handicap at Turffontein proved.

Among the other South African bred horses who distinguished

themselves, mention can be made of Nobleman a colt by Greatorex out of Peerless, whose victories included the South African Derby and the Durban July Handicap as a two-year-old, the only horse to win this important race at that age. It might, however, be added that the distance then was one mile. Nobleman's own sister Noble Lady was another brilliant performer, and the only animal to win the double of South African Derby and South African Oaks. Winnipeg by King's Favourite was another good horse. His victories included two quarterly Johannesburg Handicaps and a Durban July Handicap. Perhaps an ever better horse was Pietri's son Contentment who was very prominent in our chief races, and later got his share of winners at stud. Another brilliant filly was Dancing Wave by Greatorex, and a Prince among Sprinters was Abelard, a son of Leisure Hour who won five Merchants' Handicaps at Turffontein, and a Johannesburg Handicap. He was rated by his owner Sir Abe Bailey as the best sprinter he owned and he considered him a better horse than Camp Fire II. Perhaps the best filly ever bred in South Africa was Dignity by Minor Forfeit from Stuck Up by Suspender. She was a great success on the Turf and ranks as about the best of her sex though other good ones like Flush of Dawn and Miliza might come into the reckoning. At stud Dignity bred a lot of good stock. Her best son was Dignitary who has strong claims to be considered the best horse ever bred in South Africa, and at stud was a great success and so far is the only South African bred horse to be champion sire. Her other sons, Decorum and Manners, both won big races and her daughter Honor was in the front flight as a two-year-old. Her progeny won £22,955 in stakes at a time when stake values were less than half what they were in 1949.

Among trainers Fred Murray was among the greatest masters of his art this country has known. Jim Russell, with a large string operating over all the chief racing centres, was also very successful and, like Fred Murray, made a speciality of the Durban July Handicap. Other leading trainers might be mentioned like Jack Gard, George Weale (luckily still with us and still training winners in 1949), John Stevenson, Fred Wade, Ted Booth, " Taffy " Townsend and H. F. Seale.

There were a number of able riders. Among them special mention might be made of " Ike " Strydom, who had a fair measure of success when he tried his luck in England. Freddie Maisch rode a lot of winners as did Jackie Simpson, and Ted Shaw, now a successful trainer was always in the forefront in his time, until failing health compelled him to retire.

The latter years of World War One and the few years immediately after, marked a period of great Turf prosperity, with stakes going up from the £122,959 at the outbreak of war to the £379,426 reached in 1920-21.

For the sake of chronological convenience, the next period under review is that falling between the end of the Kaiser's War and the outbreak of Hitler's war, a period of twenty years marked by racing stability rather than by any outstanding advance. The lowest amount given in stakes over this period was the £294,698 in Season 1924-5 when the effects of the big post-war depression were felt. The highest figures were the £339,332 in 1939-40 which included a part of the war period. Racing in the Cape Province was on the up-grade, particularly in Cape Town where the two progressive Clubs, the old-established South African Turf Club racing at the picturesque Kenilworth course and the Milnerton Turf Club who control a well-appointed racecourse at Ascot, were flourishing.

It was during this period that the Union Government first imposed an import tax on horses brought into the country for racing purposes. Horses for breeding still came in free of tax. This move caused much heart-burning and was fiercely assailed in the racing press of the day, but in course of time it was accepted and its benefits generally recognised. The imposition of a tax of £100 did not stop the importation of the better class horse, but did affect the cheaper and generally less desirable animal. At a later stage when horse prices soared, this £100 tax proved totally inadequate and other measures were introduced to make effective the ban on inferior animals.

A number of very fine horses were familiar competitors on our racecourses. Among the importations was Glen Albyn, an Irish bred son of Bridge of Earn, who comes of a " short pedigree " family and is, therefore, not eligible for registration in the Stud Book. He was later acquired by Mr. Henry Nourse and did well at stud, rising to second position in the list of Winning Sires. Among his victories was a splendid effort in the Durban July Handicap, carrying top weight of 9 st. Another great galloper who could go fast and stay well, was Double Up II a son of Winalot, but, unfortunately, he did not transmit his excellence to his stock and was a stud failure as was the burly grey Roamer by Book, who won the Cape's Metropolitan Handicap two years in succession. Mr. Willie Langerman owned another very good performer in the English bred Hussein by The Vizier who won the Metropolitan and the Durban July Handicap. He, too, was a stud disappointment. The little grey horse Glolite, by the English Derby winner Cameronian out of a Tetratema mare, brought off the unusual double of Metropolitan Handicap and Johannesburg Summer Handicap, and dead-heated for third place in the Durban July Handicap. Like Double Up II, Hussein and Roamer, he failed to sire anything approaching his own class as a racehorse.

The French bred Reel II by Salmon-Trout (winner of the English St. Leger in 1924) ranked high as a racehorse and did very well as a sire though handicapped by lack of stud opportunities owing to his owner's queer ideas on breeding matters. Clove Hitch by Captain Cuttle (1922 Epsom Derby winner) was another good horse and sire, who also lacked opportunities. About the most brilliant of the imported horses was Hesperus II a son of Highborn. Among his successes was a Merchants Handicap carrying 10 st. 10 lbs. at Turffontein. He died after a few stud seasons during which he sired nothing of note. The best of the stayers among imported horses was What Next an Irish bred son of Le Prodige who won the two miles Durban Gold Cup Handicap twice, carrying over 9 stone on each occasion.

During the years between the wars South African bred horses were very much to the fore and would appear to have reached their high water mark. Three of them in Dignitary by Greatorex, Colesberg by Wilfrid and Red Ronald by Brown Ronald won the South African Triple Crown of Derby at Turffontein, Guineas and St. Leger at Benoni and all three distinguished themselves in open handicaps. Eccentric, who won £13,885 in stakes, accounted for a Durban July and a Metropolitan and was twice third in the Johannesburg Summer Handicap, and thus had the best record in the Triple Handicap Crown of South Africa. That great mare Flush of Dawn by Suneager won over £13,000 in stakes and still ranks as the biggest stake winning filly in South African Turf records. The brothers Decorum and Manners by Polystome out of Dignity (dam also of Dignitary) performed with distinction and won the Summer Handicap at Turffontein. Historian by Brown Ronald was in our top Classic and Handicap class, as was Moonlit by Cross Bow, who won two Metropolitans, carrying 10 st. 5 lbs. on the second occasion.

Other distinguished handicap horses were Vibration and Pendulum, two own brothers by Polystome out of Undulation by Greatorex, and Night Storm, by Kerasos, who died as a three-year-old, but had already accounted for the South African Derby, Nursery and Sires Produce Stakes as well as two Johannesburg Handicaps and a Germiston Holiday Handicap. Among sprinters Tenon, by Dignitary, measured up to the highest standard, among his many sprint victories being a Merchants Handicap at Turffontein with 10 st. 7 lbs. in the saddle. At the other end there was Candican, by Bird of Prey, who excelled as a stayer and is probably the best horse over a distance of ground produced in South Africa, where he could be compared to Brown Jack in England for consistency, popularity and durability.

On the breeding side we had the Nourse Studs reaching their peak, with the Vogelvlai Stud of Mr. E. V. Birch making rapid headway, until later, conducted by his sons the Birch Brothers, it ousted the Nourse Studs from premier position. It was an era of sires great in the history of the South African Turf. Polystome, a son of Polymelus imported by Mr. S. B. Joel and sold to Mr. Henry Nourse, proved his greatness by heading the South African Winning Sires list eleven times, ten of them consecutively. Sunstone, by Sunstar imported by Sir Abe Bailey and later acquired by Mr. E. V. Birch, topped the list six times if we include a second to Cameronian who stood overseas. Brown Ronald, by Dark Ronald, got many of the best class winners as did Kerasos, by Kennymore, who sired a Classic winner in every one of the seven years he stood at stud.

Other sires who did very well were St. Cyr, by St. Frusquin ; West Kent, by Polymelus ; Fenimore Cooper, by Rabelais ; Sugar Plum, by Persimmon and the South African bred Dignitary by Greatorex. In addition Pietri, by St. Frusquin, who had good juvenile form in England, sired some good horses including Contentment and in addition his daughters like those of Greatorex, Polystome, Kerasos and Sunstone made excellent broodmares and his influence on the South African Thoroughbred was considerable. In this era the best South African bred horses more than held their own against their imported brothers and sisters, due possibly to the great sires enumerated, who sired horses up to the best standards in the country, unlike their immediate successors who, with the exception of Asbestos II, could not compete with animals from overseas.

We now come to what might be termed the final phase of the present half-century, that from the outbreak of the last great war to the end of the 1948–9 racing year. It was a period of great expansion and marked the peak of the Turf's prosperity. Prior to the outbreak of war the biggest sum given in stakes was the £389,562 in 1920–1. This expanded to £988,063 in 1946–7, a figure which gives a good idea of the rise and prosperity of racing, with which was associated the prosperity of breeding. When Mr. Henry Nourse died in 1942 the demand for Thoroughbred stock was great and, with importations prohibited during the war period, there was a rush by breeders to buy the sires and mares which came into the market and prices generally ruled high. In addition to the older-established breeders, many new breeders were tempted to launch out and acquire studs. Many of these studs were founded by men with little, if any, knowledge of their subject and in addition studs were started in parts of the country unsuited to the production of horses.

The Nourse Studs, too, were in a decline, due to the vastness of the business brought about by Mr. Nourse's practice of not culling breeding stock. The result was that breeders bought anything whether good, bad or indifferent ; and many of them branched out with inferior foundations to their studs and now the results are plainly evident. There is a superfluity of inferior animals who cannot maintain themselves or their breeders by their winnings on the turf. Added to the excess production inside the country, there was also a spate of importations after the war. Prices in England and France ruled very high and buyers could not get good horses to race here and with a deterioration in the local product, there were few really outstanding performers and those there were raced in zoned areas and competed only with other horses in their zone, making it difficult to get any basis for comparison. Thus a horse racing in Natal never met horses from the Cape or the Transvaal during the critical war years.

The best horse racing through the war years was undoubtedly Royal Chaplain a son of the Eclipse Stakes winner (1934) King Salmon. He accounted for two Metropolitan Handicaps, carrying 9 st. 11 lbs. in his second effort. He raced in a zoned area so did not meet the best from the other centres, but I think it can be accepted that he was up to the best class in this country. Since the end of the war a large number of horses have been imported to race here, but it is doubtful if more than two or three can lay claim to comparison with some of the past champions. About the best of them was High Signal, an Irish bred son of Montrose, whose victories included a Clairwood Winter Handicap and a Peninsula Summer Handicap (9 st. 5 lbs.) as well as a meritorious second in the Metropolitan Handicap in which he conceded the winner, Desert Rat, over a stone. Another good horse was Thorium, an English bred colt by William of Valence, who won the Metropolitan Handicap twice. Arabian Knight II, by Furrokh Siyar, deserves honourable mention. If he had stood up to the rigours of training he might have achieved distinction. The filly Gold Shell II, by Colombo, was in the first flight among sprinters and another importation of which much might be heard is the recent Durban July Handicap winner Milesia's Pride by Montrose. A lot of other importations won good races, but few of them put up performances of real merit.

The South African bred section, especially in the first half of the last decade, included many animals of merit above the ordinary, headed by that great galloper Lenin, by Sunstone. With £15,943 to his credit he ranked as the biggest stake winner bred in South Africa. Since going to stud he has sired a number of winners, but nothing within hail of himself. Next to Lenin the best horse was probably Cape Heath, by Jubie, who put up a number of meritorious performances and like Lenin could go fast and stay well. Zamora, by Monsieur Jean, won two Metropolitan Handicaps, carrying 10 st. 7 lbs. on the second occasion, which indicates that he was a real racehorse, but his merit is difficult to gauge as he raced only against animals in his own locality, the Cape.

Four fillies deserve special mention. Miliza, by Valerius, ranks with Dignity and Flush of Dawn in the best class. Very near this class is Electrified, a daughter of Solar Cloud. Lalage, by Satyr II, was a sprinter out of the ordinary, winning fourteen races with eight places and only twice unplaced in her 24 starts, mostly in handicap events. Another brilliant filly was Preston Pan, by Fenimore Cooper, who won Durban's Merchant Handicap as a two-year-old, and others who could go very fast were Pearl Dust, by To You II, and Floater by Reel II. Other good South African bred horses through the war years include such as Authentic by Fenimore Cooper, Agricolist by Sunny View, Salmon by Salmon Leap, Ming by Hussein, Distant Call by Clustine and Dunkeld by Jugo.

In the years since the war the South African bred horses do not appear to have attained the heights of past champions. There is nothing really outstanding though such as Fire Brigade, by Extinguisher II ; Feltos, by Asbestos II ; Dazzle, by Duddingston ; Menlo, by Asbestos II ; Desert Rat, by Ballyferis ; Donate, by Asbestos II ; Danny Boy, by True Mate ; Lochiel, by Cameron Lad ; Bovidae, by Boveney and Tactful by Jubie were, at their best, all good, if not great, performers. Among sprinters Gambut, by Sunlord, ranked high and was sent to England where he failed to come up to expectations on the racecourse.

On the breeding side there has been retrogression despite the larger number of breeders. The reasons for this might be a matter of opinion, but to me it appears to be due to a lack of sires who get with some regularity the class of horse able to compete successfully with the best of the importations in the principal races in South Africa. There is no reason to suspect any deterioration in the mares used, but with the single exception of Asbestos II, no sire has been responsible for that supply of good class horses given us by Greatorex, Polystome, Sunstone, Kerasos and Brown Ronald.

Asbestos II, a French bred son of Asterus, was a good racehorse, without being by any means outstanding, but at stud he was a great success and headed the list of winning Sires regularly

GAMBUT (Sunlord-Actor), H. BERRY UP

H. WRIGHT HOLDING MILESIA'S PRIDE (Montrose-Milesia), WINNER OF
THE £12,000 DURBAN JULY HANDICAP

THE SOUTH AFRICAN OAKS AND JOHANNESBURG SUMMER HANDICAP
WINNER, ELECTRIFIED (Solar Cloud-Electric Lass)

MR. A. R. ELLIS HOLDING CAPE HEATH (Jubie-Prairie Flower), BASIL LEWIS UP

in recent years and his sons have won many big races. One of the youngest of them, Convalesce, might well develop into the best he ever sired. He is rich with promise and a worthy defender of our breeding industry. Jubie, by Biribi, has produced Tactful, Cape Heath, Coyote and Norvik, but has lacked consistency. In his younger days Boveney, by Captain Cuttle, got a lot of good horses, but like his illustrious grandsire Hurry On, did not maintain his excellence as a sire. Other sires who got their share of good horses included Solar Cloud, by Solario ; Ballyferis, by Apron ; Kipling, by Asterus ; Cockpen, by Buchan ; Clustine, by Captain Cuttle ; Marcius, by Tourbillon ; Monsieur Jean, by Hollister and Chesham by Pharos. They can all be rated as good sires but not Olympians.

Probably the biggest advance in South African Stud history has been made since the cessation of hostilities. With good prices obtaining for their products and with no good sires available, breeders imported heavily when they once more had the opportunity. Instead of relying on the horses which had finished their Turf careers, they purchased horses of a distinctly higher class than those which had graced our racecourses, and, in time, the influence of these horses is bound to be beneficial. Very few horses who gained fame on our Turf had any sort of distinguished racing record in the land of their birth and their fame rested on what they did here. The consequence was that horses that were in reality second raters, were acclaimed as champions and retired to stud. In the course of time they produced their likes and the moderate importation could still hold his own. There were, of course, a few notable exceptions like the St. Leger winners, Salmon-Trout and Royal Lancer, and the Goodwood Cup winner Salmon Leap, but they had been tried and found wanting and only became available for South Africa, because their deficiencies had been exposed.

The class of horse imported for stud purposes at the end of the war included a number of horses who were either good handicappers, some with pretensions to good weight-for-age class and some who were in the top class as two-year-olds or over sprint courses. Though not up to the best English or French Classic form, these horses represented a distinct advance over the class recruited from our racecourses. Hobo, by Fairway, proved himself at the top of the English handicap class, but unfortunately died after a few seasons at stud. Giafer, by Goya, was close to French Classic form in his native land and besides winning in very good company, also ran third in both the Grand Prix de Paris and in the Prix du Jockey Club (French Derby) and had the distinction of twice beating the English Derby winner Pearl Diver at even weights. Giafer was imported by Mr. George

U

Kramer, of the Askania Nova Stud, and probably ranks as possessing the best credentials of any horse at stud in South Africa at the time of writing.

Messrs. Birch Brothers, owners of South Africa's premier stud, have brought out four horses who should do much to rehabilitate our breed. The first horse to come out after the war was Merchant Navy, son by the 1933 Derby winner Hyperion out of the 1930 Oaks winner Rose of England, and in 1949 was the only post-war importation represented on the Turf in South Africa, and right well has he started with sons and daughters likely to win our best races in the coming season. From France Messrs. Birch Bros. brought Djask an own brother to the French Champion sire Djebel, by Tourbillon out of Loika. A good racehorse, he can be expected to make a name at stud, as should the handsome Fairthorn, by Fair Trial, out of Parity by Blandford. He boasts an excellent record in England and, at the beginning of his career in this country, demonstrated his superiority. The fourth Birch horse is the good sprinter Ranjit, by Fairway, who was in the top class as a juvenile and has demonstrated his speed in this country. With sires of this class, the famous Vogelvlei Stud should maintain its position, though competition is likely to be much more severe than in the past.

Messrs. C. & M. de Wet have imported the good stayer Felix II, by Vatellor. A good horse in France, he crossed the Channel and added the Jockey Club Cup (1946) to his meritorious record. The Hantam Studs, in the Colesberg area, imported the brilliant sprinter Mehrali, by Mahmoud out of Una, the dam of a lot of good performers including the outstanding juvenile of 1949, Palestine. This stud also has the Royal Hunt Cup winner (1945) Battle Hymn by Hyperion out of Old Melody by Sir Gallahad III, and the good horse Downrush by Bobsleigh out of Hecate a half-sister (by Felstead) to Hyperion. Mr. V. H. Russ, the owner of the Saulspoort Stud in the Orange Free State, has His Excellency by Nearco, a good horse on the English Turf in his day.

Other horses who were good performers in England and are now at stud in South Africa are Bold Devil by Horus ; Buckthorn by Umidwar ; Herald by Hyperion ; Knee Joint by Nearco ; Effervescence by Mr. Jinks ; Ramponneau by Jock and Sun Honey by Hyperion. In addition to these sires, many attractively bred mares were imported, and there is every reason to think that the quality of the South African bred horse will improve considerably as the result of the better class parent stock. An interesting addition to the sires is Montrose, by Coronach out of Accalmie. He raced with distinction in England, winning the Woodcote Stakes at Epsom, the Exeter Stakes at Newmarket, the City and Suburban at Epsom (1935 as a five-year-old), the Atlantic Cup at Liverpool and the Duke of York Handicap. Retired to stud in England in 1937, he failed to distinguish himself and, up to the time of writing, his stock in the British Isles had won about £6,000 in stakes, whereas his sons and daughters from England and Ireland have won £70,000 in stakes in South Africa, including three Durban " July " winners in Monteith, Monasterevan and Milesia's Pride, as well as other big winners like High Signal, Soundless, His Lordship, Chez Monty, Danger Zone and King's Guard. This represents an extraordinary record, probably never before equalled in getting winners of more money abroad than in the country of his domicile.

Despite the increase in stakes, no owners with big strings have come to the fore, and the most successful have been the professionals who both train and race horses. Pre-eminent among them is Syd Garrett at the Cape, while George Graham and George Azzie have been successful on the Rand, as has Howard Guinsberg and a few others. In Natal most successes have come the way of E. Shaw (who has a number of patrons), Hennie Coetzee and the veteran C. B. Clutterbuck.

The standard of jockeyship has not been very high, but in H. " Cocky " Feldman and H. W. " Tiger " Wright we have two jockeys who would probably hold their own anywhere if given the chance, and Stanley Amos is another who adorns his profession.

If the Provincial Councils who, under the Financial Relations Act, have the control of racing, will only leave the domestic control to the Jockey Club of South Africa and not kill the game by excessive taxation, there should be a bright future for racing and breeding in the Union and in Southern Rhodesia.

The Chief Clubs which cater for racing are to be commended for their admirable management and conduct of racing. The Durban Turf Club, under the able chairmanship of Mr. Ross Armstrong, has gone from strength to strength, and the other progressive Natal Club, the Clairwood Turf Club, has also made great strides under the control of Mr. Rupert Ellis-Brown and the seasoned veteran Mr. Jack Hollis. At the Cape the picturesquely-situated Kenilworth Club is the headquarters of the old-established South African Turf Club, now guided by its chairman, Mr. Hugh McKinnel, and near the Atlantic coast is the up-to-date Milnerton Turf Club's course where Mr. Sydney Benjamin and Mr. Willie Langerman are the leading lights. On the Rand the Johannesburg Turf Club has had a hard row to hoe. Taxation has been heavy and unreasonable in the Transvaal and the racing boat has been rocked by racing malcontents, but even so Colonel T. B. Clapham has done a great job of work for the senior Rand club.

The Jockey Club of South Africa, ably guided by Mr. P. M. Anderson, has had a rough passage over the years but has come out of it all very well. In 1949 a Racing Commission was appointed by the Transvaal Provincial Council and the voluminous and excellent report they issued redounded to the credit of the Jockey Club. In the Transvaal and the Cape, the Provincial ordinances lay down that all racing shall be under Jockey Club rules. Natal leaves the matter open, but actually there has been no unregistered racing and only the Orange Free State has countenanced this form of racing. With what results the future will show.

The future of Turf and Stud in South Africa is bright, providing they are not taxed or legislated out of existence or reduced to a farce by such things as night racing and other forms of horse competition which are more appropriate to the circus and exhibition than to a test of that noble creature the thoroughbred.

CHAPTER XX

HORSES, OWNERS AND BREEDERS IN U.S.A.

By Neil Newman

THOROUGHBRED racing in the United States was first established on a solid foundation in the South, principally in Louisiana, Alabama and South Carolina prior to 1860, but the outbreak of the Civil War in 1861 dealt the sport a blow from which it never wholly recovered in that section.

Racing in the North as we know it to-day had its birthplace in Paterson, New Jersey, where under the auspices of the Passaic County Fair the first Derby and the first St. Leger were run in this country. That was in 1864, the Derby being won by Robert M. Alexander's Norfolk, a bay horse by Lexington-Novice by imported Glencoe (in this race Kentucky finished unplaced). Norfolk was later sold to Theodore Winters for $15,000 and taken to California. He was never beaten and in California sired some very good horses, one of which, Emperor of Norfolk, was a racehorse of the highest type.

The New Jersey St. Leger of 1864 was won by Kentucky, a bay colt by Lexington-Magnolia by Glencoe, bred by John M. Clay who later sold Kentucky with Arcola thrown in for $6,000 to John F. Purdy who sold him by private treaty to John Hunter. After his racing days Kentucky was sold by auction to the elder August Belmont for $15,000 and retired to his new owner's stud at Babylon, Long Island, N. Y. The New Jersey Derby was the only race in which Kentucky was ever beaten in 22 starts. He was a failure at the stud.

Saratoga was established as a racing centre in 1863 ; the guns at Gettysburg were silent only about a month when the first meeting took place at Saratoga. A year later a number of stakes were contested, Kentucky winning the Travers and Sequel for three-year-olds and a year later the same horse won the first Saratoga Cup, $2\frac{1}{4}$ miles.

Jerome Park, in New York City, threw open its gates in 1867 when the first Belmont Stakes was won by Francis Morris's home-bred filly Ruthless, foaled at Throggs Neck in the environs of New York City. The antecedents of Ruthless were wholly British. Her sire was Eclipse, by the winner of the Epsom Derby of 1844, Orlando, out of the imported Simoon mare Barbarity. The Belmont Stakes is the only counterpart of the Epsom Derby run in this country, its distance is $1\frac{1}{2}$ miles, and all starters carry

scale weight. It is the most important race run in this country—
the Kentucky Derby for the past thirty-five years has been
systematically propagandized to such an extent the bewildered
public flock to Louisville annually as to a country fair—but, as a
standard, the Belmont Stakes stands alone and to the breeders
is the true yardstick for measuring the sire potentialities of the
three-year-olds.

By 1900 racing in this country was flourishing as it had never
flourished before—the sport appeared to be firmly entrenched in
California, Louisiana, Missouri, Illinois, Tennessee, Kentucky
and New York. In the short space of ten years it had been
outlawed in all of these states with the exception of Kentucky,
which was then, as it is now, the centre of the thoroughbred
breeding industry in the United States.

The first blow fell in Illinois in 1904; a year later Missouri
outlawed the sport, followed in 1906 by similar action in
Tennessee. The Louisiana solons followed suit in 1908 and in
the Spring of that year racing's centre was shaken to its foundations when the legislature of the State of New York, knouted
by a governor who was a political tool all his public life, passed
an act making it a crime to wager on racehorses in New York
State. The race tracks in New York, with the exception of
Brighton Beach which folded up like an accordion, courageously
fought a losing battle until the end of the 1910 season and then,
victims of further hostile legislation, closed their gates and did
not resume racing until May 30, 1913. Racing in California
ceased at the end of the 1910 season. The sport was not resumed
in Missouri, Tennessee, Illinois nor California for nearly a
quarter of a century while Louisiana interdicted the sport until
1920.

The Maryland Jockey Club, Pimlico, within the City limits of
Baltimore, Maryland, has conducted meetings at that course from
1870 to date with the exceptions of the years 1890 to 1893, both
inclusive, but it was not until 1912 with the opening of Havre de
Grace that racing in Maryland, outside of Pimlico, attracted any
particular attention.

The proscription of racing throughout the country with the
exception of Maryland and Kentucky resulted in the exodus of a
number of owners to Canada, England and France and the
opening of winter tracks at Ciudad Jaurez, Mexico, Havana,
Cuba and later Tijuana, Lower California.

In the early spring of 1913 Justice Gaynor, of the New York
Supreme Court, decreed that betting without writing did not
transgress the statute, and the so-called " oral betting " was
instituted on Jockey Club tracks and racing resumed May 30,
1913. Since then racing spread to all sections of the country.

States which had been fallow ground for the sport for nearly fifty years, such as New Jersey, gave racing legal sanction, other areas such as New England, where the hoof-beats of thorough-bred horses had never been heard, legalized racing under pari-mutuel betting.   States all over the country, famished for additional revenue, easy to collect through taxes on pari-mutuel betting, had no hesitation in legalizing racing.

As a result there were far too many race tracks in the United States and far too much money wagered on too many bad horses. When the pari-mutuel form of wagering was legalized in New York State about 1940, a tax of 10 per cent. was levied on every dollar wagered and this was split equally between New York State and the race tracks.   Later this was changed whereby the State now gets 6 per cent. and the racing associations 4.   In 1946 the present mayor of New York City, " imported " O'Dwyer, known throughout the city as " The Irish Ape ", imposed an additional tax of 5 per cent. on all sums wagered through the pari-mutuels.

In 1907, the first year for which statistics are available, there were 6,252 races in this country and the distribution of stake money amounted to $5,375,554.   In 1948 there were 25,388 races and $54,436,063 were distributed, the latter constituting a record sum.

When America became involved in World War II in 1941, with the consequent outpouring of money for munitions, defence measures, etc., it was immediately reflected in the sums wagered through the pari-mutuels.   In the year 1939 the revenue to the states as a whole through pari-mutuels totalled $10,369,307. In 1947 it reached its peak $97,926,984.   Figures for 1948 disclosed a recession, $95,803,363.

The National Association of State Racing Commissioners reported that in 1948 the total pari-mutuel turnover in 23 states was the almost astronomical figure of $1,600,012,159 and the combined mutuel play for the year was $106,583,529 less than in 1946.   Revenues from admissions and through the pari-mutuels have been shrinking for the past three years in New York State and this tendency persisted in 1949.   This is equally true in other sectors and is bound to be adversely reflected in the yearling sales in July and August and in the Stakes and Purses for 1950 racing.

Winter racing with the opening of Hialeah Park in 1929 under the guiding genius of the late Joseph E. Widener, and the organization of the Santa Anita track in 1935, placed the sport on a plane hitherto unknown in winter racing.   Santa Anita was followed by Hollywood in California, and Hollywood in turn by Golden Gate Park and Tanforan gave California four first class race tracks. As a racing centre California yields only to New York State.

The situation, however, is basically unsound—there are far too many race-tracks now operating in the United States and not half enough first-class horses to go around. In many instances horses race for stakes and in some instances for purses far beyond the horse's value. Stakes range in value from $5,000 to $100,000 added, and the minimum purse in New York State is $3,500, of which the winner receives $2,275.

That the tide of racing prosperity is receding cannot be controverted ; that it will recede even further seems manifest and that some tracks may have to cease operating within the next decade almost a certainty.

1900 to 1910

Two outstanding horses sired by the "Black Whirlwind", Domino, were Commando, a bay colt out of Emma C. by imp. Darebin, and Cap and Bells II, a brown filly out of imp. Ben-Ma-Chree by Galopin. They belonged to Domino's second crop of foals. In his first crop was DISGUISE II, a bay foaled in 1897 out of imp. Bonnie Gal by Galopin. Disguise's racing was confined to England. Trained by Old Sam Darling, the father of Fred, the retired Master of Beckhampton, the colt finished third in Diamond Jubilee's Derby (1900) but turned the tables on the Prince of Wales' colt in the Jockey Club Stakes. Disguise was returned to the land of his birth and did well as a sire, particularly of fillies.

All three were bred by and foaled at the Castleton Stud of James R. Keene, Lexington, Kentucky. In the fifteen years it functioned under the aegis of Major Foxhall Daingerfield, brother-in-law of Mr. Keene, Castleton gained a reputation as a thoroughbred nursery second to none in this country.

Commando and Cap and Bells were trained by James Rowe who was a leading trainer in U.S.A. for fifty years. He was a leader in 1879, when he trained the horses of the Dwyer Brothers, and also a leader up to the time of his death in 1929 when he trained for Harry Payne Whitney. In that year he trained Boojum, an unbeaten two-year-old until September, and Whichone, the best two-year-old of 1929.

Commando, who raced as a two- and three-year-old, should never have been beaten. He was ineligible for the Futurity, at two, but won five of his six races, the Zephyr, Great Trial, Montauk, Brighton Junior and Junior Champion Stakes. His only reverse was in the Matron Stakes in which his jockey Spencer became over-confident, eased his mount and Commando was caught and passed near the winning post by Beau Gallant, which won by a head. As a three-year-old Commando won the Belmont Stakes and the Carlton Stakes but broke down in his remaining start, the Lawrence Realization, in which he finished second.

Retired to the Castleton Stud, Commando became a leading sire with the unbeaten Colin, Peter Pan, Superman, Transvaal, Celt and Peter Quince to his credit. Commando was a dark bay, coarse in appearance, with great depth through the heart and flanks. He weighed about 1,100 pounds in training, had an exceptionally sweet disposition and died prematurely after four Stud seasons. Domino died after two seasons at the Stud.

Cap and Bells II retains the distinction of being the only American bred filly to win the Oaks at Epsom (1901) at the expense of Sibrinetta which was six lengths astern with Richard Croker's Minnie Dee third. Cap and Bells, like Disguise, was trained by S. Darling. As a two-year-old in America her victory in the Spinster Stakes foreshadowed her Epsom triumph. At the end of 3 furlongs she was leading by 20 lengths. She also won the Criterion Stakes but was unplaced in the Futurity which was also her fate in William the Third's Gold Cup at Ascot in 1902.

Nasturtium, a chestnut colt by imp. Watercress-Marguerique by imp. Voter, was bred by J. B. Haggin at his Rancho del Paso Stud, near Sacramento, California. The colt was sold as a yearling to Anthony Aste for $4,000. After finishing second to Blue Girl in the Great American he won the Double Event in such facile fashion that John W. Rogers, trainer for William C. Whitney, induced his employer to buy Nasturtium for $40,000. He was reckoned to be a certainty for the Futurity but was left at the post. A week later he won the Flatbush Stakes 7 furlongs beating Endurance by Right in effortless fashion. He was shipped to England to participate in Ard Patrick's Derby (1902), developed a cold in his throat and became a roarer. He was returned to this country, put to stud but, with the exception of that good filly Stamina, produced nothing of outstanding merit.

Like most of the Springfield tribe he was a gross, over-topped colt—his sire imp. Watercress weighed about 1,400 pounds at stud but was a beautifully balanced horse for all of his 17 hands odd.

Gunfire, foaled in 1899, by Hastings—imp. Royal Gun by Springfield, a brown in colour, was bred by John E. Madden and sold to William C. Whitney. She was the best daughter sired by Hastings although she won but two races in 13 starts as a two-year-old. Next season she won five out of nine, among them the Mermaid and Twin City Handicaps. As a four-year-old she won the Metropolitan Handicap and prior to 1927 she was the only filly or mare to win this stake, established in 1891. At five she completed her career by winning the Municipal Handicap, 1¾ miles, under 113 lbs., conceding 18 lbs. to the second horse. She was trained by John W. Rogers and did fairly well at Stud.

Endurance by Right was a bay filly by Inspector B.—Early Morn by Sylvester and was foaled in 1899. Prior to appearing at Saratoga in August when a two-year-old she had won eight races in nine starts in the Middle West, including the Clipsetta, Lassie, Petite and Lakeside Stakes. She was then the property of John W. Schorr who purchased her as a yearling from her breeder William S. Barnes. At Saratoga under 122 lbs. she won by two lengths, conceding as much as 24 lbs. to some of her rivals. In the Flatbush Stakes she finished third to Nasturtium and his stable-companion Goldsmith and was then purchased by William C. Whitney, turned over to John W. Rogers and was unbeaten thereafter, winning seven races in succession. Among her victories were the Great Eastern Handicap (126 lbs.) ; the Willow Stakes, the Holly Handicap (with 132 lbs.), conceding as much as 32 lbs. ; next she whipped Heno in the Third Special and in the Champagne defeated the Futurity winner Yankee and Caugnnawaga. Finally she won the White Plains Handicap of 6 furlongs with 132 lbs. She, too, contracted a cough and could not stand training as a three-year-old. At stud she produced a very good filly in Stamina.

Irish Lad, possibly the best horse bred by H. Eugene Leigh, was a brown colt foaled in 1900 by the Derby winner St. Blaise's brother imp. Candlemas-Arrowgrass by Bramble and was sold to John E. Madden as a yearling. In appearance Irish Lad left much to be desired but after winning the Great Trial Madden sold him to Harry Payne Whitney and Herman B. Duryea for $25,000 and he went to John W. Rogers to be trained. As a two-year-old he won seven of his 10 starts, one of which was the Saratoga Special. At three years he won the Saratoga Champion, the Brooklyn Handicap (beating Gunfire) and the Broadway Stakes out of six starts. At four years in six attempts he won the Metropolitan and Advance Stakes ; was second in the Brooklyn under 125 lbs. ; second in the Brighton under 127 lbs. ; third with 127 lbs. in the Suburban and third to Ort Wells with 132 lbs. in the Commonwealth Handicap. His racing days over Herman B. Duryea took Irish Lad to France, where he did well as a sire.

Beldame was one of the best fillies to race in this country in the past fifty years. A chestnut filly, decidedly masculine, Beldame, foaled in 1901, was bred by the younger August Belmont, being by Octagon-Bella Donna by Hermit. After

winning the Vernal and Great Filly Stakes for which she was trained by John J. Hyland she was leased to Newton Bennington and turned over to Fred Burlew to train. At three years she won 11 races out of 13, among them the Carter Handicap, the Ladies, Gazelle, Mermaid, Alabama, Saratoga Cup (1¾ miles beating Africander and The Picket) the Dolphin, the September, the First Special (beating Stalwart) and the Second Special. She was third in the Metropolitan Handicap, her rider Alfred Brennan being too light to do her justice and Hermis beat her a length in the Test Stakes, in which she was pocketed and hemmed in for 6 furlongs. No filly in the past fifty years has ever equalled Beldame's record as a three-year-old. She reverted to August Belmont the following season and although still trained by Burlew she lost form and won but two races, the Standard Stakes and Suburban Handicap. As a broodmare she was a failure.

It is generally conceded Artful was *the* best filly to race in this country in the past fifty years. She was a brown mare foaled in 1902 by Hamburg-Martha II by Dandy Dinmont—bred by William C. Whitney—but ran as a two-year-old in the silks of Herman B. Duryea who had leased the Whitney horses for the mourning period after Mr. Whitney's death in the late winter of 1904. At three years she ran in the " Eton blue and brown cap " of Harry Payne Whitney—she was trained by John W. Rogers. She finished second in her first two races to stable-companions and preserved her Futurity maiden allowance. She won the Futurity ; Tradition was second, Sysonby third and Tanya fourth. The second, third and fourth had never suffered defeat prior to this race and Artful and Sysonby were never beaten after it—it was the best field that ever ran in a Futurity—and it was the only race in which Sysonby was beaten. Artful next won the Great Filly Stakes, and closed the year by winning the White Plains Handicap with 130 lbs., Dandelion 100 lbs. was second. The time for the 6 furlongs, 1 min. 8 secs. had never been equalled in this country up to 1949.

A very difficult horse to train, she suffered from intermittent spells of rheumatism, Artful ran three times in her second season, winning two sprint races at 6 furlongs and in the Brighton Handicap, 1¼ miles, she ran away from Ort Wells, Beldame, Delhi, three high-class stake winners. She, too, was a failure as a broodmare.

While he never expressed the opinion openly the late Walter S. Vosburgh, official handicapper for the Jockey Club from 1894 to 1934 and associated in various capacities with racing in this country since 1866, often intimated he considered Sysonby the best racehorse he ever saw. A light bay colt, sprinkled with grey hairs, foaled in 1902 Sysonby was a son of the 1885 Derby

winner Melton-Optime by Orme. His dam was owned by Marcus
Daly and after Mr. Daly's death his bloodstock was brought from
England to this country and sold in 1901. Optime, on the insist-
ence of Foxhall P. Keene, was purchased by James R. Keene
for about $7,500—she was carrying Sysonby at the time. Turned
over to James Rowe to train Sysonby was beaten only once, in
the Futurity in 1904 finishing third to Artful and Tradition, but
the form was not true, nor was Sysonby assisted to any great
extent by his rider. At two years Sysonby won a maiden race,
the Brighton Junior, Flash, Saratoga Special and Junior
Champion. At three he ran a dead-heat with Race King IV,
in his first start, the Metropolitan Handicap, conceding the
winner a year and 10 lbs. In succession he won the eight races,
the Tidal, the Commonwealth Handicap, the Lawrence Realization, the Iroquois, the Brighton Derby, the Great Republic,
Century and Annual Champion. In the Great Republic, $1\frac{1}{4}$
miles, Sysonby was left at the post, but Nicol, his rider, steadied
him, sent him after his field, caught them at the end of a quarter
of a mile, shot to the front in another quarter and won galloping.
He won at all distances up to $2\frac{1}{4}$ miles. At four he suffered from
an attack of septic poisoning which brought about his death on
Sunday, June 17, 1906. He was buried in the stable yard at
Sheepshead Bay. His skeleton was exhumed, articulated and
now stands in the American Museum of Natural History, New
York City.

To his dying day Sysonby's trainer, James Rowe, never
doubted " Syce " was superior to Man-o'-War.

It is questionable if Harry Payne Whitney ever bred a better
horse than Burgomaster, if indeed, one as good. Burgomaster
was a dark bay son of the great Hamburg-Hurley Burley by
Riley and was bred at the Brookdale Farm, Red Bank, N. J., in
1903, and was trained by John W. Rogers. As a two-year-old
he won five races and was twice unplaced, earning $39,500.
His victories were all scored in stakes, the Great American, the
Flash, the United States Hotel, the Great Eastern Handicap with
130 pounds and the Matron, the last four in succession—he was
ineligible for the Futurity. The next season he won the Carlton
Stakes and the Belmont—his only two outings, in facile fashion.
He was a very gross colt, sadly over-topped, weighing 1,300 lbs.
in training—too heavy for his legs he was retired to the stud.
When his issue betrayed the same physical characteristics he was
sold to Chile.

Peter Pan, foaled in 1904, was one of the first of Commando's
outstanding sons. He was out of imp. Cinderella by Hermit and
boasted as his third dam Mabille, whose son Cremorne won the
Derby of 1872 and the Ascot Gold Cup in 1873. A big, burly

colt with the heart of a lion, he won three stakes in his first season, the Surf, Flash and Hopeful, the latter with 130 lbs. He was the best of his year as a three-year-old, accounting for the Belmont, the Standard, the Advance Stakes, the Brooklyn Derby and the Brighton Handicap. In the last race over 1¼ miles, his last contest, he carried 115 lbs. and defeated 13 opponents. He was practically left at the post but on being sent after his field, picked up his rivals one by one and won by a neck in 2 mins. 3⅜ secs. In the beaten field was Nealon, winner of the Suburban two weeks earlier. Peter Pan went lame after the Brighton but became a very successful stock horse, among his issue being Tryster, Black Toney (by whom his line is carried on), Vexatious, Peter Piper, Pennant, Prudery, Panoply, Puss in Boots, the last stake winner raced by Foxhall P. Keene.

Contemporaneous with Peter Pan and like him bred and raced by James R. Keene, trained by James Rowe was Ballot a son of imp. Voter—imp. Cerito by Lowland Chief foaled at the famous Castleton Stud in 1904. Among his victories were the Double Event, Neptune, Iroquois, Matron Stakes, Invincible, Standard Advance (twice) Equality and Suburban Handicap. He was unbeaten as a four-year-old and raced until he was six. In the Suburban at four years under 127 lbs. he trounced King James (98 lbs.) and Fairy Play (111 lbs.), both three-year olds. He went to England in 1909 where he won the Select Stakes, and returned to this country in 1910 and again won. At stud he was only a qualified success, his best issue being Chilhowee, Midway, Mr. Mutt and Star Voter—he was second on the list of sires in 1918. Ballot, although he was by the sprinter imp. Voter, could hold his own with the best up to 12 furlongs ; beyond that distance Salvidere was his master.

It is questionable if August Belmont's scarlet and maroon silks were ever carried by a better horse in this country than Fair Play, a most attractive-looking son of Hasting—imp. Fairy Gold by Bend Or. Certainly no horse in the current century ever played such a dominant rôle in the racing and bloodstock history of this country. Foaled in 1905 and trained by Andrew J. Joyner he was just fair as a juvenile, winning the Montauk and Flash Stakes. At three years after the enforced retirement of Colin, he won the Dwyer Stakes, the Lawrence Realization, the Jockey Club Stakes, the First Special, the Municipal Handicap with 127 lbs., the Jerome Handicap with 125 lbs.—at distances up to 2¼ miles. He was sent to England in September, 1908, where he was trained by Joyner at Ballaton Lodge, turned sour and was beaten in all his races. When returned to this country he was turned over to Tom Walsh but went wrong in 1910 and was retired to the stud where he became leading sire three times,

leading broodmare sire a number of times and three of his sons
Man-o'-War, Chatterton and Chance Place also became leading
sires.

Like Ormonde, Colin retired from the Turf with an
unblemished escutcheon—he started in 15 races and won them all,
12 as a two-year-old. A brown colt by Commando—imp.
Pastorella by Springfield foaled in 1905, bred at the Castleton
Stud of his owner, James R. Keene, trained by James Rowe,
Colin was never headed in a race. Never too sound, suffering
from bog spavins all his life, a hose was played on his hocks
daily when he was in training. At two years Colin won the
National Stallion Stakes, subsequent to his victory in his debut
in an overnight race. Next came the Great Trial and Brighton
Junior. At Saratoga only Uncle opposed him in the Saratoga
Special. These triumphs were followed by victories in the
Grand Union Hotel, Futurity, Flatbush, Brighton Produce
Stakes, the Matron and the Champagne Stakes. At three he won
the Withers beating Fair Play and King James. In the Belmont
Stakes on the verge of a breakdown, he narrowly whipped Fair
Play over a heavy track with King James third and wound up
his racing career by winning the Tidal, from Dorante and
Stamina. He was shipped to "Old Sam" Darling at Beck-
hampton and easily beat Jack Snipe in a trial, but could never be
sufficiently wound up to race—served two seasons at stud in
England, was returned to this country but failed to live up to
his racing record as a sire.

Disguise's fillies were better than his colts and Maskette was
the best. She was a brown filly, with plenty of size and substance,
out of Biturica by Hamburg and was another of the galaxy of
brilliant horses bred at Castleton by James R. Keene, raced by
him and trained by James Rowe. She was foaled in 1906 and in
her first season won five races, and was second in the Flatbush
7 furlongs trying to concede 2 lbs. to the winner, Sir Martin.
Among her victories were the Spinaway Great Filly Stakes,
Matron and Futurity. In 1909 she won the Alabama, the Ladies'
Handicap, the Gazelle Stakes, the Mermaid Stakes and the
Pierrepont Handicap with 124 lbs., beating the best of the colts.
Later she was sold to William K. Vanderbilt, shipped to France
and in 1925 her grandson, Masked Marvel, won the Cambridge-
shire in the broad red and white stripes of A. Kingsley Macomber.
In many quarters it was contended Maskette was the best filly
ever bred by James R. Keene ; superior even to Cap and Bells.

Another American-bred, not unknown to British turf
enthusiasts, is Sir Martin a chestnut son of imp. Ogden-Lady
Sterling by Hanover, bred by John E. Madden, foaled in 1906
and raced by Madden at two years. Sir Martin was the best

two-year-old of his year, winning the Great American, National Stallion Stakes, the Saratoga Special, the Double Event, the Great Trial and the Flatbush Stakes. Racing in America was then being attacked most viciously so, at the end of 1908, Madden sold Sir Martin to Louis W. Winans who turned him over to Joseph (Boxer) Cannon to train. Sir Martin started favourite for Minoru's Derby (1909) but came down at the Tattenham Corner. Next year he won the Coronation Cup at Epsom, beating Bachelor's Double, Louviers, Mustapha and Dean Swift. After Winans' death Madden re-purchased and repatriated Sir Martin and although a bit " long in the tooth " when he arrived at his birthplace, Hamburg Place, Lexington, Kentucky, he did fairly well as a sire.

Fitzherbert was one of the best three-year-olds I ever saw. He was a bay colt by Ethelbert-Morganatic by Emperor, was bred by Perry Belmont who turned him over to A. J. Joyner in cancellation of a training bill of $750. After several starts in Joyner's name he was sold to Herman Brandt and having won half a dozen races for Brandt he was sold to Samuel C. Hildreth for $10,000. Fitzherbert won 14 races out of 15 as a three-year-old, his sole defeat being at Gravesend in the autumn. He drew the inside position and had top-weight. At the start the light-weight Afflication, on the outside, crossed over, piled up the field and Fitzherbert went to his knees—he was beaten by a neck. At four he was unbeaten, winning the Brooklyn Handicap conceding Olambala, a first-class horse, 14 lbs. Fitzherbert failed as a sire.

Novelty, a bay colt foaled in 1908 by Kingston-Curiosity by Voter, bred by James W. Keene, was sold as a yearling to John E. Madden for a nominal sum and Madden in turn sold him to Samuel C. Hildreth and he developed into the best two-year-old of his year, winning the United States Hotel, Saratoga Special, the Rensselaer Handicap, the Hopeful and the Futurity—he carried 135 lbs. in the Rensselaer. At four he went to France, was then sold to Paulo Machado and became a leading sire in Brazil.

Another son of Ethelbert—out of Ionis by Magnetizer—was Dalmatian, foaled in 1907. He raced for Samuel C. Hildreth at two and three years, winning the Travers, Coney Island, Dwyer Stakes and Empire City Handicap. He was sold to Mr. Winans for whom he won the Manchester November Handicap in 1913.

1911 to 1920

When racing was resumed in New York State at Belmont Park, May 30, 1913, the sport was restricted to three days a week, and years elapsed before it attained the standards of the first decade of the present century.

The first thoroughbred to gain the adulation of the New York racing public after the resumption of the sport in 1913 was Roamer, a bay gelding foaled in 1911 by imp. Knight Errant out of imp. Rose Tree II by Bona Vista. He was bred by Woodford Clay who brought him East and sold him to Andrew Miller in the early summer of 1911. He raced for seven seasons in the "cardinal, white sash, black cap" of his new owner, starting 98 times, winning 39 races and earning $98,828. He won The Saratoga Handicap three times, the last time in 1918 when a seven-year-old with 129 lbs. in 2 mins. 2⅕ secs. He also won the Saratoga Cup, the Saratoga Special, the Travers Stakes and the Merchants' and Citizens' (all at Saratoga), the Yonkers Handicap, the Municipal Handicap, the Aqueduct Handicap, the Carter Handicap and the National Handicap. He won at various distances from one-half to 1¾ miles. On August 21, 1918, at Saratoga, Roamer, seven years old, with 110 lbs., ran an exhibition mile against time in 1 min. 34⅘ secs. the best mile on record up to that time in this country. Roamer suffered a broken leg on New Year's Day, 1920, and had to be destroyed. His owner died two days earlier.

Luke McLuke, the son of the inbred Ultimus out of Midge by Trenton, was a bay horse foaled in 1911, bred by J. R. Keene and sold as a yearling to John F. Schorr. Never too sound he could not be trained as a two-year-old, but at three he won the Kentucky Handicap, 1¼ miles in 2 mins. 2⅘ secs., defeating Rudolfo and eight older horses. Shipped East he won the Belmont Stakes without being extended and in his next race under 120 lbs. he defeated Stromboli, in receipt of 13 lbs. in the Carlton Stakes. Luke McLuke went wrong shortly after and was sold to J. O. Keene and did very well at stud.

Contemporaneous with Luke McLuke and Roamer was the gelding Old Rosebud, one of the first of the sons of Uncle, out of Ivory Bells by imp. Star Shoot, bred by John E. Madden. He began racing as a two-year-old in February, 1913, at Juarez, Mexico, and in 14 starts won 12 races and was second twice. He was unquestionably the best of his age. After winning the Kentucky Derby at three he broke down in the Withers Stakes in 1914. Patched up, he went wrong again in 1915, but in 1917 reappeared on the racecourse, starting 20 times, winning 15, among them the Clark, Latonia, Inaugural, Queens County, Carter and Delaware Handicaps, the last with 132 lbs. He was a winner as late as 1921 when ten years old.

With the resumption of racing in New York State, Harry Payne Whitney instructed A. J. Joyner to ship Whisk Broom, then six years old, and Iron Mask, also six, from Ballaton Lodge, Newmarket, to Belmont Park to James Rowe for racing in this

A CAPACITY CROWD AT JAMAICA RACECOURSE, N.Y.

KENTUCKY DERBY WINNERS.
Left to right : JOHNNY LONGDEN, WAYNE WRIGHT, CON McCREARY,
EDDIE ARCARO (3 *times*), JIMMY STOUT AND IRA HANFORD

[*Facing page* 308

THE FIRST FLYING STEWARD. A COMPLETE FILM OF EACH RACE IS
MADE, WHEREBY REPORTS OF INFRACTIONS MAY BE MADE TO THE
STEWARDS IN THE STANDS

country. Mr. Joyner had been preparing Whisk Broom, a winner
of seven races in England including the Select, Craven and
Snailwell Stakes and third to Neil Gow and Lemberg in the
2,000 Guineas (1910), for the Kempton Park Jubilee Handicap
of 1912 and was sanguine the son of Broomstick—Audience by
Sir Dixon would be returned the winner. He finished second to
Bachelor's Hope, trained by H. S. ("Atty") Persee. Less than a
month after his arrival in this country Whisk Broom won the
Metropolitan Handicap (1 mile) with 126 lbs. at Belmont Park
the day racing was resumed, May 30, 1913. A day later Iron
Mask, who accompanied Whisk Broom to this country won the
Toboggan Handicap, 6 furlongs, with 130 lbs. in 1 min. 10 secs.
Whisk Broom was unbeaten in this country. Following his
victory in the Metropolitan, he won the Brooklyn Handicap
with 130 lbs. and the Suburban Handicap, 1¼ miles with 139 lbs.
in two minutes flat, an American record. He broke down shortly
after and was relegated to the Stud and proved a successful sire.

Another horse bred by H. P. Whitney, and a good stake
winner in England in 1910 when trained by Mr. Joyner (he was
possibly the best two-year-old in England, winning the Middle
Park plate and other stakes) was Borrow, a gelding by Hamburg,
out of Forget by Exile. He was repatriated and began racing
in his native land in 1914 when he was six years old. He did
very well here despite his age, winning among other races, the
Yonkers, and Saratoga Handicap, the latter with 123 lbs. In
1915 he won the Kentucky Handicap with 126 lbs., the Ferry
and Dominion Handicaps in Canada, and the Municipal in
Belmont Park. The climax of his career in 1917 was outstanding.
He was then nine years old and won the Brooklyn Handicap,
beating his stable companion the great mare Regret, Old Rosebud,
Chicle, Roamer, Boots, Clematis, Stromboli and the Kentucky
Derby winner, Omar Khayyam, also Old Koenig. The time
1 min. 49⅖ secs. for 9 furlongs was an American record.

Possibly the best filly ever bred by H. P. Whitney was Regret.
Foaled in 1912 at the Brookdale Stud, near Red Bank, New
Jersey, she was a bright chestnut by Broomstick—Jersey
Lightning by Hamburg. She was unbeaten at two years, winning
the Saratoga Special, the Sanford Memorial and Hopeful Stakes.
At three, 1915, she was shipped to Louisville, Kentucky, for the
Kentucky Derby and crossing the Allegheny Mountains
contracted a cold that left her a bit thick winded. Despite this
she won the Kentucky Derby in effortless fashion and is the
only filly on record to win this stake. In August she won the
Saratoga Handicap, 1 mile, beating The Finn, the best three-
year-old colt. At four she did not start until August in the
Saratoga Handicap where she was favourite with 123 lbs., and

x

sustained her first defeat, finishing unplaced. Later at the same meeting she won at one mile and was retired for the year. In 1917 she ran four times, winning three ; in her remaining start in the Brooklyn Handicap under 122 lbs. she was beaten a head by her stable companion Borrow, 117 lbs.

It was Mr. H. P. Whitney's practice to send mares to England to be bred. One was Mineola by imp. Meddler. In 1914 she was bred to the Derby and Grand Prix winner Spearmint and the following year produced a colt that was to gain fame under the name of Johren. Johren could not be trained as a two-year-old, and at three he ran nine times before he won the Sweepstake at Jamaica on May 21, 1918. He was beginning to find his form and after winning another Sweepstake he unexpectedly won the Suburban Handicap at 10 to 1. Then he won the Belmont Stakes from the favourite War Cloud and on being shipped to Latonia he beat Exterminator, $1\frac{1}{2}$ miles. War Cloud turned the tables on him in the Dwyer Stakes, and at Saratoga in the Travers Stakes he was unable to concede Sunbriar's 6 lbs. He won his last three starts, the Huron Handicap, the Saratoga Cup (beating Roamer) and the Lawrence Realization. He went lame in the running of the Realization and was retired to the stud where he was an absolute failure.

Friar Rock, the best three-year-old of 1916, bred by August Belmont at the Nursery Stud, Lexington, Kentucky, was a chestnut with a large star and his quarters were liberally sprinkled with the Pantaloon spots. He was the son of a Derby winner, imp. Rocksand and the immortal Fairy Gold by Bend 'Or, the best bred mare imported into this country in the past fifty years. As a two-year-old he won five races, two of which were stakes, the Adirondack Handicap and the Wakefield Stakes. At three, his last season on the turf, he won the Belmont and went out of his class to defeat older horses, winning the Brooklyn Handicap, the Suburban Handicap and in the Saratoga Cup, he defeated Roamer and The Finn. Near the close of the season he was sold to John E. Madden for $50,000, and was a successful sire. His daughters were exceptionally good brood mares.

Cudgel, a bay son of Broomstick—Eugenia Burch by imp. Ben Strong, was bred by H. P. Whitney at his Brookdale Stud, New Jersey, and was foaled in 1914. The colt suffered from a partial paralysis of the hind leg and was sold in August, 1916, to J. F. Schorr for $1,500. In that year Cudgel won nine races in 18 starts, and was sold to J. K. L. Ross for a reported price of $30,000. Trained by Guy Bedwell for his new owner he won nine races in 17 starts in 1918, including the Merchants' Handicap with 130 lbs. (beating Johren, then three years, carrying 100 lbs.), the King's County Handicap (130 lbs.), the Brooklyn Handicap

(129 lbs.), with Roamer (120 lbs.), George Smith (122 lbs.) and five others behind him; the Schenectady Handicap (130 lbs.) and the Dixie Handicap. In 1919 he won five out of nine races.

Imported Star Shoot led the list of sires in the United States five times and his best son was SIR BARTON, a chestnut, foaled in 1916, out of Lady Sterling by Hanover, therefor a half-brother to Sir Martin, and, like him, bred by John E. Madden. Sir Barton ran six times as a juvenile without winning and was sold to J. K. L. Ross in the Autumn of 1918 for $9,000, and turned over to Guy Bedwell to train. He developed into the best three-year-old of 1919, winning eight races out of 13. He won the Kentucky Derby as a maiden, then, in succession, won the Preakness, Withers and Belmont Stakes, being the first horse in history to win these four classics. He succumbed to Purchase in the Dwyer Stakes and came back lame and had to be retired until the Autumn. At Laurel in October under 133 lbs. he won the Maryland Handicap, 1¼ miles in 2 mins. 2⅗ secs. by open daylight from Mad Hatter (106 lbs.), Audacious (118 lbs.) being a bad third. That year he also won the Potomac Handicap, Pimlico Special and Pimlico Serial. At four years he won the Rennert, Dominion, Saratoga and Merchants' Handicaps. In the Saratoga Handicap he ran 1¼ miles in the record time of 2 mins. 1⅘ secs. under 129 lbs., conceding weight to Exterminator, Mad Hatter and The Porter, winning by open daylight. In his ill-starred match with Man-o'-War he was hopelessly overmatched being lame at the time. He suffered intermittently from sore feet and it required an enormous amount of work to get him fit. As a sire he was a failure.

In 1916 Delbert Reiff sold at Saratoga a consignment of French bred yearlings. Among them was a bay colt by Sundridge—Sweet Briar by St. Frusquin, then named Sunday. Although the colt appeared to be afflicted with ring bones he was purchased by Willis Sharpe Kilmer for $6,000, the second highest price vendue, and his name was changed to SUN BRIAR. Sun Briar trained by Henry McDaniel developed into the best two-year-old of 1917, winning five races in nine starts, the Great American, The Albany Handicap, the Saratoga Special, the Grand Union and the Hopeful Stakes with 130 lbs. in a field of 18. At three he did not come to hand until August and at Saratoga won the Delaware Handicap, 1 mile in 1 min. 36½ secs., and then won the Travers Stakes, 1¼ miles, beating Johren, War Cloud and his stable companion Exterminator. At four, the last year he raced, his outstanding victory was scored by winning the Champlain Handicap with 128 lbs., Exterminator being second. As a sire Sun Briar was very successful.

Possibly the most popular gelding in the United States in

the past 30 years was Exterminator, by imp. McGee—Fair Empress by Jim Gore, bred by F. D. Knight and purchased as a yearling by J. C. Milam for $1,500. In four starts at two years he won twice. In May, 1918, he was sold to Willis Sharpe Kilmer for $9,000 along with two fillies by imp. Odgen. He raced until he was nine years old, starting in 100 races, winning 50 and earning $252,996. His first victory in the Kilmer silks " green, brown and orange " was scored in the Kentucky Derby. His outstanding victory was achieved in the Brooklyn Handicap as a seven-year-old when he carried 135 lbs. and conceded 9 lbs. to Grey Lag, beating that great son of Star Shoot a head. Among other victories Exterminator won four Saratoga cups, three Pimlico cups, two Autumn Gold cups, three Toronto Autumn cups and the Latonia cup. He won at various distances, from 6 furlongs to 2¼ miles and won handicaps with as much as 138 lbs.

Of the same age as Sir Barton was Purchase, a golden chestnut, son of Ormandale (son of the unbeaten Ormonde) out of Cherryola by imp. Tanzmeister, foaled 1916, he was bred by John E. Madden and purchased as a yearling for $1,600 by George M. Odom for George Smith. Mr. Smith retired from racing in the Autumn of 1918 and Purchase was sold to S. C. Hildreth for $12,500. At three years Purchase won nine races in 11 starts. In the Brooklyn Handicap under 117 lbs., the highest weight ever carried by a three-year-old, he succumbed to another three-year-old, Eternal. Exterminator defeated him in the Saratoga Cup under scale weights. His victories included the Stuyvesant Handicap, 124 lbs. ; the Southampton Handicap, 129 lbs. (beating Eternal with 125 lbs.) ; the Dwyer Stakes, 118 lbs. (Sir Barton 125 lbs. was second) ; Empire City Derby, the Saratoga Handicap 118 lbs., the Saranac Handicap, 133 lbs. ; the Huron Handicap, 134 lbs. and the Jockey Club Stakes. He went wrong late in September, 1919, was in retirement in 1920 but in 1921 won twice at 6 furlongs with 140 lbs. His best hostage to fortune was Chase Me, never beaten until his last start, the Suburban Handicap, in which he sustained a broken leg, necessitating his destruction.

Since 1913 to date Man-o'-War's equal as a thoroughbred has not appeared in the United States. A chestnut horse with plenty of size and scope, foaled in 1917, bred by August Belmont by Fair Play—Mahubah by imp. Rocksand, Man-o'-War raced only at two and three years, starting 21 times, winning 20 races, was second once, earning $249,465.

August Belmont was commissioned a Major in the United States Army during World War I, and this impelled him to sell at Sarratoga all his yearlings in 1918. Man-o'-War was purchased by Samuel D. Riddle for $5,000, and turned over to

Louis Feustel to train. At two he ran ten times, winning nine races. His sole defeat was sustained in the Sanford Memorial Stakes, Saratoga, August 13, 1919. Favourite at $11 to $20, carrying 130 lbs. Man-o'-War turned sideways at the start, got away in a tangle, was blocked in the stretch, taken to the outside and just failed to get up, being beaten half a length. In all his starts Man-o'-War was odds-on favourite. He won 14 stakes in succession after his defeat. At three years he dominated racing in this country, winning eleven races at various distances from 1½ to 100 lengths. On his retirement he was the holder of five time records from 1 mile to 1⅝ miles. His records for 1⅜ miles and 1⅝ miles still stand. He won the Potomac Handicap with 138 lbs., conceding 30 lbs. to the second horse Wildair, a good stakes winner. In his last race, the Kennelworth Gold Cup, 1¼ miles he defeated Sir Barton (four years) at weight for age by seven lengths for a stake of $80,000, the richest prize for which he ever ran.

Man-o'-War became the leading sire in 1926. Four of his sons and one of his daughters earned in excess of $100,000. The best son of Man-o'-War was War Admiral who was the leading sire in 1945, and five of War Admiral's progeny to date have won in excess of $100,000. This truly great horse died at the Faraway Farm, Lexington, Kentucky, of his owner Samuel D. Riddle, November 1, 1947, in his thirty-first year.

Grey Lag, bred by John E. Madden, foaled in 1918 by imp. Star Shoot—Miss Minnie by imp. Meddler was a chestnut in colour with a blaze, right fore and both hind pasterns white. He was sold as a yearling to Max Hirsch for $10,000. After winning the Champagne Stakes at two years was sold to the Rancocas Stable of Harry F. Sinclair for $60,000, and turned over to S. C. Hildreth to train. He was the best three-year-old of 1921. In 14 races that year he won nine, among them the Belmont Stakes, the Brooklyn Handicap, the Dwyer Empire City Derby, the Mt. Kisco Stakes, the International Derby and the Knickerbocker Handicap under 135 lbs., beating Careful (a very high-class filly) in receipt of 27 lbs. He won every important handicap in New York. In the Saratoga Handicap he carried 130 lbs., and the Suburban (the outstanding handicap in this country) as a five-year-old with 135 lbs. Like all the sons of Star Shoot, with the exception of Uncle, he was a failure as a sire.

It is seldom a two-year-old the equal of Morvich flashes across the racing horizon. A brown colt by Runnymede (by Voter-Running Stream by Domino) he was rather unfashionably bred in the tail female, his dam Hymir was by Dr. Leggo, and his grand dam Georgia Girl by imp. Solitaire. He was bred by A. B. Sprecles in California and on his debut at Jamaica won a selling race (entered to be sold for $5,000) by 15 lengths. Immediately after the race Max Hirsch bought him for his entered price, but on examining him critically the following day discovered the colt had a bad knee and immediately resold him to Fred Burlew for $6,000. Ten days later he won another selling race by a big margin, whereupon Mr. Burlew sold a one-half interest in the colt to Benjamin Block for $25,000. In August Block bought out Burlew's interest in Morvich for an undisclosed price. He raced thereafter in the " jade and white blocks " of Benjamin Block.

Morvich won all eleven of his starts at two years, earning $115,234, beating the best that could be mustered against him, concluding the season with a victory in the first Pimlico Futurity ever run, 1 mile, under scale weight. Morvich won the Kentucky Derby, his first race as a three-year-old, and sustained his first defeat in his thirteenth start, the Carlton Stakes, failing to concede 15 lbs. to H. P. Whitney's Whiskaway, which carried 108 lbs. Out of 16 races he won 12, was second in two, third in one, unplaced in one and earned $165,909. Retired to the stud in Kentucky he was " cold shouldered " by breeders and failed as a sire primarily from lack of opportunity. One or two of his sons raced in England in the colours of Victor Emanuel. Morvich later gravitated to California, where he died several years ago.

1920 to 1930

Mad Hatter, a bay son of Fair Play-Mad Play by imp. Rock Sand, was perhaps the second best son of his sire, inferior only to Man-o'-War. He raced from two to eight years and was a stake winner every year he raced, except as a two-year-old. He started in 98 races, winning 32, second in 22, earning $194,525 in an era when stakes were worth about half of what they are to-day. Foaled in 1916, bred by August Belmont, Mad Hatter was sold as a two-year-old to S. C. Hildreth for $5,000 and when Harry F. Sinclair assembled a racing stable and engaged S. C. Hildreth to train his horses, Mad Hatter became a unit in the Rancocas Stable. He won at various distances from 6 furlongs to 2 miles. Among his important victories were the Toboggan Handicap (6 furlongs); the Queen's County Handicap (1 mile in 1 min. 35⅖ secs.); the first Latonia Championship ever run (1¾ miles); and the Jockey Club Gold Cup, twice (2 miles). As an eight-year-old he won the Suburban with 125 lbs. in 2 mins. 3⅖ secs. His racing days over, he was purchased as a stock horse by Harry Payne Whitney for an undisclosed price, but outside of The Nut (winner of $100,470) he sired nothing of outstanding merit.

When Zev was retired to the stud in 1924 he was the leading

money winner of the world. In the three seasons he raced he
started 43 times, winning 23 races, was second in eight and third
in five, earning $313,639, and of this sum $80,600 accrued to
him as a result of his victory over the English horse Papyrus, in
the International Race, 1½ miles at Belmont Park, October 20,
1923.

Zev was a brown son of The Finn-Miss Kearney by imp.
Planudes, was bred by J. E. Madden, sold as a yearling to the
Rancocas Stable and was trained by S. C. Hildreth. Among
the events he won as a two-year-old were the Grand Union Hotel
Stakes and Albany Handicap. He wound up the year by running
third in the Hopeful and second in the Futurity Stakes. He was
at his best at three years, 1923, winning 12 of his 14 starts, was
second once and once unplaced. He began by whipping the
older horses by a neck in the Paumonok Handicap (6 furlongs),
but finished in the ruck in the Preakness. He won his next
eight starts, the Rainbow Handicap, the Kentucky Derby, the
Withers Stakes, the Queen's County Handicap, a purse, the
Lawrence Realization Stakes, the International Stakes and the
Autumn Championship Stakes. He was inexplicably and badly
beaten by In Memoriam in the Latonia Championship Stakes
(1¾ miles) finishing six lengths behind the leader. This was
followed by a victory in the Pimlico Serial weight-for-age race
No. 3. A match was then arranged with In Memoriam, each
carrying 126 lbs., but the astute Hildreth persuaded In
Memoriam's owner to make the distance, 1¼ miles. Zev won
by a nose through the splendid riding ability of his jockey, Earl
Sands. Zev was a failure at Stud.

One of the outstanding horses of the middle twenties was the
chestnut gelding Sarazen, by High Time-Rush Box by Box,
bred by Dr. Marius Johnston, Lexington, Kentucky. Col.
Phil T. Chinn purchased this gelding and another son of High
Time, later named Time Exposure, as yearlings for $2,500. At
two years in the Chicago sector Sarazen, in the " red and white "
silks of Mr. Chinn, won three races and was sold to Mrs. Graham
Fair Vanderbilt for $35,000 and turned over to Max Hirsch to
train. Sarazen was unbeaten as a two-year-old, winning seven
more races for his new owner, including the Champagne Stakes,
the Oakdale Handicap, the National Stakes and a match at Laurel
with the filly Happy Thoughts, and wound up the season by
beating older horses in the Pimlico Serial weight-for-age race
(1 mile).

His outstanding success was scored at Latonia, on October
11th, 1924, in the Internation Special No. 3 (1¼ miles) weight-for-
age, in which he ran the distance in 2 mins. 0⅘ secs.; Epinard
was second beaten 1¼ lengths, followed by Mad Play and

Altawood; Princess, Doreen and Chilhowee were among the defeated.

Sarazen raced from two to seven years, starting in 55 races, winning 27, was second in two, third in six, earning $225,000. He became cunning as a five-year-old and in a number of races refused to try. A bit on the small side, but compactly made, he carried weight well, frequently winning with as much as 130 lbs. His best distance was no further than a mile and if his racing had been confined to this distance he would have established a better record.

In the second crop of Man-o'-War's foals in 1923 appeared Crusader, a chestnut colt out of Star Fancy by imp. Star Shoot, bred by S. D. Riddle, trained by Gwin Tompkins at two and three years, and by George Conway at four. Crusader was a horse of beautiful balance. About the only place he could be faulted was his neck, it was too short. He matured slowly. In eleven starts at two years he won but five, and his only stake success was in the Manor Handicap at Laurel in October.

At three years he was beaten in his first two starts but found his form when winning the Suburban (1¼ miles) with 104 lbs. by six lengths, from his stable companion American Flag. This was followed by victories in the Belmont Stakes (1½ miles), the Dwyer Stakes, the Coney Island Derby at Cincinnati in which he met Carlaris (winner of the Tijuana Derby and Tijuana Handicap) Display and Boot to Boot. He carried Carlaris the first mile in 1 min. 36⅖ secs. and ran the 1¼ mile in 2 mins. 2 secs., winning by three lengths. Later he won the Huron Handicap, Jockey Club Gold Cup (2 miles), the Havre de Grace Handicap, the Maryland Handicap, the Riggs Handicap (1½ miles under 130 lbs.). At four years he won the Suburban Handicap for the second time with 127 lbs. In three seasons he won 18 races out of 42 starts and $203,261. He was the second best son of Man-o'-War, pride of place going to War Admiral. Like practically every horse out of Star Shoot mares he was an utter failure as a sire.

At a paddock sale at Saratoga a small owner named Willie Shea offered his mare, Ormonda, for sale to pay a $5,000 debt to a bookmaker. Joseph E. Widener purchased her for $5,500 and retired her to his Elmendorf Stud. Among her issue was that grand chestnut gelding OSMAND by imp. Sweeper II, foaled in 1924. Trained by Hamilton Keene, Osmand was the best sprinter in this country since Roseben's era (1927). In 37 starts, Osmand won 23 races, was second in four, third in four, earning $157,975. He was a horse of herculean proportions and the most popular racer of his time. He never wore blinkers, ran with his head high in the air, had a pronounced blaze and the heart of a lion. Osmand won six races in seven starts at two years, failing

only in the Saratoga Special, in which he made the running for his
stable companion Chance Shot, the winner.   His victories
included the Flash, Grab Bag and Eastern Shore.   As a three-
year-old he was as big as a bull.   But, despite the fact he was
going beyond his real distance, it was only the artistry of McAtee
on Whiskery that he was beaten a head in the Kentucky Derby
(1¼ miles).   His first stakes success as a three-year-old was in the
Saranac Handicap (1 mile).   He also won the Capital Handicap
(6 furlongs) in the Autumn.   Thereafter, with one exception,
he was never asked to race beyond one mile.   The exception was
the Havre de Grace Handicap in September (1⅛ miles) in which
he defeated Sun Beau and Crusader.   His other victories were
the Toboggan, Carter and American Legion Handicaps.   At
five he reached his zenith winning four stakes; the Toboggan
with 129 lbs., the Carter with 132 lbs. and the Fall Highweight
Handicap (6 furlongs) under 140 lbs., conceding 21 lbs. to Finite
and 22 lbs. to the accomplished Balko.

Anita Peabody, a brown filly with a narrow white stripe, by
Luke McLuke-imp. La Duphine by the Tetrarch, was beaten
but once.   She was bred in partnership by Jack Keene and John
Hertz, offered for sale as a yearling in 1926 and purchased on
behalf of Mrs. John Hertz for $11,000.   At two years she won the
Debutante Stakes, Joliette Stakes, but on going to Saratoga was
beaten into third place in the Schuylerville by Pennant Queen
and Bateau.   Later at the same meeting she won a purse and then
at Belmont Park won the Tomboy Handicap, 126 lbs., followed
by a victory in the Futurity three days later, worth $91,760 to
the winner.   She was none too sound that Autumn and her
trainer Bert Mitchell was able to get her to the post but once
at three years.   She won this race and then broke down hope-
lessly.   She started 18 times winning seven and was third once,
earning $113,105.   She died at the age of nine and produced but
three foals, one of which died early.   The others Our Count won
12 races, seven of them being stakes.   Our Raigh won 11 races.

A stable companion of Anita Peabody was Reigh Count, a
son of imp. Sunray (full brother to imp. Sun Beau who was
retired to the stud as a maiden) out of imp. Contessina by Count
Schomberg.   Bred by Willis Sharpe Kilmer at his Court Manor
Stud, New Market, Virginia, trained by Henry McDaniel, Reigh
Count won a maiden race at Saratoga, but was disqualified and
in a fit of pique Mr. Kilmer sold the colt to John Hertz for
$12,500.   For his new owner he won the Kentucky Jockey Club
Stakes (1 mile) and the Walden Handicap (1 mile) with 126 lbs.
Reigh Count proved to be the best three-year-old in training in
1928.   He was beaten but once that year in the Travers Handicap,
won by Petee Wrack, in which he finished unplaced.   He won the

Kentucky Derby, but one of his hocks was badly cut in the running and he was not seen under colours again until the Travers Stakes. He displayed a return to winning form at Saratoga when he won the Huron Handicap, and concluded the Season with the sequence of three victories; the Saratoga Cup (1¾ miles); the Lawrence Realization (1⅝ miles) and the Jockey Club Gold Cup (2 miles).

He raced in England as a four-year-old winning the Coronation Cup at Epsom from Athford and Plantago and finished second in the Ascot Gold Cup to Invershin. As a sire Reigh Count was far more successful than was anticipated. He outbred himself when he sired Count Fleet.

The sensation of the juvenile ranks in 1927 was the Wheatley Stable's bay colt Dice by Dominant-Frumpery by Chicle. He was bred by Henry Payne Whitney who sold him along with Distraction, Diavolo (all-stakes winner) and several other yearlings, to Mrs. H. C. Phipps, and her brother Odgen Mills. They began racing under the nom de course Wheatley Stable.

Dice won all his five races as a two-year-old, but during a workout at Saratoga he developed an internal hæmorrhage and died on the track.

Contemporaneous with Reigh Count, and also bred by Willis Sharpe Kilmer, at his Court Manor Stud, New Market, Virginia, was Sun Beau, a bay horse foaled in 1925 by imp. Sun Briar-Beautiful Lady by Fair Play. Sun Beau raced from two to six years, starting in 74 races, winning 33, second in 12, third in 10 and on his retirement he had earned $376,744, a world record. He was practically worthless at two years but showed vast improvement next season, winning eight races in 23 starts. He failed to win a stake until September 29th when he accounted for the Havre de Grace Cup Handicap. Next he won the Maryland Handicap, followed by a victory in the Latonia Championship Stakes (1¾ miles)—the only occasion on which he won at a distance in excess of 10 furlongs. At four he did not come to hand until the Autumn, winning his first stake in the year on September 28th, the Aqueduct Handicap. In succession he won the Havre de Grace Cup Handicap for the second time; a purse; the Hawthorne Gold Cup, 126 lbs. (1¼ miles in 2 mins. 1⅖ secs.) and the Washington Handicap.

At five years he failed to win a stake until September 20th, accounting for the Toronto Autumn Cup (1¼ miles) with 132 lbs. His remaining stake victories that year were the Hawthorne Gold Cup, the Washington Handicap and the Southern Maryland Handicap. In 1931, the last year he raced, he was shipped to lower California where he won the Fashion Stakes with 130 lbs. He was badly beaten in the Agua Caliente Handicap, finishing fifth. Three weeks later he won a purse at Havre de Grace, followed by a victory in the Philadelphia Handicap. At Arlington Park near the end of July he won the Arlington Cup (1¼ miles with 126 lbs. in 2 mins. 1⅘ secs.), followed by a victory in the Arlington Handicap with 128 lbs. by three lengths—one of his best races. He won the Lincoln Fields Handicap, August 29th, and completed his racing career by winning the Hawthorne Gold Cup for the third year in succession, with 126 lbs., conceding 6 lbs. to Mate. A peculiarity about Sun Beau was that he never won a race at Saratoga, and he never won a stake in New York other than the Aqueduct Handicap in the Autumn of 1929. As a sire Sun Beau was a bitter disappointment.

One of the best fillies, if not *the* best, racing in the last half of the decade 1920–1930, was Walter M. Jeffords's Bateau, Man-o'-War's best daughter. She was out of the French mare Escuine by Ecuon. Her fourth dam was the immortal Fairy Gold, in fact she was a double Fairy Gold. In her first season she won the Fashion and Salima Stakes, the latter over 1 mile. At three years in seven starts she won the Coaching Club, American Oaks, the Gazelle Stakes and a purse. At four she defeated the colts in the Suburban, the outstanding handicap of this country, established in 1884, and prior to Bateau the only fillies or mares to win it were Imp., " the coal black lady" in 1899 and Baldame in 1905. The Suburban was run June 1st, but Bateau retained her form to the end of the Season. On November 23rd she won the Southern Maryland Handicap, beating Victorian, Balko and Sun Beau. She was trained by Scott Harlan. In her racing career Bateau started 35 times, won 11 races, was second in five, third in nine and earned $120,760. At stud it proved impossible to get Bateau in foal and for years Mr. Jeffords used her as a hack.

Of all the horses bred by the late E. R. Bradley, Blue Larkspur was unquestionably the best. A bay son of Black Servant-Blossom dam by North Star III, Blue Larkspur was foaled in 1926 and was trained by H. C. (Dick) Thompson. Blue Larkspur was probably the best two-year-old in training in 1928. That year he won the Juvenile Stakes, the National Stallion Stakes and the Saratoga Special. He injured one of his ankles in the Futurity and pulled up lame. The training of the colt as a three-year-old was done by his owner Ed Bradley and the stable foreman " Chappy " Hastings. Blue Larkspur finished fourth in the Kentucky Derby. He started in the Withers, about four weeks later and Mr. Bradley refused to back him, saying the colt was short, which gave rise to the query " If he is short to-day, what was he for the Derby, three weeks ago ? " He won the Withers by three-quarters of a length from Chestnut Oak, with Jack High third, in 1 min 36 secs. for the mile. He started favourite for the

Belmont (1½ miles) and was all out to defeat the very moderate African which ran out at the head of the stretch. This was followed by the Dwyer Stakes (1½ miles) in which Blue Larkspur's rider Garner was accused of going to sleep and tossing the race away. The fact was Blue Larkspur was not a true stayer and stopped in the last sixteenth and was beaten a head.

For some inexplicable reason Rose of Sharon was made favourite for the Classic Stakes at Arlington Park, the track being a sea of mud, but Blue Larkspur won and Rose of Sharon finished 12th in a field of 14. Blue Larkspur struck himself in work at Saratoga and had to be retired for the Season. At four years he stood training for a while and at Arlington Park ran for the Stars and Stripes Handicap in which he was allotted 121 lbs. being in receipt of 4 lbs. from Sun Beau and 3 lbs. from Misstep and Blue Larkspur won by half a length in 1 min. 49⅗ secs. for the 9 furlongs. This was followed by a four length victory in the Arlington Gold Cup weight-for-age (1¼ miles) with Petee Wrack, Toro, Sun Beau and Reveille Boy behind him. A few days after this he went wrong for the third time and was retired to the stud, with a record of 16 starts, 10 victories, three seconds, one third and twice unplaced and earned $272,070. He was only a partial success as a sire. Far too many of his progeny were unsound, but his daughters proved pearls beyond price as broodmares.

1930 to 1940

Gallant Fox, a bay horse foaled 1927, one of the first crop of imp. Sir Gallahad III, was out of the Celt mare, Margeurite, and in the opinion of William Woodward was the best horse he ever bred. Just fair at two years, in seven starts he won the Flash Stakes at Saratoga, but in his final race, the Junior Champion Stakes, 1 mile, he emerged an easy winner by two lengths in 1 min. 38 secs. He was the horse of the year the following season. In ten starts he was beaten but once; in the Travers Stakes at Saratoga, when he finished second, beaten eight lengths by the 100–1 chance Jim Dandy—this was on August 16th. Prior to the Travers debacle Gallant Fox won the Wood Memorial, Preakness Stakes, Kentucky Derby, Belmont, Dwyer and Classic Stakes. Subsequent to the Travers, he won the Saratoga Cup, Lawrence Realization and the Jockey Club Gold Cup, carrying 4½ lbs. over the scale.

Retired to the Claiborne stud of A. B. Hancock, Gallant Fox made a most impressive start, but after his fourth crop his stock degenerated rapidly. A number of his sons raced in England, notably Flares, winner of the Ascot Gold Cup (1938) and his full brother Omaha, which finished second to Quashed in 1936.

In seventeen starts Gallant Fox won eleven races, was second in three, third in two, unplaced in one, earning $328,165, then a world's record.

Three high-class colts made their debut in 1928—George D. Widener's Jamestown; Harry Payne Whitney's Equipoise and the Greentree's Stable's Twenty Grand.

Jamestown, a son of St. James-Mlle. Dazie by Fair Play, bred by Mr. Widener, and trained by A. J. Joyner, was the best two-year-old of the year. He was beaten but once, in the Hopeful Stakes at Saratoga in which he carried 130 lbs., a short head by Epithet, 117 lbs. and suffered lack of racing room. He whipped Equipoise in the Saratoga Special at level weights, won the Grand Union Hotel Stakes with 130 lbs., the United States Hotel Stakes, and wound up the year winning the Futurity, 130 lbs., Equipoise 130 lbs. was second, Mate 122 lbs. was third. At three he won the Withers Stakes (1 mile in 1 min. 36⅗ secs.), but then completely lost his form, finishing third in the Belmont Stakes and after another defeat was retired for the year. He was a winner at four, but never reproduced the form he had displayed at two. He is the sire of Johnstown.

Equipoise, a dark liver-coloured son of Pennant-Swinging by Broomstick, was one of the most popular horses of his era. In the six seasons he raced, from two to seven years, he started 51 times, won 29 races, was second in 10, third in four, unplaced in eight, earning $338,610. His outstanding victories at two were the Youthful, Keene Memorial, Juvenile, National Stallion, Great American, Eastern Shore Stakes, and the Pimlico Futurity.

He became ill at three years, could not be properly trained and was retired after three starts. At four years he won his first eight starts, including the Harford, Toboggan, Metropolitan, Delavan, Stars and Stripes Handicaps, and the Arlington Gold Cup. He was beaten a neck in the Arlington Handicap, under 134 lbs. by Plucky Play, 111 lbs. Later he won the Wilson and the Whitney Stakes and the Havre de Grace Cup. In the Delavan Handicap, with 128 lbs. he ran 1 mile in the new American record time, 1 min. 34⅖ secs. He ran nine times at five, winning his first seven starts. They were the Philadelphia, Metropolitan, Suburban and Arlington Handicaps, the Wilson Stakes, Hawthorne Cup and the Saratoga Cup, but he was badly beaten in the Jockey Club Gold Cup, 2 miles, weight-for-age, finishing third, twelve lengths behind the winner, Dark Secret. His Suburban and Arlington triumphs were notable. In the Suburban, under 132 lbs. he ran the 10 furlongs in 2 mins 2 secs., winning by two lengths. He won the Arlington Handicap by 1½ lengths in 2 mins. 2⅗ secs. for the 1¼ miles, under 135 lbs. In 1934, at six, he won three races in six starts. The Philadelphia and Dixi Handicaps and the Whitney Gold Trophy Handicap. Retired to the stud he died after siring four crops of foals, none of which was his equal as a racehorse.

Twenty Grand was the best horse ever bred at the Greentree Stable, owned by Mrs. Helen Hay Whitney. He was a bay colt by imp. St. Germans-Bonus by imp. All Gold, and was trained in his first season by James W. Murphy. Twenty Grand, slow to mature, did not win his first stakes until October, when in receipt of 11 lbs. he defeated Equipoise in the Junior Champion Stakes. Twelve days later, at Louisville, Kentucky, under scale weights, 122 lbs., Twenty Grand defeated Equipoise a short head in the new record time for a two-year-old over a mile—1 min. 36 secs.

At three years Twenty Grand stood alone. He began by winning the Wood Memorial, but in his next start suffered repeated interference and was beaten $1\frac{1}{2}$ lengths by Mate in the Preakness. Shipped to Louisville for the Kentucky Derby ($1\frac{1}{4}$ miles), an odds on choice, he established a new race record for that distance, 2 mins. $1\frac{4}{5}$ secs., winning by four lengths; Sweep All was second and Mate a bad third. He was then trained by James Rowe, Jr., and returning East won the Belmont, $1\frac{1}{2}$ miles, by ten lengths in the new race record time, 2 mins. $29\frac{3}{5}$ secs. Next he won the Dwyer Stakes, but wrenched his back in the running. Despite being only half fit he was started in the Arlington Classic in the middle of July and was badly beaten into third place behind Mate and Spanish Play. This was a race in which he should never have been started. Five weeks later, completely recovered, he won the Travers and two weeks after he ran away from Sun Beau in the Saratoga Cup. At Belmont Park he won the Lawrence Realization by six lengths, and wound up the season by winning the Jockey Club Gold Cup by six lengths (starting at 50–1 on) in 3 mins. $23\frac{2}{5}$ secs., the race record being 3 mins. 23 secs.

His near front ankle showed signs of filling intermittently, and he went wrong in the Autumn when he was three. He was a cripple thereafter, though he started in the Fall of 1932 at Belmont Park and won, running the mile in 1 min. $36\frac{4}{5}$ secs., but pulled up lame. His connections refused to recognize the handwriting on the wall. He was started again, badly beaten, and retired to the Greentree Stud, proving sterile. Believed to be sound again he was returned to training in 1935, shipped to Santa Anita, won a race there on the disqualification of Equipoise, but finished in the ruck in the Santa Anita Handicap. Later he was shipped to England, but the change of climate and turf courses did him no good, and he came back to the Greentree

Stud, where he remained a pensioner until his death. In 25 starts he won 14 races and earned $261,790.

Top Flight, a daughter of imp. Dis Donc-Flyatit by Peter Pan, a dark brown in colour, a broad blaze extending from the forehead to the nostrils, hind legs white half-way to the hocks, trained by Thomas Healey, was unbeaten at two years, winning the Clover and the Lassie Stakes, the Saratoga Special, the Spinaway Stakes, Matron Stakes, the Futurity (with the record weight of 127 lbs.), and concluded the season by winning the Pimlico Futurity, November 7th. Her earnings that year were $170,890, the record for a two-year-old, regardless of sex.

Top Flight was foaled April 15, 1929, and was light-boned and somewhat delicate in appearance, but was possessed of abundant speed and blessed with a sweet disposition. She was winter favourite for the Kentucky Derby, but was badly beaten in her first start, the Wood Memorial, and did not make the trip to Kentucky. She won all her starts against the fillies at three, including the Coaching Club and Arlington Oaks, the Alabama and Acorn Stakes, and the Ladies Handicap. But in four starts against the colts she never finished among the first three. She broke down in her last start in September in the Potomac Handicap in Havre de Grace and never ran again. She won a total of $275,900.

After the death of Gifford A. Cochran, at the dispersal sale of his horses in training Dark Secret, a dark bay colt which later became a red roan, by Flying Ebony-Siliencia by King James, was purchased by the Wheatley Stable and turned over to James Fitzsimmons to train. He developed into one of the best stayers of his time. In his racing career in fifty-seven starts, he won twenty-three races and earned $89,375. In 1933 he won the Brooklyn, Manhattan, Empire City, Merchants' and Citizens' and Havre de Grace Handicaps, the Laurel Stakes and the Whitney Gold Trophy. In the Jockey Club Stakes (2 miles) at level weights he made Gusto, which was second, and Equipoise third, look like hacks.

In 1934 he won the Saratoga Cup (1¾ miles) the Manhattan Handicap for the second time, running the 1½ miles in 2 mins. 29⅕ secs with 122 lbs. Three days later he won the Jockey Club Gold Cup also for the second time. In the lead, 100 feet from the finish, he fractured his off fore leg, but lurched under the wire a neck in front of Faireno with Inlander third. His leg was so badly fractured it was found necessary to destroy him before he could be taken back to his stable, and an autopsy disclosed that the cannon bone was broken in eight places and some of the bone had been ground to powder. It was possibly the greatest exhibition of equine courage ever witnessed on a racecourse, and the death of this grand thoroughbred was a distinct loss to his owners and the American turf as a whole.

The New Jersey breeder, the late F. Wallis Armstrong, purchased in England the broodmare Hastily by Hurry On in 1930. She was in foal to Lancegaye. The following Spring she produced a dark brown colt that I inspected in June, 1932, when it was a yearling. Being much taken with the colt, named Cavalcade, I adjured Bob Smith to buy him at Saratoga for the Brookmeade Stable of Mrs. Isabel Dodge Sloane, leading sportswoman in this country. This Smith did, securing the colt for $1,200. At two years he won twice. One of his victories was scored in the Hyde Park Stakes and he earned over $15,000 that year. Cavalcade improved materially over the Winter and developed into the best three-year-old of 1934. At Havre de Grace he won a race at 1 mile and 70 yards in new track record time of 1 min. 41⅘ secs. He won the Chesapeake Stakes three days later in 1 min. 43⅘ secs., another track record for 1$\frac{1}{16}$ miles. A week later he won the Kentucky Derby from Discovery, and eleven others in effortless fashion. Coupled with his stable companion High Quest (the Brookmeade entry was 5/2 " on "), High Quest won by a nose in 1 min. 58⅕ secs., a new Preakness record. In the American Derby at Chicago, Cavalcade conceded Discovery 8 lbs. and won by two lengths. This was followed by his third Derby victory, that at Detroit, in which he established another track record 1 min. 58 secs. for 1$\frac{3}{16}$ miles. After a month's rest he reappeared at Chicago and won the Classic, 1¼ miles in 2 mins. 2⅘ secs., conceding Discovery 5 lbs. and beating him four lengths. When Cavalcade reached Saratoga it was discovered he was suffering from a quarter crack in his off fore heel. He never wholly recovered from this foot trouble and was retired to the stud in 1937 with a record of eight victories in 22 starts and earnings of $127,165. He was a failure as a stock horse.

Omaha, a chestnut colt, foaled March 24, 1932, was one of Gallant Fox's first crop. He was out of Flambino by imp. Wrack, was bred by William Woodward, foaled at the Claiborne Stud of A. B. Hancock, Paris, Kentucky, and was trained by Jim Fitzsimmons. Like his sire he was only fair as a two-year-old but, again like his sire, disclosed marked improvement at three years. Successful in his first start at Jamaica in April, at 1 mile and 70 yards, he was practically left at the post in the Wood Memorial, was sent off after his field and finished third. Shipped to Louisville, he won the Kentucky Derby by a length. A week later he won the Preakness at Baltimore. He was beaten by Rosemont in the Withers but reasserted himself in no uncertain fashion a week later when he won the Belmont Stakes (1½ miles)

THE START OF THE KENTUCKY DERBY, SHOWING THE AMERICAN TYPE OF GATE

A TYPICAL AMERICAN RACE: NOTE THE FLYING DIRT, JOCKEYS' GOGGLES AND BLINKERED HORSES

by $1\frac{1}{2}$ lengths from Firethorn with Rosemont ten lengths farther back. He then went out of his class and threw down the gauntlet to older horses in an effort to win the Brooklyn Handicap, $1\frac{1}{8}$ miles. He carried 114 lbs. (one under the scale) to 127 lbs. by King Saxon (one over the scale) Discovery, 123 lbs. He was "chopped" for speed as in the Withers. King Saxon led to the stretch, where Discovery ran him down in 1 min. $48\frac{1}{5}$ secs., a new American record for the distance. Omaha was third, beaten about eight lengths. He picked up the winning thread again in his next start, the Dwyer Stakes, in which he ran the 9 furlongs in 1 min. $49\frac{1}{5}$ secs. On July 20, at Arlington Park, he ran the best race of his career in the Classic, $1\frac{1}{4}$ miles, carrying 126 lbs. He went to the post at 4/1 "on" and ran past his field in the last quarter mile, winning by $1\frac{1}{2}$ lengths in 2 mins. $1\frac{2}{5}$ secs., the fastest race at 10 furlongs by a three-year-old under scale weight. Shipped back to Saratoga, Omaha went lame and was retired for the year and sent to England as a four-year-old to Captain Cecil Boyd-Rochfort at Freemason Lodge, Newmarket, his objective being the Ascot Gold Cup, in which he was beaten a head by Quashed. His rider unfortunately dropped his whip entering the straight. In 22 starts Omaha won nine races, was second in seven, third in three and earned \$153,630. As a sire he was a ghastly failure. He was a bright golden chestnut, with a stripe on his face with plenty of size and scope and stood $16\frac{1}{2}$ hands.

When Cavalcade and his stable companion High Quest were side-lined because of injuries, Alfred G. Vanderbilt's Discovery became the best three-year-old in training. A golden chestnut, standing 16.1 hands, a stripe on his face and two white feet behind, by Display-Ariadne by imp. Light Brigade, Discovery inherited his length and size from his maternal grandsire. Trained by Jack Pryce, Discovery raced in the name of Adolph Pons at two years. Mr. Pons was Mr. Salmon's general manager in his racing and breeding. Discovery's latent power was unsuspected at two. In 14 starts that year he won but two races, but Alfred G. Vanderbilt saw possibilities in the colt no one else did and buying him for \$25,000, turned him over to J. H. Stotler. As a three-year-old he won the Brooklyn Handicap, 9 furlongs with 113 lbs. by six lengths. At Saratoga he won the Kenner and Whitney Stakes; in September he won the Rhode Island and Potomac Handicaps and completed the year by winning the Maryland Handicap, $1\frac{1}{4}$ miles with 130 lbs. in 2 mins. 3 secs.

He was beaten in his first five starts at four years, but showed a return to his best form when he beat King Saxon and Omaha in the Brooklyn Handicap in the new American record time 1 min. $48\frac{1}{5}$ secs. for 9 furlongs. This was followed by seven successive

Y

victories; the Detroit Challenge Cup, Stars and Stripes Handicap, the Butler Handicap, Bunker Hill, Arlington Handicaps, and Wilson Stakes and the Merchants' and Citizens' Handicap. He won the Arlington Handicap by five lengths with 135 lbs., running the 10 furlongs in 2 mins. 1⅕ secs., won the Merchants' and Citizens' Handicap, 1⅛ miles, by two lengths with 139 lbs., equalling Whisk Broom's achievement in the Suburban Handicap in 1913. 139 lbs. is the heaviest weight ever carried to victory in the United States in a first-class handicap at 9 furlongs or further. Beaten into second place by 1½ lengths, under 139 lbs. by Top Row, 110 lbs., in the Naragansett Special, Discovery returned to winning form three days later when he won the Whitney Stakes. This was followed by victories in the Hawthorne Gold Cup and Cincinatti Handicap.

As a five-year-old Discovery retrograded slightly. In 14 starts he won six races and was twice second. His outstanding successes were his third triumph in the Brooklyn Handicap, the Saratoga Handicap, Wilson Stakes and the Whitney Stakes. He endeavoured to win the Merchants' and Citizens' Handicap for the second year in succession, but 143 lbs. proved too great a burden for his iron frame and he finished fifth. He might have been closer, but was taken up near the finish when victory was beyond his grasp. Discovery was the best weight carrying handicap horse this country has known since Exterminator. He had far more speed than Exterminator, and unquestionably was superior to Mr. Kilmer's great gelding at all distances as far as 10 furlongs irrespective of weight.

In four seasons he started in 63 races, winning 27, was second in 10, third in 10 and earned $195,287. He has proved a first-class sire, if not a great one.

Another high-class racehorse bred by William Woodward was Granville, a bay with a narrow white stripe, by Gallant Fox-Gravita by Sarmatian. His early career was almost parallel to that of his elder relative, Omaha, and the early half of his three-year-old career was dogged by misfortune. After winning his first race he was left at the post and beaten a nose by Tuefel. In the Kentucky Derby he ran out from under his jockey, Stout, and continued riderless around the course. In the Preakness he was beaten by a nose by the Derby winner Bold Venture. Many alleged this was occasioned by his rider's inability to make a strong finish. Like Omaha he went out of his class to meet older horses in the Suburban. Here again he succumbed in the last few strides to the four-year-old, Firethorn, in receipt of 11 lbs. by the scale, Granville was beaten a neck. However, in the Belmont Stakes, Granville achieved a major victory—it was a near thing, Mr. Bones went under by a neck. Granville was unbeaten thereafter.

After seven weeks rest he appeared at Arlington Park in the Classic and won by two lengths from Mr. Bones, with his ears pricked. At Saratoga he won the Kenner by a neck, followed by a success in the Travers, which he won by a head from Sun Teddy in a life and death struggle over a muddy track. His last race at Saratoga was in the Cup, $1\frac{3}{4}$ miles, weight-for-age, over a muddy track, in which he started second choice at 9/5, the remaining starter being Discovery, at 5/2 " on ". Granville led from flagfall to finish; Discovery never got near him and was beaten eight lengths. Returning to Long Island, he won the Lawrence Realization, $1\frac{5}{8}$ miles, but was all corded up after the race and was probably not himself. Later it was found he had struck himself and was retired to the stud. Like Omaha, he was a bitter disappointment as a stock horse.

Seabiscuit was termed the " from rags to riches " horse. The bay son of the Man-o'-War sire Hard Tack, out of the Whisk Broom mare Swing On, Seabiscuit was bred by the Wheatley Stable and trained by James Fitzsimmons. He was considered " small potatoes " at two years, being shipped to Hialeah, where he made his debut on January 19, 1935, in a Purse in which he finished fourth. Three days later he made one of a field in a claiming race at 3 furlongs, and was beaten two lengths by a little filly named Clapping Jane, both entered to be claimed for $2,500. Clapping Jane did not weigh more than seven hundred pounds ; she was bred by Leslie E. Keiffer at his Inverness Farm, Monkton, Maryland, and it was the only race Clapping Jane ever won. Seabiscuit failed to win until his eighteenth start, June 22nd, and four days later he won his first stake, the Watch Hill Claiming Stakes. He won three other races that year, a Purse and the Springfield and Ardsley Handicap.

At three years he won but two Purses in his first ten starts. This was followed by a victory in the Mohawk Claiming Stakes, after which he was sold to Charles S. Howard for $7,500 and turned over to Tom Smith to train. Taken to Detroit, he won the Governor's and Hendrie Handicaps. In October he won the Scarsdale Handicap at Empire City, New York, and closed the year by winning the Bay Bridge and World's Fair Handicaps. At four years, in 1937, Seabiscuit attracted national attention by winning eleven races, seven of them in succession, was second in two, third in one and unplaced but once, in 15 starts. He began the year by winning the Huntington Beach Handicap at Santa Anita, then was beaten in the Cincinnati and Santa Anita Handicaps. This was followed by a succession of seven victories, the San Juan Capistrano, Marchbank, Bay Meadows, Brooklyn, Butler, Yonkers and Massachusetts Handicaps. In the last event he carried 130 lbs. Beaten into third place in the Nara-gansett Special, under 132 lbs. behind Calumet Dick 115 lbs. and Snark 117 lbs., Seabiscuit entered the winner's circle in the Continental Handicap, Laurel Stakes (dead heat with Jacola) and the Riggs Handicap, under 130 lbs. In his last race of the year, he was beaten by Esposa, 115 lbs. in the Bowie Handicap —1⅝ miles. His rider went wide in the stretch, letting Esposa through, which accounted for Seabiscuit's defeat.

In 1938, at five years, Seabiscuit won six of his 11 races, was second in four and third in one. His outstanding successes were scored in the Agua Caliente Handicap, 130 lbs.; Bay Meadows Handicap, 133 lbs.; Hollywood Gold Cup, 130 lbs.; Havre de Grace, 128 lbs., and his famous match with War Admiral at equal weights in the Pimlico Special, 1³⁄₁₆ miles. At six years he ran but once and was retired for nearly a year. In 1940, his last season on the turf, he ran but four times, winning his last two starts, the San Antonio and the Santa Anita Handicaps. He made his farewell in a blaze of glory, winning the Santa Anita Handicap, value $86,650 under 130 lbs., in new record time of 2 mins. 1⅘ secs., finishing 1½ lengths in front of his stable companion imp. Kayak II, bred in the Argentine. The general reaction was that Kayak II might have won had the two horses been running in different interests.

The best horse ever bred by Samuel D. Riddle at the Faraway Farm, Lexington, Kentucky, was unquestionably War Admiral, a brown horse, foaled in 1934, by Man-o'-War-Brush Up by Sweep. In colour, make and shape War Admiral favoured the distaff side of his family. In racing condition he measured 15.2 hands and weighed less than one thousand pounds. He was a racehorse of the highest class, proved by the fact that in the four seasons he raced he started 26 times, winning 21 races, second in three and fourth in one, earning $273,240, during the period when stakes and purses were about one-third what they have been since 1945. Trained by George Conway War Admiral was unbeaten in eight starts as a three-year-old. He scored the " hat trick " by winning the Kentucky Derby, the Preakness and the Belmont Stakes in succession. In the latter he established a new track record, and equalled the American record, for the 1½ miles in 2 mins. 28⅗ secs. He cut his quarter in the Belmont Stakes, run early in June, and was an absentee from racing until the Autumn. He also won the Chesapeake Stakes, the Washington Handicap and the Pimlico Special, and beat the best horses of his time. At four years, he won the Widener Handicap, 1¼ miles in February under 130 lbs., the Queens County Handicap under 132 lbs., and within a period of four weeks won the Wilson Stakes, the Saratoga Handicap,

Whitney Stakes and Saratoga Cup. He won the Jockey Club Gold Cup in October, and followed this up by winning the Rhode Island Handicap. He was twice beaten at four years, finishing fourth in the Massachusetts Handicap and second to Seabiscuit in his ill-advised match at Pimlico, for which he was badly managed, trained and ridden. He was retired to the stud and developed into a very successful sire, having led the list in 1945. Among his issue were Busher, the best filly to race in this country since Regret, Bee Mac, War Jeep and War Date, all of which have won in excess of $100,000.

The best horse bred in the State of Maryland in the current century was Challedon, a brown horse by imp. Challenger II-Laura Gal by imp. Sir Gallahad III, foaled 1936, bred by William L. Brann at his Glade Valley Stud, near Frederick, Maryland. In his racing career Challedon won the Pimlico Futurity, New England Futurity, Maryland Futurity, the Preakness and Classic Stakes (beating Johnstown in both), the Yankee, Havre de Grace (twice), Maryland Handicap, the Naragansett Special, Hawthorne Gold Cup, Pimlico Special (twice), the Trantor Handicap (setting a new world's record of 1 min. 54⅖ secs. for 1 3/16 miles), the Hollywood Gold Cup (1¼ miles in 2 mins. 2 secs., a new track record), the Whitney Stakes and the Philadelphia Handicap. In all Challedon started in 44 races, winning 22, was second in seven, third in six, earning $334,660. He made an excellent start as a sire. Two of his sons, Donor and Shy Guy, in his first two crops, have each won well in excess of $100,000.

At the dispersal of W. R. Coe's Shoshone Stud, November 11, 1935, George D. Widener purchased the mare Dinner Time, then seven years old, by High Time-Sea Plane by Man-o'-War, in foal to imp. Rock Sand's grandson Pilot, for $6,000. The following year Dinner Time produced an exceptionally attractive yearling, marked with the famous " Pantaloon spots ", that was to gain fame under the name Eight Thirty. Trained by A. J. Joyner Eight Thirty raced during four seasons, starting 27 times, winning 16 races, was three times second, five times third and unplaced three times (once a disqualification, after finishing first). His earnings totalled $155,475. At two years he won the Flash and Christina Stakes, was disqualified after winning the Albany Handicap ; and was second in the Futurity, beaten a short head, the defeat being due to his rider's failure to observe the ultimate winner, Porter's Mite, which was the width of the track away from him on the outside. At three years Eight Thirty won the Diamond State, the Wilson, Travers and Whitney Stakes and the Saratoga Handicap. At four years he won the Toboggan, Suburban and Massachusetts Handicaps and the Wilson Stakes. He won his only two races at five, the Toboggan

and Metropolitan Handicaps. In the latter he carried 132 lbs.
Eight Thirty started slowly as a sire, but his stock showed marked
improvement before 1949. Among them are the stake winners
Colony Boy, Condiment, Task, Outotheblue, Slumber Song,
First Nighter, Watermill, Isa and Dinner Gong. In 1949, up to
and including the racing of June 30th, Eight Thirty's issue had
won 63 races and earned $224,660, entitling him to fifth place
on the list of leading sires.

Inferior only to Gallant Fox, among the sons of imp. Sir
Gallahad III, was the Belair Stud's Fenelon, a bay son of imp.
Sir Gallahad III-imp. Filante by Sardanaple, foaled 1937 and
trained by James Fitzsimmons. Fenelon's dam Filante was
imported to this country as a yearling by Delbert Reiff. In the
crossing she was knocked about and was not in sales condition
in August the year she was imported. Mr. William Woodward
thereupon bought her privately for $5,000. She developed into
one of the very best broodmares this country has known in the
current century. Her daughter Flying Gal II will be known to
British racegoers as a dam of the St. Leger and Eclipse winners
Boswell, Hypnotist and Gainly. In his racing career Fenelon
won thirteen races and $152,545, including the Endurance,
Empire City, Merchants' and Citizens', Brooklyn and New York
Handicaps In the last Fenelon set a new American record for
2¼ miles of 3 mins. 47 secs. He also won the Travers Stake, the
Whitney Stake, Lawrence Realization and Jockey Club Gold Cup.
Unfortunately he has sired nothing of moment to date and
breeders are beginning to look upon him with jaundiced eyes.

No horse in recent years, with the exception of Stymie, was as
popular with the racing public as Calumet Farm's home bred
Whirlaway, an exceptionally attractive-looking chestnut, son
of imp. Blenheim-Dust Whirl by Sweep. Warren Wright
purchased Dust Whirl from A. B. Hancock and from her bred
his first Kentucky Derby winner. Later he purchased from the
master of the Claiborne Stud, imp. Penicuik II by Buchan-
Pennycomequick by Hurry On, in foal to Hyperion, and the
resulting foal was Pensive, winner of the Kentucky Derby in
1944 in the Calumet " devil red and blue " silks. To carry the
parallel still farther Pensive, in his first year at stud, sired the
winner of the 1949 Kentucky Derby, Ponder, also bred by
Mr. Warren Wright. When he was retired to the stud Whirlaway
was the leading money-winning thoroughbred horse in the world
with $561,161, the winner of 32 races.

His victories included the Saratoga Cup, Breeders' Futurity,
Hopeful, and Walden Stakes at two years. At three years he
established a new track record for 1¼ miles when he won the
Kentucky Derby in 2 mins. 1⅖ secs. This was followed by

victories in the Preakness, Belmont, Dwyer, Travers Stakes, American Derby, Lawrence Realization, the Pimlico Special (walk over). He also won the Dixie, Massachusetts, Saranac, Brooklyn, Trenton, Governor Bowie, Louisana, Washington and Clark Handicaps, the Jockey Club Gold Cup and the Naragansett Special. To date he has not quite lived up to expectations as a sire. With three crops to represent him, he has sired but five stake winners; the colts Dart By, and Whirling Fox, neither of which is better than third rate, and the fillies Whirl Some, Scattered and Duchess Peg. From the standpoint of class his fillies to date are superior to his colts, nevertheless I would not suggest " selling Whirlaway short " as a potential sire. His racing class and his individuality as a racehorse make it appear he is foreordained ultimately to be a successful sire.

Market Wise, a bay horse foaled in 1938, by Broker's Tip-On Hand by On Watch, was bred by Mrs. George L. Harrison and sold as a yearling to the Brookmeade Farm for $2,100. In the Autumn of 1940 he was sold to Louis Tufano for $500, and competed in claiming races. Trained by the pint-sized George W. Carroll, he displayed marked improvement from two to three years, scoring his first stake success in the Wood Memorial Stakes. Later he accounted for the Rockingham Park, Edgemere, Governor Bowie and Gallant Fox Handicaps, the Jockey Club Gold Cup, the Pimlico Special, the Suburban Handicap, the McLennan, Massachusetts and Ballot Handicaps, and the Naragansett Special. He established new track records in winning the Edgemere and Governor Bowie Handicaps, and a new American record for two miles, 3 mins. 20$\frac{4}{5}$ secs., when he won the Jockey Club Gold Cup, beating Whirlaway at level weights. He also whipped Whirlaway in the Suburban Handicap by open daylight, running the ten furlongs in 2 mins. 1$\frac{4}{5}$ secs. Broker's Tip, the sire of Market Wise, won but one race in his life, the Kentucky Derby of 1933, and with the exception of Market Wise never sired anything that was better than a cheap plater. His first foals were of racing age in 1948, eight of them have won, but none looked impressive.

Devil Diver was the best horse to carry the " pink and black striped sleeves " of the Greentree Stable, since the retirement of Twenty Grand. A son of imp. St. Germans-Dabchick by imp. Royal Minstrel, foaled in 1939, in 47 starts he won 22 races, was second in two, third in three and earned $261,064. He was trained by John Gaver, and among his victories were the Sanford and Hopeful Stakes, the Breeder's Futurity, Phoenix, Carter, Brooklyn, Vermont, American Legion, Manhattan and Suburban Handicaps and the Whitney and Wilson Stakes. He won the Toboggan Handicap twice, on the second occasion in

1944 with 134 lbs.; and the Metropolitan Handicap three times with 117, 134 and 129 lbs. respectively. When he won with 134 lbs. he ran the mile in 1 min. 35⅘ secs. Devil Diver was handicapped from birth with a short off foreleg—it was two inches shorter than his near foreleg and he walked with a perceptible limp. Apparently it did not handicap him in his racing paces, but it was remarkable he trained at all, let alone win many of the outstanding stakes in this country. His first foals were of racing age in 1949 and include the National Stallion Stakes winner Diver.

One of the "ugly ducklings" in the yearling sales at Saratoga in 1940 was the bay colt by Good Goods-Winds Chant by Wild Air; decidedly unfashionably bred, his dam Winds Chant realized $90 in a sale by public auction. Thomas Piatt was breeder of the bay colt that sold for $700 as a yearling to Albert Sabath who named him Alsab. During the four seasons he raced this $700 yearling won 25 races, earning $350,015, the largest sum ever credited to a yearling sold by public auction. He ran 51 times and was unplaced on 10 occasions. The stake victories of Alsab include the Preakness, Withers, Lawrence Realization, American Derby, Narragansett Championship, New York Handicap, Joliet, Primer, Mayflower, Hyde Park, Washington Park, Juvenile, Prairie State, Champagne, Spalding Lowe Jenkins, and Walden Stakes and the Washington Park Futurity. He defeated Requested by 3½ lengths as a two-year-old in a match race at Belmont Park, establishing a new track record of 1 min. 16 secs. for 6½ furlongs. Incidentally this was the last race witnessed by veteran trainer Andrew Jackson Joyner, well known at Newmarket from 1908 to 1915. He occupied training quarters there at Ballaton Lodge training for the late Harry Payne Whitney. Alsab defeated Whirlaway under scale weights in a match termed the Narragansett Championship, and he also defeated the son of imp. Blenheim in the New York Handicap, 2¼ miles. Alsab's first foals were of racing age in 1948 and included the high-class fillies Myrtle Charm and Alsab's Day.

The Calumet Farm of Warren Wright, to the end of 1948, had bred fourteen horses which won from $101,105 (Twosy) to $865,150 (Citation); and the Calument sire Bull Lea by imp. Bull Dog to the end of 1948 had sired eight winners of more than $100,000, beginning with Twosy and ending with Citation.

The best filly or mare to date bred by the Calument Farm and sired by Bull Lea was Twilight Tear. Foaled in 1941 and one of Bull Lea's first crop, Twilight Tear was out of Lady Lark by Blue Larkspur, and from two to four years she ran 24 times, winning 18 races, was second twice, third twice, unplaced twice and earned $165,000. At three years she ranked with the best in training, regardless of sex; in 17 starts that year she won 14 races, was once second, once third, once unplaced and earned $167,555. Beaten in her first race, the Leap Year Handicap at Hialeah, she won her next 11 starts. In the Classic Stakes she defeated the colts and her stable companion Pensive, winner of the Kentucky Derby and the Preakness, was a badly beaten third. Twilight Tear completed the year by winning the Pimlico Special, defeating Devil Diver and Megogo under scale weight.

1940 to 1949

Calumet Farm's Armed, a brown gelding by Bull Lea-Armful by Chance Shot, foaled in 1941, was the greatest money-winning gelding in turf history. From 1944 to 1948 in 63 starts he won 36 races, was second in 14, third in five and unplaced in eight, earning $773,700. He did not race at two years and went wrong after the Hialeah Meeting (Florida) in February, 1948, and was retired for the balance of the year. He returned to training, but was only a shadow of the horse he had been.

He began to show stake quality as a four-year-old in 1945. Among his victories were the Washington Handicap and the Pimlico Special. At five, he won 11 races in 18 starts and was unplaced but once. His outstanding victories were scored in the Widener; the First and Second sections of the Double Event at Tropical Park; the Philadelphia; Dixie; Suburban; Sheridan and Washington Park Handicaps; and the Whirlaway Stakes. His most notable victory was scored in the Suburban Handicap at Belmont Park, in which he carried 130 lbs. and ran 1¼ miles in 2 mins. 2 secs. In 1947, at the age of six, he won 11 eleven races in 17 starts, and again was unplaced but once. His chief successes were the McLennan Handicap, Widener (for the second time), Gulf Stream Park, Stars and Stripes, Arlington, and Washington Park (for the second time) Handicaps; the Whirlaway Stakes (for the second time), a match race against Assault and the Sysonby Mile. In the majority of his victories he carried 130 lbs., but on the two occasions in which he carried 132 lbs., he was beaten.

Of the numerous high-class horses bred by George D. Widener, President of the Westchester Racing Association, the bay gelding Lucky Draw, foaled August 30, 1941, by Jack High-Tatanne by St. James earned the most money. In 36 starts he won 16 races, was second in six, third in four, earning $287,790. As a two-year-old he accounted for the Youthful, Juvenile, Tremont and Great American Stakes. At three he was victorious in the Second Division of the Wood Memorial Stakes, Peter Pan and the Jersey Handicaps. He went wrong after winning the Jersey Handicap and was an absentee from racing as a four-year-old in 1945. A year later he came back like a giant refreshed, winning the Butler, Monmouth, Merchants' and Citizens', the Saratoga and Olympia Handicaps and the Narragansett Special. In several of these victories he established new track records. Unfortunately he went wrong for the second time near the end of the season and despite the best efforts of his competent and conscientious trainer Bert Mulholland, it was impossible to get him back into racing condition.

Assault, a chestnut horse foaled in 1943, by the Kentucky Derby winner Bold Venture (grandson of Swynford) out of Igual by Equipoise, was the best racehorse ever bred in the State of Texas. Bred, owned and raced by the King Ranch and trained by Max Hirsch from 1945 to 1948, both years inclusive, Assault started in 33 races, winning 16, was second in five, third in five, unplaced in seven, earning $626,670. As a two-year-old he won but twice, but his improvement at three years was startling. He won the Experimental Handicap No. 1; the Wood Memorial; the Kentucky Derby; the Preakness; Belmont and Dwyer Stakes. He went amiss in the running of the Arlington Classic, July 27, and did not show a return to his best form until November 1, at Pimlico when he defeated Stymie in the Pimlico Special, and concluded the year by winning the Westchester Handicap, with Lucky Draw second. As a four-year-old he won his first five races : Grey Lag, Dixie, Suburban, Brooklyn and Butler Handicaps. He won the Brooklyn with 133 lbs.; and with 135 lbs. whipped Stymie a head in the Butler Handicap. However, under scale weights he was badly beaten into third place in the Gold Cup, July 19, won by Stymie; the distance, 1⅝ miles, appeared to be farther than he fancied.

In 1948 he won a purse at Hialeah, but was beaten off in the Widener, pulling up lame. He was retired to the stud, proved sterile and was turned out for the balance of the year. Taken up late in the Winter by his astute trainer Max Hirsch, he returned to racing apparently completely sound. He was beaten a head in his first start that year, but won the Butler Handicap, beating Vulcan's Forge (129 lbs.) which vainly tried to concede seven pounds to Assault.

The best filly to race in this country since the retirement of Beldame, about forty-five years ago, was the chestnut filly Busher, foaled in 1942 by War Admiral-Baby League by Bubbling Over, bred by the Idle Hour Stock Farm. Trained by James W. Smith, she raced as a two-year-old in the " green and white " silks of her breeder the late E. R. Bradley and won five races and was second once in seven starts.

Dubious about the future of racing by reasons of war conditions, E. R. Bradley, octogenarian owner, sold her in December, 1944 to Louis B. Mayer for $50,000. At three in the " red and light blue " silks of Mr. Mayer, trained by George M. Odom, Busher started in 13 races winning 10, was second in two, third in one, earning $273,735. Her victories that year included a Purse ; the Santa Susana Stakes, San Vicente Handicap, Santa Margarita, Cleopatra and Arlington Handicaps, in which she defeated Armed conceding him weight by the scale. Under 128 lbs. she finished third in the Beverly Handicap won by Durazna, but 11 days later in a match race under scale weights turned the tables on Durazna winning by threequarters of a length. Possibly her most meritorious performance was her victory in the Washington Park Handicap, $1\frac{1}{4}$ miles, under 115 lbs., in which she ran the distance in 2 mins. $1\frac{4}{5}$ secs. She wound up the year by winning the Hollywood Derby and the Vanity Handicap. She was injured shortly after and was unable to be trained the balance of the year. Late in 1945, Busher was purchased by Neil S. McCarthy for $135,000, and ran once in her new owner's colours on January 2, 1947 at Santa Anita Park. She failed to show any trace of her true form, finishing fifth, coming out of the race lame and was again retired. About a year later Busher was sold to Mrs. Elizabeth N. Graham for $150,000, a record price for a filly or mare.

Prior to the advent of Citation, Mrs. John Hertz's Count Fleet, a brown horse by Reigh Count-Quickly, by Haste, bred by his fair owner, was reckoned the best horse to race in this country since Man-o'-War. His dam was claimed in Florida for $2,000 by Hirsch Jacobs, who passed her along to Mrs. Hertz for $2,500 ; Count Fleet was her second foal. Trained by G. D. Cameron, Count Fleet was never unplaced in the two seasons he raced, starting 21 times, winning 16, was second in four, three in one, earning $250,300. At the close of 1942 he was reckoned the best two-year-old in training, winding up the year by winning the Champagne Stakes by six lengths, establishing the American record for one mile by a two-year-old, 1 min. $34\frac{4}{5}$ secs., the Thunderclap Purse by six lengths ; the Pimlico Futurity (with Occupation, which had defeated Count Fleet in The Futurity, five lengths away) and he concluded the year by winning the Walden Stakes by 30 lengths in the track record time for $1\frac{1}{16}$ miles, of 1 min. $44\frac{4}{5}$ secs.

Count Fleet won all his six races as a three-year-old. His first stake victory of the year was scored in the Wood Memorial, in which he was jumped upon at the post, and was more or less lame the balance of the year. " Don " Cameron displayed skill of the highest degree in keeping Count Fleet in condition to win his four remaining starts. They were the Kentucky Derby, by three lengths ; the Preakness Stakes by eight lengths ; the Withers Stakes by five lengths ; and the Belmont Stakes, $1\frac{1}{2}$ miles, equalling the track record time 2 mins. $28\frac{1}{5}$ secs. by 25 lengths. In running for the Belmont he went completely wrong and could never be trained thereafter. Count Fleet, however, whose first stock raced in 1948 made a most auspicious start as a sire ; three of his two-year-olds being stake winners.

Gallorette, a chestnut mare by imp. Challenger II-Gallette by imp. Sir Gallahad III, after five seasons retired at the end of 1948 with the credit of being the biggest money-winning mare in history. Bred by Preston M. Burch, raced by W. L. Brann and trained by E. A. Christmas, Gallorette started 72 times, winning 21 races, second in 20, third in 13, unplaced in 18, earning $445,535. Her form at two years was not particularly striking, although she won three races. At three, however, she displayed marked improvement. Among her victories were : The Acorn Stakes ; the Pimlico Oaks, the Delaware and Empire City Stakes, beating the colts. At four she won the Metropolitan ; Nimba ; Brooklyn ; Bay Shore and Beldame Handicaps. In the Brooklyn Handicap she defeated Stymie a neck. In 1947 she won the Queens County and Capra Handicap and the Wilson Stakes. In 1948, the last year she raced, she won the Carter Handicap ; the Wilson and Whitney Stakes. Galorette was one of the best looking mares that ever raced in this country. She stood 16 hands, was beautifully proportioned, with a sweet head, the best of legs and feet. She never took a lame step in her racing career.

For four racing seasons, 1945 to 1948, the idol of the racing world was the chestnut horse Stymie by Equestrian-Stop Watch by On Watch, bred by Max Hirsch in Texas. By midsummer 1948, Stymie had started in 126 races, had won 35, was second in 32, third in 26 and unplaced in 33, earning $911,335, the greatest sum credited to a horse in racing history. On July 24, 1948 in the Monmouth Handicap, Stymie under 129 lbs. fractured a bone in his off forefoot, which necessitated his retirement for the year. He was bred to about 14 mares in 1949, and then put back in training. Stymie's career is most dramatic. He is far from fashionably bred. His sire Equestrian, was an ordinary racehorse albeit a well bred one. His dam Stop Watch, never won a race and never produced a winner other than Stymie. His second dam, Sunset Gun by Man-o'-War never won a race and never produced a winner. In Stymie's pedigree are two crosses of the great producer imp. Fairy Gold. Stymie is one of the most handsome horses that has raced in this country in the present century. A bright chestnut with a blaze face, he stands about 15.3 hands, has plenty of scope, an intelligent head, widely spaced between the eyes, with a perfect disposition. Although he has won at all distances up to 2½ miles, he has never been worked farther than a mile at speed. One work-out a week at one mile in about 1 min. 40 secs. served to keep him in racing condition. As a matter of record, he has only worked a mile faster than 1 min. 40 secs. once; this on a Wednesday in 1 min. 38⅖ secs., and was soundly beaten the following Saturday.

Stymie was claimed from the King Ranch on his third appearance under colours at Belmont Park, June 2, 1943 for $1,500 by Hirsch Jacobs, whose superior as a judge and trainer of horses does not exist in this country. Racing in the " salmon and green hoops " of Mrs. Ethel D. Jacobs, wife of his trainer, Stymie failed to win a race until his fourteenth start, on August 18, 1943 at Belmont Park ; it was a claiming race and Stymie could have been claimed for $3,300 that afternoon. Stymie failed to win a stake until he was a four-year-old ; this being the Grey Lag Handicap, 1⅛ miles on June 2, 1945, at Jamaica. This was followed by a victory in the Brooklyn Handicap 1¼ miles in 2 mins. 2⅖ secs., worth $39,120 to the winner., His remaining stake victories that year were scored in the Butler Handicap, Saratoga Cup, Continental, Westchester, Riggs and Pimlico Cup Handicaps. In 1946 his victories included the Grey Lag Handicap, for the second time, the Whitney Stakes, the Edgemere Handicap, Manhattan, New York and Gallant Fox Handicaps. In 1947 he won the Metropolitan (one mile), the Questionnaire, Sussex, Massachusetts, Aqueduct, and the Gallant Fox Handicap for the second time. He also won the International Gold Cup, 1⅝ miles, with Assault badly beaten into third place. Incidentally, in 1945, 1946 and 1947, Stymie won over $225,000 each year. In 1948, the last year he appeared under colours, he won the Metropolitan Handicap for the second time, the Aqueduct Handicap and the Sussex Handicap for the second time. In the Sussex under 130 lbs. he established a new track record of 2 mins. 2 secs. for the 1¼ miles. He has won with various weights up to 132 lbs.

The form displayed by the Calumet Farm's Citation, bay colt foaled in 1945 by Bull Lea-Hydroplane II by Hyperion, as a three-year-old in 1949 caused him to be hailed in some quarters as superior to Man-o'-War. However, those loudest in this claim had never seen Man-o'-War race. Citation was a first-class two-year-old. Trained by B. A. Jones, one of the most competent at that period, he started in nine races, winning eight, was second in one, earning $155,690. His sole defeat was at the heels of his stable companion, the brilliant filly, Bewitch.

At three years, Citation was practically invincible. In 20 starts he won 19 races, was second once, and earned $709,470, the greatest sum ever won by a racehorse in one season. His sole defeat was suffered on the occasion of his fourth start, the Chesapeake Trial, six furlongs, at Havre de Grace, April 12, in which he succumbed to the three-year-old Saggy, in which he carried 126 lbs., conceding 4 lbs. to the winner. This marked Citation's first race in six weeks and it is generally held he was a " short horse " for the Chesapeake Trial. After this he was never defeated, winning 13 races in succession. Shortly after his last victory he popped an osselet, was retired, but returned to training.

That Citation was one of the very best horses that ever raced in this country admits of no contradiction. The number of truly outstanding horses, or to use a Hollywood term, super-horses, to race in this country in the current century, taking them in chronological order, to my mind, are Sysonby, Colin, Man-o'-War, Count Fleet and Citation among the colts ; and Beldame, Artful and Busher among the fillies. B. A. Jones and Hirsch Jacobs never over-worked their horses. If any-thing, Jones erred on the easy side. He will frequently start a horse known to be short, relying upon his class to carry him through, and in the majority of cases the soundness of this logic is borne out in the races.

As an example, Citation in his preparation for his Fall engage-ments in late September and early October, was never worked at speed at a distance beyond six furlongs. His best work for the Sysonby Mile, scale weights, was 6 furlongs in 1 min. 12 secs. Going to the post he looked as big as a bull and galloping behind his field to the threequarter pole he squatted like a big black leopard, put in a series of leaps that quickly carried him to the front ; he won from First Flight and Coaltown, in 1 min. 36 secs. This contest tightened him up sufficiently to win the Jockey Club Gold Cup, 2 miles, in 3 mins. 21⅗ secs., four-fifths of a second off the track record.

With Citation on the sidelines the Calumet Farm has pro-duced another horse little, if at all, inferior in 1949 to Citation. This is Coaltown, a bay colt by Bull Lea-Easy Lass by imp. Blenheim II, bred and owned by the Calumet Farm and trained by B. A. Jones. Coaltown suffered from a throat affliction at two and could not be brought up to racing condition. In 1948, at three, he started in 13 races, won eight, was second in three, third in two, never unplaced, earning $104,650. He began by winning the Phoenix Handicap and the Bluegrass

Stakes and then finished second to his stable companion Citation in the Kentucky Derby.   Brought East he won the Swift Stakes, seven furlongs, but was beaten by Vulcan's Forge in the Withers Stakes, one mile, in which he bled slightly.   Nothing more was seen of him for a month, when he finished third in the Skoki Handicap.   After another rest of six weeks, he won the Drexel Handicap, but was beaten in the Great Western Handicap. In the Autumn, at Belmont Park, he won the Jerome Handicap, one mile, under 126 lbs. in 1 min. 36 secs., and concluded the year by finishing third in the Sysonby Mile.

Coaltown proved to be the best horse in training in 1949. He is a "Triton" among minnows, although I am frank to confess I have never seen fewer first-class horses under silks. To the end of July, Coaltown started in 11 races, won 10, and finished second in the other.   His stake victories in 1949 include the McLennan and Widener Handicaps, at Hialeah; the Edward Burke Handicap at Havre de Grace; the Gallant Fox Handicap, under 130 lbs. at Jamaica; the Roger Williams at Narragansett; the Stars and Stripes and the Arlington Handicap, at Arlington Park.   His earnings for the year amount to $215,925.   The only set-back he has suffered to date was in the Equipoise Mile at Arlington, June 25, in which he carried 132 lbs. and was beaten into second place by Star Reward under 116 lbs.   Here again it is believed Coaltown was a bit "short", if so it was no place to start a "short" horse.   In his last start in the Arlington Handicap, Coaltown, under 130 lbs. experienced no difficulty in turning the tables on Star Reward, 116 lbs., winning in effortless fashion by three lengths, leading all the way.

A rule was enacted several years ago at Arlington and Washington Parks, whereby no horse in a handicap at one mile should be forced to carry in excess of 132 lbs., and in a handicap at a distance beyond one mile, 130 lbs.   This in effect handcuffs the handicappers, but was devised to keep the weight off the backs of the Calumet Farm horses, and the trainer of this organization, B. A. Jones, refused to start any of his charges in handicaps with weights in excess of those prevailing at Arlington and Washington Parks.

CLASSIC WINNERS

1900

2,000 GUINEAS

1. **Diamond Jubilee**
(St. Simon–Perdita II)
H. Jones 11–4
2. **Bonarosa**
(Bonavista–Rose Madder)
L. Reiff 50–1
3. **Sidus**
(St. Simon–Star of Fortune)
T. Loates 100–1
4 L.; $\frac{3}{4}$ L. 10 ran.
Time 1 m. $41\frac{3}{5}$ s.
Owner—H.R.H. Prince of Wales.
Trainer—R. Marsh.

1,000 GUINEAS

1. **Winifreda**
(St. Simon–Melody)
S. Loates 11–2
2. **Inquisitive**
(Hampton–None the Wiser)
T. Sloan 100–7
3. **Vain Duchess**
(Isinglass–Sweet Duchess)
J. H. Martin 4–1 (fav.)
$\frac{3}{4}$L.; 2 L. 10 ran.
Time 1 m. 46 s.
Owner—Mr. L. Brassey
Trainer—T. Jennings, jun.

THE DERBY

1. **Diamond Jubilee**
H. Jones 6–4 (fav.)
2. **Simondale**
(St. Simon–Ismay)
M. Cannon 100–6
3. **Disguise II**
(Domino–Bonnie Gal)
T. Sloan 8–1
$\frac{3}{4}$ L.; 4 L. 14 ran.
Time 2 m. 42 s.
Owner—H.R.H. Prince of Wales
Trainer—R. Marsh

THE OAKS

1. **La Roche**
(St. Simon–Miss Mildred)
M. Cannon 5–1
2. **Merry Gal**
(Galopin–Mary Seaton)
K. Cannon 100–7
3. **Lady Schomberg**
(Aughrim–Clonavarn)
T. Sloan 3–1 (co-fav.)
3 L.; Bad. 14 ran.
Time 2 m. $45\frac{1}{5}$ s.
Owner—Duke of Portland.
Trainer—J. Porter.

ST. LEGER

1. **Diamond Jubilee**
H. Jones 2–7 (fav.)
2. **Elopement**
(Rightaway–Maid of Lorn)
M. Cannon 100–7
3. **Courian**
(Gallinule–Clarion)
T. Sloan 25–1
1 L.; 2 L. 11 ran.
Time 3 m. $9\frac{1}{5}$ s.
Owner—H.R.H. Prince of Wales
Trainer—R. Marsh

1901

2,000 GUINEAS

1. **Handicapper**
(Matchmaker–Agnes Osborne)
W. Halsey 33–1
2. **Doricles**
(Florizel II–Rosalie)
K. Cannon 4–1
3. **Osboch**
(Oberon–St. Isabela)
H. Jones 40–1
2 L.; Neck. 17 ran.
Time 1 m. 43 s.
Owner—Sir E. Cassel
Trainer—F. W. Day

1,000 GUINEAS

1. **Aida**
(Galopin–Queen Adelaide)
D. Maher 13–8
2. **Fleur D'ete**
(St. Florian–Summerdale)
W. Halsey 10–1
3. **Santa Brigida**
(St. Simon–Bridger)
J. Reiff 10–1
Neck; 2 L. 15 ran.
Time 1 m. $44\frac{3}{5}$ s.
Owner—Sir J. Miller
Trainer—G. Blackwell

THE DERBY

1. **Volodyovski**
(Florizel II–La Reine)
L. Reiff 5–2 (fav.)
2. **William The Third**
(St. Simon–Gravity)
M. Cannon 100–7
3. **Veronese**
(Donovan–Maize)
F. Rickaby 40–1
$1\frac{1}{2}$ L.; 6 L. 25 ran.
Time 2 m. $40\frac{4}{5}$ s.
Owner—Mr. W. Whitney
Trainer—J. Huggins

THE OAKS

1. **Cap and Bells II**
(Domino–Ben-Ma-Chree)
M. Henry 9–4 (fav.)
2. **Sibrinetta**
(Kilmartin–Sabra)
C. Jenkins 50–1
3. **Minnie Dee**
(Fitzsimon–King's Daughter)
L. Reiff 10–1
6 L.; 2 L. 21 ran.
Time 2 m. $44\frac{3}{5}$ s.
Owner—Mr. F. Keene
Trainer—S. Darling

ST. LEGER

1. **Doricles**
K. Cannon 40–1
2. **Volodyovoski**
L. Reiff 5–6 (fav.)
3. **Revenue**
(Blairfind–Income)
H. Jones 100–8
Neck; 3 L. 13 ran.
Time 3 m. $8\frac{3}{5}$ s.
Owner—Mr. L. de Rothschild
Trainer—A. Hayhoe

1902

2,000 GUINEAS

1. **Sceptre**
(Persimmon–Ornament)
H. Randall 4–1 (co-fav.)
2. **Pistol**
(Carbine–Wenonah)
J. H. Martin 50–1
3. **Ard Patrick**
(St. Florian–Morganette)
K. Cannon 9–2
2 L.; 3 L. 14 ran.
Time 1 m. 39 s.
Owner and Trainer—Mr. R. Sievier

1,000 GUINEAS

1. **Sceptre**
H. Randall 1–2 (fav.)
2. **St. Windeline**
(St. Simon–Queen of Spring)
W. Lane 100–7
3. **Black Fairey**
(Ladas–Black Duchess)
J. Childs 33–1
$1\frac{1}{2}$ L.; 4 L. 15 ran.
Time 1 m. $40\frac{1}{5}$ s.
Owner and Trainer—Mr. R. Sievier

THE DERBY

1. **Ard Patrick**
J. H. Martin 100–14
2. **Rising Glass**
(Isinglass–Hautesse)
G. McCall 40–1
3. **Friar Tuck**
(Friar's Balsam–dam by Gallinule)
M. Cannon 100–7
3 L.; 3 L. 18 ran.
Time 2 m. $42\frac{1}{5}$ s.
Owner—Mr. J. Gubbins
Trainer—S. Darling

THE OAKS

1. **Sceptre**
H. Randall 5–2 (fav.)
2. **Glass Jug**
(Isinglass–Amphora)
G. McCall 10–1
3. **Elba**
(Prisoner–Simoon)
3 L.; $1\frac{1}{2}$ L. 14 ran.
D. Maher 25–1
Time 2 m. $46\frac{3}{5}$ s.
Owner and Trainer—Mr. R. Sievier

ST. LEGER

1. **Sceptre**
F. Hardy 100–30 (fav.)
2. **Rising Glass**
W. Halsey 9–1
3. **Friar Tuck**
H. Randall 7–1
3 L.; 2 L. 12 ran.
Time 3 m. $12\frac{3}{5}$ s.
Owner and Trainer—Mr. R Sievier

1903

2,000 GUINEAS

1. **Rock Sand**
   (Sainfoin–Roquebrune)
   J. H. Martin 6–4 (fav.)
2. **Flotsam**
   (St. Frusquin–Float)
   D. Maher 7–1
3. **Rabelais**
   (St. Simon–Satirical)
   K. Cannon 8–1

$1\frac{1}{2}$ L.; 2 L. 11 ran.
Time 1 m. 42 s.
Owner—Sir J. Miller
Trainer—G. Blackwell

1,000 GUINEAS

1. **Quintessence**
   (St. Frusquin–Margarine)
   H. Randall 4–1
2. **Sun-Rose**
   (Sheen–Nina)
   W. Halsey 20–1
3. **Skyscraper**
   (Velasquez or Ayrshire–) Chelandry
   D. Maher 9–4 (fav.)

$1\frac{1}{2}$ L.; 2 L. 12 ran.
Time 1 m. 48 s.
Owner—Ld. Falmouth
Trainer—J. Chandler

THE DERBY

1. **Rock Sand**
   D. Maher 4–6 (fav.)
2. **Vinicius**
   (Masque–Wandora)
   G. Thompson 11–2
3. **Flotsam**
   W. Halsey 100–14

2 L.; 2 L. 7 ran.
Time 2 m. $42\frac{4}{5}$ s.
Owner—Sir J. Miller
Trainer—G. Blackwell

THE OAKS

1. **Our Lassie**
   (Ayrshire–Yours)
   M. Cannon 6–1
2. **Hammerkop**
   (Gallinule–Concussion)
   J. H. Martin 2–1 (fav.)
3. **Skyscraper**
   D. Maher 100–7

3 L.; Head. 10 ran.
Time 2 m $44\frac{3}{5}$ s.
Owner—Mr. J. B. Joel
Trainer—C. Morton

ST. LEGER

1. **Rock Sand**
   D. Maher 2–5 (fav.)
2. **William Rufus**
   (Melton–Simena)
   O. Madden 100–9
3. **Mead**
   Persimmon–Meadow Chat
   M. Cannon 7–2

4 L.; $\frac{1}{2}$ L. 5 ran.
Time 3 m. $9\frac{3}{5}$ s.
Owner—Sir J. Miller
Trainer—G. Blackwell

1904

2,000 GUINEAS

1. **St. Amant**
   (St. Frusquin–Lady Loverule)
   K. Cannon 11–4 (fav.)
2. **John O'Gaunt**
   (Isinglass–La Fleche)
   Mr. G. Thursby 10–1
3. **Henry The First**
   (Melton–Simena)
   O. Madden 8–1

4 L.; 2 L. 14 ran.
Time 1 m. $38\frac{3}{5}$ s.
Owner—Mr. L. de Rothschild
Trainer—A. Hayhoe

1,000 GUINEAS

1. **Pretty Polly**
   (Gallinule–Admiration)
   W. Lane 1–4 (fav.)
2. **Lencadia**
   (Marlagan–Santa Maura)
   H. Aylin 33–1
3. **Flamma**
   (Florizel II–Hand Grenade)
   D. Maher 100–1

3 L.; 4 L. 7 ran.
Time 1 m. 49 s.
Owner—Major E. Loder
Trainer—P. Gilpin

THE DERBY

1. **St. Amant**
   K. Cannon 5–1
2. **John O'Gaunt**
   Mr. G. Thursby 4–1
3. **St. Denis**
   (St. Simon–Brooch)
   W. Halsey 50–1

3 L.; 6 L. 8 ran.
Time 2 m. $45\frac{4}{5}$ s.
Owner—Mr. L. de Rothschild
Trainer—A. Hayhoe

THE OAKS

1. **Pretty Polly**
   W. Lane 8–100 (fav.)
2. **Bitters**
   (St. Serf–Mara)
   K. Cannon 20–1
3. **Finance**
   (St. Frusquin–Wise Virgin)
   J. Watts 100–7

3 L.; Bad. 4 ran.
Time 2 m. $46\frac{1}{5}$ s.
Owner Major E. Loder
Trainer—P. Gilpin

ST. LEGER

1. **Pretty Polly**
   W. Lane 2–5 (fav.
2. **Henry The First**
   O. Madden 50–1
3. **Almscliff**
   (Wolf's Crag–Lighthead)
   D. Maher 100–6

3 L.; 6 L. 6 ran.
Time 3 m. $5\frac{4}{5}$ s.
Owner—Major E. Loder
Trainer—P. Gilpin

1905

2,000 GUINEAS

1. **Vedas**
   (Florizel II–Agnostic)
   H. Jones 11–2
2. **Signorino**
   (Best Man–Signorina)
   B. Dillon 25–1
3. **Llangibby**
   (Wildflower–Concussion)
   O. Madden 4–1

2 L.; Head. 13 ran.
Time 1 m. $41\frac{3}{5}$ s.
Owner—Mr. W. F. de Wend-Fenton
Trainer—W. Robinson

1,000 GUINEAS

1. **Cherry Lass**
   (Isinglass–Black Cherry)
   G. McCall 5–4 (fav.)
2. **Koorbaan**
   (Kilcock–Sabre)
   B. Dillon 33–1
3. **Jongleuse**
   (Juggler–Grand Prix)
   H. Pike 33–1

1 L.; 3 L. 19 ran.
Time 1 m. $43\frac{3}{5}$ s.
Owner—Mr. W. Hall-Walker
Trainer—W. Robinson

THE DERBY

1. **Cicero**
   Cyllene–Gas
   D. Maher 4–11 (fav.)
2. **Jardy**
   (Flying Fox–Airs and Graces)
   G. Stern 4–1
3. **Signorino**
   K. Cannon 66–1

$\frac{3}{4}$ L.; Head. 9 ran.
Time 2 m. $39\frac{3}{5}$ s.
Owner—Ld. Rosebery
Trainer—P. Peck

THE OAKS

1. **Cherry Lass**
   H. Jones 4–5 (fav.)
2. **Queen of the Earth**
   (Flying Fox–Lonely)
   W. Higgs 100–14
3. **Amitie**
   (Chaleureux–La Sagesse)
   D. Maher 100–14

3 L.; 6 L. 12 ran.
Time 2 m. 38 s.
J Owner—Mr. W. Hall-Walker
Trainer—W. Robinson

ST. LEGER

1. **Challacombe**
   (St. Serf–Lady Chansellor)
   O. Madden 100–6
2. **Polymelus,**
   (Cyllene–Maid Marion)
   M. Cannon 10–1
3. **Cherry Lass**
   H. Jones 4–6 (fav.)

3 L.; 3 L. 8 ran.
Time 3 m. $5\frac{3}{5}$ s.
Owner—Mr. W. Singer
Trainer—A. Taylor

1906

2,000 GUINEAS

1. **Gorgos**
   (Ladas–The Gorgon)
   H. Jones 20–1
2. **Sancy**
   (Diamond Jubilee–Dame Agnetta)
   O. Madden 100–8
3. **Ramrod**
   (Carbine–Esk)
   W. Higgs 100–7

Head; Neck. 12 ran.
Time 1 m. $43\frac{4}{5}$ s.
Owner—Mr. A. James
Trainer—R. Marsh

1,000 GUINEAS

1. **Flair**
   (St. Frusquin–Glare)
   B. Dillon 10–11 (fav.)
2. **Lischana**
   (Orvieto–Escalade)
   W. Higgs 20–1
3. **Paid Up**
   (St. Simon–Settlement)
   H. Randall 20–1

3 L.; $\frac{3}{4}$ L. 12 ran.
Time 1 m. $40\frac{3}{5}$ s.
Owner—Sir D. Cooper
Trainer—P. Gilpin

THE DERBY

1. **Spearmint**
   (Carbine–Maid of the Mint)
   D. Maher 6–1
2. **Picton**
   (Orbieto–Hecuba)
   Mr. G. Thursby 18–1
3. **Troutbeck**
   (Ladas–Royal Mount)
   J. H. Martin 33–1

$1\frac{1}{2}$ L.; 2 L. 22 ran.
Time 2 m. $36\frac{4}{5}$ s.
Owner—Major E. Loder
Trainer—P. Gilpin

THE OAKS

1. **Keystone II**
   (Persimmon–Lock and Key)
   D. Maher 5–2 (fav.)
2. **Gold Raich**
   (Bend Or–Wasp)
   O. Madden 5–1
3. **Snow Glory**
   (Ayrshire or Nimus–Perce-Neige)
   W. Halsey 100–9

3 L.; $1\frac{1}{2}$ L. 12 ran.
Time 2 m. $38\frac{3}{5}$ s.
Owner—Ld. Derby
Trainer—G. Lambton

ST. LEGER

1. **Troutbeck**
   G. Stern 5–1
2. **Prince William**
   (Bill of Portland–La Vierge)
   W. Halsey 25–1
3. **Beppo**
   (Marco–Petti)
   W. Higgs 100–9

Head; Head. 12 ran.
Time 3 m. $4\frac{1}{5}$ s.
Owner—Duke of Westminster
Trainer—W. Waugh.

1907

2,000 GUINEAS

1. **Slieve Gallion**
   (Gallinule–Reclusion)
   W. Higgs 4–11 (fav.)
2. **Bezonian**
   (Velasquez–Gas)
   D. Maher 100–9
3. **Linacre**
   (Wolf's Crag–Lismaine)
   W. Halsey 100–6

3 L.; $\frac{3}{4}$ L. 10 ran.
Time 1 m. $41\frac{4}{5}$ s.
Owner—Capt. Greer
Trainer—S. Darling

1,000 GUINEAS

1. **Witch Elm**
   (Orme–Canny Lassie)
   B. Lynham 4–11 (fav.)
2. **Frugality**
   (St. Frusquin–Wise Virgin)
   G. McCall 20–1
3. **Sixty**
   (Diamond Jubilee–Lucina)
   W. Halsey 20–1

3 L.; $1\frac{1}{2}$ L. 17 ran
Time 1 m. $42\frac{3}{5}$ s.
Owner—Mr. W. H. Walker
Trainer—W. Robinson

THE DERBY

1. **Orby**
   (Orme–Rhoda B.)
   J. Reiff 100–9
2. **Wool Winder**
   (Martagan–St. Windeline)
   O. Madden 100–9
3. **Slieve Gallion**
   W. Higgs 8–13 (fav.)

2 L.; $\frac{1}{2}$ L. 9 ran.
Time 2 m. 44 s.
Owner—Mr. R. Croker
Trained in Ireland

THE OAKS

1. **Glass Doll**
   (Isinglass–Fota)
   H. Randall 25–1
2. **Laomedia**
   (St. Serf–Great Dame)
   O. Madden 10–1
3. **Lady Hasty**
   (Desmond–Molly Morgan)
   J. Thompson 100–14

$\frac{1}{2}$ L.; $\frac{3}{4}$ L. 14 ran.
Time 2 m. 42 s.
Owner—Mr. J. B. Joel
Tralner—C. Morton

ST. LEGER

1. **Wool Winder**
   W. Halsey 11–10 (fav.)
2. **Baltinglass**
   (Isinglass–Sibola)
   B. Dillon 100–8
3. **Acclaim**
   (Amphion–Claque)
   W. Higgs 8–1

6 L.; $\frac{1}{2}$ L. 12 ran.
Time 3 m. $5\frac{3}{5}$ s.
Owner—Col. E. Baird
Trainer—H. Enoch

1908

2,000 GUINEAS

1. **Norman III**
   (Octagon–Nineveh)
   O. Madden 33–1
2. **Sir Archibald**
   (Desmond–Arc Light)
   Mr. G. Thursby 5–1
3. **White Eagle**
   (Gallinule–Merry Gal)
   L. Hewitt 100–7

3 L.; $\frac{3}{4}$ L. 17 ran
Time 1 m. $44\frac{3}{5}$ s.
Owner—Mr. A. Belmont
Trainer—J. Watson

1,000 GUINEAS

1. **Rhodora**
   (St. Frusquin–Rhoda)
   L. Lyne 100–8
2. **Bracelet**
   (Collar–Isis Belle)
   B. Lynham 5–1
3. **Ardentrive**
   (William the Third–View)
   W. Halsey 100–6

2 L.; Neck. 19 ran.
Time 1 m. $43\frac{4}{5}$ s.
Owner—Mr. R. Croker
Trainer—Allen

THE DERBY

1. **Signorinetta**
   (Chaleureux–Signora)
   W. Bullock 100–1
2. **Primer**
   (St. Simon–Breviary)
   B. Dillon 40–1
3. **Llangwm**
   (Musselthrush–Llangarren Lass)
   D. Maher 100–8

2 L.; Neck. 18 ran.
Time 2 m. $39\frac{4}{5}$ s.
Owner and Trainer—Chev. E. Ginistrelli

THE OAKS

1. **Signorinetta**
   W. Bullock 3–1
2. **Courtesy**
   (Isinglass–Cortegar)
   Wm. Griggs 100–7
3. **Santeve**
   (Santoi–Wedding Eve)
   W. Higgs 100–7

$\frac{3}{4}$ L.; 2 L. 13 ran.
Time 2 m. $42\frac{3}{5}$ s.
Owner and Trainer—Chev. E. Ginistrelli

ST. LEGER

1. **Your Majesty**
   (Persimmon–Yours)
   Wal. Griggs 11–8 (fav.)
2. **White Eagle**
   D. Maher 100–7
3. **Santo Strato**
   (Victor Wild or St. Frusquin–Pie Powder)
   O. Madden 100–6

$\frac{1}{2}$ L.; 4 L. 10 ran.
Time 3 m. 6 s.
Owner—Mr. J. B. Joel
Trainer—C. Morton

1909

2,000 GUINEAS

1. **Minoru**
   (Cyllene–Mother Siegel)
   H. Jones 4–1
2. **Phaleron**
   (Gallinule–Mrs. Butterick)
   W. Earl 33–1
3. **Louviers**
   (Isinglass–St. Louvaine)
   G. Stern 100–7

2 L.; $1\frac{1}{2}$ L. 11 ran.
Time 1 m. $37\frac{3}{5}$ s.
Owner—King Edward VII
Trainer—R. Marsh

1,000 GUINEAS

1. **Electra**
   (Eager–Sirenia)
   B. Dillon 9–1
2. **Princess de Galles**
   (Gallinule–Ecila)
   H. Jones 5–2 (fav.)
3. **Perola**
   (Persimmon–Edmeee)
   F. Wootton 3–1

1 L.; 4 L. 10 ran.
Time 1 m. $40\frac{2}{5}$ s.
Owner—Mr. L. Neumann
Trainer—P. Gilpin

THE DERBY

1. **Minoru**
   H. Jones 7–2
2. **Louviers**
   G. Stern 9–2
3. **William the Fourth**
   (William the Third–Lady Sevinton)
   W. Higgs 20–1

Short Head; $\frac{1}{2}$ L. 15 ran.
Time 2 m. $42\frac{2}{5}$ s.
Owner—King Edward VII
Trainer—R. Marsh

THE OAKS

1. **Perola**
   F. Wootton 5–1
2. **Princess de Galles**
   H. Jones 11–2
3. **Verne**
   (Bill of Portland–La Vierge)
   Wal. Griggs 25–1

2 L.; 2 L. 14 ran.
Time 2 m. $39\frac{4}{5}$ s.
Owner—Mr. W. C. Cooper
Trainer—G. S. Davies

ST. LEGER

1. **Bayardo**
   (Bay Ronald–Galicia)
   D. Maher 10–1
2. **Valens**
   (Lavenu–Valenza)
   F. Wootton 100–8
3. **Miradon**
   (Marco–Semitone)
   B. Dillon 20–1

$1\frac{1}{2}$ L.; $\frac{1}{2}$ L. 7 ran.
Time 3 m. $8\frac{3}{5}$ s.
Owner—Mr. Fairie
Trainer—A. Taylor

1910

2,000 GUINEAS

1. **Neil Gow**
   (Marco–Chelandry)
   D. Maher 2–1 (fav.)
2. **Lemberg**
   (Cyllene–Galicia)
   B. Dillon 7–2
3. **Whisk Broom**
   (Broomstick–Audience)
   J. H. Martin 100–7

Short head; 2 L. 13 ran.
Time 1 m. $40\frac{2}{5}$ s.
Owner—Ld. Rosebery
Trainer—P. Peck

1,000 GUINEAS

1. **Winkipop**
   (William the Third–Conjure)
   B. Lynham 5–2 (fav.)
2. **Maid of Corinth**
   (Cyllene–Sceptre)
   H. Jones 100–8
3. **Rosedrop**
   (St. Frusquin–Rosaline)
   C. Trigg 20–1

$1\frac{1}{2}$ L.; Head. 13 ran.
Time 1 m. 41 s.
Owner—Mr. W. Astor
Trainer—W. Waugh

THE DERBY

1. **Lemberg**
   B. Dillon 7–4 (fav.)
2. **Greenback**
   (St. Frusquin–Evergreen)
   F. Templeman 100–8
3. **Charles O'Malley**
   (Desmond–Goody Two Shoes)
   S. Donoghue 33–1

Neck; 2 L 15 ran.
Time 2 m. $35\frac{1}{5}$ s.
Owner—Mr. Fairie
Trainer—A. Taylor.

THE OAKS

1. **Rosedrop**
   C. Trigg 7–1
2. **Evolution**
   (Marco–Ste Perpetual)
   J. Thompson 25–1
3. **Pernelle**
   (Persimmon–Nuneaton)
   W. Higgs 25–1

4 L.; Neck. 11 ran.
Time 2 m. $38\frac{1}{5}$ s.
Owner—Sir W. Bass
Trainer—A. Taylor

ST. LEGER

1. **Swynford**
   (John O'Gaunt–Canterbury Pilgrim)
   F. Wootton 9–2
2. **Bronzino**
   (Marco–Flitters)
   F. Fox 20–1
3. **Lemberg**
   D. Maher 4–5 (fav.)

Head; $1\frac{1}{2}$ L. 11 ran.
Time 3 m. 4 s.
Owner—Ld. Derby
Trainer—G. Lambton

1911

2,000 GUINEAS

1. **Sunstar**
   (Sundridge–Doris)
   G. Stern 5–1
2. **Stedfast**
   (Chaucer–Be Sure)
   F. Wootton 100–9
3. **Lycaon**
   (Cyllene–La Vierge)
   E. Shaw 50–1

2 L.; $\frac{1}{2}$ L. 14 ran.
Time 1 m. $37\frac{3}{5}$ s.
Owner—Mr. J. B. Joel
Trainer—C. Morton

1,000 GUINEAS

1. **Atmah**
   (Galeazzo–Mrs. Kendal)
   F. Fox 7–1
2. **Radiancy**
   (Sundridge–Queen Elizabeth)
   J. H. Martin 25–1
3. **Knockfeerna**
   (Desmond–Adula)
   F. O'Neill 100–8

Short head; 2 L. 16 ran.
Time 1 m. $38\frac{2}{5}$ s.
Owner–Mr. J. A. de Rothschild
Trainer—F. Pratt

THE DERBY

1. **Sunstar**
   G. Stern 13–8 (fav.)
2. **Stedfast**
   B. Lynham 100–8
3. **Royal Tender**
   (Persimmon–Tender and True)
   S. Donoghue 25–1

2 L.; 4 L. 26 ran.
Time 2 m. $36\frac{4}{5}$ s.
Owner—Mr. J. B. Joel
Trainer—C. Morton

THE OAKS

1. **Cherimoya**
   (Cherry Tree–Swelt)
   F. Winter 25–1
2. **Tootles**
   (John O'Gaunt–Lady Drake)
   S. Donoghue 7–2 (fav.)
3. **Hair Trigger II**
   (Fowling Piece–Altcar)
   F. Wootton 9–1

3 L.; 5 L 21 ran.
Time 2 m. $41\frac{3}{5}$ s.
Owner–Mr. W. Broderick Clotes
Trainer—C. Marsh

ST. LEGER

1. **Prince Palatine**
   (Persimmon–Lady Lightfoot)
   F. O'Neill 100–30
2. **Lycaon**
   G. Stern 100–30
3. **King William**
   (William III–Glasalt)
   F. Wootton 6–4 (fav.)

6 L.; 3 L. 8 ran.
Time 3 m. 6 s.
Owner—Mr. T. Pilkington
Trainer—J. Beardsley

1912

2,000 GUINEAS

1. **Sweeper II**
   (Broomstick–Ravello II)
   D. Maher 6–1
2. **Jaeger**
   (Eager–Mesange)
   Wal. Griggs 100–1
3. **Hall Cross**
   (Desmond–Altesse)
   W. Saxby 9–2

1 L.; ½ L. 14 ran.
Time 1 m. 38⅗ s.
Owner—Mr. H. Duryea
Trainer—H. Persse

1,000 GUINEAS

1. **Tagalie**
   (Cyllene–Tegale)
   L. Hewitt 20–1
2. **Alope**
   (Gallinule–Altoviscar)
   B. Carslake 20–1
3. **Belleisle**
   (Isinglass–Virginal)
   H. Jones 7–4 (fav.)

1½ L.; ¾ L. 13 ran.
Time 1 m. 39⅗ s.
Owner—Mr. W. Raphael
Trainer—D. Waugh

THE DERBY

1. **Tagalie**
   J. Reiff 100–8
2. **Jaeger**
   Wal. Griggs 8–1
3. **Tracery**
   (Rock Sand–Tapiary)
   G. Bellhouse 66–1

4 L.; 2 L. 20 ran.
Time 2 m. 38⅘ s.
Owner—Mr. W. Raphael
Trainer—D. Waugh

THE OAKS

1. **Mirska**
   (St. Frusquin–Musa)
   J. Childs 33–1
2. **Equitable**
   (St. Frusquin–Themes)
   F. O'Neill 33–1
3. **Bill and Coo**
   (William the Third–Cooee)
   F. Wootton 10–1

3 L.; ¾ L. 14 ran.
Time 2 m. 43 s.
Owner—Mr. J. Prat
Trained in France

ST. LEGER

1. **Tracery**
   G. Bellhouse 8–1
2. **Maiden Erlegh**
   (Polymelus–Plum Tart)
   G. Stern 100–8
3. **Hector**
   (St. Amant–Necuba)
   A. Escott 10–1

5 L.; ¾ L. 14 ran.
Time 3 m. 11⅘ s.
Owner—Mr. A. Belmont
Trainer—J. Watson

1913

2,000 GUINEAS

1. **Louvois**
   (Islinglass–St. Louvaine)
   J. Reiff 25–1
2. **Craganour**
   (Desmond–Veneration II)
   W. Saxby 3–1 (fav.)
3. **Meeting House**
   (Voter–Noonday)
   F. O'Neill 50–1

Head; 2 L. 15 ran.
Time 1 m. 38⅘ s.
Owner—Mr. W. Raphael
Trainer—D. Waugh

1,000 GUINEAS

1. **Jest**
   (Sundridge–Absurdity)
   F. Rickaby 9–1
2. **Taslett**
   (William the Third–Burgonet)
   E. Wheatley 6–1 (fav.)
3. **Prue**
   (Cicera–Prune)
   D. Maher 9–1

Head; 1 L. 22 ran.
Time 1 m. 40⅘ s.
Owner—Mr. J. B. Joel
Trainer—C. Morton

THE DERBY

1. **Aboyeur**
   (Desmond–Pawky)
   E. Piper 100–1
2. **Louvois**
   W. Saxby 10–1
3. **Great Sport**
   (Gallinule–Gondolette)
   G. Stern 20–1

Craganour came in first, head in front of Aboyeur, but was disqualified. Louvois neck behind. 15 ran.
Time 2 m. 37⅗ s.
Owner—Mr. A. P. Cunliffe
Trainer—T. Lewis

THE OAKS

1. **Jest**
   F. Rickaby 8–1
2. **Depeche**
   (Gallinule–Petit Bleu)
   Wal. Griggs 20–1
3. **Arda**
   (St. Frusquin–Ardmore)
   W. Earl 100–8

2 L.; ½ L. 12 ran.
Time 2 m. 37⅗ s.
Owner—Mr. J. B. Joel
Trainer—C. Morton

ST. LEGER

1. **Night Hawk**
   (Gallinule–Jean's Folly)
   E. Wheatley 50–1
2. **White Magic**
   (Sundridge–La Vierge)
   F. Wootton 33–1
3. **Seremond**
   (Desmond–Serenata)
   N. Spear 33–1

2 L.; 3 L. 12 ran.
Time 3 m. 3⅗ s.
Owner—Col. Hall-Walker
Trainer—W. Robinson

1914

2,000 GUINEAS

1. **Kennymore**
   (John O'Gaunt–Croceum)
   G. Stern 2–1 (fav.)
2. **Corcyra**
   (Polymelus–Permain)
   F. O'Neill 7–2
3. **Black Jester**
   (Polymelus–Absurdity)
   H. Randall 20–1

Short head; 2 L. 18 ran.
Time 1 m. 38 s.
Owner—Sir J. Thursby
Trainer—A. Taylor

1,000 GUINEAS

1. **Princess Dorrie**
   (Your Majesty–Doria)
   W. Huxley 100–9
2. **Glorvina**
   (Desmond–Veneration II)
   F. Rickaby 100–7
3. **Torchlight**
   (John O'Gaunt–Lesbia)
   G. Stern. Evens (fav.)

¾ L.; Neck. 13 ran.
Time 1 m. 42 s.
Owner—Mr. J. B. Joel
Trainer—C. Morton

THE DERBY

1. **Durbar II**
   (Rabelais–Armenia)
   M. MacGee 20–1
2. **Hapsburg**
   (Desmond–Altesse)
   C. Foy 33–1
3. **Peter the Hermit**
   (St. Petersburg–Carlin)
   R. Watson 100–1

3 L.; 1½ L. 30 ran.
Time 2 m. 38⅗ s.
Owner—Mr. H. Duryea
Trainer—T. Murphy (France)

THE OAKS

1. **Princess Dorrie**
   W. Huxley 11–4 (fav.)
2. **Wassilissa**
   (Eager–Missovaja)
   E. Huxley 100–6
3. **Torchlight**
   G. Stern 10–1

2 L.; 4 L. 21 ran.
Time 2 m. 38⅕ s.
Owner—Mr J. B. Joel
Trainer—C. Morton

ST. LEGER

1. **Black Jester**
   Wal. Griggs 10–1
2. **Kennymore**
   F. Templeman 7–2 (fav.)
3. **Cressingham**
   (John O'Gaunt–Manda)
   H. Jelliss 100–1

5 L.; 3 L. 18 ran.
Time 3 m. 2⅗ s.
Owner—Mr. J. B. Joel
Trainer—C. Morton

1915

2,000 GUINEAS

1. **Pommern**
   (Polymelus–Merry Agnes)
   S. Donoghue 2–1 (fav.)
2. **Tournament**
   (Spearmint–Sirenia)
   Wal. Griggs 100–6
3. **The Vizier**
   (Valais–Cambrea)
   F. Bullock 25–1

3 L.; Head. 16 ran.
Time 1 m. 43⅖ s.
Owner—Mr. S. Joel
Trainer—C. Peck

1,000 GUINEAS

1. **Vaucluse**
   (Dark Ronald–Valve)
   F. Rickaby 5–2 (fav.)
2. **Silver Tag**
   (Sundridge–Silver Fowl)
   S. Donoghue 4–1
3. **Bright**
   (Sundridge–Doris)
   F. Fox 10–1

¾ L.; 1½ L. 15 ran.
Time 1 m. 40⅘ s.
Owner—Lord Rosebery
Trainer—F. Hartigan

THE DERBY

(Run at Newmarket)

1. **Pommern**
   S. Donoghue 11–10 (fav.)
2. **Let Fly**
   (White Eagle–Gondolette)
   J. Childs 10–1
3. **Rossendale**
   (St. Frusquin–Menda)
   J. Clark 40–1

2 L.; 3 L. 17 ran.
Time 2 m. 32⅘ s.
Owner—Mr. S. Joel
Trainer—C. Peck

THE OAKS

(Run at Newmarket)

1. **Snow Marten**
   (Martagon–Siberia)
   Wal. Griggs 20–1
2. **Bright**
   W. Huxley 7–1
3. **Silver Tag**
   S. Donoghue 11–4

4 L.; Head. 11 ran.
Time 2 m. 36⅕ s.
Owner—Mr. L. Neumann
Trainer—P. Gilpin

ST. LEGER

(Newmarket, as September Stakes)

1. **Pommern**
   S. Donoghue 1–3 (fav.)
2. **Snow Marten**
   Wal. Griggs 9–1
3. **Achtoi**
   (Santoi–Achray)
   C. Trigg 25–1

2 L.; 6 L. 7 ran.
Time 2 m. 55⅗ s.
Owner—Mr. S. Joel
Trainer—C. Peck

1916

2,000 GUINEAS

1. **Clarissimus**
   (Radium–Quintessence)
   J. Clark 100–7
2. **Kwang Su**
   (Cicero–Galicia)
   F. Templeman 10–1
3. **Nassovian**
   (William the Third–Veneration)
   N. Spear 20–1

½ L.; 3 L. 17 ran.
Time 1 m. 39⅘ s.
Owner—Lord Falmouth
Trainer—W. Waugh

1,000 GUINEAS

1. **Canyon**
   (Chaucer–Glasalt)
   F. Rickaby 9–4
2. **Fifinella**
   (Polymelus–Silver Fox)
   J. Childs 11–10 (fav.)
3. **Salamandra**
   (St. Frusquin–Electra)
   A. Whalley 10–1

¾ L.; 3 L. 10 ran.
Time 1 m. 40 s.
Owner—Lord Derby
Trainer—G. Lambton

THE DERBY

(Run at Newmarket)

1. **Fifinella**
   J. Childs 11–2
2. **Kwang Su**
   F. Templeman 3–1
3. **Nassovian**
   F. O'Neill 11–2

Neck; head. 10 ran.
Time 2 m. 30⅗ s.
Owner—Mr. E. Hulton
Trainer—R. Dawson

THE OAKS

(Run at Newmarket)

1. **Fifinella**
   J. Childs (8–13 (fav.)
2. **Salamandra**
   A. Whalley 8–1
3. **Market Girl**
   (Martagon–Coster Girl)
   S. Donoghue 20–1

5 L.; ½ L. 7 ran.
Time 2 m. 35 s.
Owner—Mr. E. Hulton
Trainer—R. Rawson

ST. LEGER

(Newmarket, as September Stakes)

1. **Hurry On**
   (Marconi–Tout–Suite)
   C. Childs 11–10 (fav.)
2. **Clarissimus**
   F. Bullock 5–2
3. **Atheling**
   (Desmond–Wood Daisy)
   J. Childs 4–1

3 L.; 5 L. 5 ran.
Time 2 m. 59⅗ s.
Owner—Mr. J. Buchanan
Trainer—F. Darling

1917

2,000 GUINEAS

1. **Gay Crusader**
   (Bayardo–Gay Laura)
   S. Donoghue 9–4 (fav.)
2. **Magpie**
   (Dark Ronald–Popinjay)
   O. Madden 6–1
3. **Athdara**
   (Desmond–Lady Jess)
   J. Evans 25–1

Head; 3 L. 14 ran.
Time 1 m. 40 ⅘ s.
Owner—Mr. Fairie
Trainer—A. Taylor

1,000 GUINEAS

1. **Diadem**
   (Orby–Donnetta)
   F. Rickaby 6–4 (fav.)
2. **Sunny Jane**
   (Sunstar–Maid of the Mist)
   R. Cooper 25–1
3. **Nonpareil**
   (Radium–Quintessence)
   A. Whalley 25–1

½ L.; 4 L. 14 ran.
Time 1 m. 43 s.
Owner—Lord d'Abernon
Trainer—G. Lambton

THE DERBY

(Run at Newmarket)

1. **Gay Crusader**
   S. Donoghue (7–4 (fav.)
2. **Dansellon**
   (Chaucer–Tortor)
   R. Watson 7–1
3. **Dark Legend**
   (Dark Ronald–Golden Legend)
   J. Childs 100–15

4 L.; Head. 14 ran.
Time 2 m. 40⅘ s.
Owner—Mr. Fairie
Trainer—A. Taylor

THE OAKS

(Run at Newmarket)

1. **Sunny Jane**
   O. Madden 4–1
2. **Diadem**
   F. Rickaby 7–4 (fav.)
3. **Moravia**
   (Minoru–Via)
   E. Wheatley 100–8

½ L.; 4 L. 11 ran.
Time 2 m. 43⅗ s.
Owner—Major W. Astor
Trainer—A. Taylor

ST. LEGER

(Newmarket, as September Stakes)

1. **Gay Crusader**
   S. Donoghue 2–11 (fav.)
2. **Kingston Black**
   (Royal Realm–Black Cherry)
   T. Burns 33–1
3. **Dansellon**
   F. Rickaby 100–15

6 L.; Bad. 3 ran.
Time 2 m. 59⅗ s.
Owner—Mr. Fairie
Trainer—A. Taylor

	2,000 GUINEAS	1,000 GUINEAS	THE DERBY (Run at Newmarket)	THE OAKS (Run at Newmarket)	ST. LEGER (Newmarket, as September Stakes)
1918	1. **Gainsborough** 4-1 (Bayardo–Rosedrop) J. Childs 2. **Somme Kiss** 8-1 (Sunstar–Stolen Kiss) J. H. Martin 3. **Blink** 100-8 (Sunstrad–Winkipop) G. Colling 1½ L.; 6 L., 13 ran. Time 1 m. 44½ s. Owner—Lady J. Douglas Trainer—A. Taylor	1. **Ferry** 50-1 (Swynford–Gondolette) B. Carslake 2. **My Dear** (Beppo–Silesia) S. Donoghue 6-4 (fav.) 3. **Herself** 20-1 (Neil Gow–Aida) F. Fox 2 L.; 3 L., 8 ran. Time 1 m. 48 s. Owner—Lord Derby Trainer—G. Lambton	1. **Gainsborough** 8-13 (fav.) J. Childs 2. **Blink** 100-8 R. Collins 3. **Treclare** 20-1 (Tredennis–Clare) W. Langford 1½ L.; 2 L., 13 ran. Time 2 m. 33½ s. Owner—Lady J. Douglas Trainer—A. Taylor	1. **My Dear** 3-1 (fav.) S. Donoghue { **Ferry** 100-6 B. Carslake **Silver Bullet** 33-1 (Swynford–Saintly Lady) O. Madden Stony Ford (J. H. Martin) came in first by a length but was disqualified. A dead heat for third place. 15 ran. Time 2 m. 34½ s. Owner—Mr. A. W. Cox Trainer—A. Taylor	1. **Gainsborough** 4-11 (fav.) J. Childs 2. **My Dear** 100-6 S. Donoghue 3. **Prince Chimay** 9-1 (Chaucer–Gallorette) O. Madden 100-14 3 L.; 4 L., 5 ran. Time 3 m. 4 s. Owner—Lady J. Douglas Trainer—A. Taylor
1919	1. **The Panther** 10-1 (Tracery–Countess Zia) R. Cooper 2. **Buchan** 100-8 (Sunstar–Mamoaze) V. Smyth 3. **Dominion** 100-6 (Polymelus–Osyrna) A. Smith Neck; ¾ L., 12 ran. Time 1 m. 44½ s. Owner—Sir A. Black Trainer—G. Manser	1. **Roseway** 2-1 (fav.) (Stornoway–Rose of Ayre) A. Whalley 2. **Britannia** 6-1 (Sunstar–Red Lily) F. Fox 3. **Glaciale** 20-1 (Polymelus–Glacier) G. Colling 6 L.; 1½ L., 15 ran. Time 1 m. 47½ s. Owner—Sir E. Hulton Trainer—F. Hartigan	(Run at Epsom) 1. **Grand Parade** 33-1 (Orby–Grand Geraldine) F. Templeman 2. **Buchan** 7-1 F. B. Brennan 3. **Paper Money** 8-1 (Greenback–Epping Rose) S. Donoghue ½ L.; 2 L., 13 ran. Time 2 m. 35½ s. Owner—Lord Glanely Trainer—F. B. Barling	(Run at Epsom) 1. **Bayuda** 100-7 (Bayardo–Jessica) J. Childs 2. **Roseway** 4-7 (fav.) S. Donoghue 3. **Mapledurham** 25-1 (Bayardo–Montem) G. Hulme 1½ L.; 1½ L., 10 ran. Time 2 m. 37½ s. Owner—Lady J. Douglas Trainer—A. Taylor	1. **Keysoe** 100-8 (Swynford–Keystone II) B. Carslake 2. **Dominion** 7-1 A. Smith 3. **Buchan** 8-1 J. Childs 6 L.; 2 L., 10 ran. Time 3 m. 6½ s. Owner—Lord Derby Trainer—G. Lambton
1920	1. **Tetratema** 2-1 (fav.) (The Tetrarch–Scotch Gift) B. Carslake 2. **Allenby** 100-7 (Bayardo–Tagalie) F. Slade 3. **Paragon** 8-1 (Radium–Quintessence) A. Smith ½ L.; 3 L., 17 ran. Time 1 m. 40½ s. Owner—Major D. McCalmont Trainer—H. Persse	1. **Cinna** 4-1 (Polymelus–Baroness 1a Fleche) Wm. Griggs 2. **Cicerole** 100-8 (Cicero–Casetta) J. Childs 3. **Valescure** 25-1 (Swynford–Valve) G. Preece 3 L.; 1 L., 21 ran. Time 1 m. 40½ s. Owner—Sir R. W. Jardine Trainer—T. Waugh	1. **Sylon Kop** 100-6 (Spearmint–Hammerkop) F. O'Neill 2. **Archaic** 10-1 (Polymelus–Keystone II) G. Bellhouse 3. **Orpheus** 50-1 (Orby–Electra) F. Leach 2 L.; 1½ L., 19 ran. Time 2 m. 34½ s. Owner—Major G. Loder Trainer—P. Gilpin.	1. **Charlebelle** 7-2 (Charles O'Malley–Bushey Belle) A. Whalley 2. **Cinna** 2-1 (fav.) Wm. Griggs 3. **Roselet** 25-1 (Stornoway–Rose of Ayrshire) V. Smyth Neck; 4 L., 17 ran. Time 2 m. 38½ s. Owner—Mr. A. P. Cunliffe Trainer—H. Braine	1. **Caligula** 100-6 (The Tetrarch–Snoot) A. Smith 2. **Silvern** 8-1 (Polymelus–Silver Fowl) F. Templeman 3. **Manton** 33-1 (Bayardo–Jane Grey II) F. Lane ½ L.; 3 L., 14 ran. Time 3 m. 7½ s. Owner—Mr. M. Goculdas Trainer—H. Leader

1921

2,000 GUINEAS

1. **Craig an Eran**
(Sunstar–Maid of the Mist)
J. Brennan 100–6
2. **Lemonora**
(Lemberg–Honora)
J. Childs 100–7
3. **Humorist**
(Polymelus–Jest)
S. Donoghue 3–1 (fav.)

$\frac{3}{4}$ L.; $\frac{3}{4}$ L. 26 ran.
Time 1 m. $41\frac{3}{5}$ s.
Owner—Lord Astor
Trainer—A. Taylor

1,000 GUINEAS

1. **Bettina**
(Swynford–Bobbina)
G. Bellhouse 33–1
2. **Petrea**
(St. Amant–Doro)
B. Carslake) 33–1
3. **Pompadour**
(Bayardo–Popinjay)
J. Brennan 7–1

$1\frac{1}{2}$ L.; $\frac{3}{4}$ L. 24 ran.
Time 1 m. $44\frac{3}{5}$ s.
Owner—Mr. W. Raphael
Trainer—P. Linton

THE DERBY

1. **Humorist**
S. Donoghue 6–1
2. **Craig an Eran**
J. Brennan 5–1
3. **Lemonora**
J. Childs 8–1

Neck; 3 L. 23 ran.
Time 2 m. $35\frac{3}{5}$ s.
Owner—Mr. J. B. Joel
Trainer—C. Morton

THE OAKS

1. **Love in Idleness**
(Bachelor's Double–Cornfield)
J. Childs 5–1
2. **Lady Sleipner**
(Sleipner–Lady Charmain)
P. Mason 25–1
3. **Long Suit**
(Lemberg–Third Trick)
F. Lane 10–1

3 L.; Neck. 22 ran.
Time 2 m. $38\frac{2}{5}$ s.
Owner—Mr. Joe Watson
Trainer—A. Taylor

ST. LEGER

1. **Polemarch**
(The Tetrarch–Pomace)
J. Childs 50–1
2. **Franklin**
(Volta–Cambric)
E. Gardner 100–6
3. **Westward Ho**
(Swynford–Blue Tit)
B. Carslake 8–1

$1\frac{1}{2}$ L.; 3 L. 9 ran.
Time 3 m. $6\frac{4}{5}$ s.
Owner—Lord Londonderry
Trainer—T. Green

1922

2,000 GUINEAS

1. **St. Louis**
(Louvois–Princess Sterling)
G. Archibald 6–1
2. **Pondoland**
(Pommern–Gourouli)
F. O'Neill 5–1
3. **Captain Cuttle**
(Hurry On–Bellavista)
V. Smyth 4–1

3 L.; 4 L. 22 ran.
Time 1 m. $43\frac{3}{5}$ s.
Owner—Lord Queenborough
Trainer—P. Gilpin

1,000 GUINEAS

1. **Silver Urn**
(Juggernaut–Queen Silver)
B. Carslake 10–1
2. **Soubriquet**
(Lemberg–Silver Fowl)
V. Smyth 100–12
3. **Golden Corn**
(Golden Son–Corn Crackle)
S. Donoghue 7–4 (fav.)

2 L.; $\frac{3}{4}$ L. 20 ran.
Time 1 m. 40 s.
Owner—Mr. B. W. Parr
Trainer—H. Persse

THE DERBY

1. **Captain Cuttle**
S. Donoghue 10–1
2. **Tamar**
(Tracery–Hamoaze)
F. Bullock 10–1
3. **Craigengower**
(Polymelus–Fortuna)
M. Beary 20–1

4 L.; 3 L. 30 ran.
Time 2 m. $34\frac{3}{5}$ s.
Owner—Lord Woolavington
Trainer—F. Darling

THE OAKS

1. **Pogrom**
(Lemberg–Popingoal)
E. Gardner 5–4 (fav.)
2. **Soubriquet**
S. Donoghue 7–2
3. **Mysia**
(Bachelor's Hope–Mitylene)
G. Archibald 100–8

$\frac{3}{4}$ L.; 3 L. 11 ran.
Time 2 m. $36\frac{1}{5}$ s.
Owner—Lord Astor
Trainer—A. Taylor

ST. LEGER

1. **Royal Lancer**
(Spearmint–Royal Favour)
R. A. Jones 33–1
2. **Silurian**
(Swynford–Glacier)
E. Gardner 100–8
3. **Ceylonese**
(Willonyx–Excelita
F. Bullock 20–1

2 L.; 2 L. 24 ran.
Time 3 m. $14\frac{1}{5}$ s.
Owner—Lord Lonsdale
Trainer—A. Sadler, jun.

1923

2,000 GUINEAS

1. **Ellangowan**
(Lemberg–Lammermuir)
C. Elliott 7–1
2. **Knockando**
(Pharlaris–Spean Bridge)
G. Archibald 25–1
3. **D'Orsay**
(Son-in-Law–My Dame)
R. Jones 50–1

Head; $\frac{1}{2}$ L. 18 ran.
Time 1 m. $37\frac{4}{5}$ s.
Owner—Lord Rosebery
Trainer—J. Jarvis

1,000 GUINEAS

1. **Tranquil**
(Swynford–Serenissima)
E. Gardner 5–2 (fav.)
2. **Cos**
(Flying Ore–Renaissance)
G. Hulme 10–1
3. **Shrove**
(Pommern–Silver Tag)
W. McLachlan 100–6

$1\frac{1}{2}$ L., 1 L. 16 ran.
Time 1 m. 39 s.
Owner—Lord Derby
Trainer—G. Lambton

THE DERBY

1. **Papyrus**
(Tracery–Miss Malley)
S. Donoghue 100–15
2. **Pharos**
(Phalaris–Scapa Flow)
E. Gardner 6–1
3. **Parth**
(Polymelus–Willia)
A. Walker 33–1

1 L.; $1\frac{1}{2}$ L. 19 ran.
Time 2 m. 38 s.
Owner—Mr. B. Irish
Trainer—B. Jarvis

THE OAKS

1. **Brownhylda**
(Stedfast–Valkyrie)
V. Smyth 10–1
2. **Shrove**
C. Elliott 100–7
3. **Teresina**
(Tracery–Blue Tit)
G. Hulme 8–1

Neck; Head. 12 ran.
Time 2 m. 37 s.
Owner—Vicomte de Fontarce
Trainer—R. Dawson

ST. LEGER

1. **Tranquil**
T. Weston 100–9
2. **Papyrus**
S. Donoghue 15–8 (fav.)
3. **Teresina**
G. Hulme 100–7

2 L.; $\frac{1}{2}$ L. 13 ran.
Time 3 m. 5 s.
Owner—Lord Derby
Trainer—C. Morton

	2,000 GUINEAS	1,000 GUINEAS	THE DERBY	THE OAKS	ST. LEGER
1924	1. **Diophon** (Grand Parade–Donetta) G. Hulme 11–2 2. **Bright Knight** (Gay Crusader–Sunny Jane) F. Bullock 100–9 3. **Green Fire** (Sunstar–Green Cloth) S. Donoghue 100–8 Head; Neck. 20 ran. Time 1 m. 39 s. Owner—H.H. Aga Khan Trainer—R. Dawson	1. **Plack** (Hurry On–Groat) 8–1 C. Elliott 2. **Mumtaz Mahal** (The Tetrarch–Lady Josephine) G. Hulme 6–5 (fav.) 3. **Straitlace** (Son-in-Law–Stolen Kiss) F. O'Neill 7–2 $\frac{1}{2}$ L.; Same. 16 ran. Time 1 m. $39\frac{3}{5}$ s. Owner—Lord Rosebery Trainer—J. Jarvis	1. **Sansovino** (Swynford–Gondolette) T. Weston 9–2 (fav.) 2. **St. Germans** (Swynford–Hamoaze) F. Bullock 100–7 3. **Hurstwood** (Gay Crusader–Bleasdale) V. Smyth 20–1 6 L.; Neck. 27 ran. Time 2 m. $46\frac{3}{5}$ s. Owner—Lord Derby Trainer—G. Lambton	1. **Straitlace** F. O'Neill 100–30 2. **Plack** C. Elliott 11–10 (fav.) 3. **Mink** (Marten–Cuptosser) R. A. Jones 100–7 $1\frac{1}{2}$ L.; Head. 12 ran. Time 2 m. 47 s. Owner—Sir E. Hulton Trainer—D. Waugh	1. **Salmon Trout** (The Tetrarch–Salamandra) B. Carslake 6–1 2. **Santorb** (Santoi–Countess Torby) G. Hulme 40–1 3. **Polyphontes** (Polymelus–St. Josephine) W. McLachlan 100–30 2 L.; $\frac{1}{2}$ L. 17 ran. Time 3 m. $13\frac{1}{5}$ s. Owner—H.H. Aga Khan Trainer—R. Dawson
1925	1. **Manna** (Phalaris–Waffles) S. Donoghue 100–8 2. **St. Becan** (Hurry On–The Cyprian) C. Elliott 9–1 3. **Oojah** (Bachelor's Double–Confey) C. Smirke 10–1 2 L.; 4 L. 13 ran. Time 1 m. $39\frac{3}{5}$ s. Owner—Mr. H. Morriss Trainer—F. Darling	1. **Saucy Sue** (Swynford–Good and Gay F. Bullock 1–4 (fav.) 2. **Miss Gadabout** (Cylgad–Popingaol) J. Brennan 20–1 3. **Firouze Mahal** (The Tetrarch–Grey Tip) B. Carslake 7–1 6 L.; 2 L. 11 ran. Time 1 m. $42\frac{3}{5}$ s. Owner—Lord Astor Trainer—A. Taylor	1. **Manna** S. Donoghue 9–1 2. **Zionist** (Spearmint–Judea) B. Carslake 10–1 3. **The Sirdar** (McKinley–Gibbs) A. Ealing 50–1 8 L.; 2 L. 27 ran. Time 2 m. $40\frac{3}{5}$ s. Owner—Mr. H. Morriss Trainer—F. Darling	1. **Saucy Sue** F. Bullock 30–100 (fav.) 2. **Miss Gadabout** J. Brennan 100–8 3. **Riding Light** (Galloper Light–Zobiska) S. Donoghue 20–1 8 L.; Same. 12 ran. Time 2 m. $38\frac{1}{5}$ s. Owner—Lord Astor Trainer—A. Taylor	1. **Solario** (Gainsborough–Sunworship) J. Childs 7–2 2. **Zambo** (Sunster–Airashii) B. Carslake 6–1 3 **Warden of the Marches** (Phalaris–Mary Mona) W. Wells 18–1 3 L.; Same. 15 ran. Time 3 m. $4\frac{3}{5}$ s. Owner—Sir J. Rutherford Trainer—R. Day.
1926	1. **Colorado** (Phalaris–Canyon) T. Weston 100–8 2. **Coronach** (Hurry On–Wet Kiss) J. Childs 5–4 (fav.) 3. **Apple Sammy** (Pommern–Lady Phoebe) H. Jelliss 10–1 5 L.; 3 L. 19 ran. Time 1 m. $43\frac{3}{5}$ s. Owner—Lord Derby Trainer—G. Lambton	1. **Pillion** (Chaucer–Double Back) R. Perryman 25–1 2. **Trilogy** (Son-in-Law–Triniestral) F. Lane 8–1 3. **Short Story** (Buchan–Long Suit) J. Brennan 20–1 1 L.; $\frac{1}{2}$ L. 29 ran. Time 1 m. 42 s. Owner—Mr. A. de Rothschild Trainer—J. Watson	1. **Coronach** J. Childs 11–2 2. **Lancegaye** (Swynford–Flying Spear) R. Perryman 40–1 3. **Colorado** T. Weston 2–1 (fav.) 5 L.; Short head. 19 ran. Time 2 m. $47\frac{4}{5}$ s. Owner—Lord Woolavington Trainer—F. Darling	1. **Short Story** R. Jones 5–1 2. **Resplendent** (By George–Sunbridge) T. Burns 100–6 3. **Gay Bird** (Lady Crusader–Popinjay) J. Brennan 100–8 4 L.; 2 L. 16 ran. Time 2 m. $43\frac{3}{5}$ s. Owner—Lord Astor Trainer—A. Taylor	1. **Coronach** J. Childs 8–15 (fav.) 2. **Caissot** (Gay Crusader–Keysoe) B. Carslake 100–9 3. **Foliation** (Tracery–Eglantine II) J. Brennan 100–7 2 L.; 6 L. 12 ran. Time 3 m. $1\frac{3}{5}$ s. Owner—Lord Woolavington Trainer—F. Darling

2,000 GUINEAS	1,000 GUINEAS	THE DERBY	THE OAKS	ST. LEGER
1927 **1. Adam's Apple** (Pommern–Mount Whistle) J. Leach 20–1 **2. Call Boy** (Hurry On–Comedienne) C. Elliott 5–2 (fav.) **3. Sickle** (Phalaris–Selene) T. Weston 10–1 Short head ; $\frac{1}{2}$ L. 23 ran. Time 1 m. 38$\frac{1}{5}$ s. Owner—Mr. C. W. Whitburn Trainer—H. Cottrill	**1. Cresta Run** (Hurry On–Bridgemount) A. Balding 10–1 **Book Law** (Buchan–Popingaol) H. Jelliss 13–2 **Endowment** (Silvern–Enrichment) J. Childs 3–1 (fav.) 2 L. ; Dead heat. 28 ran. Time 1 m. 38 s. Owner—Col. G. Loder Trainer—P. Gilpin	**1. Call Boy** C. Elliott 4–1 (fav.) **2. Hot Night** (Gay Crusader–Tubbercurry) H. Wragg 9–2 **3. Shian Mor** (Buchan–Arlass) F. Lane 22–1 2 L. ; 8 L. 23 ran. Time 2 m. 34$\frac{2}{5}$ s. Owner—Mr. F. Curzon Trainer—J. Watts	**1. Beam** (Galloper Light–Mustrella) T. Weston 4–1 **2. Booklaw** H. Jelliss 5–2 (fav.) **3. Grand Vitesse** (Hurry On–Lanessa) S. Donoghue 25–1 Head ; 6 L. 16 ran. Time 2 m. 34$\frac{3}{5}$ s. Owner—Lord Durham Trainer—Frank Butters	**1. Booklaw** H. Jelliss 7–4 (fav. **2. Hot Night** H. Wragg 4–1 **3. Son and Heir** (Son-in-Law–Cinderella) B. Carslake 25–1 3 L. ; 5 L. 16 ran. Time 3 m. 14$\frac{3}{5}$ s. Owner—Lord Astor Trainer—A. Taylor
1928 **1. Flamingo** (Flamboyant–Lady Peregrine) C. Elliott 5–1 **2. Royal Minstrel** (Tetretema–Harpischord) H. Beasley 7–2 **3. O'Curry** (Abbots Trace–La Paloma) P. Beasley 33–1 Head ; 1$\frac{1}{2}$ L. 17 ran. Time 1 m. 38$\frac{4}{5}$ s. Owner—Sir L. Phillips Trainer—J. Jarvis	**1. Scuttle** (Captain Cuttle–Stained Glass) J. Childs 15–8 (fav.) **2. Jurisdiction** (Abbots Trace–Lady Juror) G. Richards 100–8 **3. Toboggan** (Hurry On–Glacier) T. Weston 11–2 1 L. ; 6 L. 14 ran. Time 1 m. 44$\frac{1}{5}$s . Owner—His Majesty Trainer—W. Jarvis	**1. Felstead** (Spion Kop–Felkington) H. Wragg 33–1 **2. Flamingo** C. Elliott 9–2 **3. Black Watch** (Black Gauntlet–Pucka III) C. Smirke 33–1 1$\frac{1}{2}$ L. ; 6 L. 19 ran. Time 2 m. 34$\frac{2}{5}$ s. Owner—Sir H. Cunliffe-Owen Trainer—O. Bell.	**1. Toboggan** T. Weston 100–15 **2. Scuttle** J. Childs Evens **3. Flegere** (Grand Parade–Corrie) R. Jones 100–8 4 L. 6 L. 13 ran. Time 2 m. 37$\frac{3}{5}$ s. Owner—Lord Derby Trainer—Frank Butters	**1. Fairway** (Phalaris–Scapa Flow) T. Weston 7–4 (fav. **2. Palais Royal II** (Bruleur–Puntarenas) M. Allemond 100–6 **3. Cyclonic** (Hurry On–Volcanic) R. A. Jones 100–15 1$\frac{1}{2}$ L. ; 1 L. 13 ran. Time 3 m. 3 s. Owner—Lord Derby Trainer—Frank Butters
1929 **1. Mr. Jinks** (Tetratema–False Piety) H. Beasley 5–2 (fav.) **2. Cragadour** (Craig an Eran–Pompadour) H. Jelliss 4–1 **3. Gay Day** (Gay Crusader–Silver Tag) S. Donoghue 20–1 Head ; 1$\frac{1}{2}$ L. 22 ran. Time 1 m. 39$\frac{4}{5}$s Owner—Major D. McCalmont Trainer—H. Persse	**1. Taj Mah** (Lemberg–Taj Mahal) W. Sibbritt 33–1 **2. Sister Anne** (Son-in-Law–Dutch Mary) J. Childs 5–2 (fav.) **3. Ellanvale** (Ellangowan–Valini) C. Elliott 20–1 $\frac{3}{4}$ L. ; Short Head. 19 ran. Time 1 m. 40$\frac{3}{5}$ s. Owner—M. Simon Guthmann Trainer—J. Torterolo	**1. Trigo** (Blandford–Athasi) J. Marshall 33–1 **2. Walter Gay** (Capt. Cuttle–William's Pride) F. Fox 100–8 **3. Brienz** (Blink–Blue Lake) R. Jones 50–1 1$\frac{1}{2}$ L. ; 2 L. 26 ran. Time 2 m. 36$\frac{3}{5}$ s. Owner—Mr. W. Barnett Trainer—R. Dawson	**1. Pennycomequick** (Hurry On–Plymstock) H. Jelliss 11–10 **2. Golden Silence** (Swynford–Molly Desmond) C Ray 20–1 **3. Sister Anne** J. Childs 7–2 5 L. ; 2 L. 13 ran. Time 2 m. 35$\frac{4}{5}$ s. Owner—Lord Astor Trainer—J. Lawson	**1. Trigo** M. Beary 5–1 **2. Bosworth** (Son-in.Law–Serefrissima) T. Weston 9–1 **3. Horus** (Papyrus–Lady Peregrine, C. Elliott 25–1 Short head ; $\frac{3}{4}$ L. 14 ran. Time 3 m. 3$\frac{3}{5}$ s. Owner—Mr. W. Barnett Trainer—R. Dawson

Year	2,000 GUINEAS	1,000 GUINEAS	THE DERBY	THE OAKS	ST. LEGER
1930	1. **Diolite** (Diophon–Needle Rock) F. Fox 10–1 2. **Paradine** (Grand Parade–Jesting Maid) R. Perryman 33–1 3. **Silver Flare** (Pharos–Silver Hand) C. Elliott 25–1 2 L.; 1 L. 28 ran. Time 1 m. 42$\frac{3}{5}$ s. Owner—Sir H. Hirst Trainer—F. Templeman	1. **Fair Isle** (Phalaris–Scapa Flow) T. Weston 7–4 (fav.) 2. **Torchere** (Pomme de Terre–Torchlight) R. Perryman 10–1 3. **Silver Clover** (Friar Marcus–Miss Sainfoin) J. Sirett 10–1 Short head; Neck. 19 ran. Time 1 m. 42 s. Owner—Lord Derby Trainer—Frank Butters	1. **Blenheim** (Blandford–Malva) H. Wragg 18–1 2. **Iliad** (Swynford–Pagan Sacrifice) R. A. Jones 25–1 3. **Diolite** C. Ray 11–4 1 L.; 2 L. 17 ran. Time 2 m. 38$\frac{1}{5}$ s. Owner—H.H. Aga Khan Trainer—R. Dawson	1. **Rose of England** (Teddy–Pierce Heige) G. Richards 7–1 2. **Wedding Favour** (Son-in-Law–Red Rosette) M. Wing 33–1 3. **Micmac** (Sansovino–Celiba) C. Ray 33–1 3 L.; 2 L. 15 ran. Time 2 m. 39 s. Owner—Lord Glanely Trainer—T. Hogg	1. **Singapore** (Gainsborough–Tetrabbazia) G. Richards 4–1 2. **Parenthesis** (Son-in-Law–Bracket) F. Fox 4–1 3. **Rustom Pasha** (Son-in-Law–Cos) H. Wragg 20–1 1$\frac{1}{2}$ L.; $\frac{3}{4}$ L. 13 ran. Time 3 m. 9$\frac{1}{5}$ s. Owner—Lord Glanely Trainer—T. Hogg
1931	1. **Cameronian** (Pharos–Una Cameron) J. Childs 100–8 2. **Goyescas** (Gainsborough–Zariba) C. Elliott 8–1 3. **Orpen** (Solario–Harpy) R. A. Jones 18–1 2 L.; 3 L. 24 ran. Time 1 m. 39$\frac{3}{5}$ s. Owner—Mr. J. A. Dewar Trainer—F. Darling	1. **Four Course** (Tetratema–Dinner) C. Elliott 100–9 2. **Lady Marjorie** (Sansovino–Florena) G. Richards 4–1 3. **Lindos Ojos** (Buen Ojo–Fourfold) H. Beasley 10–1 Head; 1 L. 20 ran. Time 1 m. 39$\frac{4}{5}$ s. Owner—Lord Ellesmere Trainer—F. Darling	1. **Cameronian** F. Fox 7–2 2. **Orpen** R. A. Jones 9–1 3. **Sandwich** (Sansovino–Waffles) H. Wragg 8–1 $\frac{3}{4}$ L.; Same. 25 ran. Time 2 m. 36$\frac{3}{5}$ Owner—Mr. J. A. Dewar Trainer—F. Darling	1. **Brulette** (Bruleur–Seaweed) C. Elliott 7–2 2. **Four Course** F. Fox 6–1 3. **Links Tor** (Lancegaye–Leighon Tor) R. A. Jones 10–1 1 L.; $\frac{3}{4}$ L. 15 ran. Time 2 m. 39$\frac{1}{5}$ s. Owner—Lt.-Col. C. Birkin Trainer—F. Carter (France)	1. **Sandwich** H. Wragg 9–1 2. **Orpen** J. Childs 11–2 3. **Sir Andrew** (Sir Galahad III–Gravitate) P. Beasley 20–1 4 L.; 1 L. 10 ran. Time 3 m. 11$\frac{1}{5}$ s. Owner—Lord Rosebery Trainer—J. Jarvis
1932	1. **Orwell** (Gainsborough–Golden Hair) R. A. Jones Evens(fav.) 2. **Dastur** (Solario–Friar's Daughter) M. Beary 10–1 3. **Hesperus** (Phalaris–Sweet Rocket) C. Elliott 25–1 2 L.; 1$\frac{1}{2}$ L. 11 ran. Time 1 m. 42$\frac{3}{5}$ s. Owner—Mr. W. M. Singer Trainer—J. Lawson	1. **Kandy** (Alcantara II–Kiao Tehau) C. Elliott 33–1 2. **Thorridean** (Hurstwood–Lady Ethel R. A. Jones 20–1 3. **Safe Return** (Stratford–Flying Home) G. Richards 100–6 1 L.; Same. 19 ran. Time 1 m. 44 s. Owner—M. E. de St. Alary Trainer—V. Gilpin	1. **April the Fifth** (Craig an Eran–Sold Again) F. Lane 100–6 2. **Dastur** M. Beary 18–1 3. **Miracle** (Manna–Brodrick Bay) H. Wragg 100–9 $\frac{3}{4}$ L.; Short head. 21 ran. Time 2 m. 43 s. Owner—Mr. T. Walls Trainer—Mr. T. Walls	1. **Udaipur** (Blandford–Uganda) M. Beary 10–1 2. **Will o' the Wisp** (Hurry On–William's Pride) G. Richards 9–4 3. **Giudecca** (Galloper Light–Piazzetta) T. Weston 10–1 2 L.; same. 12 ran. Time 2 m. 43$\frac{1}{5}$ s. Owner—H.H. Aga Khan Trainer—Frank Butters	1. **Firdaussi** (Pharos–Brownhylda) F. Fox 20–1 2. **Dastur** M. Beary 6–1 3. **Silvermere** (The Winter King–Demurrage) R. Dick 33–1 Neck; 4 L. 19 ran. Time 3 m. 4$\frac{3}{5}$ s. Owner—H.H. Aga Khan Trainer—Frank Butters.

	2,000 GUINEAS	1,000 GUINEAS	THE DERBY	THE OAKS	ST. LEGER
1933	**1. Rodosto** (Epinard–Ramondie) R. Brethes 9–1 **2. King Salmon** (Salmon Trout–Malva) H. Wragg 25–1 **3. Gino** (Tetratema–Teresina) C. Elliott 100–6 1 L.; $\frac{3}{4}$ L. 27 ran. Time 1 m. $40\frac{3}{5}$ s. Owner—Princess de Faucigny-Lucinge) Trainer—H. Count (France)	**1. Brown Betty** (Friar Marcus–Garpal) J. Childs 8–1 **2. Fur Tor** (Apelle–Leighon Tor) R. A. Jones 100–6 **3. Myrobelia** (Tetratema–Dolabella) G. Richards 5–1 $\frac{1}{2}$ L.; $\frac{3}{4}$ L. 22 ran. Time 1 m. $39\frac{3}{5}$ s. Owner—Mr W. Woodward Trainer—C. Boyd-Rochfort	**1. Hyperion** (Gainsborough–Selene) T. Weston 6–1 **2. King Salmon** H. Wragg 7–1 **3. Statesman** (Blandford–Dail) B. Carslake 20–1 4 L.; 1 L. 24 ran. Time 2 m. 34 s. Owner—Lord Derby Trainer—G. Lambton	**1. Chatelaine** (Phalaris–Herself) S. Wragg 25–1 **2. Solfatara** (Solario–Panic) S. Donoghue 20–1 **3. Fur Tor** R. A. Jones 100–8 $1\frac{1}{2}$ L.; 2 L. 14 ran. Time 2 m. $36\frac{4}{5}$ s. Owner—Mr. E. Thornton-Smith Trainer—F. Templeman	**1. Hyperion** T. Weston 6–4 (fav.) **2. Felicitation** (Colorado–Felicita) M. Beary 22–1 **3. Scarlet Tiger** (Colorado–Trilogy) B. Carslake 100–8 3 L.; Neck. 14 ran. Time 3 m. $6\frac{4}{5}$ s. Owner—Lord Derby Trainer—G. Lambton
1934	**1. Colombo** (Manna–Lady Nairne) W. Johnstone 2–7 (fav.) **2. Easton** (Dark Legend–Phaona C. Semblat 20–1 **3. Badruddin** (Blandford–Mumtaz Mahal) F. Fox 50–1 1 L.; $1\frac{1}{2}$ L. 12 ran. Time 1 m. 40 s. Owner—Lord Glanely Trainer—T. Hogg.	**1. Campanula** (Blandford–Vesper Bell) H. Wragg 2–5 (fav.) **2. Light Brocade** (Galloper Light–Trilogy) B. Carslake 100–6 **3. Spend A Penny** (Apron–Lady Earn) R. Perryman 100–9 1 L.; 6 L. 10 ran. Time 1 m. 39 s. Owner—Sir G. Bullough Trainer—J. Jarvis.	**1. Windsor Lad** (Blandford–Resplendent) C. Smirke 15–2 **2. Easton** G. Richards 100–9 **3. Colombo** W. Johnstone 11–8 (fav.) 1 L.; neck. 19 ran. Time 2 m. 34 s. Owner—H.H. Maharaja of Rajpipla. Trainer—M. Marsh.	**1. Light Brocade** B. Carslake 7–4 (fav.) **2. Zelina** (Blandford–Zoza) S. Donoghue 9–4 **3. Instantaneous** (Hurry On–Picture) R. Dick 20–1 $1\frac{1}{2}$ L.; 1 L. 8 ran. Time 2 m. $35\frac{1}{5}$ s. Owner—Lord Durham Trainer—Frank Butters	**1. Windsor Lad** C. Smirke 4–9 fav. **2. Tiberius** (Foxlaw–Glenapatrick) R. A. Jones 20–1 **3. Lo Zingaro** (Solario–Love in Idleness) G. Richards 100–9 2 L.; 2 L. 10 ran. Time 3 m. $1\frac{3}{5}$ s. Owner—H.H Maharaja of Rajpipla Trainer—M. Marsh.
1935	**1. Bahram** (Blandford–Friar's Daughter) F. Fox 7–2 (2nd fav.) **2. Theft** (Tetratema–Voleuse) G. Richards 11–2 **3. Sea Bequest** (Legatee–Ocean Light) E. Smith 100–7 $1\frac{1}{2}$ L.; 2 L. 16 ran. Time 1 m. $41\frac{3}{5}$ s. Owner—H.H. Aga Khan Trainer—Frank Butters	**1. Mesa** (Kircubbin–Mackwiller) W. Johnstone 8–1 **2. Hyndford Bridge** (Beresford–Portree) H. Wragg 20–1 **3. Caretta** (Phalaris or Solario–Daumont) G. Richards 9–4 (fav.) 3 L.; $1\frac{1}{2}$ L. 22 ran. Time 1 m. 43 s. Owner—M. Pierre Wertheimer Trainer—A. Swann (France)	**1. Bahram** F. Fox 5–4 (fav.) **2. Robin Goodfellow** (Son and Heir–Eppie Adair) T. Weston 50–1 **3. Field Trial** (Felstead–Popingaol) R. Dick 9–1 2 L.; $\frac{1}{2}$ L. 16 ran. Time 2 m. 36 s. Owner—H.H. Aga Khan Trainer—Frank Butters	**1. Quashed** (Obliterate–Verdict) H. Jelliss 33–1 **2. Ankaret** (Blandford–Sister Stella) F. Fox 100–6 **3. Mesa** W. Johnstone 5–4 (fav.) Short head; 1 L. 17 ran. Time 2 m. $41\frac{3}{5}$ s. Owner—Lord Stanley Trainer—C. Leader	**1. Bahram** C. Smirke 4–11 (fav.) **2. Solar Ray** (Solario–Trincomalee) J. Sirett 100–6 **3. Buckleigh** (Sansovino–Surbine) H. Wragg 25–1 5 L.; 3 L. 8 ran. Time 3 m. $1\frac{3}{5}$ s. Owner—H.H. Aga Khan Trainer—Frank Butters

1936

2,000 GUINEAS

1. Pay Up
(Fairway–Book Debt)
R. Dick 11–2
2. Mahmound
(Blenheim–Mah Mahal)
S. Donoghue 100–8
3. Thankerton
(Manna–Verdict)
T. Burns 40–1
Short head; 3 L. 19 ran.
Time 1 m. 39 $\frac{3}{5}$ s.
Owner—Lord Astor
Trainer—J. Lawson

1,000 GUINEAS

1. Tide-Way
(Fairway–Drift)
R. Perryman 100–30
2. Feola
(Friar Marcus–Aloe)
F. Fox 28–1
3. Ferrybridge
(Ballyferis–Sunbridge)
G. Richards 11–4
$1\frac{1}{2}$ L.; Neck. 22 ran.
Time 1 m. 42 s.
Owner—Lord Derby
Trainer—C. Leader

THE DERBY

1. Mahmoud
C. Smirke 100–8
2. Taj Akbar
(Fairway–Taj Shirin)
G. Richards 6–1
3. Thankerton
T. Burns 33–1
3 L.; $\frac{3}{4}$ L. 22 ran.
Time 2 m. 33 $\frac{4}{5}$ s.
Owner—H. H. Aga Khan
Trainer—Frank Butters

THE OAKS

1. Lovely Rosa
(Tolgus–Napoule)
T. Weston 33–1
2. Barrow Glen
(Hurstwood–Flower Show)
P. Beasley 22–1
3. Feola
F. Fox 10–1
$\frac{3}{4}$ L.; 2 L. 17 ran.
Time 2 m. 36 s.
Owner—Sir A. Bailey
Trainer—H. Cottrill

ST. LEGER

1. Boswell
(Bosworth–Flying Gal II)
P. Beasley 20–1
2. Fearless Fox
(Foxlaw–Molly Adare)
E. Smith 100–6
3. Mahmoud
C. Smirke 5–1
$\frac{3}{4}$ L.; 3 L. 13 ran.
Time 3 m. $8\frac{3}{5}$ s.
Owner—Mr. W. Woodward
Trainer—C. Boyd-Rochfort

1937

2,000 GUINEAS

1. Le Ksar
(Ksar–Queen Iseult)
C. Semblat 20–1
2. Goya II
(Tourbillon–Zariba)
C. Elliott 7–1
3. Mid-Day Sun
(Solario–Bridge of Allan)
T. Lowrey 25–1
4 L.; $\frac{1}{2}$ L. 18 ran.
Time 1 m. $44\frac{3}{5}$ s.
Owner—M. E. St. Alary
Trainer—F. Carter (France)

1,000 GUINEAS

1. Exhibitionist
(Solario–Lady Wembley)
S. Donoghue 10–1
2. Spray
(Blandford–Tilia)
P. Beasley 100–6
3. Gainsborough Lass
(Gainsborough–Golden Hair)
E. Smith 10–11 (fav.)
$\frac{1}{2}$ L.; Head. 20 ran.
Time 1 m. $43\frac{4}{5}$ s.
Owner—Sir V. Sassoon.
Trainer—J. Lawson

THE DERBY

1. Mid-Day Sun
M. Beary 100–7
2. Sandsprite
(Sandwich–Wood Nymph)
J. Crouch 100–1
3. Le Grand Duc
(Blenheim–La Douairiere)
C. Smirke 100–9
$1\frac{1}{2}$ L.; $1\frac{1}{2}$ L. 21 ran.
Time 2 m. $37\frac{1}{5}$ s.
Owner—Mrs. G. H. Miller
Trainer—F. S. Butters

THE OAKS

1. Exhibitionist
R. Jones 3–1 (fav.)
2. Sweet Content
(Salmon Trout–Belle Soleil)
W. Sibbritt 33–1
3. Sculpture
(Sansovino–Picture)
R. A. Jones 20–1
3 L.; Head. 13 ran.
Time 2 m. $36\frac{4}{5}$ s.
Owner—Sir V. Sassoon
Trainer—J. Lawson

ST. LEGER

1. Chumleigh
(Singapore–Rose of England)
G. Richards 18–1
2. Fair Copy
(Fairway–Composure)
R. Perryman 6–1
3. Mid-Day Sun
M. Beary 3–1 (fav.)
$\frac{1}{2}$ L.; 3 L. 15 ran.
Time 3 m. $7\frac{3}{5}$ s.
Owner—Lord Glanely
Trainer—T. Hogg

1938

2,000 GUINEAS

1. Pasch
(Blandford–Pasca)
G. Richards 5–2 (fav.)
2. Scottish Union
(Cameronian–Trustful)
B. Carslake 9–1
3. Mirza II
(Blenheim–Mumtaz Mahal)
H. Wragg 7–1
2 L.; $1\frac{1}{2}$ L. 18 ran.
Time 1 m. 38 $\frac{4}{5}$ s.
Owner—Mrs. H. Morriss
Trainer—F. Darling

1,000 GUINEAS

1. Rockfel
(Felstead–Rockliffe)
S. Wragg 8–1
2. Laughing Water
(Walter Gay–Duchess of Mars)
W. Stephenson 20–1
3. Solar Flower
(Solario–Serena)
R. Perryman 20–1
$1\frac{1}{2}$ L.; 3 L. 20 ran.
Time 1 m. 38 s.
Owner—Sir H. Cunliffe-Owen
Trainer—O. Bell

THE DERBY

1. Bois Roussel
(Vatout–Plucky Liege)
E. C. Elliott 20–1
2. Scottish Union
B. Carslake 8–1
3. Pasch
G. Richards 9–4 (fav.)
4 L.; 2 L. 22 ran.
Time 2 m. $38\frac{1}{5}$ s.
Owner—Mr. P. Beatty
Trainer—F. Darling

THE OAKS

1. Rockfel
H. Wragg 3–1 (fav.)
2. Radiant
(Blandford–Resplendent)
C. Smirke 100–7
3. Solar Flower
R. Perryman 100–9
4 L.; $1\frac{1}{2}$ L. 14 ran.
Time 2 m. 37s
Owner—Sir H. Cunliffe-Owen
Trainer—O. Bell

ST. LEGER

1. Scottish Union
B. Carslake 7–1
2. Challenge
(Apelle–Molly Adare)
E. Smith 100–8
3. Pasch
G. Richards 6–5 (fav.)
Neck; 4 L. 9 ran.
Time 3 m. $11\frac{3}{5}$ s.
Owner—Mr. J. V. Rank
Trainer—N. Cannon

	2,000 GUINEAS	1,000 GUINEAS	THE DERBY	THE OAKS	ST. LEGER
1939	1. **Blue Peter** (Fairway–Fancy Free) E. Smith 5–1 (co-fav.) 2. **Admiral's Walk** (Hyperion–Tabaris) H. Wragg 100–7 3. **Fairstone** (Fairway–Rosetta) M. Beary 13–2 $\frac{1}{2}$ L.; $\frac{3}{4}$ L. 25 ran. Time 1 m. 40 s. Owner—Lord Rosebery Trainer—J. Jarvis	1. **Galatea II** (Dark Legend–Galaday) R. A. Jones 6–1 2. **Aurora** (Hyperion–Red Rose) R. Perryman 7–1 3. **Olien** (Colombo–Grand Peace) T. Lowrey 9–2 (fav.) 3 L.; $\frac{1}{2}$ L. 16 ran. Time 1 m. 38$\frac{3}{5}$ s. Owner—Mr. H. S. Clark Trainer—J. Lawson	1. **Blue Peter** E. Smith 7–2 (fav.) 2. **Fox Cub** (Foxhunter–Dorina) G. Richards 100–6 3. **Heliopolis** (Hyperion–Drift) R. Perryman 100–9 4 L.; 3 L. 27 ran. Time 2 m. 36$\frac{3}{5}$ s. Owner Lord Rosebery Trainer—J. Jarvis	1. **Galatea II** R. A. Jones 10-11(fav.) 2. **White Fox** (Foxhunter–Bipearl) E. C. Elliott 9–1 3. **Superbe** (Bosworth–Surbine) P. Beasley 20–1 Head; 3 L. 21 ran. Time 2 m. 4$\frac{3}{5}$ s. Owner—Mr. H. S. Clark Trainer—J. Lawson	Abandoned owing to outbreak of War.
1940	1. **Djebel** (Tourbillon–Loika) C. Elliott 9–4 (fav.) 2. **Stardust** (Hyperion–Sister Stella) H. Wragg 100–9 3. **Tant Mieux** (Asterus–Tantine) G. Richards 13–2 2 L.; Head. 21 ran. Time 1 m. 42$\frac{3}{5}$ s. Owner—M. Boussac Trained in France	1. **Godiva** (Hyperion–Carpet Slipper) D. Marks 10–1 2. **Golden Penny** (Hyperion–Pennycomequick) G. Richards 8–11 (fav.) 3. **Allure** (Sir Cosmo–Simonella) M. Beary 10–1 5 L.; 4 L. 11 ran. Time 1 m. 40$\frac{3}{5}$ s. Owner—Lord Rothermere Trainer—W. R. Jarvis	(Run at Newmarket) 1. **Pont L'Eveque** (Barneveldt–Ponteba) S. Wragg 10–1 2. **Turkhan** (Bahram–Theresina) C. Smirke 100–7 3. **Lighthouse II** (Pharos–Pyramid) R. Perryman 85–40 (fav.) 3 L.; Short head. 16 ran. Time 2 m. 30$\frac{3}{5}$ s. Owner—Mr. F. Darling Trainer—F. Darling	(Run at Newmarket) 1. **Godiva** D. Marks 7–4 (fav.) 2. **Silverlace II** (Hotweed–Straitlace) G. Richards 100–8 3. **Valeraine** (Tiberius–Haintovette) T. Weston 33–1 3 L.; 4 L. 14 ran. Time 2 m. 30$\frac{3}{5}$ s. Owner—Lord Rothermere Trainer—W. R. Jarvis	(Run at Thirsk as Yorkshire St. Leger) 1. **Turkhan** G. Richards 4–1 2. **Stardust** H. Wragg 9–4 (fav.) 3. **Hippens** (Hyperion–Edgelaw) E. Smith 4–1 $\frac{3}{4}$ L.; $\frac{3}{4}$ L. 6 ran. 3 m. 32$\frac{3}{5}$ s. Owner—H.H. Aga Khan Trainer—Frank Butters
1941	1. **Lambert Simnel** (Fair Trial–Simnel) C. Elliott 10–1 2. **Morogoro** (Felicitation–Moti Begum) H. Wragg 100–30 3. **Sun Castle** (Hyperion–Castle Gay) P. Beasley 100–7 2 L.; $1\frac{1}{2}$ L. 19 ran. Time 1 m. 42$\frac{3}{5}$ s. Owner—Duke of Westminster Trainer—F. Templeman	1. **Dancing Time** (Colombo–Show Girl) R. Perryman 100–8 2. **Beausite** (Bora Archer–Orama) H. Wragg 7–1 3. **Keystone** (Umidwar–Rosetta) G. Richards 11–2 1 L.; 2 L. 13 ran. Time 1 m. 40$\frac{4}{5}$ s. Owner—Lord Glanely Trainer—J. Lawson	(Run at Newmar;et) 1. **Owen Tudor** (Hyperion–Mary Tudor II) W. Nevett 25–1 2. **Morogoro** H. Wragg 11–2 3. **Firoze Din** (Fairway–La Voulsie) W. Stephenson 100–1 $1\frac{1}{2}$ L.; 2 L. 20 ran. Time 2 m. 32 s. Owner—Mrs. Macdonald-Buchanan Trainer—F. Darling	(Run at Newmarket) 1. **Commotion** (Mieuxce–Riot) H. Wragg 8–1 2. **Turkana** (Firdaussi–Ticca Rani) P. Evans 100–8 3. **Dancing Time** R. Perryman 4–7 (fav.) 2 L.; $\frac{3}{4}$ L. 12 ran. Time 2 m. 37 s. Owner—Mr. J. A. Dewar Trainer—F. Darling	(Run at Manchester) 1. **Sun Castle** G. Bridgland 10–1 2. **Chateau Larose** (Chateau-Bouscaut–Pasca) R. Jones 11–2 3. **Dancing Time** M. Beary 25–1 Head; 1 L. 16 ran. Time 3 m. 4$\frac{3}{5}$ s. Owner—Lord Portal Trainer—C. Boyd-Rochfort

1942

2,000 GUINEAS

1. **Big Game**
   (Bahram–Myrobella)
   G. Richards 8–11 (fav.)
2. **Watling Street**
   (Fairway–Ranai)
   S. Ellis 13–2
3. **Gold Nib**
   (Dastur–Gold Race)
   R. Jones 100–7

4 L.; 2 L. 14 ran.
Time 1 m. $40\frac{4}{5}$ s.
Owner—King George VI
Trainer—F. Darling

1,000 GUINEAS

1. **Sun Chariot**
   (Hyperion–Clarence)
   G. Richards Evens (fav.)
2. **Perfect Peace**
   (Colombo–Grand Peace)
   R. Jones 5–1
3. **Light of Day**
   (Hyperion–Leger Day)
   S. Ellis 25–1

4 L.; 2 L. 18 ran.
Time 1 m. $39\frac{3}{5}$ s.
Owner—King George VI
Trainer—F. Darling

THE DERBY

(Run at Newmarket)

1. **Watling Street**
   H. Wragg 6–1
2. **Hyperides**
   (Hyperion–Priscilla)
   E. Smith 9–2
3. **Ujiji**
   (Umidwar–Theresina)
   C. Richards 18–1

Neck; 2 L. 13 ran.
Time 2 m. $29\frac{3}{5}$ s.
Owner—Lord Derby
Trainer—W. Earl

THE OAKS

(Run at Newmarket)

1. **Sun Chariot**
   G. Richards 1–4 (fav.)
2. **Afterthought**
   (Obliterate–Plack)
   E. Smith 10–1
3. **Feberion**
   (Hyperion–Februa)
   T. Carey 20–1

1 L.; $1\frac{1}{2}$ L. 12 ran.
Time 2 m. $33\frac{1}{5}$ s.
King George VI
Trainer—F. Darling

ST. LEGER

(Run at Newmarket)

1. **Sun Chariot**
   G. Richards 9–4
2. **Watling Street**
   H. Wragg 2–1 (fav.)
3. **Hyperides**
   E. Smith 9–2

3 L; 5 L. 8 ran.
Time 3 m. $8\frac{1}{5}$ s.
King George VI
Trainer—F. Darling

1943

2,000 GUINEAS

1. **Kingsway**
   (Fairway–Yenna)
   S. Wragg 18–1
2. **Pink Flower**
   (Oleander–Plymstock)
   T. Lowrey 100–9
3. **Way In**
   (Fairway–Instantaneous)
   C. Richards 100–9

Short head; Head. 19 ran.
Time 1 m. $37\frac{3}{5}$ s.
Owner—Mr. A. Saunders
Trainer—J. Lawson

1,000 GUINEAS

1. **Herringbone**
   (King Salmon–Schiaparelli)
   H. Wragg 15–2
2. **Ribbon**
   (Fairway–Bongrace)
   E. Smith 6–4 (fav.)
3. **Cincture**
   (Hyperion–Cinnabar)
   W. Nevett 100–7

Neck; $1\frac{1}{2}$ L. 12 ran.
Time 1 m. 41 s.
Owner—Lord Derby
Trainer—W. Earl

THE DERBY

(Run at Newmarket)

1. **Straight Deal**
   (Solario–Good Deal)
   T. Carey 100–6
2. **Umiddad**
   (Dastur–Udiapur)
   C. Elliott 100–8
3. **Nasrullah**
   (Nearco–Mumtaz Begum)
   G. Richards 9–1

Head; $\frac{1}{2}$ L. 23 ran.
Time 2 m. $30\frac{3}{5}$ s.
Owner—Miss D. Paget
Trainer—W. Nightingall

THE OAKS

(Run at Newmarket)

1. **Why Hurry**
   (Precipitation–Cybiane)
   C. Elliott 7–1
2. **Ribbon**
   E. Smith 5–2
3. **Tropical Sun**
   (Hyperion–Brulette)
   G. Richards 7–4 (fav.)

Neck; 1 L. 13 ran.
Time 2 m. $33\frac{1}{5}$ s.
Owner—Mr. J. V. Rank
Trainer—N. Cannon

ST. LEGER

(Run at Newmarket)

1. **Herringbone**
   H. Wragg 100–6
2. **Ribbon**
   E. Smith 10–1
3. **Straight Deal**
   T. Carey 100–30

Short head; $\frac{3}{4}$ L. 12 ran.
Time 3 m. $5\frac{4}{5}$ s.
Owner—Lord Derby
Trainer—W. Earl

1944

2,000 GUINEAS

1. **Garden Path**
   (Fairway–Ranai)
   H. Wragg 5–1 (fav.)
2. **Growing Confidence**
   (Blue Peter–Tornadic)
   K. Mullins 20–1
3. **Tehran**
   (Bois Roussel–Stafaralla)
   P. Gomez 50–1

Head; $1\frac{1}{2}$ L. 26 ran.
Time 1 m. $39\frac{4}{5}$ s.
Owner Lord Derby
Trainer—W. Earl

1,000 GUINEAS

1. **Picture Play**
   (Donatello II–Amuse)
   C. Elliott 15–2
2. **Grande Corniche**
   (Panorama–Joy Ride)
   P. Evans 100–6
3. **Superior**
   (Scottish Union–Supervisor)
   T. Weston 100–9

4 L.; 2 L. 11 ran.
Time 1 m. $40\frac{3}{5}$ s.
Owner—Mr. H. J. Joel
Trainer—J. Watts

THE DERBY

(Run at Newmarket)

1. **Ocean Swell**
   (Blue Peter–Jiffy)
   W. Nevett 28–1
2. **Tehran**
   E. Smith 8–1
3. **Happy Landing**
   (Windsor Lad–Happy Morn)
   R. Jones 22–1

Neck; Short head. 20 ran.
Time 2 m. $28\frac{1}{5}$ s.
Owner Lord Rosebery
Trainer—J. Jarvis

THE OAKS

(Run at Nermarket)

1. **Hycilla**
   (Hyperion–Priscilla)
   G. Bridgland 8–1
2. **Monsoon**
   (Umidwar–Heavenly Wind)
   P. Maher 33–1
3. **Kannabis**
   (Phideas–Hempseed)
   A. Richardson 18–1

$1\frac{1}{2}$ L.; $1\frac{1}{2}$ L. 16 ran.
Time 2 m. $31\frac{1}{5}$ s.
Owner—Mr. W. Woodward
Trainer—C. Boyd-Rochfort

ST. LEGER

(Run at Newmarket)

1. **Tehran**
   G. Richards 9–2
2. **Borealis**
   (Brumeux–Aurora)
   H. Wragg 11–2
3. **Ocean Swell**
   E. Smith 11–2

$1\frac{1}{2}$ L.; 1 L. 17 ran.
Time 3 m. $6\frac{3}{5}$ s.
Owner—H.H. Aga Khan
Trainer—Frank Butters

	2,000 GUINEAS	1,000 GUINEAS	THE DERBY	THE OAKS	ST. LEGER
1945			(Run at Newmarket)	(Run at Newmarket)	(Run at York)
	1. Court Martial (Fair Trial–Instantaneous) C. Richards 13–2 **2. Dante** (Nearco–Rosy Legend) W. Nevett Evens (fav.) **3. Royal Charger** (Nearco–Sun Princess) R. Jones 40–1 Neck; 2 L. 20 ran. Time 1 m. $40\frac{3}{5}$ s. Owner—Lord Astor Trainer—J. Lawson	**1. Sun Stream** (Hyperion–Drift) H. Wragg 5–2 (fav.) **2. Blue Smoke** (Blue Peter–Fireplace) E. Smith 25–1 **3. Mrs. Feather** (Fairway–My Pet A. Wragg 4–1 3 L.; 2 L. 14 ran. Time 1 m. $45\frac{3}{5}$ s. Owner—Lord Derby Trainer—W. Earl	**1. Dante** W. Nevett 100–30 (fav.) **2. Midas** (Hyperion–Coin of the Realm) E. Smith 6–1 **3. Court Martial** C. Richards 100–9 2 L.; Head. 27 ran. Time 2 m. $26\frac{3}{5}$ s. Owner—Sir E. Ohlson Trainer—M. Peacock	**1. Sun Stream** H. Wragg 6–4 (fav.) **2. Naishapur** (Nearco–Udaipur) D. Smith 20–1 **3. Solar Princess** (Solario–Mary Tudor II) G. Richards 20–1 Short head; $\frac{3}{4}$ L. 16 ran. Time 2 m. 30 s. Owner—Lord Derby Trainer—W. Earl	**1. Chamossaire** (Precipitation–Snowberry) T. Lowrey 11–2 **2. Rising Light** (Hyperion–Bread Card) D. Smith 9–2 **3. Stirling Castle** (Scottish Union–Town Kate) H. Wragg 7–1 2 L.; $\frac{3}{4}$ L. 10 ran. Time 2 m. $55\frac{4}{5}$ s. Owner—Mr. Stanhope Joel Trainer—R. Perryman
1946			(Run at Epsom)	(Run at Epsom)	(Run at Doncaster)
	1. Happy Knight (Colombo–Happy Morn) T. Weston 28–1 **2. Khaled** (Hyperion–Eclair) R. Jones 100–30 **3. Radiotherapy** (Hyperion–Belleva) T. H. Carey 100–6 4 L.; Head. 13 ran. Time 1 m. $38\frac{1}{5}$ s. Owner—Sir W. Cooke Trainer—H. Jelliss	**1. Hypericum** (Hyperion–Feola) D. Smith 100–6 **2. Neolight** (Nearco–Sansonnet) G. Richards 4–6 (fav.) **3. Iona** (Hyperion–Jiffy) E. Smith 9–1 $1\frac{1}{2}$ L.; $\frac{3}{4}$ L. 13 ran. Time 1 m. $41\frac{3}{5}$ s. Owner—His Majesty Trainer—C. Boyd-Rochfort	**1. Airborne** (Precipitation–Bouquet) T. Lowrey 50–1 **2. Gulf Stream** (Hyperion–Tide-Way) H. Wragg 7–1 **3. Radiotherapy** T. H. Carey 8–1 1 L.; 2 L. 17 ran. Time 2 m. $44\frac{3}{5}$ s. Owner—Mr. J. E. Ferguson Trainer—R. Perryman	**1. Steady Aim** (Felstead–Quick Arrow) H. Wragg 7–1 **2. Iona** E. Smith 2–1 (fav.) **3. Nelia** (Nearco–Springtime) M. Beary 7–1 3 L.; 3 L. 10 ran. Time 2 m. 41 s. Owner—Sir A. Butt Trainer—Frank Butters	**1. Airborne** T. Lowrey 3–1 (fav.) **2. Murren** (Mieuzce–Renate) T. Weston 40–1 **3. Fast and Fair** (Fairway–Quixotic) C. Richards 100–9 $1\frac{1}{2}$ L.; 3 L. 11 ran. Time 3 m. 10 s. Owner—Mr. J. E. Ferguson Trainer—R. Perryman
1947					
	1. Tudor Minstrel (Owen Tudor–Sansonnet) G. Richards 11–8 (fav.) **2. Saravan** (Legend of France–Way) Wong) C. Elliott 25–1 **3. Sayajirao** (Nearco–Rosy Legend) E. Britt 33–1 8 L.; Short head. 15 ran. Time 1 m. 37 s. Owner—Mr. J. A. Dewar Trainer—F. Darling	**1. Imprudence** (Canot–Indiscretion) W. Johnstone 4–1(fav.) **2. Rose O'Lynn** (Pherozshah–Rocklyn) S. Smith 100–8 **3. Wild Child** (Casanova–Lionelle) T. Lowrey 20–1 Neck; Head. 20 ran. Time 1 m. 46 s. Owner—Mme P. Corbiere Trainer—J. Lieux	**1. Pearl Diver** (Vatellor–Pearl Cap) G. Bridgland 40–1 **2. Migoli** (Bois Roussel–Mah Iran) D. Smith 20–1 **3. Sayajirao** E. Britt 13–2 4 L.; $\frac{3}{4}$ L. 15 ran. Time 2 m. $38\frac{3}{5}$ s. Owner—Baron G. de Waldner Trainer—W. Halsey	**1. Imprudence** W. Johnstone 7–4(fav.) **2. Netherton Maid** (Nearco–Phase) W. Rickaby 7–1 **3. Mermaid** (Blue Peter–Sonsie Wench) E. Smith 6–1 5 L.; 2 L. 11 ran. Time 2 m. 40 s. Owner—Mme Corbiere Trainer—J. Lieux	**1. Sayajirao** E. Britt 9–2 **2. Arbar** (Djebel–Astronomic) C. Elliott 5–1 **3. Migoli** G. Richards 9–4 (fav.) Head; 3 L. 11 ran. Time 3 m. $7\frac{4}{5}$ s. Owner—H.H. Maharaja of Baroda Trainer—F. Armstrong

1948

2,000 GUINEAS

1. **My Babu**
   (Djebel–Perfume)
   C. Smirke 2–1 (fav.)
2. **The Cobbler**
   (Windsor Slipper–Overture)
   G. Richards 100–30
3. **Pride of India**
   (Colombo–The Bud)
   E. Britt 20–1

Head ; 4 L. 18 ran
Time 1 m. 35⅘ s
(equals Course record)
Owner—The Maharaja of Baroda
Trainer—F. Armstrong

1,000 GUINEAS

1. **Queenpot**
   (Big Game–Poker Chip)
   G. Richards 6–1
2. **Ariostar**
   (Solario–Co-Star)
   J. Marshall 100–6
3. **Duplicity**
   (Nearco–Doubleton)
   W. Nevett 33–1

Head ; 1½ L. 22 ran.
Time 1 m. 41⅘ s.
Owner—Sir P. Loraine
Trainer—N. Murless

THE DERBY

1. **My Love**
   (Vatellor–For My Love)
   W. R. Johnstone 100–9
2. **Royal Drake**
   (Admiral Drake–Hurrylor)
   J. Doyasbere 25–1
3. **Noor**
   (Nasrullah–Queen of Baghdad)
   T. Weston 22–1

1½ L. ; 4 L. 32 ran.
Time 2 m. 40 s.
Owner—H.H. Aga Khan
Trainer—R. Carter (France)

THE OAKS

1. **Masaka**
   (Nearco–Majidel)
   W. Nevett 7–1
2. **Angelola**
   (Donatello II–Feola)
   W. H. Carr 20–1
3. **Folie II**
   (Deiri–Follette V)
   J. Doyasbere 33–1

6 L. ; 3 L. 25 ran
Time 2 m. 40⅗ s.
Owner—H.H. Aga Khan
Trainer—Frank Butters

ST. LEGER

1. **Black Tarquin**
   (Rhodes Scholar–Vagrancy)
   E. Britt 15–2
2. **Alycidon**
   (Donatello II–Aurora)
   D. Smith 20–1
3. **Solar Slipper**
   (Windsor Slipper–Solar Flower)
   E. Smith 13–2

1½ L . ; 5 L. 14 ran.
Time 3 m. 8⅗ s.
Owner—Mr. W. Woodward
Trainer—C. Boyd-Rochfort

1949

2,000 GUINEAS

1. **Nimbus**
   (Nearco-Kong)
   E. C. Elliott 10–1
2. **Abernant**
   (Owen Tudor–Ruston Mahal)
   G. Richards 5–4 (fav.)
3. **Barnes Park**
   (Nasrullah-Battlestown)
   W. Cook 100–1

Sh. Hd. ; 4 L. 13 ran.
Time 1 m. 38 s.
Owner—Mrs. M. Glenister
Trainer—G. Colling

1,000 GUINEAS

1. **Musidora**
   (Nasrullah–Painted Vale)
   E. Britt 100–8
2. **Unknown Quantity**
   (Blue Peter–Firegall)
   W. Rickaby 7–2 (fav.)
3. **Solar Myth**
   (Hyperion–Keystone)
   T. Gosling 100–8

1½ L. ; 2 L. 18 ran.
Time 1 m. 40 s.
Owner—Mr. N. P. Donaldson
Trainer—C. F. Elsey

THE DERBY

1. **Nimbus**
   E. C. Elliott 7–1
2. **Amour Drake**
   (Admiral Drake–Vers l'Amour)
   W. Johnstone 10–1
3. **Swallow Tail**
   (Bois Roussel–Schiaparelli)
   D. Smith 100–8

Hd. ; Hd. 32 ran.
Time 2 m. 42 s.
Owner—Mrs. M. Glenister
Trainer—G. Colling

THE OAKS

1. **Musidora**
   E. Britt 4–1
2. **Coronation V**
   (Djebel-Esmeralda)
   E. C. Elliott 6–1
3. **Vice Versa II**
   (Verso II–Nica)
   W. Johnstone 5–1

Nk. ; 2 L. 17 ran.
Time 2 m. 40 s.
Owner—Mr. N. P. Donaldson
Trainer—C. F. Elsey

ST. LEGER

1. **Ridge Wood**
   (Bois Roussel-Hanging Fall)
   M. Beary 100–7
2. **Dust Devil**
   (Stardust–Udaipur)
   W. Johnstone 40–1
3. **Lone Eagle**
   (Isolater-Marigal)
   W. Carr 6–1

3 L. ; ¾ L. 16 ran.
Time 3 m. 8⅕ s.
Owner—Mr. G. R. H. Smith.
Trainer—N. Murless.